THE ILLUSTRATED ATLAS OF
JEWISH
CIVILIZATION

THE ILLUSTRATED ATLAS OF
JEWISH
CIVILIZATION

JOSEPHINE BACON
CONSULTANT EDITOR MARTIN GILBERT

Quantum
Books

A QUANTUM BOOK

This book is produced by
Quantum Books Ltd
6 Blundell Street
London N7 9BH

Copyright © MCMXC
Quarto Publishing plc

This edition printed 2006

ISBN-10: 0-681-28922-8
ISBN-13: 978-0-68128-922-2

QUMIJC

Maps prepared for Quarto by Arka Cartographics Ltd

Printed in Singapore by
Star Standard Industries (Pte) Ltd.

CONTENTS

INTRODUCTION

MAPPING JEWISH HISTORY

More than thirty-five years ago I gave a lecture at Oxford entitled "The Jews versus Geography." It seemed to me that it was the Jewish ability not only to survive repeated physical persecution but also to survive constant territorial dispersion, that was remarkable.

Subsequently I drew more than a hundred maps to illustrate the theme of Jewish movement, whether through expulsion, trade, or the desire to return to Zion. In due course, I published these maps as a *Jewish History Atlas* which, over thirty years later, is still in print. This new book draws together my work in this field and subsequent research into the history of the Jewish people. It reflects my belief that so varied and mobile a people can have its story told not only in words, but also in maps, the pictorial representation of world-wide movement.

In every generation since the first destruction of the Temple in Jerusalem, Jews have been on the move. Sometimes tyrants forced them on the road. Sometimes it was the pressure of economic hardship. Sometimes it was the lure of commerce, or the prospect of advancement through travel to new lands, to distant horizons.

Nor did the attraction of a return to Zion ever fully fade. From the moment of the first dispersal to Babylon, it was a powerful impetus, preserved and stimulated in prayer and song. It was the Psalmist who first encapsulated the pain of exile when he wrote: "By the rivers of Babylon, there we sat down; yea, we wept, when we remembered Zion."

In every century, Jewish travelers, pilgrims, and settlers were to be found making their way, often with considerable hardship, toward the Land of Israel. In the past century, the movement for the return of the exiles found its full force in political Zionism,

which, after many tribulations, including those imposed by outside forces and hostile nations, found its culmination in the establishment of a Jewish State, Israel.

Not all Jewish communities were able to preserve their identity or their longings. By the end of the nineteenth century, the Jews of China, once relatively numerous, had dwindled to a virtually unrecognizable remnant. Many centuries earlier, the Jews of Provence – in southern France – had assimilated into the richness of their local landscape and traditions. The converted Jews of Spain became an integral part of the vibrant life and culture of the Iberian Peninsula and its widening Empire, a loss to Jewish life, but a gain for Spanish culture.

The fate of every Jewish wandering is not known. The mystery of the ten lost tribes has always intrigued scholars and laymen. Where did those tribes go? How long did they preserve their identity as Jews? In what form, if any, do they survive today?

The recent return to Israel of so many thousands of black Jews from Ethiopia was a reminder of how scattered the Jews had become, and how much they had become a part of distant and different cultures, traditions, and even races. Yet they had never ceased to be Jews, never lost the essence of Judaism, never lost the will to be Jews.

An equally remarkable phenomenon has also been seen in our time: the emergence of more than two million Jews from behind the black night of the Iron Curtain and Communism, still preserving their sense of being Jews, and still capable of learning, from a blank base, the rudiments of Jewish history, tradition and identity. In 1990, in the aftermath of the collapse of Communism, more than a hundred Jews arrived in Israel from the Soviet Union every day.

For millions of other Jews, however,

through the ages, assimilation was complete, and all contact with Judaism lost. It may well be that for every Jew who passed on some inkling of his heritage to his children, another Jew did not. Intermarriage has taken place in every generation; in the United States today, more than a third of all Jews who marry choose a non-Jewish partner.

Yet it would seem that the Jews will not disappear. None of the efforts against them, by tyrants intent on wiping them out, have succeeded. The most terrible of those attempts, the Nazi German mass murder plan, succeeded in destroying one third of the Jewish people. Over large areas of Europe it totally destroyed Jewish life, as well as Jewish lives. Yet this terrible slaughter failed in its aim. Even from the fire, there were survivors, who were able to bear witness to what had happened, and to recount tales of heroism and fortitude.

In the modern world of mass communications, Jews are no longer cut off, as they were even a century ago, from their fellow-Jews in what were then distant lands. Today, air travel, television, and the telephone, as well as computer-based communications, cover Jews in a protective shield. An indignity or a danger to one community can be known about within hours, and combatted within days. World-wide Jewish organizations can protect Jews the world over. An insult in Ireland can be parried in Rome. A threat in Damascus can be challenged at Geneva. A libel in Alberta can be answered in Jerusalem.

The Jews are a varied as well as a scattered people. Different cultural and historical traditions affect their daily life. Political differences are also considerable, even within the narrow geographic confines of the Jewish State. Jews have fought in many opposing armies, and have contributed to many conflicting political systems. Yet the sense of Jewish identity remains, and remains strong.

Rooted in a common spiritual heritage, spread through diverse historical experiences, the Jewish identity has survived for more than five thousand years, as the Jewish calendar attests: it is the longest-running calendar in the world today.

The year 1996 marked the three-thousandth anniversary of the establishment of Jerusalem as David's city, the spiritual and temporal focus of the Jewish nation. Many of the nations against whom David's descendants fought have faded from history. The Jews have not. The celebrations in Jerusalem marked, not the end of the Jewish story, but another remarkable milestone along its colorful and creative path.

Martin Gilbert
Merton College
Oxford

CHAPTER ONE

From Abraham to the Destruction of the Second Temple

T he survival of the Jewish people down through the ages has been an extraordinary and unparalleled phenomenon. There is hardly another people on earth who can trace a continuous history that covers 4000 years. It can be argued that Chinese civilization is just as old, but the Chinese have always been geographically remote. The true miracle of Jewish survival is that it occurred first in the most fought-over region of the world – the crossroads of Europe, Asia, and Africa – and, after the Diaspora, in many nations throughout the world. The Jews have managed to survive every crisis, every hardship.

The Middle East has not only been the cradle of civilizations – it has also been their graveyard. The Babylonian, Sumerian, Egyptian, Assyrian, and Hittite cultures were swallowed up by later conquests until virtually every trace of them disappeared. Yet the Jews have remained a self-defined ethnic group, in direct descent from the ancient Hebrews who came to be called the Children of Israel.

The Jews' unique religious system is more than a religion. Besides the belief in a single, indivisible deity, it embraces a set of ethical and moral precepts covering every aspect of daily life, from hygiene and behavior to justice and equality before God and the law. Not all the concepts that make up what is known as Judaism were new and original – many were echoes of other ancient cultures – but it was the Jews who brought them together for the first time. Although the Jews have always been a minority in all lands outside Israel, the sheer power of these

concepts has contributed to the shaping of both Christianity and Islam, as well as inspiring the secular philosophy of the West. Jerusalem itself is a center of three world religions.

LEFT: *Abraham and the three angels, from the* St. Louis Psalter. *The founding father of the Jewish people and of Judaism, Abraham's unswerving devotion to God, led him to obey divine commandments without question, as in his willingness to sacrifice Isaac, his son. His reward was the covenant between God and the Jews and the promise of Canaan as their home.*

LEFT: *Rameses III is depicted in an Egyptian glazed relief, dating from around 1200 B.C.E. and found at his temple at Tel el Jahudiye. According to tradition, the Exodus from Egypt took place under one of his predecessors; in fact, Rameses, the last powerful ruler of his dynasty, maintained Egyptian influence in Palestine, which did not wane until after his reign.*

The Early Semites

The Bible claims that the Semitic people who later became the Jews are descended from Abraham, who left his homeland – "Ur of the Chaldees," or "Ur of the Babylonians" – and wandered westward with his flocks at least 4000 years ago. Although there is no archaeological evidence for the existence of Abraham as a person, the Bible story is very plausible. Many aspects of early Hebrew culture as described in the Bible bear traces of the influence of Babylonian/Mesopotamian culture, which flourished in the rich lands that are nourished by the Tigris and Euphrates rivers in what is now southern Iraq. For example, Bible stories about the Flood, the demand of a deity for the ultimate sacrifice of a loved one (Isaac), and the finding of a child in the bulrushes who is actually a prince (Moses) are all versions of Mesopotamian myths. The story of the Flood was actually found engraved on a stele at Nippur dating from 3000 B.C.E., and it also occurs in the *Epic of Gilgamesh,* which was written down in about 1700 B.C.E., 500 years before the exodus from Egypt.

What archaeology tells us is that a semi-nomadic people speaking a proto-Semitic language, an early version of Hebrew, lived in the northern deserts of Arabia some three to four thousand years ago. Perhaps because they were shepherds looking for better grazing for their flocks after a drought, some moved north and settled in Canaan (later to be called Palestine), while others traveled west and east to found the two great Bronze Age civilizations of Egypt and the Mesopotamian city-states of Sumer and Akkad, later known collectively as Babylonia. A fourth group, the Phoenicians, settled on the Mediterranean coast around Tyre and Sidon (now in modern Lebanon), where they reached the apogee of their power through the exploits of King Hiram (c. 970–40 B.C.E.). They were the ancestors of colonists who eventually moved into North Africa and founded Carthage in the ninth century B.C.E.

The earliest town so far discovered in the area is Jericho, an oasis in the Judaean desert, where archaeologists have unearthed remains dating from 7500 B.C.E., 4000 years older than the earliest Babylonian examples. Jericho lies below sea level at a convenient crossing point over the River Jordan, and thus it was on a major trade route. It had its own spring, so water was plentiful, and

BELOW: *According to Jewish tradition, Abraham, the first Patriarch, left his home in Ur to migrate westward through the so-called Fertile Crescent, eventually reaching Canaan. Though there is no scientific evidence to support the existence of Abraham as a person, archaeology confirms that Semitic shepherds lived a nomadic life at this time – probably seeking a suitable homeland in which to establish permanent settlements. Some settled in Canaan; others traveled east and west to settle in Egypt and Mesopotamia respectively.*

paleobotanists have recently discovered that large stands of wild grain were to be found nearby. It would have been a natural thing for the first farmers to store seed from these wild plants and sow it close to their houses. The Semites of Jericho, who lived in round, brick-built houses, even practiced crop rotation and irrigation; they also reared livestock.

Jericho was unaccountably abandoned in about 4000 B.C.E. By this time the Semites of the city-state of Akkad were becoming powerful in Babylonia, having settled there about 4000 years before. In approximately 3500 B.C.E., they were conquered by the Sumerians, a non-Semitic race that probably originated in central Asia. After dominating Babylonian culture for 1000 years, the Sumerians were finally driven out by Sargon the Great, also known as Sargon of Akkad, the first truly Babylonian king. After reconquering his homeland, he extended his empire – the world's first – through battle until it covered almost all of the Semitic

world, from the Mediterranean to the Gulf. During his reign, Semitic culture received a new lease on life: mathematics and astronomy flourished and architecture reached new levels of sophistication.

Sargon died in about 2300 B.C.E., while subduing a revolt. Nearly three centuries later, a new wave of Semitic invaders appeared in Babylonia. These were the Amurru or Amorites ("Westerners"), who may have come from Canaan, which the Babylonians called "The West." The Amorites later captured the old Sumerian city-states, including Ur, Abraham's birthplace. According to the Bible (Genesis 11:31) Abraham and his father, Terah, left Ur. No doubt the Amorite invasion, about 2000 B.C.E., was a powerful incentive.

The Patriarchs and Moses

Abraham, Isaac, and Jacob (collectively known as the Patriarchs) and Moses are the four major figures of the Torah, the first five

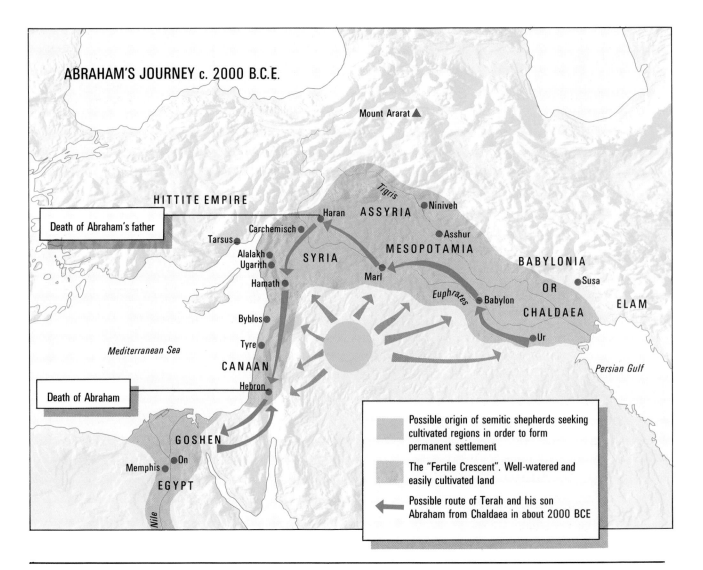

ABRAHAM'S JOURNEY c. 2000 B.C.E.

Mount Ararat ▲

HITTITE EMPIRE

Death of Abraham's father

Tarsus

Carchemisch

Haran

ASSYRIA

Niniveh

Asshur

MESOPOTAMIA

Tigris

Alalakh
Ugarith

SYRIA

BABYLONIA

Hamath

Marl

Susa

OR

Euphrates

Byblos

Babylon

CHALDAEA

ELAM

Tyre

Mediterranean Sea

CANAAN

Ur

Persian Gulf

Hebron

Death of Abraham

GOSHEN

On

Memphis

EGYPT

Nile

☐ Possible origin of semitic shepherds seeking cultivated regions in order to form permanent settlement

☐ The "Fertile Crescent". Well-watered and easily cultivated land

← Possible route of Terah and his son Abraham from Chaldaea in about 2000 BCE

books of the Bible (Genesis, Exodus, Leviticus, Numbers, Deuteronomy). Each of them "discovered" God for himself, and each time anew. In the cases of Abraham and Moses, theirs was a violent reaction against the pagan beliefs of their contemporaries.

The Patriarchs continued the nomadic traditions of their ancestors. Genesis 12–46 recounts the wanderings of Abraham, Isaac, and Jacob through the land first promised to Abraham in the covenant that God made with him (Genesis 15:18) and repeatedly promised to his descendants and then to Moses (Exodus 33:1). It is for this reason that the territory defined in the Bible as the area between the Nile and the Euphrates is known to the Jews as the "promised land."

It is because of Jacob that the name "Israel" became synonymous with the Jews. At Peniel, he fought with something that he first took for a man but then realized was a supernatural being, either an angel or God Himself. Afterwards he was given the nickname "Israel," which in Hebrew means "fighter with God" (Genesis 32:24–30). It was in memory of Jacob that his descendants – the Hebrews – took the name of "Children of Israel."

It was only with Joseph, son of Jacob and Rachel, that these Semitic nomads moved into a more restricted area. The Bible tells how Joseph was sold to slave traders by his brothers and taken to Egypt, later to be followed by his family. These same brothers became the founders of ten of the Twelve Tribes of Israel (the remainder were founded by two of Joseph's sons).

The Hebrews in Egypt

The settlement of Hebrew peoples in Egypt may have begun as early as 1800 B.C.E. Some historians believe that they fled before the advance of the Hyksos, an Asiatic people who conquered Egypt in about 1650 B.C.E. and dominated Upper and Lower Egypt, Palestine and Syria for the next 200 years. However, the Hyksos appear to have contained some Semitic elements, and these may well have been Hebrews, who were by now gaining a definite identity. A people called *Habiru, Hapiru,* or *Apiru* are mentioned in cuneiform tablets, and they seem to be the same as the *Pwr* found in Egyptian hieroglyphics. Historians are divided as to whether these are the same as the *Ibr,* or Hebrews, also found in Egyptian writing. It may be significant that this latter name, like "Amorite," also means "Westerner" in Semitic languages. In Egypt, the Habiru appear to have been a social class, and they crop up in

ABOVE: *The presentation of tribute by Semitic envoys from Syria is shown in this Egyptian wall-painting from the tomb of Sebek Lotep at Thebes and dating from around 1420 B.C.E. The relationship between the Jews and Egyptians during this period is extremely complex. Whether the Hebrews were expelled from Egypt or left of their own accord is a matter of conjecture; certainly, no archaeological evidence has been found, as yet, to support the Biblical version of the Exodus.*

RIGHT: Israel in Egypt, *as painted by Sir Edward Poynter in the nineteenth century. The descent of the Jews in Egypt into slavery is thought by some historians to be the story of the defeat and overthrow, by the Egyptians, of a people living in Egypt called the Hyksos. What is clear is that the Biblical account of the Exodus is not supported by any Egyptian records yet discovered, the sole exception being an inscription on a stele at Thebes which claims an Egyptian victory over the Jews in the desert.*

RIGHT: *Rameses II, dressed for war. This depiction comes from the Valley of the Kings, Thebes. Under him, Egypt's boundaries expanded, but the mercenaries he employed to bring this about and the huge cost of his lavish building program, for which the Jews were conscripted as slave labor, both contributed to Egypt's decline. He is probably the pharaoh of the Exile mentioned in Exodus.*

various functions and roles – both lowly and high ranking, within and outside the law – throughout the second millennium B.C.E.

The Jewish historian Josephus (Flavius Josephus, c. C.E. 38–c. 100), in his *Jewish Antiquities*, equates the Egyptian revolt against the foreign rule of the Hyksos in about 1550 B.C.E. with the exodus of the Jews from Egypt, thus firmly identifying the Hyksos with the ancient Hebrews. This seems unlikely, both from what is known today and from biblical chronology. However, the descent of the Hebrews into slavery may have been linked to the overthrow of the Hyksos. This situation found echoes down the centuries of history: a minority group such as the Jews is identified with a conqueror and finds itself on the losing side when the conqueror is overthrown.

Egyptian life was strictly ordered and dominated by a priest caste that wielded almost unlimited power. Surrounded by mystifying phenomena such as the changing seasons, the annual flooding of the Nile, and death – the greatest mystery of all – the Egyptians focused all their energies on the

called himself, is fairly obscure, but it is known that all the gods were ousted except Ra, the sun god – represented in the form of the Aton, or sun disk. The name *Aton* is significantly similar to the Hebrew word for "Lord" – *Adon* – used in the Bible. It is not surprising that Akhnaton's faith and its possible influence on Moses is a subject that has intrigued scholars for many centuries – including Sigmund Freud, who set out his theories in *Moses and Monotheism*.

Overthrowing the old order in Egypt, Akhnaton established a new capital in Akhetaten (Tel el-Amarna), but his ambitious reforms were thwarted by his untimely death at the age of only 30. His successors abandoned Akhnaton's beliefs and attempted to restore Egypt's prestige abroad. This was accomplished through the efforts of Rameses II, who came to the throne in 1292 B.C.E. and ruled for the next 67 years. He expanded Egypt's power by making conquests in Syria and Palestine and concluded a treaty with the Hyksos – now known as Hittites – who were still powerful in that region. This is almost certainly the pharaoh mentioned in the Bible who enslaved the Jews and forced them to build Pithom and the city of Raamses.

afterlife. Another explanation for this preoccupation may be the harshness of life in that merciless climate. Mummies recently subjected to rigorous medical examination have shown that even the most aristocratic Egyptians suffered from a range of unpleasant conditions and diseases caused by the heat and the physical environment – for instance, ground-down teeth and abscess-afflicted jaws were both results of the presence of grains of sand in food.

The Egyptians were ruled by a pantheon of gods and goddesses with animal heads and human bodies. Humans themselves were treated by these gods with contempt and, like their counterparts in Greece and Rome, were toyed with at the deities' whim. The gods had to be placated with sacrifices, and their physical likenesses on earth were revered.

In the mid-fourteenth century B.C.E., about 100 years before the time of Moses, a pharaoh ascended the throne who utterly rejected the established religion as practiced by the priestly hierarchy and introduced one of his own to replace it. The nature of the religion of Amenhotep IV, or Akhnaton as he

Moses and the Exodus

According to some theories, Moses was an Egyptian prince who decided to convert the caste of untouchables known as the Habiru to his Akhnaton-inspired religious beliefs. He knew that in order for them to practice this new religion they would have to leave Egypt; the priests and the pharaohs would surely destroy these supporters of a rival creed. Other theorists contend that this slave caste already practiced a form of monotheism, and this perceptive but rather eccentric member of the royal family became interested in it and adopted it. Still others believe the Bible story to be closest to the truth: Moses was a Hebrew who was "adopted" by a royal princess and brought up as an aristocrat, but he instinctively recognized his roots when he grew up. As to why he was forced to flee the royal court, the Bible says that it was because he killed an Egyptian whom he witnessed beating a Hebrew slave.

An interesting sidelight on the psychology of the authors of the Bible is the fact that the

ABOVE: *This carving outside the synagogue at Kfar Nachum (Capernaum) depicts the Ark of the Covenant. This started life as a portable shrine, tended by a priestly family. Eventually, it was installed by Solomon in the great Temple he built in Jerusalem. It was overlaid with gold both inside and out and was kept heavily veiled; only the high priest could look at the uncovered surface. Touching the ark was an offense punishable by death.*

heroes and villains they describe are never cardboard characters. Neither completely pure nor totally evil, they are many-faceted – in other words, *human*. Even when they repent and affirm their belief in the One God, as did Jacob, this does not turn them into models of perfection.

All the Bible heroes strayed occasionally from the divine path, for which transgression they were suitably punished. For instance, when Moses was arrogant enough to try to perform a miracle in a more spectacular way than God had commanded – he struck a rock twice to cause water to spring from it, rather than talking to it as God had ordered him to do – he was punished by being denied the privilege of leading his people into the promised land (Deuteronomy 32:50–52). As for David, his lust for Bathsheba made him deliberately send her husband Uriah the Hittite to the front line to be killed in battle. As punishment for his behavior, God caused the death of the child that David had fathered while Bathsheba had still been married to Uriah (2 Samuel 11, 12:15–19). Nor would He let David build the Temple in Jerusalem, a task that would be fulfilled by his son Solomon.

The heroes of the Bible made no proud boasts for themselves but attributed all their victories and triumphs to a single, unique, and all-powerful deity. And this God – unlike the pagan gods of the Middle East, for whom the affairs of humans were usually a matter of supreme indifference – took a direct interest in their progress.

Whether the Hebrews were expelled from Egypt or whether they left of their own accord is a matter for conjecture. The exodus is a major biblical event for which no definitive corroboration has been found in other texts or archaeological remains. Certainly their numbers could not have been as great as the 600,000 Hebrews of fighting age claimed by the Bible. If this were true, the total Hebrew population would have numbered as many as 2.5 million – greater than the population of Egypt as a whole.

The one plausible explanation for the lack of documentation about the exodus is that the numbers involved were far too small and the Hebrews themselves too insignificant to warrant mention in the official records. In fact, outside the pages of the Bible, the only reference to what might have been the exodus is an inscription on a stele at the ancient

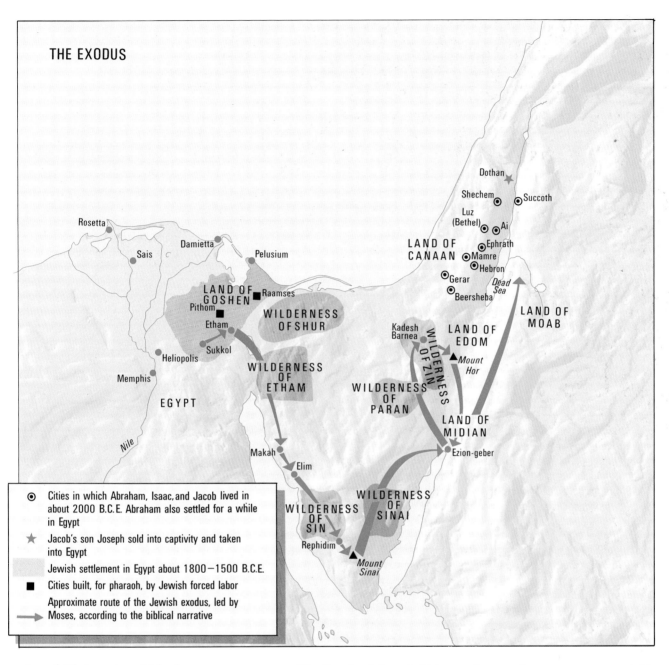

city of Thebes, in which the successor to Rameses II, Pharaoh Merneptah (reigned c. 1224–1214 B.C.E.), boasts:

**Israel lies desolate; its seed is no more...
All the lands in their entirety are at peace,
Everyone who was a nomad has been
curbed by King Merneptah.**

This allegedly refers to an Egyptian military victory. However, it would have been quite possible for the pharaoh's troops to battle with the Hebrews in the desert and then return with false tales of winning. Throughout history, there have been many examples of armies claiming victory when, in fact, they had been defeated.

The fact that Moses led his people on such a tortuous route through Goshen and Sinai is not as surprising as it would at first appear. At the time, the Egyptians were waging military campaigns in Palestine and Syria, and recent evidence has shown that they had established a flourishing colony in what is today the Gaza Strip. The Hebrews would have wanted to avoid any contact with their former masters. Historians are very divided as to the actual route taken by the Hebrews, and they cannot even agree on where the crossing of the Sea of Reeds (the Red Sea in the Bible) took place. Only the site of Kadesh Barnea – called Mount Hor in the Bible, and the place where the Jews halted after the revelation on

ABOVE: *Historians hold conflicting views about the nature of the exodus of the Jews from Egypt; though this is a major Biblical incident, no archaeological evidence, as yet, has been found to confirm its scale or the route taken by the Jews. It seems reasonable to suppose that the numbers involved were relatively small and that the tortuous route Moses apparently chose was to avoid the Egyptian armies then fighting in Canaan and Syria.*

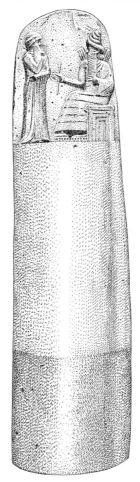

Mount Sinai (Exodus 19) and where Moses's brother and sister Aaron and Miriam died – has been positively identified through recently discovered evidence of a Hebrew presence there. Whether or not it took 40 years to travel such a short distance should be judged in the light of the Bible's exaggerated use of statistics as a whole (Abraham, it says, was 100 years old when Isaac was born, and he died at the age of 175).

The Giving of the Law

The revelation on Mount Sinai (also known as Mount Horeb) and the giving of the Law mark a turning point, not only in Jewish history but also in world culture. However, it cannot be seen as a unique event. It can be judged only against parallel developments in contemporary Middle Eastern societies, since the Hebrews were not the first to have codified laws.

The best-known pre-Mosaic lawgiver was the Babylonian king Hammurabi (c. 1728–1686 B.C.E.), but his code – as written on the great stele bearing his likeness discovered at Susa (now in modern Iran) in 1901 – was just one of a number that were compiled in the

ancient world once writing had been invented. Mosaic law, revealed in about 1350 B.C.E., is the distillation of these codes, but it is more than this. Whereas the previous codes had dealt in a matter-of-fact way with such legal matters as sale and purchase, inheritance, theft, and manslaughter, Mosaic law can be seen as based on fundamental moral principles. Moreover the basic laws – the Ten Commandments – were given to the Jews directly by God in the form of the tablets Moses received on Sinai; according to the Susa stele, Hammurabi was simply commissioned by Shamash, the Babylonian sun god and god of justice, to write them himself.

Besides the Ten Commandments (also known as the Decalogue), which have governed civilized societies down through the ages, hundreds of other commandments – to be found in Exodus, Leviticus, and Deuteronomy – are also attributed to Moses himself. They cover almost every aspect of human life, from Temple ritual and ethics to the treatment of animals, sexual morality, and the rules of good hygiene. The closest parallels with earlier Semitic laws lie in the areas of trade and compensation for injuries.

It is the latter concept – also incorporated by the Romans into their laws as *lex talionis* – that has caused considerable controversy over the years. "An eye for an eye, a tooth for a tooth" (Exodus 21:23) has often been quoted out of context by those who seek to show the God of the Old Testament as vengeful and devoid of love, mercy, and forgiveness. In fact, financial compensation for causing injury was such a well-known legal concept at the time that it was considered unnecessary to define it in greater detail. Another aspect of the *lex talionis* often overlooked is the fact that it set a limit to the amount of compensation that could be demanded (no more than an eye for an eye, a tooth for a tooth).

The Laws of Moses are most notable for the way they define specific principles of justice and mercy, which not only appear here for the first time but would not be incorporated into the legislation of other nations until many centuries later. The most important of these is equality before the law. Under the laws of Hammurabi and his predecessors, the people were strictly divided into three classes: the nobility, commoners,

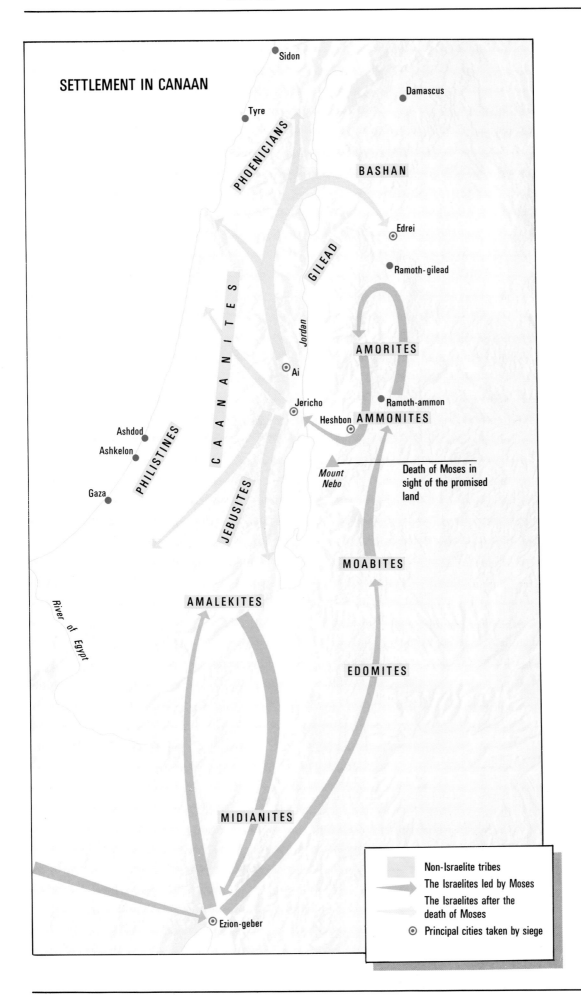

SETTLEMENT IN CANAAN

Sidon

Damascus

Tyre

PHOENICIANS

BASHAN

Edrei

GILEAD

Ramoth-gilead

Jordan

AMORITES

Ai

C A A N A N I T E S

Jericho

Ramoth-ammon

Heshbon AMMONITES

Ashdod

Ashkelon

PHILISTINES

Mount
Nebo

Death of Moses in
sight of the promised
land

Gaza

JEBUSITES

MOABITES

River of Egypt

AMALEKITES

EDOMITES

MIDIANITES

Ezion-geber

Non-Israelite tribes

The Israelites led by Moses

The Israelites after the
death of Moses

⊙ Principal cities taken by siege

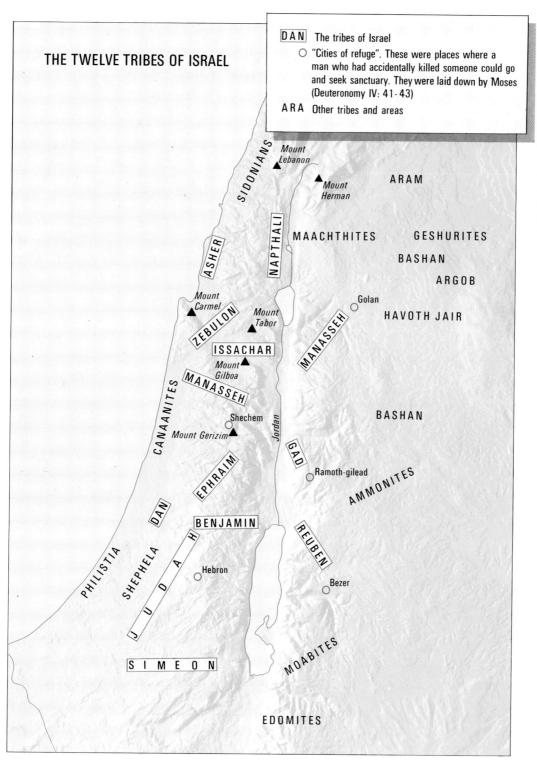

THE TWELVE TRIBES OF ISRAEL

DAN The tribes of Israel

○ "Cities of refuge". These were places where a man who had accidentally killed someone could go and seek sanctuary. They were laid down by Moses (Deuteronomy IV: 41-43)

ARA Other tribes and areas

LEFT: Despite their single, shared religious belief, the new Israelites stubbornly preserved their original tribal structure, which they traced back to the original Patriarchs. The idea of forming a single national unit under one king was alien to them. It took outside influence to make them change their views, although, even then, the powers of the king were severely limited.

and slaves. If a nobleman killed or injured a commoner or slave, his punishment would have been paltry compared to what he might have received had he killed or maimed one of his own class. This difference in treatment before the law remained a cornerstone of the world's judicial systems for centuries. It provides a stark contrast with the Laws of Moses, where nowhere is there any hint of a legal distinction between rich and poor.

The word "slave," as used in the Bible, has led to some misunderstanding. In fact, the Hebrew word *eved* means an indentured servant, a status similar to that of a serf or villein in the Middle Ages. However, in the King James version of the Hebrew Bible, it is translated as "slave," "servant," or "bondsman," depending on the context and the meaning the translator wished to convey. It is important to realize that "slavery" in biblical times was nothing like the enslavement practiced later, in Romanov Russia before the emancipation of the serfs by Tsar Alexander II, or as in the American South before the Civil War, when a slave's status was often lower than that of an animal and his only worth was as an item of property. The Laws of Moses insist that "slaves" have the same rights before the law as everyone else and that they must be set free of their obligations after a certain period.

A new attitude toward the sanctity of human life and what modern psychologists would call "interpersonal relationships" is also apparent in Mosaic law. Even the treatment of strangers was considered:

Thou shalt neither vex a stranger, nor oppress him; for ye were strangers in the land of Egypt. EXODUS 22:20

The Greeks, who did not encounter the Jews until about 375 B.C.E., were to express amazement at – and even admiration for – some of the manifestations of this life-enhancing concept. The Jews, whom Aristotle's pupil Theophrastus and his contemporaries called "philosophers by race," were even commended for failing to expose newborn babies to the elements to kill off the weakest. The Roman historian Tacitus, however, expressed contempt for the fact that "the Jews even consider it a crime to kill a newborn infant."

Health and hygiene are also matters that were enshrined in law for the first time. The Mosaic realization of the potential for contamination by corpses, vermin, and excrement was far in advance of its time; some aspects were not recognized in Europe until the discovery of microbes in the eighteenth century. In addition, the Jewish customs of washing the hands before a meal and refraining from eating certain foods that are easily contaminated, such as pork and shellfish, are all given the status of a divine command in Mosaic law. Admittedly food taboos were by no means unknown in other contemporary cultures – there is even a reference to the food taboos of the ancient Egyptians in Genesis 43:32 – but few seem to have had the same logical basis as those of the Jews. The Jewish preoccupation with health has been the butt of jokes through the ages, but countless non-Jewish medical sources have noted that,

when people have been forced to live in adverse conditions, it is the Jewish community that has remained the healthiest.

Another innovation was the introduction of an official day of rest: the Sabbath. Jews have always considered the Sabbath so important that they have given it a status equal to that of a major festival, even though it occurs every week. The idea of allowing everyone, even "slaves," to have a day of rest, is now virtually universal, though in many cultures it only became established less than 100 years ago.

It is hardly surprising that among the hundreds of laws contained in the Mosaic canon some are considered offensive or incompatible with modern ways of thinking. Among these are the imposition of the death penalty for crimes other than murder and such occasional bizarre and obscure pronouncements as *"Thou shalt not suffer a witch to live"* (Exodus 22:18). However, it is one thing to stipulate penalties and another to impose them. In practice, the death penalty was hardly ever resorted to by Jewish courts of law in the Holy Land, and it is doubtful whether it was even imposed in Moses's day.

The Laws bestowed the habits of diet and lifestyle which set the Jews apart.

The Conquest of Canaan

Moses himself was not destined to enter the Holy Land. It was left to his young general Joshua to lead a military campaign against the Canaanites, the tribes who inhabited Canaan, the land that had been promised to the Hebrews. The biblical impression that this conquest was swift is not the whole story; some sections of the native population held out and it took centuries to subdue them. Although no trace of God's destruction of the walls has been found at Jericho, the city of Hatzor does bear the marks of Joshua's military might in the late thirteenth century B.C.E.

Joshua, named by Moses as his successor to lead the Children of Israel into the promised land, was the first of the "judges." While acting partly as legal authorities, these were really administrators and military leaders who held their posts for life and who, according to the book of the Bible that bears their title, were appointed by God. Their achievements in the military field reached a climax when the last major Canaanite ruler, Jabin (or Javin), was defeated in northern Galilee in the twelfth century B.C.E. The Hebrew general responsible for the victory was Barak, acting on behalf of Deborah, the only woman judge and indeed the only example of a female ruler in her own right in Hebrew history.

The phenomenon of Deborah is especially surprising when one realizes that the status of women in Judaism, inherited from previous Semitic cultures, is such a lowly one. The usual explanation for this is that the pagan goddesses were frequently connected with such practices as fertility rites and sacred prostitution, which (like all sexual deviation) were considered an abomination in Mosaic law. As a result, women could not be appointed priests and had no inheritance rights, although they were allowed to keep their dowries. Although, in the centuries that followed, this tradition was upheld by the rabbis and even reinforced by them (as will be seen later), in practice Jewish women have enjoyed greater independence and authority than their non-Jewish counterparts, even though this may merely have been as a result of the circumstances in which they found themselves.

The period of the judges lasted for about 200 years. By now, the Children of Israel had conquered the land of Canaan, which they called "Israel" after themselves. The Bible, too, gives the Hebrews a new name: "Israelites." They had learned much from their neighbors and their enemies about agriculture, art, and a settled way of life. However, they often absorbed the bad with the good, and the Bible reports repeated falls from grace and lapses into idolatry.

The Israelites, despite their uniform beliefs, were still a collection of tribes, without an organized state, and they seem to have rejected the idea of a sovereign ruler out of hand. However, a new type of leader was soon to emerge to lead them out of this amorphous situation.

The Prophets

Although the term "prophet" is also used for such prominent biblical figures as Moses and David, the first true prophet in Israel was Samuel. He was the son of Elkanah and

ABOVE: *A carving of grapes and a wine chalice from the synagogue at Capernaum on Lake Tiberius.*

RIGHT: *A winged bull from Nineveh, the capital of the Assyrian Empire, which was one of the Jews' chief foes.*

Hannah, whose career began, in the late eleventh century B.C.E., as an acolyte to the then high priest, Eli.

The Israelite prophets were not merely fortune tellers, although they did occasionally prophesy the future (often a gloomy one). They were primarily involved in interpreting God's will to their contemporaries, and as such would remonstrate with reigning monarchs and point out the error of their ways, which made them less than popular with those in power. Despite this, they were held in the highest esteem and even awe. The

RIGHT: *With his military successes against the Philistines and other potential rivals, David laid the foundations of a strong state and extended his rule over many peoples in the area; his successor, Solomon, built on this to lead the Jews into what is popularly believed to have been a golden age.*

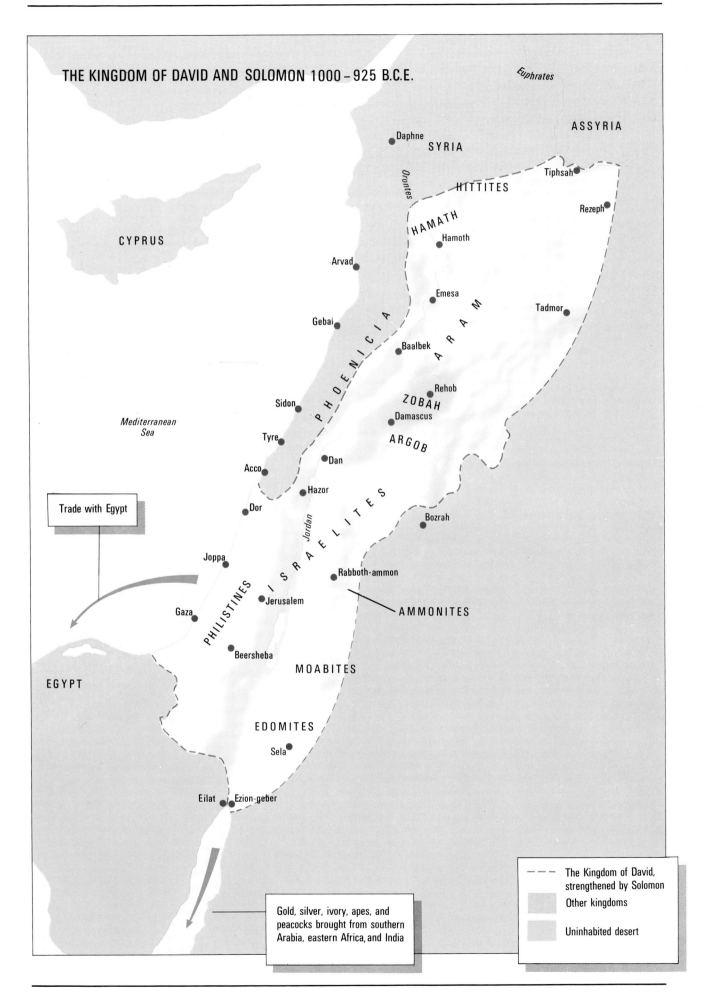

THE KINGDOM OF DAVID AND SOLOMON 1000 – 925 B.C.E.

Euphrates

ASSYRIA

Daphne

SYRIA

Tiphsah

HITTITES

Rezeph

Orontes

HAMATH

Hamoth

CYPRUS

Arvad

Emesa

A R A M

Tadmor

Gebal

Baalbek

Rehob

Mediterranean Sea

Z O B A H

Sidon

Damascus

Tyre

A R G O B

Dan

Acco

Hazor

I S R A E L I T E S

Trade with Egypt

Dor

Bozrah

Jordan

Joppa

Rabboth-ammon

P H I L I S T I N E S

Jerusalem

AMMONITES

Gaza

Beersheba

EGYPT

MOABITES

EDOMITES

Sela

Eilat

Ezion-geber

Gold, silver, ivory, apes, and peacocks brought from southern Arabia, eastern Africa, and India

- - - The Kingdom of David, strengthened by Solomon

Other kingdoms

Uninhabited desert

meekness of David, for example, when the prophet Nathan denounced him for the immorality of his behavior over Bathsheba (2 Samuel 12:1–13) is astonishing by the standards of any period. At the height of Samuel's power, as the Bible puts it:

> **The Lord was with him and did let none of his words fall to the ground. And all Israel from Dan even to Beersheba knew that Samuel was established even to be a prophet of the Lord.**
>
> 1 SAMUEL 3: 19–20.

In Samuel's day, the most formidable of the Israelites' enemies were the Philistines, who are almost certainly the "peoples of the sea" referred to in contemporary Egyptian documents. Although depicted as barbarians by the Israelites (a reputation that has long outlived them), they were, in fact, a highly developed race, who may well have been an offshoot of the Minoan civilization of Crete. They were definitely not Semites for they did not practice circumcision, a pan-Semitic custom to this day. The Philistines held tenaciously to a coastal strip that extended from what is today the Gaza Strip right up to Jaffa in the north – land that was, as now, the most fertile region of Israel. They even, in one battle, had the temerity to capture the Ark of the Covenant from the Israelites.

The Ark of the Covenant, a gilded acacia-wood chest carried on poles, was a portable shrine which was carried into battle by Joshua and the judges-appointed generals who succeeded him. When the Philistines captured it, it allegedly brought them nothing but harm – the image of their chief god, Dagon (a fertility symbol whose name lives on in the Hebrew word for "grain" or "silage"), even fell flat on its face before it (1 Samuel 5:1–6). The Ark was recovered during the Israelite victory at Mizpeh, and Samuel erected a standing stone, which he called *Eben-ezer* (which means "stone of assistance"), to commemorate the event.

As Samuel grew older, the people of Israel, no doubt influenced by their neighbors, changed their minds about the type of leadership they wanted. They saw the advantages of royal rule, and turned to Samuel to choose a king for them. Samuel reluctantly asked God to help, and God told him to choose Saul, the son of Kish.

The Kings of Israel

The fact that Saul was chosen and anointed by Samuel, who continued to maintain his authority over Saul until the end of the king's days, demonstrates the importance of the prophets and the nature of kingship in Israel. There never was even a whisper of the divine right of kings. If a king tried to claim too much power, he would soon face the opposition of the prophets and the people. Saul, for example, could not choose his own successor, and David was not considered fit to build the Temple in Jerusalem, though he longed to do so. These limits placed on men in power – which we could call "democracy" – are characteristic of Jewish life down through the ages.

Saul fell out of favor with the aging Samuel when he refused to destroy the hostile tribe of the Amalekites. This was a foretaste of further disobedience. Samuel then rejected Saul and vowed not to let his heirs rule Israel. Instead, Saul was succeeded by his son-in-law David – a trained sling-shooter who had distinguished himself in single combat against the Philistine giant Goliath. After him came Solomon, and together they would inspire some of the greatest works of art in the Christian world, representing the apotheosis of the mighty sovereign. David and Solomon represent the Golden Age of the Israelite monarchy.

The Bible paints a more complete portrait of David than of any other figure. He was a complex character: an innocent young shepherd boy; close friend of the king's son Jonathan; a talented psalmist and musician; and, later, a fierce fighter and implacable enemy, as well as a lusty lover. David, chosen through Samuel, is described more than once in the Bible as "the Lord's anointed." He was the first embodiment of the Messianic concept in Judaism: one of his descendants would return to save the Jews in their hour of need. It is indicative of the Jewish attitude toward David that, although he could not have written all of the Psalms, some of which were composed about 1000 years after his death, all of them have been attributed to him, as the founder of Jerusalem, the spiritual home of the Jews.

Jerusalem and its eastern suburb, known as Zion, had been inhabited for at least 2000 years before David's conquest. Jerusalem is

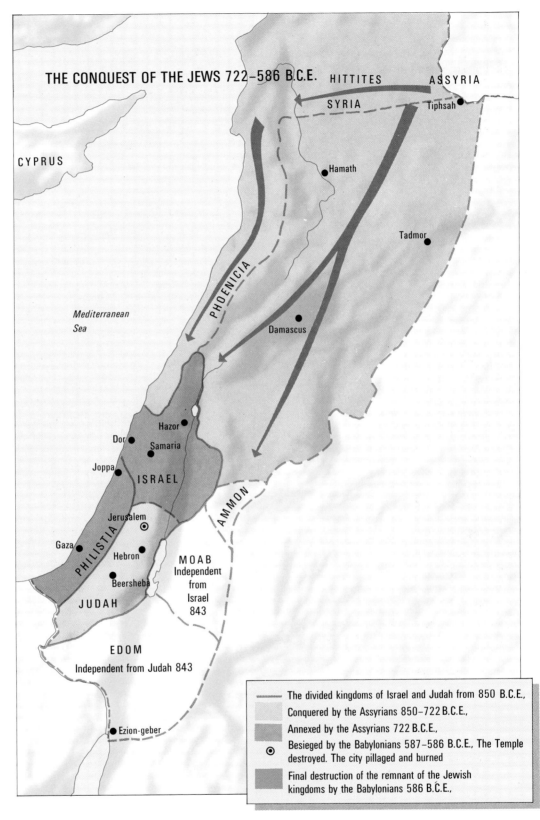

THE CONQUEST OF THE JEWS 722–586 B.C.E.

CYPRUS

HITTITES

ASSYRIA

SYRIA

Tiphsah

Hamath

Tadmor

PHOENICIA

Mediterranean Sea

Damascus

Hazor

Dor

Samaria

Joppa

ISRAEL

Jerusalem ⊙

Gaza

Hebron

PHILISTIA

Beersheba

AMMON

JUDAH

MOAB
Independent from Israel 843

EDOM
Independent from Judah 843

Ezion-geber

The divided kingdoms of Israel and Judah from 850 B.C.E.,

Conquered by the Assyrians 850–722 B.C.E.,

Annexed by the Assyrians 722 B.C.E.,

⊙ Besieged by the Babylonians 587–586 B.C.E., The Temple destroyed. The city pillaged and burned

Final destruction of the remnant of the Jewish kingdoms by the Babylonians 586 B.C.E.,

mentioned in the Bible as the territory of the Jebusites, one of the Canaanite peoples. David bought a threshing floor in the city from Araunah the Jebusite (2 Samuel: 21–23), where he set up an altar; it was on this site that the Temple was eventually built by Solomon. Jerusalem was not only an easily defensible mountain stronghold but also located in a neutral area between the northern and southern territories of the Twelve Tribes of Israel, a sort of "federal district" shared between the Tribes.

Solomon has been depicted through the centuries as the archetype of a great king. There are the stories of his legendary wealth, his thousands of wives and concubines, his trading ships and his dealings with neighboring monarchs who, like the Queen of Sheba, came to pay their respects to him. Solomon's building program was to be rivaled only by that of the later Herod the Great, and its crowning glory was the Temple. The expensive building materials – including cedars of Lebanon – came largely from Tyre, and Solomon forged important strategic alliances, notably with the powerful Phoenician king Hiram, to attain his goal of making the Temple the most magnificent structure in the region.

The Bible goes into the minutest detail about the Temple's architecture and the ritual that was carried out within its precincts; the vast sacrifices of grain and beasts; the specially baked "shew-bread" for sacrifice, arrayed under the magnificent cloths on the altar tables (Jews still bake special breads for the Sabbath in memory of this shew-bread); the *"sounding brass and tinkling cymbal"* of the musicians; and the priests and high priest garbed in spectacular robes. The innermost sanctuary – the Holy of Holies – housed the Ark of the Covenant; even the high priest himself could enter it only once a year. The precise meanings of some aspects of Temple ritual have been forgotten; these include the *urim* and the *thummim*, which were worn by the priests around the neck and seem to have been used for divination.

The Two Kingdoms

When Solomon died in about 930 B.C.E., he left a land almost bankrupted by his excessive spending, in which the difference between rich and poor had increased. Solomon's son and heir, Rehoboam, refused to placate the disgruntled tribes in the north of the kingdom, and his brother, the rebel general Jeroboam, who had led an unsuccessful revolt in the last year of Solomon's reign, returned to lead these tribes into secession.

The kingdom was split in two. The two tribes of the south – Judah and Benjamin – held on to Jerusalem, Hebron, and Beersheba, and called themselves Judah. The remaining ten tribes of the north – Reuben, Simeon, Issaschar, Zebulun, Gad, Asher, Dan, Naph-

ABOVE: *Scenes from the life of David, from a twelfth-century English manuscript. In the sequence's first picture (top left), David is being ordered forth by Saul to fight the Philistine giant Goliath; in the fourth (middle section, right), he is being anointed king by the prophet Samuel; in the last (bottom right), he is mourning the death of his rebellious son Absalom.*

LEFT: *Solomon reading the Torah, from a late thirteenth-century Hebrew Bible and prayer book.*

SOLOMON'S GREAT TEMPLE

Before archaeology was established as a science, artists recreated Solomon's Temple in the image of their own age, as these architectural fantasies show.

What Solomon intended was quite clear. His new Temple was to be more than a permanent home for the Ark of the Covenant, it also signaled that the nomadic way of life was over and that centralized government had come to the Jewish people.

The Temple itself stood in a great court, which also housed the royal palace. As it was not designed to accommodate worshipers, it was a comparatively small building entered via a porch, between two ceremonial pillars, which led into the Hekhal, or main hall. This connected with the Debir, the innermost shrine, which housed the Ark of the Covenant. The whole interior was elaborately paneled with cedar wood.

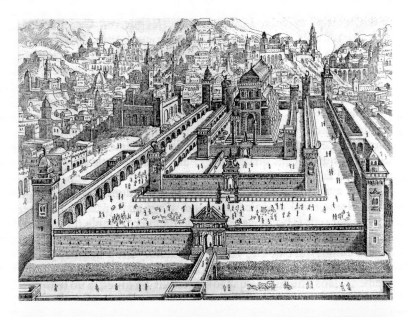

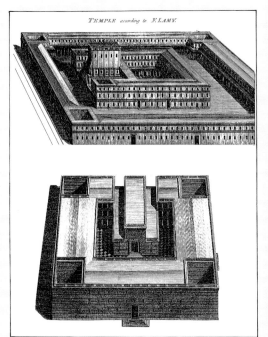

The Destruction of the Kingdom of Israel

The end of the northern kingdom of Israel began when King Omri (876–869 B.C.E.) gave his son Ahab in marriage to Jezebel, the daughter of the king of Tyre. Jezebel proved to be a much stronger character than her husband, a particular misfortune since she also was a militant adherent of the Phoenician deities Melkart, Astarte, and above all, Baal. She conducted a mission of conversion until Israel had more followers of Baal than of

ABOVE: *Food being sold to the citizens of beseiged Samaria, from the first edition of the Luther Bible (1534). Though in this instance, as predicted by the prophet Elisha, the besieging Assyrian forces mistook the city's starving lepers for reinforcements and withdrew, the divided Jews were no match for Assyria's military might in the long term.*

tali, Manasseh, and Ephraim – had their capital at Shechem (modern Nablus) on Mount Ephraim, also called Mount Gerizim, and they retained the name Israel. This northern kingdom, sometimes also referred to in the Bible as Ephraim or Samaria, was thus deprived of the city that had become the focus of Jewish worship.

In a desperate attempt to deflect the focus of worship away from Jerusalem, the capital of Judah, Jeroboam established two new temples – one at Bethel and the other in the territory of the Tribe of Dan – and had two golden calves made to rival the golden cherubim in the Temple at Jerusalem. The Bible is unclear as to whether Jeroboam was actually trying to establish a rival religion, but his efforts were not altogether popular with his subjects. Eventually, however, the faith of the tribes that constituted the new Israel proved unable to withstand assimilation with that of other nations.

The Bible records the open hostility between Judah and Israel which existed as long as the two Jewish kingdoms themselves managed to survive. Judah, however, not only had the advantage of the shrine of Jerusalem but also proved to have abler rulers than its northern rival. A number of kings of Israel were assassinated over frantic struggles for power, during which the kingdom changed hands three times in 50 years. During this period (913–869 B.C.E.), Judah was ruled peacefully by King Asa and his son Jehoshaphat. The kingdom's damaged fortunes and trade position improved.

RIGHT: *With the worldwide diaspora of the Jews, it is hardly surprising that many myths arose concerning the nature of the dispersion. One of the most widespread of these is the belief in the ten lost tribes of Israel, whose disappearance dates back to the Assyrian deportation of 740 to 700 B.C.E..*

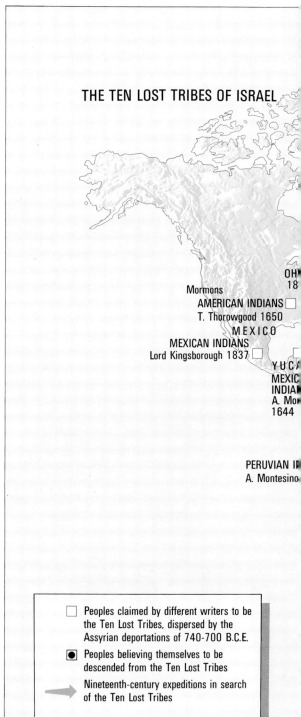

THE TEN LOST TRIBES OF ISRAEL

Mormons
OH
18
AMERICAN INDIANS ☐
T. Thorowgood 1650
MEXICO
MEXICAN INDIANS
Lord Kingsborough 1837 ☐
YUCA
MEXIC
INDIA
A. Mo
1644
PERUVIAN I
A. Montesino

☐ Peoples claimed by different writers to be the Ten Lost Tribes, dispersed by the Assyrian deportations of 740-700 B.C.E.

◉ Peoples believing themselves to be descended from the Ten Lost Tribes

➤ Nineteenth-century expeditions in search of the Ten Lost Tribes

the Jewish God. Jezebel's fiercest enemy was Elijah, chief among the prophets, whom she hated and feared and who correctly prophesied her eventual destruction. He was joined by the prophets Amos and Hosea in condemning the corruption of the kingdom.

Israel, being closer to the Assyrians in the north, was the first to fall victim to their onslaughts. Despite incredibly brave resistance in a series of wars that lasted for ten years, the Israelites were finally unable to withstand the force of Tiglath-Pileser III, the Assyrian king who had captured Babylon, and the country fell in 722 B.C.E. The kingdom was broken up and its people dispersed, becoming the "Ten Lost Tribes of Israel."

The Fall of Judah

Even in Judah, the lure of idolatry was proving strong. This kingdom was also under threat from the Assyrian empire to the north.

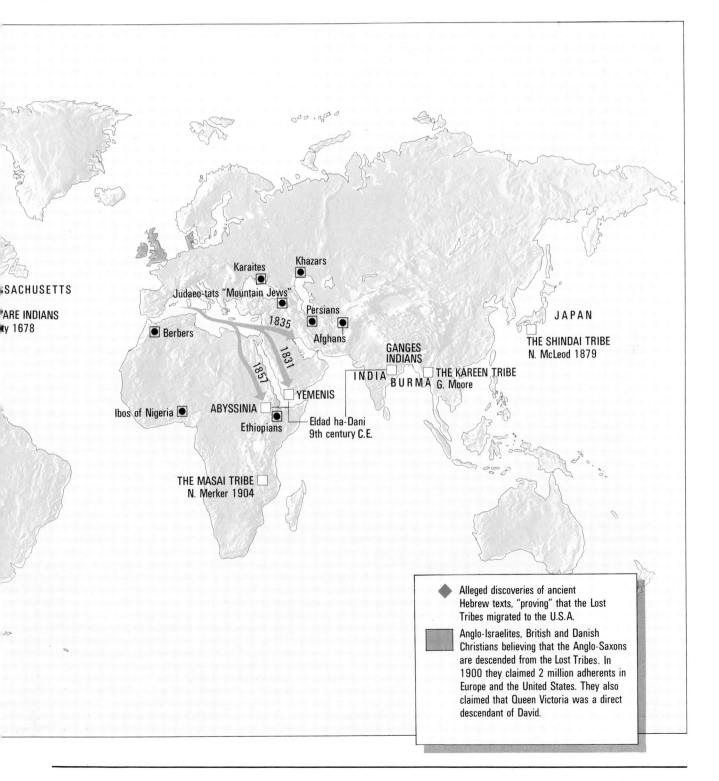

Karaites

Khazars

SACHUSETTS

'ARE INDIANS
ty 1678

Judaeo-tats "Mountain Jews"

Persians

1835

Afghans

JAPAN

THE SHINDAI TRIBE
N. McLeod 1879

Berbers

GANGES
INDIANS

1831

INDIA

THE KAREEN TRIBE
G. Moore

BURMA

1857

YEMENIS

Ibos of Nigeria

ABYSSINIA

Ethiopians

Eldad ha-Dani
9th century C.E.

THE MASAI TRIBE
N. Merker 1904

◆ Alleged discoveries of ancient Hebrew texts, "proving" that the Lost Tribes migrated to the U.S.A.

▢ Anglo-Israelites, British and Danish Christians believing that the Anglo-Saxons are descended from the Lost Tribes. In 1900 they claimed 2 million adherents in Europe and the United States. They also claimed that Queen Victoria was a direct descendant of David.

ABOVE: *The vanquished Jehu pays homage to the Assyrian ruler Shalmaneser III in this detail from the so-called Black Obelisk. The tribute Jehu was forced to concede included "silver, gold, a golden bowl, a golden vase, golden cups, golden buckets, tin, a staff for the royal hand, and purahati fruits," according to the inscription at the base. He was also forced to concede Israel's territories to the east of Jordan to Assyria.*

RIGHT: *Diaspora means "scattering" or "dispersal," and following the Assyrian and Babylonian conquests, Jewish communities were established in many of the key cities of the east. By the sixth century B.C.E. the influence of the Jews was widespread; they had risen to high status in Babylonia, where they were allowed to practice their religion freely.*

However, the Jews had a strong leader in King Josiah (reigned 638–608 B.C.E.), who probably had a greater influence on the practice of Judaism as we know it today than did David or Solomon.

Josiah ascended the throne at the age of eight. The regents who held the reins of power for him until he came of age tried to placate their threatening northern neighbor: they were extremely tolerant of idolatrous practices including intermarriage and the erection of temples to Assyrian deities. Wisely, they decided against helping Israel in its war against the Assyrians, which saved Judah from the same fate.

In 629/8 B.C.E., when Josiah reached the age of 20, he launched a massive revival of Judaism, beginning with the renovation of the Temple. During the restoration work, in the eighteenth year of Josiah's reign, a curious incident occurred (2 Kings 22:8–20 and 2 Chronicles 34:15–24). The high priest, Hilkiah, claimed to have found a manuscript described as "the book of the Law," and its authenticity was vouched for by an obscure prophetess called Huldah. Scholars believe that this was, in fact, the first written version of the book of Deuteronomy. Hitherto, what were called the "five books of Moses" – the

As

Mediter.

Alexandria

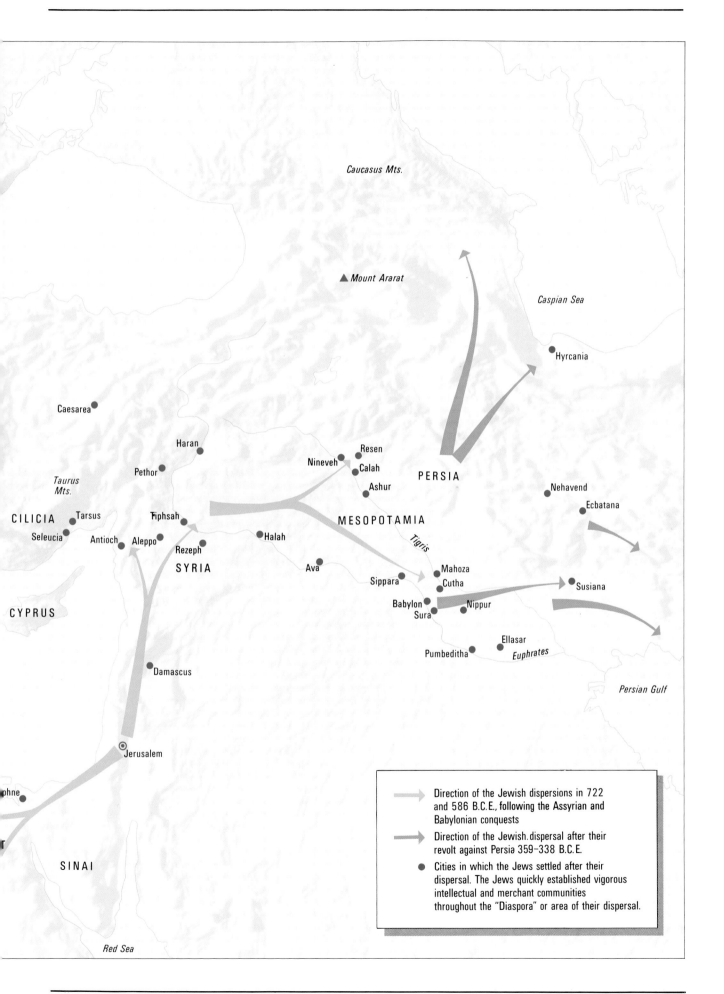

Caucasus Mts.

▲ Mount Ararat

Caspian Sea

Hyrcania

Caesarea

Haran

Resen
Nineveh
Calah
Ashur

PERSIA

Nehavend
Ecbatana

Taurus
Mts.

Pethor

CILICIA   Tarsus

Tiphsah

MESOPOTAMIA

Tigris

Seleucia
Antioch   Aleppo
Rezeph

SYRIA

Halah

Ava

Mahoza
Cutha
Sippara
Babylon   Nippur
Sura

Susiana

CYPRUS

Ellasar
Pumbeditha   Euphrates

Persian Gulf

Damascus

Jerusalem

phne

SINAI

Direction of the Jewish dispersions in 722
and 586 B.C.E., following the Assyrian and
Babylonian conquests

Direction of the Jewish dispersal after their
revolt against Persia 359–338 B.C.E.

● Cities in which the Jews settled after their
dispersal. The Jews quickly established vigorous
intellectual and merchant communities
throughout the "Diaspora" or area of their dispersal.

Red Sea

Pentateuch – had been handed down orally.

Although it is clear that the chief of the prophets, Jeremiah, was more than a little skeptical, he nevertheless applauded the religous reawakening that the find generated and approved of Josiah's campaign against various idolatrous practices. One of the commandments in the manuscript was the observance of the Passover. Josiah turned the traditional spring pilgrimage to the Temple into a celebration of the exodus from Egypt, an observance that Jews everywhere around the world have continued uninterrupted down through the centuries.

Judah's renewed glory was shortlived. In 612 B.C.E., Nineveh, the Assyrian capital, fell to a Babylonian upstart, and Babylon regained its old domination of the region. Then in 608 B.C.E., Josiah was killed in battle against the combined forces of the Assyrians and Egyptians at Megiddo – a battle that was to give its name to the prophetic world battle in the Book of Revelation in the New Testament: Armageddon.

Josiah's son Jehoiakim kept the voracious new enemy Babylon at bay by allying Judah with the Egyptians (against Jeremiah's advice) and paying tribute to the Babylonians. But when he became bolder and withheld payments, the Babylonians invaded. After replacing Jehoiakim with Jehoiachin, the invaders left, but the new ruler, too, proved unsatisfactory to the enemy. In 597 B.C.E., their king Nebuchadnezzar captured Jerusalem. The wealthiest families were carried off into captivity, Jehoiachin among them, leaving behind his son Zedekiah on the throne.

In the years that followed, Jeremiah repeatedly urged Zedekiah not to provoke the Babylonian conquerors, but in vain. Two synchronized Jewish uprisings, one in Judah and one in Babylon itself, brought the full might of Nebuchadnezzar's armies to bear against Jerusalem. The siege lasted two years, but on the ninth day of the month of Av, 586 B.C.E., the Babylonian general Nebuzar-adan captured the Temple, carried away the sacred vessels, and razed the building to the ground. He then forced Zedekiah to witness the murders of his sons before having his eyes put out. The king was then bound in chains and sent with most of the remaining population of Judah into captivity, where he died.

Only the poorest peasants were left behind.

The Babylonian Captivity

The words of the prophets at this time introduced a new dimension to Judaism. They preached on two levels: universal truths that were to spread throughout the civilized world; and a nationalistic cry exhorting the Judaeans – or "Jews" as they were now called – to retain their identity in the face of every adversity. In this, they were helped, curiously enough, by the Babylonian exile. Instead of destroying Judaism, as the conquerors intended, it probably saved the religion from degenerating into just another Semitic cult, focused on a shrine (the Temple in Jerusalem) and ruled by a priestly class.

The exiled Jews learned an important lesson from their prophets: they discovered

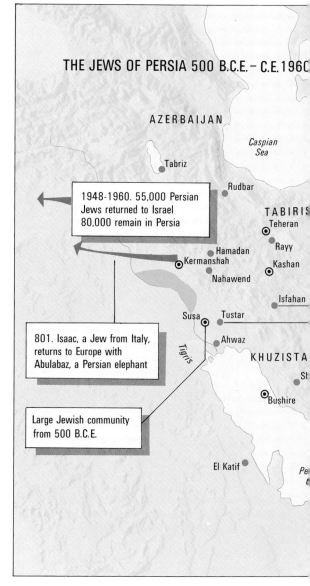

THE JEWS OF PERSIA 500 B.C.E. – C.E. 1960

AZERBAIJAN

Caspian Sea

Tabriz

Rudbar

TABIRIS
Teheran

1948-1960. 55,000 Persian Jews returned to Israel 80,000 remain in Persia

Rayy

Hamadan
Kermanshah
Kashan

Nahawend

Isfahan

Susa
Tustar

801. Isaac, a Jew from Italy, returns to Europe with Abulabaz, a Persian elephant

Ahwaz

Tigris

KHUZISTA

Large Jewish community from 500 B.C.E.

Bushire

El Katif

that Judaism did not depend solely on the Temple for its practice. In fact, some prophets, who found the rituals of the Temple suspiciously similar to the pagan variety, actually abhorred them. For example, Hosea proclaimed:

> **They sacrifice flesh for the sacrifices of mine offerings, and eat it; but the Lord accepteth them not ... For Israel hath forgotten his Maker and buildeth temples ...** HOSEA 7:13–14.

Now, for the first time, meeting places *(batei-knesset)* or synagogues were established where Jews could meet to worship, and sacrifices were replaced by prayer, a direct communication with God. Judaism had existed before the Temple and its priests, and it was destined to survive even after the Temple's destruction.

Despite the prominence given to the Babylonian exile in the Bible, it lasted only 48 years. During this time, Jeremiah, who had been imprisoned for sedition by King Zedekiah, was released by the Babylonians and managed to find shelter with other Jews who had succeeded in escaping captivity. However, the Babylonians were keeping a careful watch on the population of Judah in case of unrest, and especially on Jeremiah whom they knew to be influential. Eventually, he was persuaded by friends to flee to Egypt with others. Ironically, all his traveling companions soon began to practice the local religion – unlike the exiles in Babylonia who clung tenaciously to their faith.

The Babylonian captivity can be said to be the start of the diaspora – a Greek word for "scattering" or "dispersal." Surprisingly, despite their lamentations and despair, comparatively few of the exiled Jews volunteered to return to their homeland when such a return eventually became possible. During the intervening years, they had risen to high status in Babylonia – as they were to later under the Persians – and were allowed to practice their religion freely. Jews had also become highly placed in Egypt and Asia Minor. Thus, in the sixth century B.C.E., the influence of the Jews had begun to reach beyond the boundaries of the promised land.

The Return to Jerusalem under Persian Rule

Another empire rose to overwhelm Babylon, which fell for the last time. The Medes and the Persians, two closely related nations, were descended from Aryans from central Asia. Cyrus of Persia conquered the Medes in 550 B.C.E. and captured Babylon 11 years later, to become the ruler of a vast empire extending from the Mediterranean in the west to the Hindu Kush in the east.

Although an Aryan himself, Cyrus introduced Aramaic, a Semitic tongue, as the *lingua franca* of his empire. This language – still spoken by small Christian communities in Iraq, Syria, and Jordan – was to become for the Jews a tongue second in importance only to their native Hebrew. The books of Daniel and Esther were written partly in Aramaic, and it remained current in the Middle East for nearly 1,000 years.

The Persians quickly identified with their

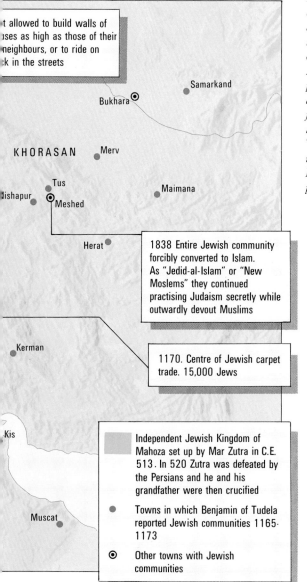

LEFT: *With the emergence of Persia as the dominant military power in the east, and the eclipse of Babylon, the Jews settled there and prospered. Cyrus the Great allowed them religious freedom and encouraged the rebuilding of the Temple in Jerusalem. It was only much later, under Muslim rule, that persecution began.*

t allowed to build walls of ses as high as those of their neighbours, or to ride on k in the streets

Samarkand

Bukhara

KHORASAN   Merv

Tus

Jishapur Meshed   Maimana

Herat

1838 Entire Jewish community forcibly converted to Islam. As "Jedid-al-Islam" or "New Moslems" they continued practising Judaism secretly while outwardly devout Muslims

Kerman

1170. Centre of Jewish carpet trade. 15,000 Jews

Kis

Independent Jewish Kingdom of Mahoza set up by Mar Zutra in C.E. 513. In 520 Zutra was defeated by the Persians and he and his grandfather were then crucified

Muscat

● Towns in which Benjamin of Tudela reported Jewish communities 1165-1173

◉ Other towns with Jewish communities

ABOVE: *The siege of Lachish, shown in a relief from Sennacherib's palace in Nineveh. With the death in battle of Josiah against the combined forces of Assyria and Egypt at Megiddo, the fall of Judah could not be long delayed.*

would be an asset. However, although he encouraged the return of the Jews to their land, he had no intention of allowing them complete independence from Persian rule. Instead, Judah became the Persian "satrapy," or province, of Yahud.

The first to return were a small group of Jews led by Sheshbazzar, who had been appointed governor of Yahud. Once there, Zerubabbel – probably a grandson of Jehoiakim, the last legitimate king of Judah (some historians believe Sheshbazzar and Zerubabbel to have been the same person) – and Joshua, son of the last high priest of the Temple, constructed an altar on its former site. Temple sacrifices were renewed on the first day of the month of Tishri 538 B.C.E., at a festival then known as the Feast of Trumpets (the date is now celebrated as the Jewish New Year). Seven months later, work began on building the Second Temple itself, using cedarwood ordered from Lebanon. The older Jews present, who remembered the First Temple, must have wept bitter tears over Solomon's glories, which would never be fully restored.

The pagan population of Yahud – the Edomites (or Idumeans) and the nomadic tribes who had filled the vacuum left by the exiled Jews – were as strongly opposed to renewed Jewish occupation as the Arabs were to be, more than 2400 years later. They appealed to Cyrus and to his son and successor, Cambyses II, claiming that the Temple would become the focus for a Jewish uprising. Cambyses, who had inherited none of his father's wisdom or tolerance, was persuaded by their arguments and ordered all restoration work to come to a halt.

Nine years went by, during which the Jews concentrated on rebuilding other parts of their devastated land. Finally, the prophets Haggai and Zachariah urged that work on the Temple be restarted. Meanwhile, a new king had ascended the Persian throne: Darius I. When the satrap (governor) of Trans-Euphrates remonstrated with him over the resumption of the building works in Jerusalem, he received an astonishing reply. "The Jews are the servants of the God of Heaven and Earth," said Darius, "and this Temple ... has been rebuilt on the order given by Cyrus."

The satrap demanded proof of this order,

Jewish subjects, for they, too, adhered to a monotheistic religion, unlike the surrounding pagan nations. Zoroaster (also known as Zarathustra), a religious reformer, had arisen in the previous generation to "purify" belief (somewhat like Akhnaton's venture in Egypt), and he converted the Persian royal family. Soon Zoroastrianism, with its worship of the supreme deity, Ahuramazda, and its cult of fire, became the state religion. Tolerance was one of its tenets, and Cyrus permitted all forms of worship – including Judaism – within his empire.

Cyrus also had a very practical reason for helping the Jews and for issuing his famous edict for the restoration of the vessels stolen from Jerusalem and assistance in rebuilding the Temple. Judah straddled the border between the Persian and Egyptian empires, and having friends in this strategic zone

and a search was made of the summer palace, which duly produced a copy of Cyrus's edict. The king's treasury even helped to finance the cost of the rebuilding of the ruined Temple, which was finally completed on the 3rd of Adar (February–March) 515 B.C.E.

Ezra and Nehemiah

Despite this new beginning, the Jews of Yahud squabbled among themselves, and the land was neglected and the walls of Jerusalem fell into disrepair. It was not for another 50 years that order was restored and further progress made in the practice of Judaism. All this was the result of the arrival of a new idealistic group from Babylon under Ezra the scribe.

Ezra had been an important official at the court of Artaxerxes I of Persia (reigned 464–24 B.C.E.). Arriving in Jerusalem with presents from the king for the Temple and its priests, he wept when he saw the lamentable state into which his religion had fallen. His first demand was that intermarriage with pagan women should cease, a practice of which even the priests had been guilty.

Ezra was assisted in his work of spiritual renewal by Nehemiah, a former minister of the Persian court. Learning of the poor state of Jerusalem, he asked for and was granted permission to emigrate to Yahud as its new governor. Hastening to Jerusalem with more gifts, he immediately set about restoring the city to its former glory, beginning by building up its walls.

Ezra's most important contribution to Judaism was his codification of the four books of the Bible – Genesis, Exodus, Leviticus and Numbers – that, with Deuteronomy ("discovered" in Josiah's time), make

LEFT: *The prophet Ezra rewriting the Sacred Records, from the* Codex Amiatinus, *created at Jarrow in the early eighth century. He had been commanded by Artaxerxes I to restore Jewish law; his most important contribution was the codification of the first four books of the Bible. These, together with* Deuteronomy, *make up the Jewish Torah.*

ABOVE: *A modern rabbi with a Torah scroll. The tradition Ezra founded of public readings of the Torah is still maintained in Judaism today.*

up the Pentateuch or *Torah*. When, on the Feast of Trumpets, Nehemiah finished his rebuilding work, Ezra read to the people from the now-completed Hebrew text of the Torah, and spent the whole morning explaining its meaning in Aramaic, the common tongue since the time of Cyrus. He also decreed that the Torah should be read on the Sabbath, as well as at the Monday and Thursday markets in major towns.

Thus was born the tradition of the public reading of the Torah and the vast explanatory literature that has surrounded it. The trans-

lations of and commentaries on the Torah in the vernacular are known as the *Targum* (the Aramaic word for "translation"). Several versions exist today, and besides explanation, they contain many legends and stories about biblical heroes.

Ten days after the Feast of Trumpets, the Jews again gathered in the Temple, this time to repent of their sins and mourn for the fate of Judah. Ezra and Nehemiah turned this into an annual event: the Day of Atonement, or Yom Kippur *(Yom Ha-kippurim)*. Ezra also revived the Feast of Tabernacles —

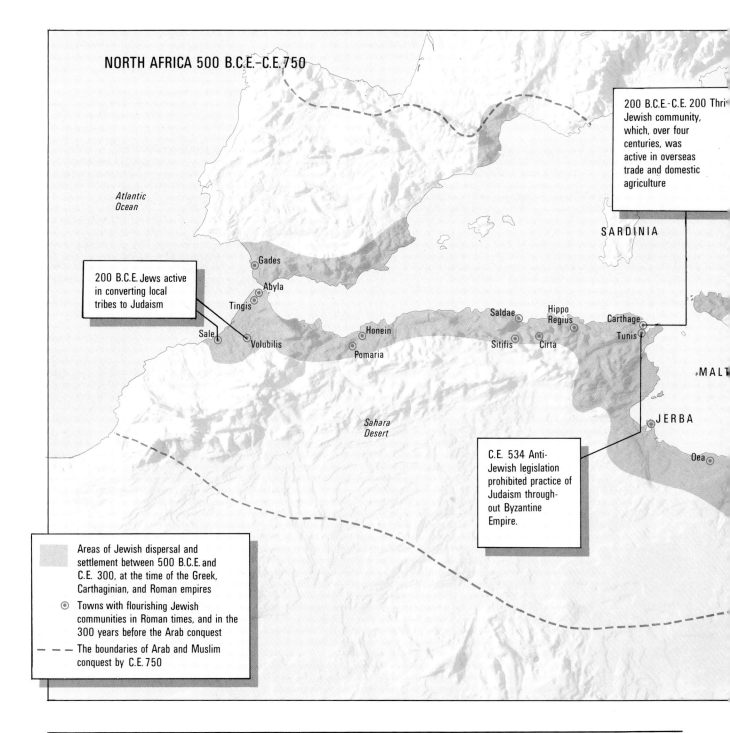

NORTH AFRICA 500 B.C.E.–C.E. 750

200 B.C.E.-C.E. 200 Thri[ving] Jewish community, which, over four centuries, was active in overseas trade and domestic agriculture

Atlantic Ocean

SARDINIA

Gades

200 B.C.E. Jews active in converting local tribes to Judaism

Abyla

Tingis

Saldae · Hippo Regius · Carthage

Honein · Sitifis · Cirta · Tunis

Sale · Volubilis

Pomaria

MALT[A]

Sahara Desert

JERBA

C.E. 534 Anti-Jewish legislation prohibited practice of Judaism throughout Byzantine Empire.

Oea

Areas of Jewish dispersal and settlement between 500 B.C.E. and C.E. 300, at the time of the Greek, Carthaginian, and Roman empires

⊚ Towns with flourishing Jewish communities in Roman times, and in the 300 years before the Arab conquest

— — The boundaries of Arab and Muslim conquest by C.E. 750

Sukkot – in commemoration of the temporary dwellings erected by the Hebrews after the exodus, and thus of their wandering through the desert wilderness.

The Hellenistic Period

Two centuries after the death of Artaxerxes I, the Persian empire fell easy prey to a new world conqueror – Alexander of Macedon, known to history as Alexander the Great (reigned 336–23 B.C.E.). It is not known for certain if he ever visited the Holy Land, although he certainly did travel (possibly overland) from Tyre to Egypt in 332 B.C.E. In any event, he rapidly conquered the whole of the Middle East and beyond – from the Indus to the Nile – opening up the east to all things Greek.

Through the influence of Alexander and his successors, the Asiatic and Semitic peoples became hellenized (from the Greek word *Hellenizo*, "to make Greek"). They adopted Greek dress, lifestyles, and culture, and absorbed the vast amounts of knowledge found in the Greek libraries that Alexander had placed at their disposal. The Greek gods

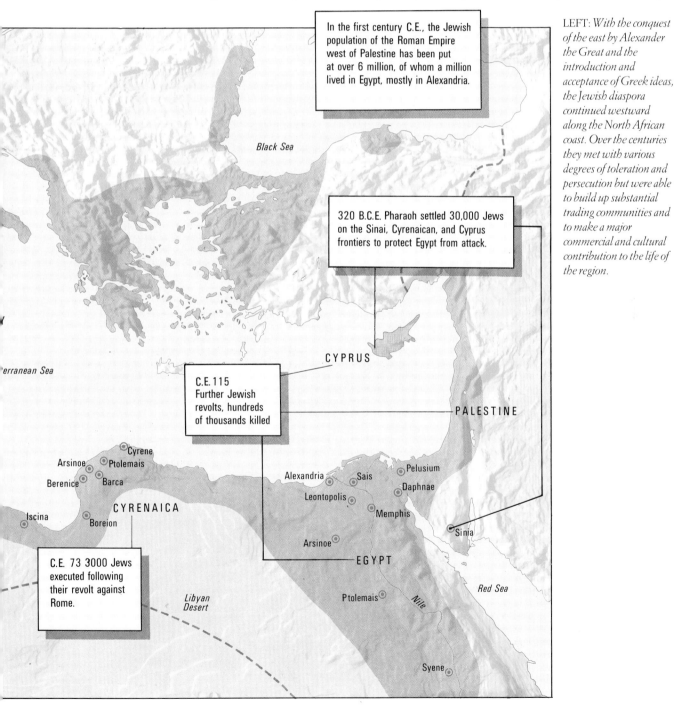

In the first century C.E., the Jewish population of the Roman Empire west of Palestine has been put at over 6 million, of whom a million lived in Egypt, mostly in Alexandria.

320 B.C.E. Pharaoh settled 30,000 Jews on the Sinai, Cyrenaican, and Cyprus frontiers to protect Egypt from attack.

C.E. 115 Further Jewish revolts, hundreds of thousands killed

C.E. 73 3000 Jews executed following their revolt against Rome.

Black Sea

Mediterranean Sea

CYPRUS

PALESTINE

Cyrene
Arsinoe
Ptolemais
Berenice
Barca
Iscina
Boreion
CYRENAICA

Alexandria
Sais
Pelusium
Daphnae
Leontopolis
Memphis
Arsinoe
Sinia

EGYPT

Libyan Desert

Ptolemais

Nile

Red Sea

Syene

LEFT: *With the conquest of the east by Alexander the Great and the introduction and acceptance of Greek ideas, the Jewish diaspora continued westward along the North African coast. Over the centuries they met with various degrees of toleration and persecution but were able to build up substantial trading communities and to make a major commercial and cultural contribution to the life of the region.*

were also adopted with enthusiasm by the Semitic peoples – with one notable exception. Although many Jews, and especially those of the upper classes, embraced Greek ideas and customs, they drew the line at the Greek religion; those of the lower classes simply regarded these new ideas and fashions with suspicion.

Despite this, Greek influence on the Jews was to prove pervasive. This can be seen from the number of Greek words that were absorbed into Hebrew, and the adoption of Greek as the vernacular outside Palestine. The Jews of Cyprus and those of Alexandria in Egypt, for instance, who in the first century B.C.E. were more numerous than those in Palestine, spoke and wrote Greek to the exclusion of Hebrew (the language of prayer) and even Aramaic, until then the common speech of the Middle East.

Judah became the vassal province of Judea, ruled by the direct and indirect heirs of Alexander. First came the Ptolemies, Egyptian kings of Macedonian descent who controlled Judea from 301 to 198 B.C.E.

Legend has it that when Ptolemy II (reigned 285–46 B.C.E.) decided that he wanted to know more about the religion of the Jews who were his subjects, he commissioned each of 70 scholars to translate the Scriptures – which by now consisted of the Torah and some subsequent writings – into Greek. All 70 scholars, it was said, miraculously produced identical translations. Despite the fact that it was probably the Jews of Alexandria who sponsored the Greek translation, this version of the Bible has become known as the "Septuagint," from the Latin word for "seventy."

The Seleucids
Another family that carved themselves a piece of Alexander's Middle Eastern empire were the Seleucids, descended from Seleucus, one of the conqueror's Macedonian generals. The Seleucids, making their home in Babylonia (modern Iraq) and Syria, engaged in constant squabbling with the Ptolemies in Egypt. Naturally enough, Judea became a battleground, with its own pro-Ptolemy and pro-Seleucid factions, and all the internal disunity that this unwelcome development generated.

Judea finally fell to one of the Seleucids –

Antiochus III – in 198 B.C.E., and became part of "Coele-Syria and Phoenicia," the province that comprised all the territory previously held by the Ptolemies. Antiochus issued decrees favorable to the Jews, forbidding strangers from entering the Temple precincts and offering help to renew their land, which had been laid waste by years of war.

His grandson Antiochus IV Epiphanes ("The Magnificent"; reigned 175–63 B.C.E.) was not so tolerant. Called Antiochus Epimanes ("The Mad") by his enemies, he was a megalomaniac who eventually forced his

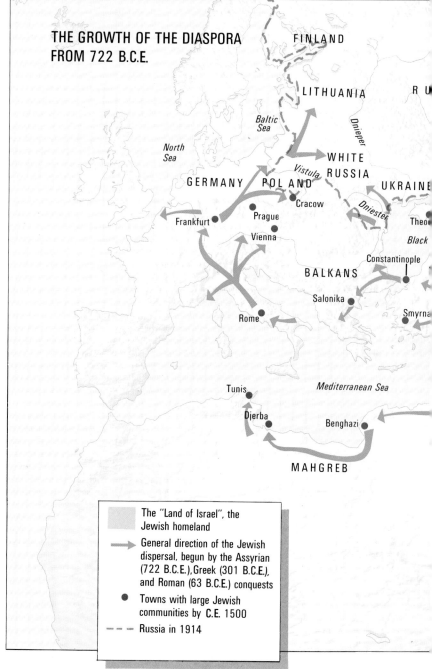

THE GROWTH OF THE DIASPORA FROM 722 B.C.E.

The "Land of Israel", the Jewish homeland

General direction of the Jewish dispersal, begun by the Assyrian (722 B.C.E.), Greek (301 B.C.E.), and Roman (63 B.C.E.) conquests

● Towns with large Jewish communities by C.E. 1500

– – – Russia in 1914

subjects to adopt every aspect of hellenism, even those which he knew to be repugnant to the Jews; he also renamed Jerusalem "Antioch in Jerusalem" and had a stadium built there.

Antiochus continued the war against Egypt and the Ptolemies, but by now the latter had won the support of a new and powerful ally: Rome. On a march against Egypt, the Seleucid king was waylaid by Roman troops. The Roman ambassador to Egypt drew a circle in the sand around Antiochus and ordered him to stay within it – that is, to keep to his own territories.

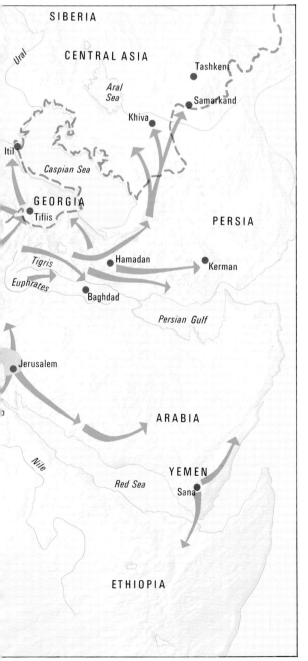

ABOVE: *The entry of Ptolemy Soter (the "Preserver") into Jerusalem. One of the leading generals of Alexander the Great, Ptolemy received Egypt when the Greek empire Alexander had created was divided after his death. Ptolemy did much to make Alexandria a cultural and artistic center, founding the city's great library; under him Alexandria's Jewish community grew in size, strength, and prestige.*

LEFT: *From the time of the Assyrian conquests of 722 B.C.E., the Jews were a people on the move, as their homeland, and later their adopted countries, fell under the control of successive alien empires or became places of prejudice and persecution. However, in each generation some sought to return to the promised land, Israel.*

The humiliated monarch retreated. Jerusalem lay in his path. The city was looted and virtually destroyed and the Temple desecrated. Decrees were issued abolishing Temple worship and outlawing the practice of Judaism on pain of death. In December 167 B.C.E., an altar to Zeus was erected inside the Temple, on which the flesh of a sow was offered as a sacrifice.

The Early Hasmoneans

Jewish resistance to these Seleucid decrees was courageous. Of the many tales of martyrdom, some are to be found in the story of Esther and the book of Daniel, as well as in the books of the Maccabees.

An underground movement was established in Judea to fight Antiochus and perpetuate a purified form of Judaism. These Hasideans ("Pious"), hiding in caves in the desert, were led by a member of the Hasmonean family. Mattathias, a priest from Modiin in southwestern Samaria, had already defied Seleucid officials who had tried to force him to sacrifice to Zeus; now he and his five sons raised an open rebellion.

ABOVE: *Judas Maccabeus rededicates the altar of the Temple, following his defeat of the Syrians and occupation of Jerusalem in 164 B.C.E. The Hasmoneans, whom Maccabeus led, were at the forefront of Jewish resistance to Seleucid occupation.*

OPPOSITE PAGE: *Resistance to the Seleucids culminated in a successful guerilla war led by the Hasmonean family. Finally an outright military victory liberated Jerusalem in 164 B.C.E.. The Hasmoneans became priest-kings of Judea, but subsequent civil war led to Roman intervention. Pompey invaded Judea in 67 B.C.E. and the country became a client state in 63 B.C.E.*

Incredibly, a little band led by Mattathias's third son, Judas – nicknamed "Maccabeus" ("The Hammer"), began to win skirmishes with the Seleucid forces, and using guerilla tactics, they eventually defeated them outright. Judas marched triumphantly into Jerusalem and set about cleansing and purifying the Temple, and in December 164 B.C.E., three years to the day after its desecration, it was rededicated. One year later, Antiochus IV was dead.

Although Judas defeated their commander, Nicanor, at Beth Horon in 161 B.C.E., the Seleucids continued hostilities, and soon afterward Judas himself was killed in battle. This was followed by the murder of his brother Jonathan – who had by then been recognized by the Seleucids as a minor king – at the hands of local tribesmen in 143 B.C.E. The last surviving brother, Simon, managed to rid the Acra fortress in Jerusalem of the Seleucid garrison installed there. He then had himself declared hereditary high priest,

military commander, and ethnarch (governor) – the beginning of the priest-king dynasty of the Hasmoneans.

The Hasmoneans and Rome

The Jewish writer Max Dimont has described the Hasmoneans as "petty tyrants, vengeful fanatics and sybaritic playboys." However these rulers may have gained time for their people. Since their tiny country had for centuries been a pawn in the power games of empires – a role it would continue to play until its ultimate destruction by the Romans – a more forceful leader might have provoked the struggle against Rome at an even earlier date, causing the downfall of Judea that much sooner.

At first, the Romans treated Judea as an independent, sovereign state and honored its rulers. In the late autumn of 134 B.C.E., John Hyrcanus, younger son of Simon and his successor, sent three delegates to Rome to negotiate with the *praetor* Lucius Valerius

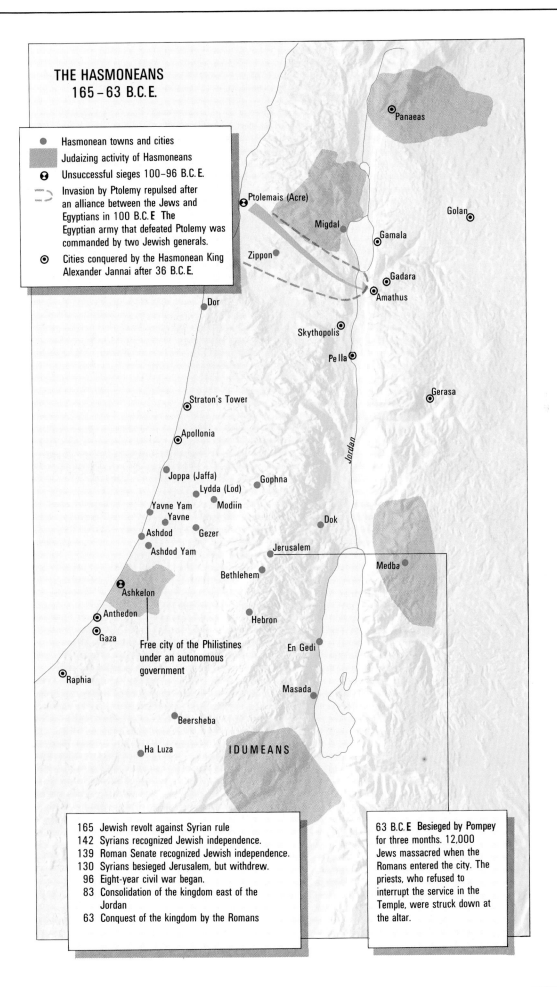

THE HASMONEANS
165 – 63 B.C.E.

- **Hasmonean towns and cities**
- **Judaizing activity of Hasmoneans**
- **Unsuccessful sieges 100–96 B.C.E.**
- **Invasion by Ptolemy repulsed after an alliance between the Jews and Egyptians in 100 B.C.E. The Egyptian army that defeated Ptolemy was commanded by two Jewish generals.**
- **Cities conquered by the Hasmonean King Alexander Jannai after 36 B.C.E.**

Panaeas

Ptolemais (Acre)

Golan

Migdal

Gamala

Zippon

Gadara

Amathus

Dor

Skythopolis

Pella

Straton's Tower

Gerasa

Apollonia

Jordan

Joppa (Jaffa)

Gophna

Lydda (Lod)

Modiin

Yavne Yam

Yavne

Dok

Ashdod

Gezer

Jerusalem

Ashdod Yam

Medba

Bethlehem

Ashkelon

Anthedon

Hebron

Gaza

Free city of the Philistines under an autonomous government

En Gedi

Raphia

Masada

Beersheba

Ha Luza

IDUMEANS

165 Jewish revolt against Syrian rule
142 Syrians recognized Jewish independence.
139 Roman Senate recognized Jewish independence.
130 Syrians besieged Jerusalem, but withdrew.
96 Eight-year civil war began.
83 Consolidation of the kingdom east of the Jordan
63 Conquest of the kingdom by the Romans

63 B.C.E Besieged by Pompey for three months. 12,000 Jews massacred when the Romans entered the city. The priests, who refused to interrupt the service in the Temple, were struck down at the altar.

Flavius. Roman help was important because both the Ptolemies and the Seleucids continued to threaten Judea. In fact, in that year Antiochus VII began a siege of Jerusalem, but the city valiantly resisted. Two years later, with both armies exhausted, a peace treaty was concluded.

John Hyrcanus conquered Idumea, south of the Dead Sea (now partly in modern Jordan), as well as Samaria. These conquests were to have serious repercussions. The Samaritans were – and still are – followers of a religion that is almost a sect of Judaism, having (it is believed) descended from the Jews who remained in Israel and Judah during the Babylonian exile. They have their own versions of the Pentateuch and the book of Joshua, and in the second century B.C.E. they had their own Temple on Mount Gerizim. John Hyrcanus razed this to the ground. The Samaritans never forgave this hostile act and have dissociated themselves from the Jews ever since.

John Hyrcanus's other mistake was the forcible conversion of the Idumeans to Judaism. Although some fully embraced the faith, others diluted it with their own beliefs, causing an eventual schism with the Jews.

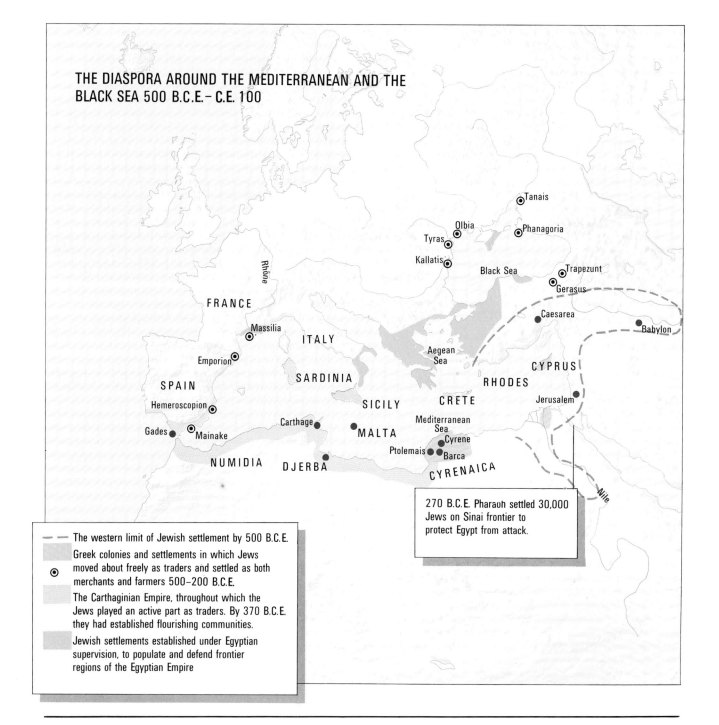

THE DIASPORA AROUND THE MEDITERRANEAN AND THE BLACK SEA 500 B.C.E.– C.E. 100

270 B.C.E. Pharaoh settled 30,000 Jews on Sinai frontier to protect Egypt from attack.

— — — The western limit of Jewish settlement by 500 B.C.E.

Greek colonies and settlements in which Jews moved about freely as traders and settled as both merchants and farmers 500–200 B.C.E.

The Carthaginian Empire, throughout which the Jews played an active part as traders. By 370 B.C.E. they had established flourishing communities.

Jewish settlements established under Egyptian supervision, to populate and defend frontier regions of the Egyptian Empire

The Hasmonean kingdom reached its zenith under Alexander Jannai, John Hyrcanus's third son, who ascended to the high priesthood in 103 B.C.E. However, in that year, civil war broke out between two of the country's three political factions.

Sadducees, Pharisees, and Essenes

The three main political factions of the Hasmonean kingdom were the Sadducees, Pharisees, and Essenes. The Sadducees, supporters of the Hasmonean priest class, pressed for a continuation of the primacy of the Temple "cult." The Pharisees, on the other hand, deplored the wealth and arrogance of the priests – including Alexander Jannai – and promoted synagogue (as opposed to Temple) worship. Some would go out to teach and help the people; such individuals were called *rav* ("master" or "teacher"), and are the forerunners of the rabbis of today.

The greatest of the Pharisees was Hillel, a poor woodcutter, who in about 40 B.C.E. traveled from Babylon to Judea to learn from the leading Jewish sages of the day. When he was asked by a pagan to summarize Judaism while standing on one leg, he said: "Do not do unto others as you would not have them do unto you. The rest is commentary. Now go and learn."

This story is related in the Talmud Shabbat, one of the tractates of the Talmud (*see* Chapter 2), which contains the oral law of Judaism, comprising codification and interpretation of the Scriptures. It was this oral law that was, in fact, at the heart of the dispute between the Sadducees and the Pharisees: the former refused to recognize it, while the latter were developing it for the new age. The first leaders of the rabbinic movement, Hillel and Shammai (who lived at the end of the first century B.C.E.), both issued rulings on important questions of religious law; it is significant that the high priests never enjoyed this legal authority. Fortunately for Judaism, the Pharisees prevailed over the Sadducees and the rabbinic structure has survived to this day.

Unfortunately, most of what is commonly known of the Pharisees today derives from the Christian Gospels, in which they appear as villains. The Gospel writers were most anxious not to offend the Romans, who were both their masters and the largest reserve of potential converts to Christianity. Instead of making them solely responsible for the execution of Jesus, the Gospel writers pinned the larger share of blame on the Jews – and after the destruction of the Second Temple in C.E. 70 *(see below)* and the disappearance of the Sadducees, the term "Pharisees" had become synonymous with "Jews." However, far from castigating the Pharisees, Jesus had himself been one – a worker-rabbi – and his wrath had actually been directed against the priest class that the Sadducees represented.

The ascetic Essenes were a more obscure faction, and may have been only one of a number of groups of men and women who, as the temporal situation grew worse, sought a spiritual and Messianic solution to the problems of Judaea. The Essenes' practice of total sexual abstinence places them outside the mainstream of Jewish tradition, which does not recognize chastity as a virtue in itself and has no use for monastic orders. The practice also undoubtedly contributed to the Essenes' eventual decline.

Although the adherents themselves soon died out, some of the Essenes' writings remained. In 1947, at their former settlement near Qumran on the Jordanian shore of the Dead Sea, leather and papyrus scrolls were discovered dating from between 100 B.C.E. and C.E. 50. What have come to be called the "Dead Sea Scrolls" include the Essenes' *Manual of Discipline*, some legends about a war between the Sons of Light and the Sons of Darkness, two copies of the book of Isaiah, and other texts and commentaries. These are still being deciphered and interpreted.

In the bitter civil war, Alexander Jannai executed hundreds of his Pharisaic opponents and thousands more fled the country. There was a brief respite during the reign of Alexander's widow, the wise Queen Salome, whose own brother was the Pharisaic leader Simeon ben Shetah. However, the worst effect of the civil strife was the excuse it gave the Romans under Pompey – who were at war with the Seleucids across the border in Syria – to intervene. Pompey invaded Judea in 67 B.C.E. and, after a three-month siege of Jerusalem, occupied the Temple in 63 B.C.E. Judea now became a Roman client-state, with Hyracanus II, a Hasmonean, as high priest and Antipater, an Idumean convert to Judaism, as governor.

When Julius Caesar defeated Pompey in 48 B.C.E., he rejected the Hasmonean succession and nominated Antipater's sons, Phasael and Herod, to inherit the throne of Judea.

Herod the Great

The Hasmonean fall from power was inevitable. The family's last attempt to regain their lost status was a Parthian-sponsored invasion of Judea by Antigonus, son of the banished Aristobulus II, the last independent Hasmonean priest-king. Herod fled to Rome, his brother Phasael having committed suicide. There, Herod ingratiated himself with Octavian (later to become the Emperor Augustus)

CHRISTIAN CONVERTS C.E. 45–300

MACEDONIA
Beroea
Thessalonica
Neapolis
Philippi
THRACE
Samothrace
Nicomedia
Prusa
MYSIA
Troas
Assos
Dory
Pergamum
Myteline
LYDIA
Thyatira
Antioch
Sardis
Philadelphia
Smyrna
Samos
Ephesus
Laod
Miletus
Larissa
GREECE
ACHAIA
Delphi
Patrae
Athens
Corinth
Halicarnassus
Kos
Sparta
Patora
Pharae
Rhodes

CRETE
Gnossos
Gortyna

MEDITERRANEAN SEA

Cyrene
Barca
CYRENAICA
Berenice

and Mark Antony, who in 40 B.C.E. persuaded the Roman Senate to confirm Herod as king of Judea and remove Hyrcanus II as high priest. Herod returned, defeated Antigonus (who had managed to hold out for three years), and in 37 B.C.E. captured Jerusalem. Antigonus and his Sanhedrin, or Jewish parliament, were put to death, an ominous start to Herod's reign.

Herod ruled for 33 years, an ally and friend of the Romans but loathed and feared by his Jewish subjects. He was a cruel and evil despot who stopped at nothing to fulfill his insane desire for power and prestige. After Herod murdered three of his sons – and many others, including his wife Mariamne, when he felt even remotely threatened – the Emperor Augustus commented, "It were better to be such a man's swine than his son."

Evidence of Herod's megalomania can be seen today in the remains of his huge building program. This included the new seaport of Caesarea, a chain of fortresses (e.g. Masada), the most magnificent palace in the Middle East, and even embellishments to the Temple in Jerusalem (the Western Wall he had constructed still stands), although these latter were more of a sop to the traditionalists than any sign of personal devotion.

On his death, which occurred in 4 B.C.E., Herod had intended that Judea would be divided between his remaining sons. Instead, as one son, Herod Antipas, succeeded to the throne of Galilee – a region in the north bounded by the River Jordan and the Sea of Galilee on the east and the Plain of Esdraelon on the south – a Roman legion arrived to keep order in Jerusalem. The Romans then seized the opportunity to impose direct rule on Judea, making it a Roman province in C.E. 6. Until the governorship of Pontius Pilate (C.E. 26–36), the new rulers did not greatly offend the Jews. However, Pilate proved to be a corrupt and vicious ruler, who installed pagan symbols in Jerusalem and tried to rob the Temple of its treasures.

With the loss of independence and the burden of Roman rapacity, it is hardly surprising that the situation in Judea gave rise to so many Messianic movements. A number of visionaries and anti-establishment leaders emerged, including Barabbas, John the Baptist, Jesus of Nazareth, and even an Egyptian whose name has been lost. All, with the possible exception of the first, were executed as rebels against imperial rule.

The Destruction of the Second Temple

Pontius Pilate was dismissed in C.E. 36, and the following year, Caligula succeeded to the imperial throne. He decided to have himself declared a god and ordered the Romans and all their subjects, including the Jews, to worship him. This blasphemy – the denial of

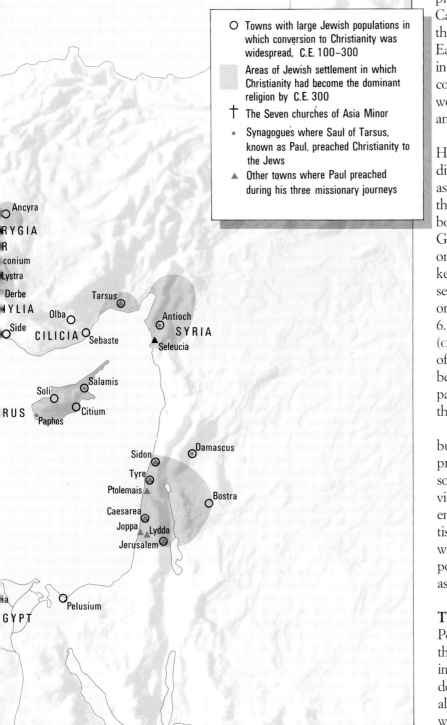

○ Towns with large Jewish populations in which conversion to Christianity was widespread, C.E. 100–300

▨ Areas of Jewish settlement in which Christianity had become the dominant religion by C.E. 300

† The Seven churches of Asia Minor

• Synagogues where Saul of Tarsus, known as Paul, preached Christianity to the Jews

▲ Other towns where Paul preached during his three missionary journeys

Ancyra
RYGIA
R
conium
Lystra
Derbe
MYLIA   Olba
Side   CILICIA   Sebaste   Tarsus
Soli   Salamis   Antioch   SYRIA
RUS   Citium   Seleucia
Paphos
Sidon   Damascus
Tyre
Ptolemais   Bostra
Caesarea
Joppa   Lydda
Jerusalem
Pelusium
GYPT

everything the Jews (and the Christians) held sacred – caused outrage in Judea, especially when the people learned of Caligula's command that a statue of him be erected and worshipped in the Temple.

To forestall the inevitable uprising, a delegation of prominent Jews arrived in Rome in C.E. 40 to try to persuade Caligula to change his mind. Among the delegation was the leading Jewish philosopher of the diaspora – Philo of Alexandria. Unfortunately, little of Philo's work has survived, and what is known of his thinking comes primarily from Christian sources. However, he seems to have combined rationality with a belief in God, a synthesis of Greek philosophy and Jewish humanitarianism that was centuries ahead of its time. As for the success or failure of the delegation, this became a moot point when Caligula was murdered the following year.

LEFT: *The synagogue at Masada. The fortress stood on a spur of rock overlooking the Dead Sea; the sheer cliffs falling away from it on three sides made it practically impregnable. The Zealots held out here against the Romans for three years, following the fall of Jerusalem.*

RIGHT: *By the time Titus defeated the last of the Zealots at Masada in C.E. 74, this Jewish revolt had lasted for nearly eight years. The areas of major Zealot activity are shaded on the map. No doubt political uncertainties in Rome, following the suicide of Nero in C.E. 68, played a part in lessening the effectiveness of Roman response.*

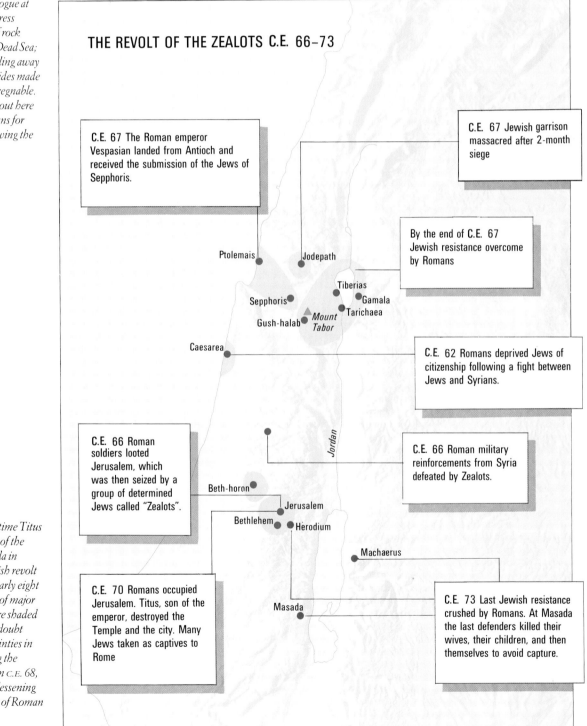

THE REVOLT OF THE ZEALOTS C.E. 66–73

C.E. 67 The Roman emperor Vespasian landed from Antioch and received the submission of the Jews of Sepphoris.

C.E. 67 Jewish garrison massacred after 2-month siege

By the end of C.E. 67 Jewish resistance overcome by Romans

C.E. 62 Romans deprived Jews of citizenship following a fight between Jews and Syrians.

C.E. 66 Roman soldiers looted Jerusalem, which was then seized by a group of determined Jews called "Zealots".

C.E. 66 Roman military reinforcements from Syria defeated by Zealots.

C.E. 70 Romans occupied Jerusalem. Titus, son of the emperor, destroyed the Temple and the city. Many Jews taken as captives to Rome

C.E. 73 Last Jewish resistance crushed by Romans. At Masada the last defenders killed their wives, their children, and then themselves to avoid capture.

Ptolemais
Jodepath
Tiberias
Sepphoris
Gamala
Tarichaea
Gush-halab
Mount Tabor
Caesarea
Jordan
Beth-horon
Jerusalem
Bethlehem
Herodium
Machaerus
Masada

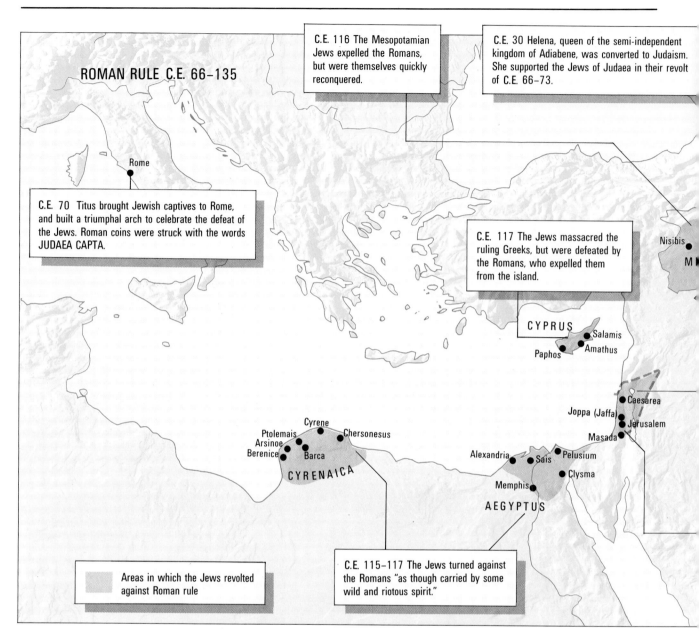

ROMAN RULE C.E. 66–135

C.E. 116 The Mesopotamian Jews expelled the Romans, but were themselves quickly reconquered.

C.E. 30 Helena, queen of the semi-independent kingdom of Adiabene, was converted to Judaism. She supported the Jews of Judaea in their revolt of C.E. 66–73.

C.E. 70 Titus brought Jewish captives to Rome, and built a triumphal arch to celebrate the defeat of the Jews. Roman coins were struck with the words JUDAEA CAPTA.

C.E. 117 The Jews massacred the ruling Greeks, but were defeated by the Romans, who expelled them from the island.

Rome

Nisibis

M

CYPRUS

Salamis
Amathus
Paphos

Caesarea
Joppa (Jaffa)
Jerusalem
Masada

Cyrene
Ptolemais
Arsinoe
Berenice
Barca
Chersonesus

CYRENAICA

Alexandria
Sais
Pelusium
Clysma
Memphis

AEGYPTUS

Areas in which the Jews revolted against Roman rule

C.E. 115–117 The Jews turned against the Romans "as though carried by some wild and riotous spirit."

LEFT: *Remains of a house of the Roman period show the marks of destruction by fire, when it was sacked by the triumphant legions of Titus in C.E. 70.*

66–73 Revolt of the Zealots.

132-135 Bar Kochba's
It. Suppressed by Hadrian,
ea almost depopulated of
s and renamed SYRIA
AESTRINA

LEFT: *The death of Herod Agrippa in C.E. 44 and his replacement by a succession of unsympathetic Roman procurators led first to riots and then to an outright military revolt in C.E. 66; it took the Romans nearly eight years to suppress this. The unrest spread to other Jewish communities within the empire, followed by another outbreak in Judea itself, which was suppressed by Hadrian.*

Caligula had removed Herod Antipas from the Galilean throne in C.E. 39 and replaced him with his boyhood companion Herod Agrippa, the grandson of Herod the Great. Despite his friendship with the crazed Roman emperor, Herod Agrippa proved a popular ruler. On his death in C.E. 44, however, he was replaced by a series of venal Roman procurators and law and order broke down.

In C.E. 64, one of these procurators, Florus, seized gold from the Temple treasury, provoking a riot which was brutally repressed. In response, Roman sympathizers in Judea were murdered by gangs of Jewish terrorists known as *Sicarii* (after the short daggers they plunged into their victims), and a political faction called the Zealots (*Kanaim*) vowed to destroy all supporters of Rome. Attacks on Jews by the local non-Jewish population of Galilee and Samaria also became more frequent and vicious, culminating in a massacre of Jews by Greeks in Caesarea. Riots flared up all over the country.

For the next three years, Roman troops were attacked by bands of Jewish rebels with increasing frequency. However, the army under the Roman general Vespasian managed to win back control of Galilee in C.E. 67. The Jewish rebel commander, one Joseph ben Mattathias, surrendered to the enemy and even assumed a Roman name: Flavius Josephus, "Flavius" being Vespasian's family name. He was to become the historian Josephus, whose *The Jewish War*, although biased in favor of Rome and the Sadducees, is one of the few contemporary accounts of the Jews of this period.

Vespasian marched south in the spring of C.E. 68. He was about to begin the siege of Jerusalem when word arrived that the Emperor Nero had committed suicide and that the Roman army in the East was backing Vespasian's claims to succeed to the imperial throne. Before leaving for Alexandria (where he was declared emperor) and then Rome, he put his son Titus in charge of the siege.

A few days before Passover C.E. 70, Titus set up camp outside Jerusalem. Although the defenders fought with great courage – the various Jewish factions for once united against the enemy – the Temple precincts were eventually stormed and burned down. According to tradition, this occurred on the 9th of Av, the anniversary of the fall of the First Temple to the Babylonians in 586 B.C.E.

It took another month of fighting for Jerusalem to be subdued completely, after which Titus razed it to the ground with the exception of the towers of Herod's palace. The following year, Titus and Vespasian celebrated the victory with a triumphal march through Rome, parading the stolen Temple vessels and thousands of captured Jews, now slaves. This triumph was later commemorated in the victory arch of Titus, which still stands in Rome.

The parade was, however, somewhat premature, for several pockets of resistance still held out in Judea. When, after a two-year siege, the Romans finally stormed Herod the Great's fortress at Masada in April C.E. 73, they found that the last of the *Sicarii* who had defended it had committed suicide rather than surrender.

Titus was convinced that once the Temple had been destroyed, Judaism would cease to exist. As if to make sure, he had exterminated 25 per cent of the Jewish population of Judea and enslaved a further 10 per cent, reducing the Jews to almost a minority in their own land. Although the Temple and the high priesthood did vanish forever, Titus was as mistaken as the despots that came before and after him. It was the Roman empire that would cease to exist, Titus's triumphal arch remaining as just another relic of a once-mighty civilization. In the meantime, the Jews survived.

CHAPTER TWO

THE AGE OF PRAYER AND THOUGHT: C.E. 70 TO THE SPANISH INQUISITION

W ith the destruction of the Second Temple and the massacre or exile of a large part of the Jewish population, Judea became merely a Roman province governed by a legate. The Tenth Legion was stationed permanently in this potentially unruly territory, garrisoned in the ruins of what had once been the upper part of the once glorious city of Jerusalem.

Yet the fall of Jerusalem's holy shrine did not signal the end of Judaism. The roots of Jewish culture had become far too firmly embedded for that. This was due in no small part to the work of the rabbinic movement and, in particular, the Pharisees, the reforming rabbis of their day.

The Tannaim and the Yavne Academy
The leading Pharisees followed in the footsteps of Hillel, Shammai, and others of the first-century B.C.E. school of rabbis, carrying on the tradition of giving judgments and interpreting the Scriptures for laymen who considered themselves unqualified. The teachings of these early rabbis and Pharisees, who are known as the *Tannaim* ("those who hand down by word of mouth"), have been preserved thanks to the efforts of the brilliant scholar and rabbi Yohanan ben Zakkai.

Rabbi ben Zakkai had an immensely practical and far-sighted view of Judaism and its place in the world. He refused to abandon himself to the belief in a messiah who might come at any moment to deliver the Jews from

RIGHT: *Despite Roman hopes at the time, the fall and sack of Jerusalem did not spell the end of Judaism. The rabbinic movement was receiving new energy from the reforms of the Pharisees and this ensured that Jewish learning survived and flourished. As the importance of the rabbi grew so did that of the synagogue; this synagogue floor, for example, is decorated with a mosaic telling the story of Isaac. It dates from the sixth century.*

LEFT: *Rome had conquered the Jews physically, but it was the Greeks who had the greater cultural and intellectual influence. This continued into the days of Byzantium, as this fifth-century mosaic, decorating the floor of a synagogue in Galilee, demonstrates.*

the Romans, a belief with which many less courageous people comforted themselves during those desperate times. "If you are holding a seedling in your hand and the coming of the Messiah is announced," he said, "first plant your seedling, then go to greet the Messiah." On the other hand, his approach to Roman rule was never confrontational; instead, he advocated non-violent resistance through the intensification of Jewish spirituality, condemned open rebellion, and predicted its disastrous outcome. His outspokenness was an act of great courage: the Zealots had been known to murder those who, with far less reason, they considered "traitors" to the Jewish cause.

Ben Zakkai was an old man when he slipped out of Jerusalem in C.E. 68, secreted in a coffin, and, with the permission of the Romans, established a school at Yavne, on the coast near Jaffa. This religious academy – which, among Jews, has become a byword for learning – kept the torch of Jewish teaching alight in those dark days. It was the forerunner of all the great religious academies (*yeshivot*) which have kept Jewish scholarship alive.

When Yohanan ben Zakkai died, he was succeeded by the equally eminent leader Gamaliel, usually known as "The Master" (*Rabban*) Gamaliel II. The first Gamaliel, his grandfather, had been patriarch under Herod Agrippa and a descendant of the great teacher Hillel. "Patriarch" was the title given to the spiritual leader of the Jews once the Temple had been destroyed and there was no longer a high priest. The Romans recognized the position and accorded succeeding patriarchs temporal power and honors until, in 418, the Byzantine emperor Theodosius II abolished the title.

During these years, Yavne in lower Galilee became the chief center of Jewish learning. This was the case not only for the Judean Jews but also for the great number of those who were now scattered all over the "civilized" world and beyond.

The Emerging Diaspora

In addition to the major settlements in Egypt and Mesopotamia (Babylonia), which had grown up over the previous 700 years, Jews now lived all over the Roman Empire, and there was a sizable community in Rome itself. The destruction of Judea had resulted in a major Jewish exodus. The élite fled to their co-religionists in Mesopotamia, now part of the Parthian Empire, Rome's greatest enemy, and the rest emigrated to the lands around the Mediterranean. Even at this stage, the diaspora was many times larger than the Jewish population of Judea, yet all still turned to the rabbis in the Holy Land for advice and guidance.

In 114, the Emperor Trajan attacked the Parthian Empire, invading Mesopotamia. Although the Roman legions easily overcame the Parthians, they met fierce resistance from

RIGHT: *One prominent area of Jewish settlement was Iraq; by C.E. 634, the year of the Muslim conquest, there were about 806,000 of them settled in hundreds of towns and villages. After that conquest, they continued to prosper, despite spasmodic and, at times, severe persecution. In C.E. 800, for instance, they were heavily taxed, subjected to residence restrictions, and forced to wear a yellow star as an identifying symbol.*

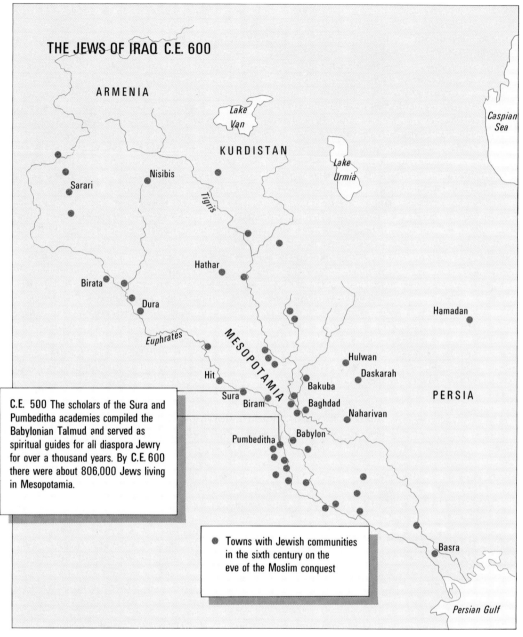

THE JEWS OF IRAQ C.E. 600

ARMENIA

Lake Van

KURDISTAN

Lake Urmia

Caspian Sea

Sarari

Nisibis

Tigris

Hathar

Hamadan

Birata

Dura

Euphrates

MESOPOTAMIA

Hulwan

Daskarah

Hit

Bakuba

PERSIA

Sura

Baghdad

Biram

Naharivan

Pumbeditha

Babylon

Basra

Persian Gulf

C.E. 500 The scholars of the Sura and Pumbeditha academies compiled the Babylonian Talmud and served as spiritual guides for all diaspora Jewry for over a thousand years. By **C.E. 600** there were about 806,000 Jews living in Mesopotamia.

● Towns with Jewish communities in the sixth century on the eve of the Moslim conquest

the large Jewish settlements, where the people were enraged that the destroyers of the Temple were now trying to conquer them. Jewish fighting forces were recruited at Nisibis and even in the frontier kingdom of Adiabene (in what is now Kurdistan), whose rulers had recently been converted to Judaism.

The struggle in Mesopotamia was a signal to Jews throughout the Roman Empire to revolt. The rising started at Cyrene (in modern Libya) and spread to Alexandria and Cyprus. There was unrest in Judea, too, but the Jews there, still suffering the effects of their grievous defeat of 75 years before, felt unable to incur the wrath of Rome by risking

open rebellion. The Romans eventually, and with great difficulty, quelled the Jewish revolt, in the process annihilating the Jewish community in Cyprus and burning the main synagogue in Alexandria. Trajan died shortly before an uneasy peace was restored. His successor, Hadrian, withdrew from Mesopotamia and made peace with Parthia; the Roman Empire would never again extend beyond the Euphrates.

The Bar Kochba Revolt

Hadrian introduced many repressive measures against non-pagans – including, for the Jews, a complete ban on circumcision and instruction in the Law. This enraged the Jews and provoked another armed rebellion in the Holy Land, the last in Judean history. It was "sponsored" by another great teacher and thinker, Rabbi Akiva, who appointed as its leader the statesman and soldier Simeon ben Kozba. In 132, the latter crushed the Roman legions in a surprise victory, and an independent Jewish state was re-established with Simeon ben Kozba as head of state and Eleazar of Modiin in the revived post of high priest. Rabbi Akiva renamed ben Kozba – whom he claimed to be the Messiah – *Bar Kochba*, "son of the star." This refers to the prophecy, "A star shall come forth from Jacob."

The Jews' success was shortlived. Rome sent reinforcements to put down the revolt, and Bar Kochba was finally defeated after a two-year siege of the fortress of Bet Their (Betar), southwest of Jerusalem. Symbolically, Bet Their fell on 9 Av 135, the anniversary of the destruction of both the First and the Second Temples. The Romans massacred everyone found at Bet Their, and sold many Jews from other parts of the country into slavery. Rabbi Akiva was executed: according to unconfirmed reports, he was first hideously tortured, then flayed alive and finally torn to death with metal combs.

The most lasting consequence of the Bar Kochba revolt was one that must have seemed of little significance at the time. The Romans banned the name "Judea," which was derived from the Latin word for "Jewish"; henceforth, the province was to be known as "Syria-Palaestina," the second word being a reference to the Philistines who had once inhabited the coastal strip but had long since disappeared. The name *Palaestina*, or Palestine, has lasted until the twentieth century – a name that is, in itself, a negation of the Jewish right to the Holy Land. Before his death in 138, Hadrian also renamed Jerusalem – *Colonia Aelia Capitolina* – and dedicated the city to Jupiter, a temple to whom was erected on the site of the ruined Temple of the Jews.

The new emperor, Antoninus Pius, had a completely different, benign attitude toward the Jews. This spirit of toleration was to last through a succession of Roman emperors until the death of Alexander Severus in 235, reaching its apogee in the positively philo-Semitic Septimus Severus (reigned 193–211), who was himself a Semite from North Africa. Nevertheless the Jews of Judea were never again to achieve independence under the Romans.

The Beginnings of the Talmud

Although Jews were forbidden to live in Jerusalem, their places being taken by Greeks and others from Samaria and Caesarea, they did not disappear from the Holy Land. The center of Jewish settlement transferred to Galilee, and Gamaliel III established an academy at Usha, in Lower Galilee, which carried on the traditions of Yavne. Despite the restrictions placed upon subjects by rulers, relations between the Jews and the Romans improved – for example, Gamaliel III's son Rabbi Judah actually became a friend of a Roman emperor (probably Marcus Aurelius).

Gamaliel III and his successors were to have a most profound effect on the practice of Judaism. In about the year C.E. 100, they finalized the compilation of the third section of the Torah known as the Writings or Hagiography (*Ketuvim*) – comprising the Psalms and Proverbs, the Song of Songs and the books of Job, Ruth, Lamentations, Ecclesiastes, Esther, Daniel, Ezra, Nehemiah, and the Chronicles – and laid down a daily order of prayer. They also revolutionized religious practice by transferring to the synagogue the rites that, before, had been practiced only in the Temple. The blowing of the ram's horn (*shofar*) on the New Year would now take place in all synagogues, and the Day of Atonement would become a fast day for individual repentence, to replace the act of atonement for the whole people which had previously been carried out by the high priest in the Temple.

Above all, the rabbis of Yavne and, later, Usha began the process of codifying the "oral law" known as the *Mishnah*. The "oral law" had arisen from the Tannaim's interpretations of the biblical laws – known as the "written law" – and much of it resulted from the questions sent by Jews from all over the Diaspora to the rabbis of the Holy Land and the answers that the latter gave. This form of rabbinic literature – called *responsa* – has continued ever since.

The rabbi Judah Hanasi (*c.*170–*c.*219) did not approve of the way in which the Scrip-

ABOVE: *This map of Jerusalem is part of a mosaic, found at Madaba in Jordan. Despite the various attempts to destroy Jerusalem – notably by the Babylonians and the Romans – the city survived, to be rebuilt and extended over the centuries. Under Muslim rule, it became the chief Islamic shrine after Mecca, since it was believed Mohammed had visited the city.*

tures were being interpreted in the light of new circumstances – the essence of the oral law. To counter this, he ordered that the Mishnah be written down in a definitive form, and he died secure in his belief that this would terminate its development. He was, of course, quite wrong. The written Mishnah simply became the foundation for many other writings and commentaries.

At the time of Rabbi Hanasi's death, Judea and much of the rest of the Middle East was in disorder. The frequent struggles for the reins of Roman power (in the 73 years between the death of Septimus Severus and the accession of Diocletian in 284, there were 27 emperors) and the increasing number of invasions on distant frontiers meant that the Roman legions had to be deployed farther afield. This uneasy state of affairs prompted many Jews in Galilee to emigrate to Persian-ruled Babylon, where they enjoyed enormous prestige and prosperity. Eventually, at the end of the third century, order was restored

to the Roman Middle East by Diocletian, who, having defeated the Persians in 298, now held Mesopotamia.

In both Galilee and Babylon, this may well have been the most productive period of Jewish scholarship of all time. For three centuries, the wise men of Yavne, Usha, Sepphoris, and Bet Shearim in Galilee and their Mesopotamian counterparts in Sura, Pumbeditha, and Nahardea on the banks of the Euphrates labored to perfect and codify the oral tradition of questions and answers, interpretations and glosses on the Scriptures, all of which would be collected in the vast work known as the Talmud.

The Talmud originally consisted of the Mishnah – 200 years of the teachings of the Tannaim – and a commentary upon it called the *Gemarrah* (from the Hebrew word *gamar*, meaning "finished," "complete"). The Gemarrah also includes *Aggadah* – legends, stories, proverbs, parables, and anecdotes. The aspects of the Talmud that deal with Jewish law, ceremony, and rites are known as the *Halachah*, "the way of going."

The two sets of scholars, working in their respective countries, produced two versions of this material: the Palestinian or Jerusalem Talmud, finalized in about C.E. 400, and the Babylonian Talmud, which followed about a century later. The latter, four times the size of the Jerusalem Talmud and containing 39 tractates, or volumes, is generally accepted as the more authoritative.

Persecution in the Christian Empire

The decline in Jewish influence in the Holy Land was accelerated by the accession of Constantine to the Roman throne. Attributing his victory over one of his rivals in 312 to a vision of the Christian cross, he subsequently gave Christianity the status of official religion of the Empire. The Christians, hitherto a persecuted minority, immediately began persecuting those of other religions, particularly the Jews, who at that time were actively encouraging conversions and were thus perceived as competition.

Judaism had been fashionable in the Roman Empire in the years between the death of Marcus Aurelius in 180 and the assassination in 235 of the 27-year-old Alexander Severus, who had installed a statue of Abraham in his private temple. Now proselytizing of and conversions to Judaism were banned and Jews were encouraged to convert to Christianity.

There was a brief lull in the persecution when, in 361, the Christian-born Emperor Julian – later known as "the Apostate" – converted to the old pagan Roman religion. He forbade anti-Jewish activity, although he had no love for the Jews themselves, but rather a virulent hatred of the Christians. Julian even proposed allowing the Jews to re-build the Temple, but on his death in 363, he was succeeded by the Christian, Valentinian I, and the plan was dropped.

Despite their adherence to Christianity, Valentinian and one of his successors, Theodosius ("The Great"), frequently intervened to prevent the destruction of synagogues and attacks on Jews, and they both offered Jews the protection of the law. However, St. Ambrose, the bishop of Milan – who, as a theologian, ranks as one of the fathers of the Roman Catholic Church – remonstrated with Theodosius when, in 388, the Emperor insisted on the rebuilding of a synagogue that had been burned down on the orders of the bishop of Edessa (in northern Iraq). St. Ambrose's Eastern contemporary St. John Chrysostom (another

BELOW: Paradoxically, the Jews of the east found that their new Islamic rulers were more tolerant than their Christian overlords had been. For instance, the Jews were allowed their own courts of law and exempted from military service. There were nothing like the frequent massacres and expulsions which were the lot of Jews living in Christendom; in Muslim-ruled Spain the Jews enjoyed a golden age.

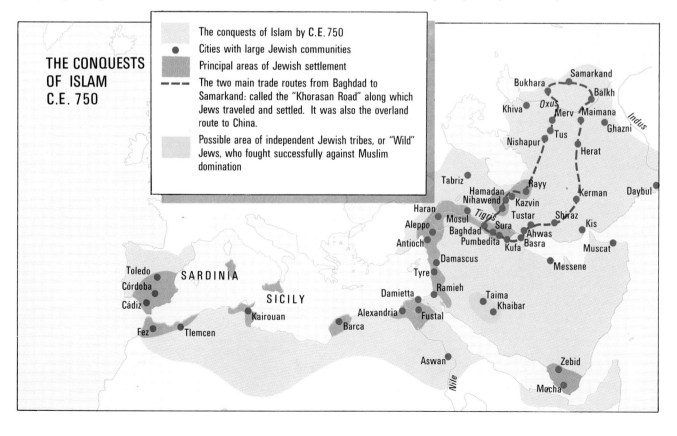

THE CONQUESTS OF ISLAM C.E. 750

The conquests of Islam by C.E. 750
Cities with large Jewish communities
Principal areas of Jewish settlement
The two main trade routes from Baghdad to Samarkand: called the "Khorasan Road" along which Jews traveled and settled. It was also the overland route to China.
Possible area of independent Jewish tribes, or "Wild" Jews, who fought successfully against Muslim domination

time, the Sassanids were Zoroastrians and tolerant of the Jews as fellow monotheists.

Like the rest of the Diaspora, the Mesopotamian Jews were faced with the challenge of adapting to living in a completely non-Jewish environment under laws not of their own making. Samuel, head of the academy at Nahardea, whose teachings are still obeyed by Jews all over the world, placed these circumstances in a religious context with his decree *Dina de-malchuta dina* – a pithy Aramaic phrase that meant that, in any matter not directly involving religion, the law

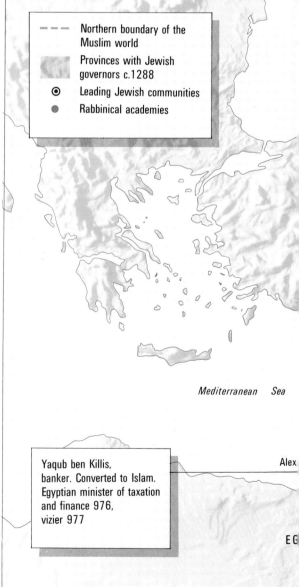

INTEGRATION UNDER ISLAM 908-1318

- Northern boundary of the Muslim world
- Provinces with Jewish governors c.1288
- ⊙ Leading Jewish communities
- ● Rabbinical academies

Mediterranean Sea

Alex

Yaqub ben Killis, banker. Converted to Islam. Egyptian minister of taxation and finance 976, vizier 977

E G

father of the Church) preached against any fraternization between Christians and Jews.

In 285, Diocletian had divided the Roman Empire into two administrative halves – West and East. Although the Empire was briefly united under both Constantine and Julian, by 363 the division had become permanent. Most Jews lived in the Eastern Empire, the capital of which was Byzantium, refounded as Constantinople by Constantine (now modern Istanbul). Successive restrictive measures were introduced against the Jews. In 415, Orestes, prefect of Alexandria, expelled all the Jews, and the patriarchate of Judea (Palestine) was abolished in 418. Synagogues were systematically destroyed and their rebuilding forbidden (although Theodoric the Great, the Ostrogoth king of Italy from 493 to 526, did protect the Jews against the synagogue destroyers). In 553, Justinian, the Emperor of the Eastern Empire, even issued an edict forbidding the study of the Mishnah.

The Sassanids

In Mesopotamia (modern Iraq), the tradition of Jewish scholarship continued through successive conquests, first by the princes of Palmyra, and then, from 226 onward, by the Sassanid rulers of Persia (modern Iran). Like their forerunners, the Persians of Cyrus's

ABOVE: *The remains of Esh Temoah, a synagogue on the west bank of the Jordan which was destroyed during the Byzantine period. At this time, the rulers of Byzantium launched a number of edicts against the Jews; this contrasted with the tolerant attitude of the Sassanid rulers of Persia.*

RIGHT: *Jews found Muslim rule tolerant. They were encouraged to settle in towns, and their interest in trade and banking developed. Jewish bankers and merchants established networks of contacts in Islamic cities, which increased in size with the growth of the Muslim sphere of influence. Quick to recognize ability, Islamic rulers also advanced suitable Jews to prominence in their governments.*

of the state shall be the law of the Jews. For their part, the Sassanids conferred the title of *resh galuta* or "exilarch" on the leader of the Jews under their rule, a post that had much status and authority. Their benevolent rule lasted until the seventh century and gave the Jewish communities of Mesopotamia the chance to prosper and produce prodigious scholarship.

The End of Roman Rule in the Holy Land
In 614, Jerusalem fell to the Persian army (which included many Jews), and the Holy Land was occupied. At first, the Persians returned Jerusalem to the Jews, but later changed their minds and sided with the Christians in persecuting them. The Eastern, or Byzantine, Emperor Heraclius briefly reconquered the Holy Land in 629, but he was soon overthrown by the Muslim Arabs (called "Saracens" by their Christian enemies) who, after a series of battles, finally took the Holy Land in 641.

The centuries of persecution had left their mark on the resident Jews: at the time of the Muslim conquest, only one-tenth of the

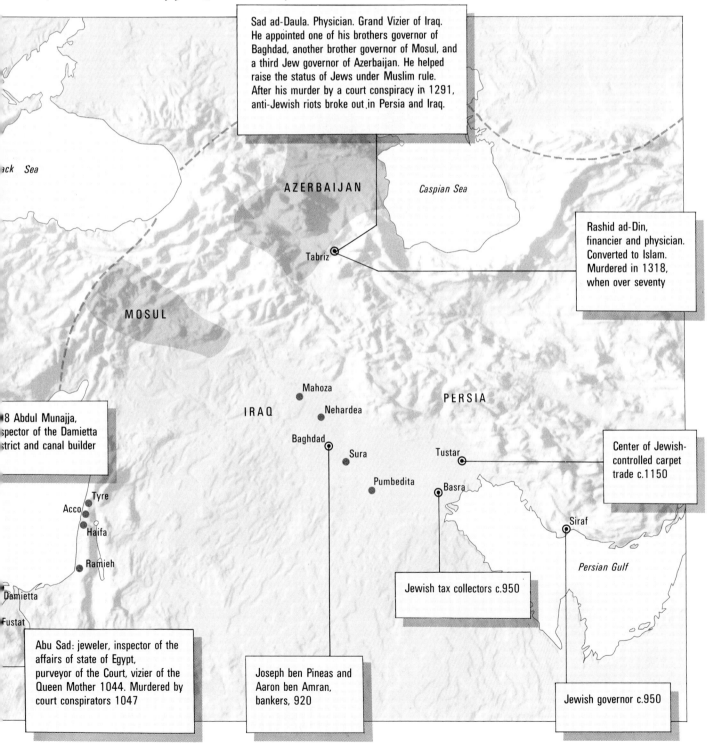

Sad ad-Daula. Physician. Grand Vizier of Iraq. He appointed one of his brothers governor of Baghdad, another brother governor of Mosul, and a third Jew governor of Azerbaijan. He helped raise the status of Jews under Muslim rule. After his murder by a court conspiracy in 1291, anti-Jewish riots broke out in Persia and Iraq.

Rashid ad-Din, financier and physician. Converted to Islam. Murdered in 1318, when over seventy

8 Abdul Munajja, inspector of the Damietta district and canal builder

Center of Jewish-controlled carpet trade c.1150

Jewish tax collectors c.950

Jewish governor c.950

Abu Sad: jeweler, inspector of the affairs of state of Egypt, purveyor of the Court, vizier of the Queen Mother 1044. Murdered by court conspirators 1047

Joseph ben Pineas and Aaron ben Amran, bankers, 920

population was Jewish. Now the center of Jewish spiritual leadership passed to the Jews of the Diaspora.

Judaism under Islam

In 622, Mohammed fled from his birthplace, Mecca, and settled with his followers in Medina. The new monotheistic religion he founded – Islam – was to have a spectacular success. His successors, the caliphs, spread it through their conquests all over western Asia and north Africa, and only 12 years after Mohammed's death in 632, Syria, Palestine, Egypt, Mesopotamia, and Persia were ruled from Mecca by the Umayyad dynasty.

For the next four centuries, Jewish life was centered in the lands under Islamic rule. The earliest Muslims in Arabia had been as intolerant of the Jews – whose influence they feared – as had the early Christians. Yet, after Mohammed's death, Jews and Christians, who shared the common traditions of the Bible with Muslims, discovered that Islamic rule was relatively benign. Jews and Christians – together called the *dhimmi* – were granted exemption from military service, the right to their own courts of law, and a guarantee of the safety of their property. However, they were not allowed to build their own houses of worship, to make converts, or to erect houses higher than those of their Muslim neighbors, and the farmers and

peasants among them were subjected to extra taxation.

This taxation caused Jews to abandon the land and congregate in towns, where they took up crafts such as dyeing, weaving, and metalwork – trades that they have carried on ever since. Allowed to acquire wealth, Jewish merchants and bankers established networks of contacts in Muslim cities, and they traveled widely, visiting and establishing communities in such far-flung corners of the Muslim world as the Iberian peninsula and north Africa. They even ventured beyond its borders – to the Volga (where Jewish travelers converted the Khazar people to Judaism in the ninth century) and into Christian Europe. Jews from the Mediterranean moved northward and settled along the Rhine and in northern France.

The Last Years of the Babylonian Academies

The Mesopotamian community remained the focus of spiritual leadership for all Jews until the eleventh century. The directors of the academies at Sura and Pumbeditha were known as *geonim*, which in the singular – *gaon* – means "genius" in modern Hebrew, but is actually the abbreviation of the Hebrew title "head of the academy which is the pride of Jacob." The *geonim*, who ruled from 689 to 1038, were the supreme judges, ruling

SETTLEMENT ON THE BLACK SEA AND IN CENTRAL ASIA

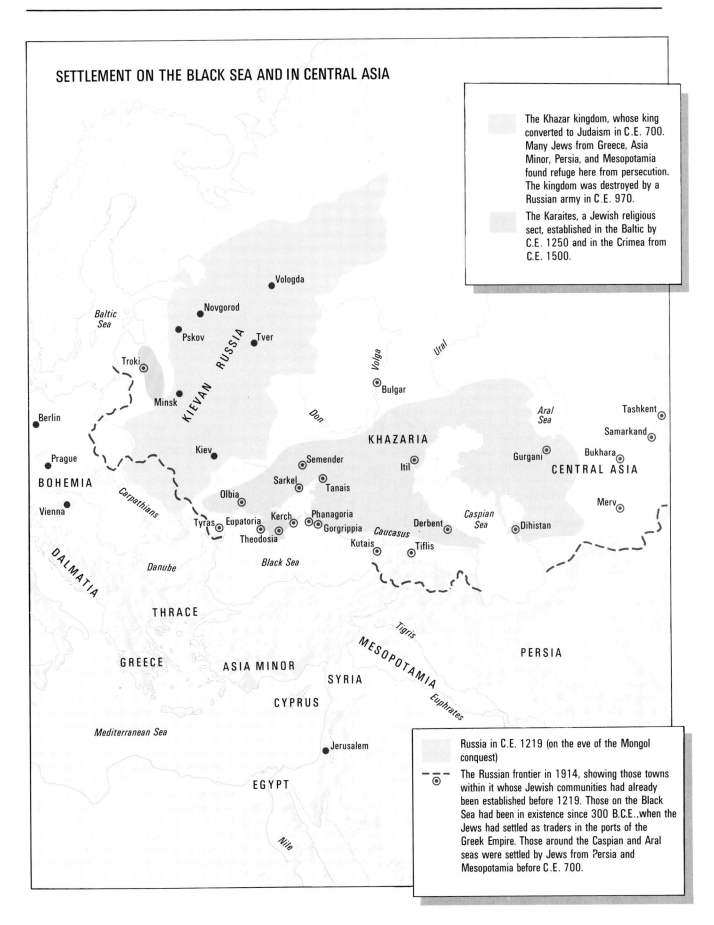

The Khazar kingdom, whose king converted to Judaism in C.E. 700. Many Jews from Greece, Asia Minor, Persia, and Mesopotamia found refuge here from persecution. The kingdom was destroyed by a Russian army in C.E. 970.

The Karaites, a Jewish religious sect, established in the Baltic by C.E. 1250 and in the Crimea from C.E. 1500.

Russia in C.E. 1219 (on the eve of the Mongol conquest)

The Russian frontier in 1914, showing those towns within it whose Jewish communities had already been established before 1219. Those on the Black Sea had been in existence since 300 B.C.E., when the Jews had settled as traders in the ports of the Greek Empire. Those around the Caspian and Aral seas were settled by Jews from Persia and Mesopotamia before C.E. 700.

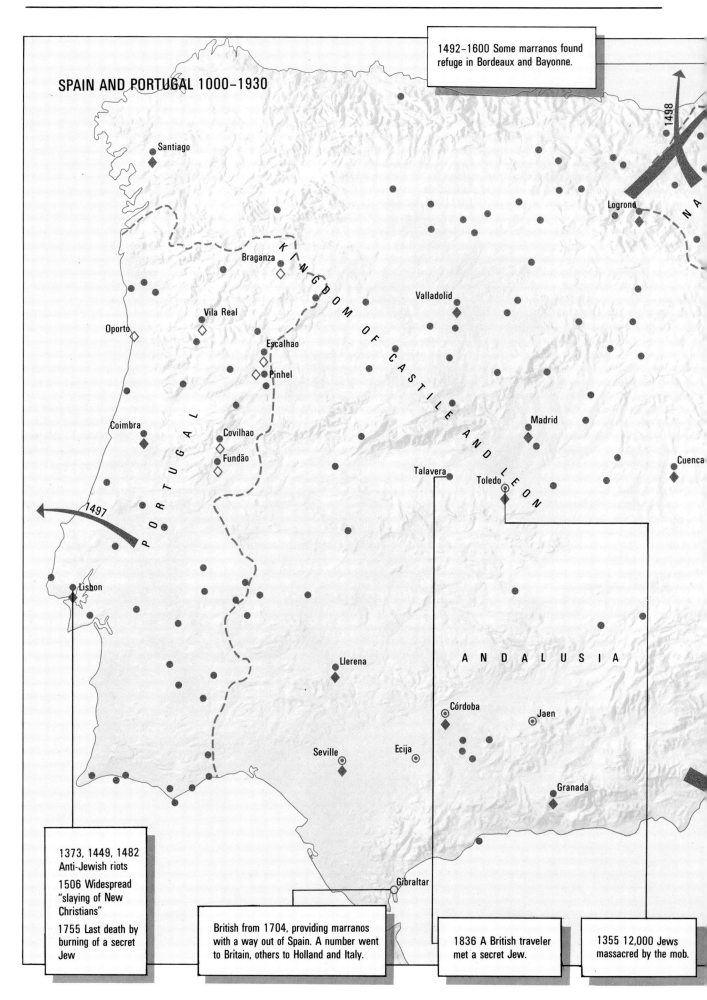

SPAIN AND PORTUGAL 1000–1930

1492–1600 Some marranos found refuge in Bordeaux and Bayonne.

Santiago

Braganza

KINGDOM OF CASTILE AND LEON

Valladolid

Vila Real

Oporto

Escalhao

Pinhel

Logrono

PORTUGAL

Coimbra

Covilhao

Fundão

Madrid

Cuenca

Talavera

Toledo

1497

Lisbon

ANDALUSIA

Llerena

Córdoba

Jaen

Seville

Ecija

Granada

Gibraltar

1373, 1449, 1482
Anti-Jewish riots

1506 Widespread
"slaying of New
Christians"

1755 Last death by
burning of a secret
Jew

British from 1704, providing marranos
with a way out of Spain. A number went
to Britain, others to Holland and Italy.

1836 A British traveler
met a secret Jew.

1355 12,000 Jews
massacred by the mob.

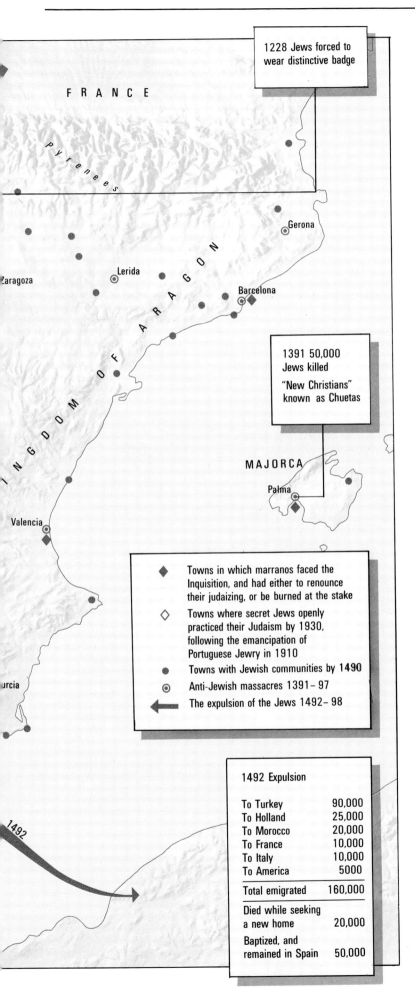

1228 Jews forced to wear distinctive badge

FRANCE

Pyrenees

Gerona

Zaragoza

Lerida

Barcelona

KINGDOM OF ARAGON

1391 50,000
Jews killed
"New Christians"
known as Chuetas

MAJORCA

Palma

Valencia

urcia

◆ Towns in which marranos faced the Inquisition, and had either to renounce their judaizing, or be burned at the stake

◇ Towns where secret Jews openly practiced their Judaism by 1930, following the emancipation of Portuguese Jewry in 1910

● Towns with Jewish communities by **1490**

◉ Anti-Jewish massacres 1391–97

← The expulsion of the Jews 1492–98

1492

1492 Expulsion	
To Turkey	90,000
To Holland	25,000
To Morocco	20,000
To France	10,000
To Italy	10,000
To America	5000
Total emigrated	160,000
Died while seeking a new home	20,000
Baptized, and remained in Spain	50,000

on civil and criminal matters, issuing codes of ethics – in short, concerning themselves with every sort of religious and non-religious matter, about which they were consulted by Jews all over the world.

Much of our knowledge about Jewish life in the Diaspora of that time comes from the *responsa* and writings of these *geonim*. The replies began as merely "yes" or "no" answers to questions. Then, primarily under the leadership of the blind *gaon* Yehudai ben Nahman (*c.*690–761), they developed into lengthy discussions and dissertations. Although he was in office for only four short years – during which time he wrote *Decided Laws*, the first attempt to codify the Talmud – Ben Nahman was very influential. Two other *geonim* are of major importance to the history of Judaism, and they were among the last: Saadyah and Hai.

Saadyah (882–946), like Rabbi Akiva before him, was of humble birth and also reputed to be the son of a convert to Judaism. A brilliant scholar – he published a Hebrew dictionary at the age of 20 and translated the Bible into Arabic – Saadyah eventually rose to become the head of the academy at Sura. His rabbinical interpretations were very much in the liberal tradition. Although he claimed to be against scientific as opposed to spiritual thought, he favored inquiry over theorizing, writing, "It is inconceivable that honest investigation should be forbidden to us." Unfortunately, Saadyah was prone to violent fits of temper, and these eventually degenerated into the madness that caused his death. In the meantime, he conducted bitter feuds with both the *resh galuta* and the sect known as the Karaites.

The Karaites were the only major divergence within Judaism until the progressive movement of the nineteenth century. Originally arising from a dispute between village

LEFT: *Under Islamic rule, the Jews of the southern part of the Iberian peninsula enjoyed a golden age, but the Christian reconquista was to totally reverse their fortunes. Successive persecutions culminated in the final expulsion of the Jews in 1492 (for Spain) and 1498 (for Portugal). The alternative was conversion, though many of the marranos, as the converts were termed, continued to practice Judaism in secret. The penalty for this was the Inquisition and death at the stake.*

and city Jews in Mesopotamia, the Karaites came to reject the Talmud, with its glosses on and interpretations of biblical law, instead interpreting biblical law literally and following it to the letter. They finally broke away to form a sect when their leader, Anan ben David, was imprisoned on the orders of the rabbis for preaching heresy and was sentenced to death by the caliph. The Karaite communities scattered like those of the Jews, but unlike the latter, they declined. Until recently, their largest concentrations were in the Crimea and Egypt, but today they live mainly in Israel.

Hai Gaon of Pumbeditha was so liberal in his views that he, too, was thrown into jail (in Damascus) by the orthodox rabbis. This, however, did not detract from his reputation as a *gaon* and as one of the international authorities on commercial law. In his great work *Buying and Selling*, he followed Talmudic precepts by recommending legislation to govern the prices of scarce goods and prevent a situation in which the poor could not afford to buy essentials. His interpretations are still put into practice today.

When Hai died in 1038 at the age of 99, the Pumbeditha academy closed its doors for the last time, signaling the end of the flowering of Babylonian Jewry, whose supremacy had lasted for 600 years. Although for the next four centuries, academies continued to exist in Mesopotamia and to be consulted by Jews on religious matters, the initiative now passed to Spain, France, and Germany.

The Jewish Golden Age in Spain

By the middle of the eighth century, the eastern half of the Byzantine Empire, together with Persia, north Africa, and the southern Iberian peninsula, were in the hands of the Muslim caliphs. Having no traditions of their own, they drew liberally on those of other civilizations, including the Hellenistic and Byzantine. They also employed Jewish scholars in the exercise of their love of science and the spread of knowledge. Thus began the Jewish golden age in Spain, during which poets, doctors, and scholars combined secular and religious knowledge in a way that has never been achieved since. Although the era is generally known as the golden age of Arab civilization, its greatness was, in fact, influenced by Jews

living throughout the Islamic world. Jews even occupied the highest posts in the Muslim world, including those of viziers (prime ministers) to the caliphs.

In southern Spain, the great cities of Córdoba, Toledo, and Lucena all had large Jewish populations – the latter two are even reputed to have been founded by Jews. Among the most illustrious names of the period are the Jews Ibn Daud, who in the mid-twelfth century, translated Hebrew, Greek, and Arabic scientific and philosophical works into Latin, and Judah ben Samuel ha-Levi (1075–1141), who was born in Toledo and studied at Lucena. His poetry, in Arabic and Hebrew, was very diverse and, for the first time since the Song of Songs, introduced sexual themes in Hebrew. Above all, he is remembered for his epic poem about the conversion of the Khazars, and for his proto-Zionism: "I am at the tip of the Western world, but my heart is in the East." Others who became justly famous were the poets and philosophers Solomon ibn Gabirol (*c.* 1021–*c.* 1058), Moses ibn Ezra (*c.* 1055– *c.* 1155), and Judah al-Harizi (1170–1235), as well as Benjamin ben Jonah of Tudela, for his diary of his travels from Castile to the Middle East in 1165–73.

Three of the greatest scholars of Muslim north Africa and Spain were Jews. Isaac Alfasi (sometimes given as Alphesi; 1013– 1103) was, as the Arabic translation of his name implies, born in Fez (now in modern Morocco), but fled from there to Lucena in his old age. He was the first rabbi to interpret the laws of the Babylonian Talmud in the light of contemporary life. Moses Maimonides (Rabbi Moses ben Maimon, sometimes Rambam; 1135–1204) was forced, because of persecution by the fanatical Muslim Almohads, to escape from his native Córdoba to Cairo, where he combined Jewish scholarship with his work as court physician to Saladin. He was a prodigious writer, whose most famous religious and philosophical works include the *Mishneh Torah* (the repetition of the Torah) and *The Guide to the Perplexed (Moreh Nevukhim)*, and his medical texts are full of good advice and common sense. Although less well known than these two, Hasdai Crescas (1340–1410), born in Barcelona, had an extraordinary influence on early Renaissance thought. Applying Talmu-

BELOW: *Born in Tudela, in Spain, Benjamin ben Jonah recorded his adventures in his* Book of Travels, *an unparalleled record of medieval Jewish and Gentile life. He is thought to have been the first European to have visited China and is certainly the first to mention the country by its modern name.*

BENJAMIN OF TUDE
1165–73

SPA

Regions described by Benjamin of Tudela

Towns visited or described by Benjamin

RIGHT: *A statue of Maimonides, one of the greatest Hebrew scholars of all time, in his birthplace, Córdoba. Maimonides was born there in 1135; he died in Cairo in 1204, where he became court physician to Saladin. His greatest works are the* Mishneh Torah, *in which he tried to codify Jewish oral law, and the* Moreh Nevukhim (The Guide to the Perplexed), *which deeply influenced subsequent Jewish and Christian philosophers.*

dic reasoning, he disproved some of the more far-fetched theories of Aristotle and, as such, was a precursor of Galileo, who demonstrated by experiment the errors of Aristotelian philosophy.

The Muslim Empire in Spain shrank under the onslaught of the Christians, and the Moorish provinces gradually fell under their rule. Although not all Christian rulers were hostile to the Jews, many persecuted them, and in the fifteenth century, a series of repressive measures were enacted. The impetus for this was provided by wandering fanatical Dominican friars who, surrounded by flagellants, preached against non-believers. In 1412, the Jews of Castile were forced into separate quarters (*juderías*), forbidden to engage in crafts or medicine and made to wear badges designating them as Jewish. Two years later, a ludicrously unfair debate between Christianity and Judaism was staged at the instigation of Ferdinand I ("The Just") of Aragon. This charade, which lasted

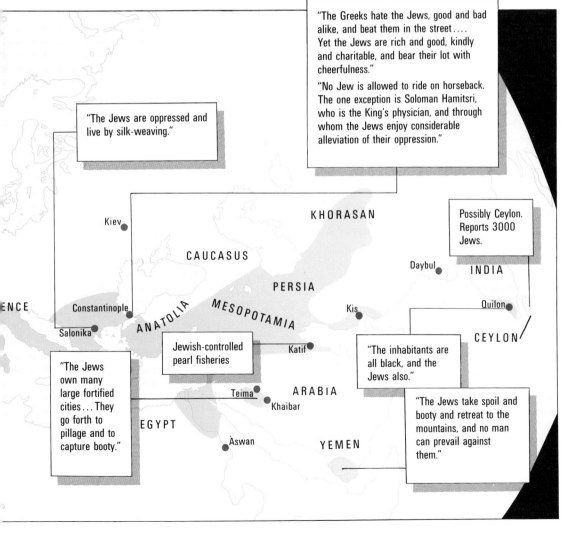

"The Greeks hate the Jews, good and bad alike, and beat them in the street....
Yet the Jews are rich and good, kindly and charitable, and bear their lot with cheerfulness."

"No Jew is allowed to ride on horseback. The one exception is Soloman Hamitsri, who is the King's physician, and through whom the Jews enjoy considerable alleviation of their oppression."

"The Jews are oppressed and live by silk-weaving."

KHORASAN

Kiev

Possibly Ceylon. Reports 3000 Jews.

CAUCASUS

Daybul   INDIA

PERSIA

ENCE   Constantinople   Kis   Quilon

ANATOLIA   MESOPOTAMIA   CEYLON

Salonika

Jewish-controlled pearl fisheries   Katif   "The inhabitants are all black, and the Jews also."

"The Jews own many large fortified cities... They go forth to pillage and to capture booty."   Teima   ARABIA   "The Jews take spoil and booty and retreat to the mountains, and no man can prevail against them."

Khaibar

EGYPT

Aswan   YEMEN

from February to November, ended when the advocate for Christianity – Geronimo de Santa Fé, the king's physician, who himself was a convert from Judaism – proclaimed himself the victor.

The preaching of "holy hatred" against the Jews by an itinerant monk, St. Vincent Ferrer (1350–1419), resulted in the forced baptism of thousands, especially in Castile and Aragon. Jews who had been forced to convert to Christianity did not do so with any great sincerity, and many continued to practice their own religion, or aspects of it, in secret. When this was realized – and, with it, the enhanced prosperity of these ersatz Christians, to whom all walks of life had suddenly been opened – the envy and hatred of the "Old" Christians for the "New" erupted into clashes between the two, beginning in Toledo in 1467.

The culmination of the Jewish persecution came with the accession, in 1474, of Ferdinand II of Aragon and Isabella of Castile – the so-called "Catholic Monarchs" – who were idolized for having united Spain. (Ironically, the royal marriage had been arranged by a Jew, Abraham Senior.) Ferdinand and Isabella gave their consent to the campaign by the Spanish clergy to root out any remaining non-Christian influences in Spain.

The Spanish Inquisition

The very first inquisition had been set up in 1229 in the French city of Toulouse as a tribunal to suppress heresy generally. Consisting largely of the trials and torture of "witches" and those "in league with the Devil," it had been able to deal only with people who professed to be Christians. The early advocates of such tribunals had not called for the death of heretics, nor had they concerned themselves with Jews, who were not considered heretics, only non-believers. All this changed when the Roman Catholic Church realized that the so-called New Christians of Spain were practicing their old religion in secret. In November 1478, Pope Sixtus IV issued a bull to establish a national inquisition there – an institution that was to last until 1820.

The Spanish Inquisition was directed mainly against the great number of Jews – called *conversos* or, less politely, *marranos* ("swine") – who had converted to Christianity for the sake of convenience, many of whom had become powerful, even within the Church. It began with a series of trials in 1480. The first of these was held in Barcelona, on the main street known as the Ramblas – today, a plaque marks the spot. All the victims were tortured, and any sign that the accused might have Jewish habits – such as the wearing of fresh linen on Saturday, the Jewish Sabbath, or a dislike of pork – was

RIGHT: *The Islamic caliphs employed and encouraged Jewish scholars and scientists. One such figure, Moses Maimonides, rose to become court physician to the Great Saladin. In the Rhineland, despite Christian persecution, Gershom ben Judah codified Talmudic law. Later thinkers, such as Spinoza, fell foul of the Jews themselves, while others, such as Marx, rejected their Jewish roots.*

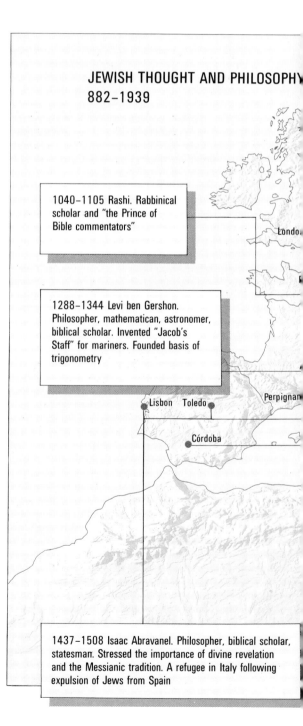

JEWISH THOUGHT AND PHILOSOPHY 882–1939

1040–1105 Rashi. Rabbinical scholar and "the Prince of Bible commentators"

1288–1344 Levi ben Gershon. Philosopher, mathematican, astronomer, biblical scholar. Invented "Jacob's Staff" for mariners. Founded basis of trigonometry

London

Perpignan

Lisbon Toledo

Córdoba

1437–1508 Isaac Abravanel. Philosopher, biblical scholar, statesman. Stressed the importance of divine revelation and the Messianic tradition. A refugee in Italy following expulsion of Jews from Spain

taken as proof of heresy. Within a year, 300 had been burned at the stake.

Rome protested these excesses, which had not been intended when the Inquisition had been established. However, the situation only worsened, especially when, in 1483, Tomás de Torquemada was appointed inquisitor-general for Castile and Aragon. Increasing numbers of people met their deaths in the fire, and even the dead were exhumed and tried so that their fortunes could be confiscated by the state. No one was safe: many genuine Christians, who had the misfortune to have annoyed a neighbor or fallen foul of the authorities in some way, were consigned to the flames.

Expulsion from Spain and Portugal
Until now, Spanish Jews who had been able to adhere to their original faith had been

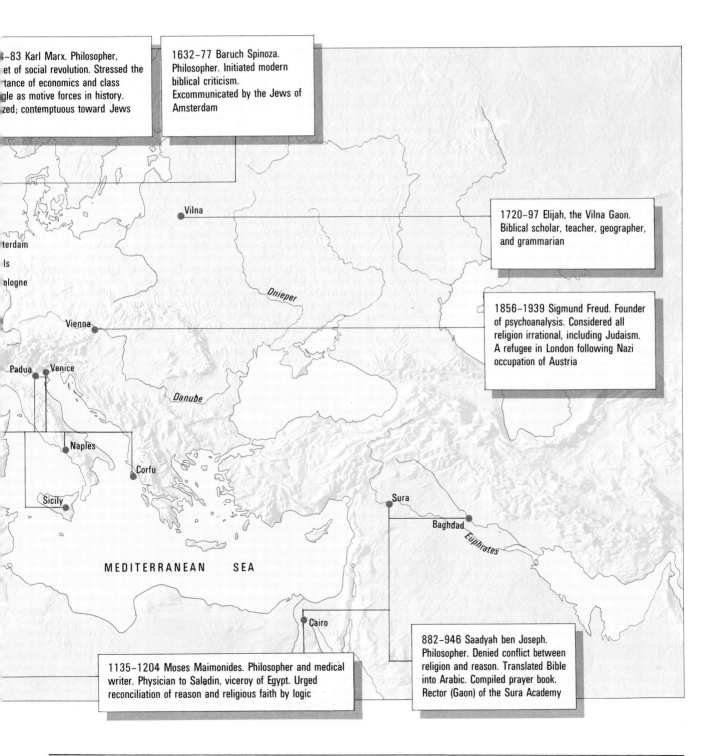

–83 Karl Marx. Philosopher, et of social revolution. Stressed the tance of economics and class gle as motive forces in history. zed; contemptuous toward Jews

1632–77 Baruch Spinoza. Philosopher. Initiated modern biblical criticism. Excommunicated by the Jews of Amsterdam

1720–97 Elijah, the Vilna Gaon. Biblical scholar, teacher, geographer, and grammarian

1856–1939 Sigmund Freud. Founder of psychoanalysis. Considered all religion irrational, including Judaism. A refugee in London following Nazi occupation of Austria

Vilna

terdam

ls

ologne

Vienna

Dnieper

Padua Venice

Danube

Naples

Corfu

Sicily

Sura

Baghdad

Euphrates

MEDITERRANEAN SEA

Cairo

882–946 Saadyah ben Joseph. Philosopher. Denied conflict between religion and reason. Translated Bible into Arabic. Compiled prayer book. Rector (Gaon) of the Sura Academy

1135–1204 Moses Maimonides. Philosopher and medical writer. Physician to Saladin, viceroy of Egypt. Urged reconciliation of reason and religious faith by logic

LEFT AND RIGHT:
Isabella and Ferdinand,
rulers of Aragon and
Castile, brought national
unity to Spain and
completed the work of the
Christian reconquista. *For*
the Jews, however, their
reign was an unmitigated
disaster, culminating in
their edict of 1492,
ordering the Jews to
embrace Christianity or
leave their kingdom.

The 100,000 Jews who had left had been led out by Don Isaac Abrabanel. He, like many of his fellows, settled in Italy – first in Naples and then in Venice, where he became adviser to the Doge. Other Jews fled to Portugal, hoping for sanctuary. Resident Jews bribed King João II ("The Perfect") to let them stay, but he would agree only to their remaining for eight months. When the deadline was reached, a few ships arrived to take some of the refugees to Portuguese possessions overseas, where many perished from tropical diseases. The majority, however, were left in Portugal.

unaffected by the Inquisition. Then Torquemada, not satisfied with exterminating the crypto-Jews, demanded the expulsion of the professing Jews. First, he asked the Pope to issue the order, but when he refused, Torquemada turned to Ferdinand and Isabella. While they hesitated, Don Isaac Abrabanel, a leading rabbi who was also the court financier, interceded for his people.

According to legend, Torquemada was listening at the door when Abrabanel offered the royal couple a handsome payment in gold to let his people stay in Spain. The inquisitor-general then rushed into the room, holding up a crucifix, and cried: "Behold the Saviour whom the wicked Judas sold for 30 pieces of silver. If you approve this deed, then you sell Him for a great sum!" This was enough to persuade the devoutly Catholic monarchs to expel the Jews.

In 1492, as Columbus set out across the Atlantic, Ferdinand and Isabella issued the *General Edict on the Expulsion of the Jews from Aragon and Castile*, the excuse for its issue being that the Jews were leading the New Christians astray and persuading them to follow their old religion. Any Jew who wished to could still convert rather than be expelled, and 50,000 did. Double that number left: by July 31, 1492, the specified date for full expulsion, not one professing Jew was left in Spain or its dominions.

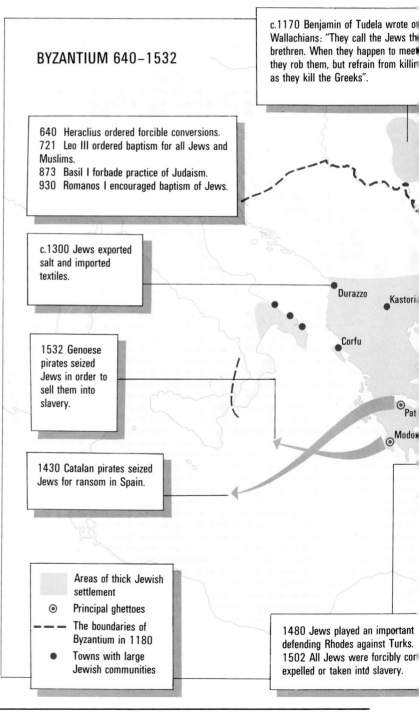

BYZANTIUM 640–1532

c.1170 Benjamin of Tudela wrote o[f] Wallachians: "They call the Jews th[eir] brethren. When they happen to mee[t] they rob them, but refrain from killi[ng] as they kill the Greeks".

640 Heraclius ordered forcible conversions.
721 Leo III ordered baptism for all Jews and Muslims.
873 Basil I forbade practice of Judaism.
930 Romanos I encouraged baptism of Jews.

c.1300 Jews exported salt and imported textiles.

1532 Genoese pirates seized Jews in order to sell them into slavery.

1430 Catalan pirates seized Jews for ransom in Spain.

Durazzo

Kastori[a]

Corfu

Pat[ras]

Modo[n]

1480 Jews played an important [role in] defending Rhodes against Turks.
1502 All Jews were forcibly con[verted,] expelled or taken into slavery.

⬛ Areas of thick Jewish settlement
⊙ Principal ghettoes
– – – The boundaries of Byzantium in 1180
● Towns with large Jewish communities

João II died in 1495, and his successor, Manoel I ("The Fortunate"), decided to allow the remaining refugees to stay. Unfortunately, circumstances were to alter this favorable attitude. The year after his accession to the Portuguese throne, Manoel signed a marriage contract with the Infanta Isabella of Spain. One of its clauses ordered the expulsion of all the Jews in Portugal – both those who had fled Spain and those who had been living there for centuries.

Manoel hoped that the Portuguese Jews would ease matters by accepting baptism. When they did not, he had all Jewish children

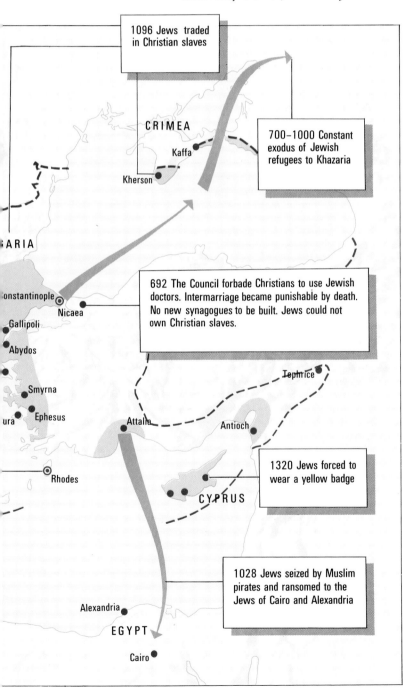

1096 Jews traded in Christian slaves

CRIMEA
Kaffa
Kherson

700–1000 Constant exodus of Jewish refugees to Khazaria

ARIA

onstantinople
Nicaea
Gallipoli
Abydos
ura
Smyrna
Ephesus
Attalia
Rhodes

692 The Council forbade Christians to use Jewish doctors. Intermarriage became punishable by death. No new synagogues to be built. Jews could not own Christian slaves.

Tephrice
Antioch

1320 Jews forced to wear a yellow badge

CYPRUS

1028 Jews seized by Muslim pirates and ransomed to the Jews of Cairo and Alexandria

Alexandria

EGYPT

Cairo

between the ages of four and twenty seized and forcibly baptized. He then ordered that the Jews could leave only by ship from Lisbon; when no ships materialized and the deadline for expulsion had passed, the Jewish adults who had congregated in Lisbon were also forcibly baptized. When they resisted, many were killed, but most survived, although only after a spell in prison. Finding that even this ploy had failed, Manoel finally ordered ships to take them all away, and by 1498, not a Jew was left in Portugal. They had fled anywhere that was willing to take them, principally the Netherlands, the Ottoman Empire, and Poland.

From Sepharad to Ashkenaz

In the rest of Europe in the meantime, Jewish fortunes had fluctuated wildly between tolerance, acceptance, and persecution. A succession of "barbarians" – Goths, Vandals,

LEFT: *In Byzantium, repressive measures against the Jews started as early as 415, with the expulsion of the Jews from Alexandria, and continued over the following centuries. From 700, there was a constant flow of Jewish refugees to Khazaria, which ended only with the fall of that kingdom to Islam; in the west, Jewish communities were also threatened by Christian pirates from Italy and Spain.*

SEPHARDIM AND ASHKENAZIM

By this time, the Jews of the diaspora had divided into a number of groups, the chief of these being known as the Sephardim and Ashkenazim. The former was the name given to Jews settled in Spain and Portugal; the latter was applied to the Jews in Germany, though later, it was used to describe all the Jews of northern and eastern Europe. Both sets of Jews experienced wavering fortunes during the Middle Ages. Under Islamic rule the Sephardim experienced a golden age, but the Christian *reconquista* was to bring this to an end. The Ashkenazim faced waves of persecution, but their scholars contributed greatly to the development of Jewish thought. The synagogues illustrated here are (right) a German synagogue in Alsace with walls painted with folk art motifs; (below right) a synagogue in Worms; (below) the church of Santa Maria la Blanca in Toledo. This was built as a synagogue in 1203 but converted to a church in 1411 at a time of anti-Jewish persecution.

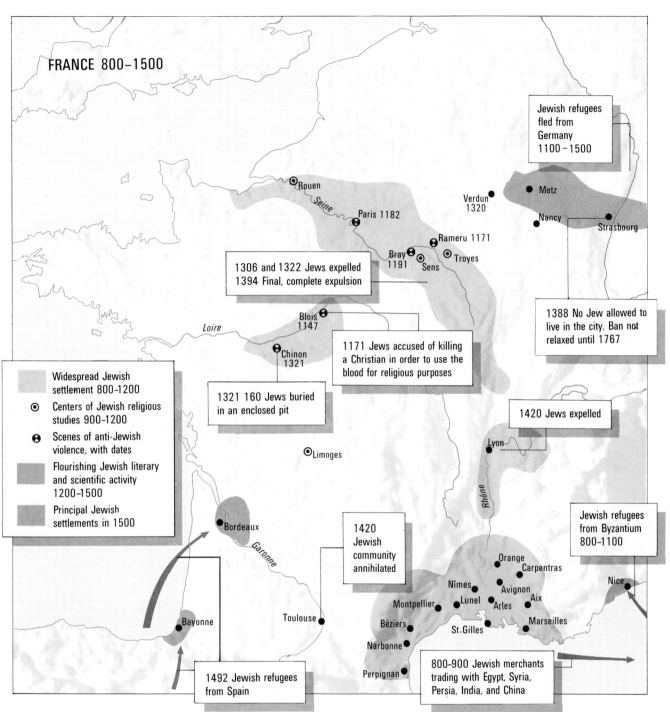

FRANCE 800–1500

Jewish refugees
fled from
Germany
1100–1500

Verdun
1320

Metz

Nancy

Strasbourg

Rouen

Seine

Paris 1182

Rameru 1171

Bray
1191

Sens

Troyes

1306 and 1322 Jews expelled
1394 Final, complete expulsion

1388 No Jew allowed to
live in the city. Ban not
relaxed until 1767

Blois
1147

Loire

1171 Jews accused of killing
a Christian in order to use the
blood for religious purposes

Chinon
1321

1321 160 Jews buried
in an enclosed pit

Widespread Jewish
settlement 800–1200

Centers of Jewish religious
studies 900–1200

Scenes of anti-Jewish
violence, with dates

Flourishing Jewish literary
and scientific activity
1200–1500

Principal Jewish
settlements in 1500

Limoges

1420 Jews expelled

Lyon

Rhône

Jewish refugees
from Byzantium
800–1100

Bordeaux

Garonne

1420
Jewish
community
annihilated

Orange

Carpentras

Nîmes

Avignon

Nice

Montpellier

Lunel

Arles

Aix

Bayonne

Toulouse

Béziers

St.Gilles

Marseilles

Narbonne

1492 Jewish refugees
from Spain

Perpignan

800–900 Jewish merchants
trading with Egypt, Syria,
Persia, India, and China

Franks, and others – had invaded the western half of the Roman Empire, and some had even attacked Rome itself. The earliest of these invaders had merely been plunderers, hostile to anyone who got in their path, but two great sovereigns had emerged. The Ostrogoth Theodoric the Great (c.454–526), ruler of Italy, and the Frankish Charlemagne (742–814), ruler of France and western Germany, had both invited Jews to settle throughout their kingdoms and, with their skills, craftsmanship, and knowledge of languages, bring new prosperity.

The Vikings, too, had been tolerant of Jews in the places they had settled during their invasions of Europe in the ninth and tenth centuries. One of their descendants – William the Conqueror, who as Duke of Normandy invaded England in 1066 – is believed to have brought Jews with him to revive the English economy. Certainly there were Jews in England under the Angevin kings in the twelfth and thirteenth centuries. One of them – Aaron – financed part of the building of Canterbury Cathedral.

This is the period commonly known as

ABOVE: *Charlemagne had encouraged Jewish settlement in France to help rekindle the prosperity of his empire, but his tolerant policies were not continued by his successors. By 1500, the principal Jewish settlements were concentrated on France's eastern frontier, where they were joined by Jews fleeing from persecution within Germany.*

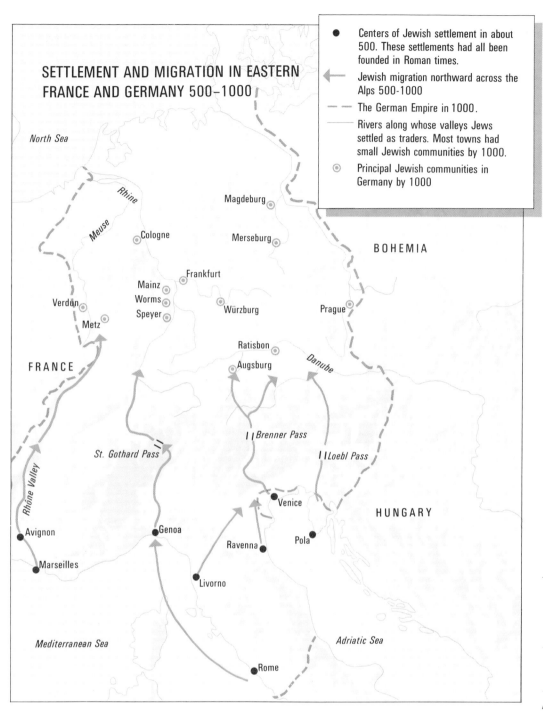

SETTLEMENT AND MIGRATION IN EASTERN FRANCE AND GERMANY 500–1000

Legend:
- ● Centers of Jewish settlement in about 500. These settlements had all been founded in Roman times.
- ← Jewish migration northward across the Alps 500-1000
- – – – The German Empire in 1000.
- —— Rivers along whose valleys Jews settled as traders. Most towns had small Jewish communities by 1000.
- ⊙ Principal Jewish communities in Germany by 1000

North Sea
Rhine
Meuse
Magdeburg
Cologne
Merseburg
BOHEMIA
Frankfurt
Mainz
Worms
Verdun
Würzburg
Speyer
Prague
Metz
FRANCE
Ratisbon
Augsburg
Danube
Brenner Pass
St. Gothard Pass
Loebl Pass
Rhône Valley
Venice
HUNGARY
Avignon
Genoa
Ravenna
Pola
Marseilles
Livorno
Mediterranean Sea
Adriatic Sea
Rome

RIGHT: *The house of Aaron the Jew in Lincoln, said to be the oldest inhabited house in England. In common with their continental brothers, the Jews of England faced the risk of persecution and pogrom during the Middle Ages. One of the chief reasons for their unpopularity was their role as moneylenders to the king, though, in many cases, such loans were coerced, rather than freely offered or negotiated.*

BELOW RIGHT: *A Jewish scholar depicted in a woodcut of 1508. Just as Christian philosophy was greatly developed during the Middle Ages, so was Talmudic scholarship in the Jewish world.*

LEFT: *With the fall of the western Roman empire, Jewish fortunes fluctuated throughout the Dark Ages until the emergence of Charlemagne, who encouraged Jewish settlement throughout his empire. By 1000, the Jews were well established in the central region and had penetrated as far east as Prague.*

Europe's "Middle Ages." For the Jews, however, it was, despite outbreaks of persecution, a time of spiritual growth.

The Jewish communities had by now divided into a number of different groups. The two main ones were the Sephardi (from *Sepharad*, a biblical word believed to refer to Spain) and the Ashkenazi (from *Ashkenaz*, a similarly biblical name for France and Germany, although its tradition came to embrace the whole of northern and eastern Europe). In a few areas – in what is now modern Italy,

Romania, and Yugoslavia – mixed Ashkenazi and Sephardi communities developed. Other smaller groups included the Italians, who could trace their origins back to the Romans and beyond, and the Orientals, or Easterners, mainly in what was to become Iraq, some of whom could trace their ancestry to the Babylonian exile.

The Ashkenazi scholars of this era were among the greatest Jewish thinkers of all time. Gershom ben Judah (960–1040), who lived in the Rhineland, is often referred to as

"Our Rabbi Gershom, Light of the Exile," so great was his influence. At a council summoned by Gershom at Mainz in the year 1000, he made public a series of edicts (e.g. forbidding Jewish men from marrying more than one wife) and moral precepts (e.g. forbidding the divorcing of a wife without her consent and forbidding the opening and reading of other people's letters). These were all strictly observed throughout the Ashkenazi world.

Rabbi Shlomo Itzhaki (1040–1105), better known as "Rashi," was born in the French city of Troyes, where his father owned a vineyard. Rashi's commentary on the Torah and Talmud is considered so definitive that it is still included with the Talmud whenever the latter is printed. His grandsons Samuel ben Meir and Rabbenu Tam carried on this great tradition of biblical and Talmudic interpretation, as did Rabbi Jacob ben Asher (1270–1343), who fled from Germany to Toledo in Spain to escape religious persecution. He wrote commentaries on the Talmud and codified it in his book *Four Rows (Arba'a Turim)* – and, in so doing, united the two

strands of Sephardi and Ashkenazi learning.

The centers of Jewish scholarship in Europe switched from country to country, according to where it was safest and permissible for Jews to live. Talmudic law was to make one of its largest impacts in England. The Jewish financiers under the Angevin kings were responsible for the entry into the English legal system of the Talmudic property law, which the Jews used in commercial transactions. Some of these laws are actually enshrined in the guarantees of rights and privileges granted by King John in the Magna Carta of 1215. Although trial by combat remained on British statute books until as late as 1817, its place was gradually taken by the rule of law to which the Jews had always subjected themselves: the right to be judged on the facts alone. Through the English legal system, Talmudic law went on to influence legislation throughout the English-speaking world.

CHAPTER THREE

THE HIGH MIDDLE AGES TO MOSES MENDELSSOHN

The High Middle Ages – from the thirteenth century until well into the Reformation in the early sixteenth century – were the Dark Ages for the Jews of Europe. All over northern and southern Europe and, later, as the Muslim tide retreated, in Spain and Portugal, their fortunes waned as those of the Christian Church rose. The pagans and the heretical Christian sects having been largely eliminated in "holy" wars, the Jews remained the only non-Christians in a Europe that was being systematically forced to follow Catholicism.

The puzzle is why the Jews were allowed to exist at all. Certainly there were many brutal attempts to convert them – the wife and child of Rabbi Gershom ben Judah, the "Light of the Exile," were both forcibly baptized by Christians in retaliation for a local priest's decision to adopt Judaism – as well as many massacres of Jews by those who wished to exterminate them.

The Birth of Banking

One reason why the Jews were allowed to remain in certain places – although often in humiliating conditions – is that their existence had become an economic necessity. The Jews were outside the feudal system: they could not belong to the craftsmen's guilds; nor were they tied to the land, as were the serfs and villeins who served – as the Jews could not – in the private armies of their lords. Since they were not under the vassalage of any of the feudal lords, the Jews were directly answerable to the kings.

The Jews, excluded from respectable professions, were condemned to follow only the lowliest of occupations. For instance, they had to provide hangmen from their communities, and public hangings always took place in Jewish cemeteries. With almost all other avenues of economic activity closed to them, they were encouraged to engage in what the Christians could not – usury.

In 1179, the Third Lateran Council had forbidden all Roman Catholics to lend money at interest, threatening to refuse Christian burial to any who did so. However, it was soon realized that no healthy economy could exist without moneylending. The Jews, too, were forbidden, by the Bible, to lend money at interest, at least to each other, and the Talmud extended that prohibition to charging interest to anyone. However, because in Judaism, the preservation of human life is considered a holy act, and because they soon found themselves having to choose between becoming moneylenders or losing their lives; invariably, the Jews took the former course. By following the laws of the Talmud with regard to commercial transactions, they behaved fairly and justly. In this way, they became the merchants and financiers of Christian Europe.

Prior to the Middle Ages, Jews had been craftsmen and even soldiers (the class of Roman *equites*, or knights, included Jews), but they had never been considered part of the merchant class. They nevertheless thrived in their new profession, having many natural advantages as merchants, especially in international trade. Unlike others who only spoke their own local language, the Jews could

RIGHT: *Medieval Italy was the battleground between Judaism and the Papacy, though Catholic persecution was by no means continuous. The chief period of papal pressure was in the mid-sixteenth century, with the decrees of 1555; the Popes also pressed for the setting up of ghettoes and other controls on Jewish activity.*

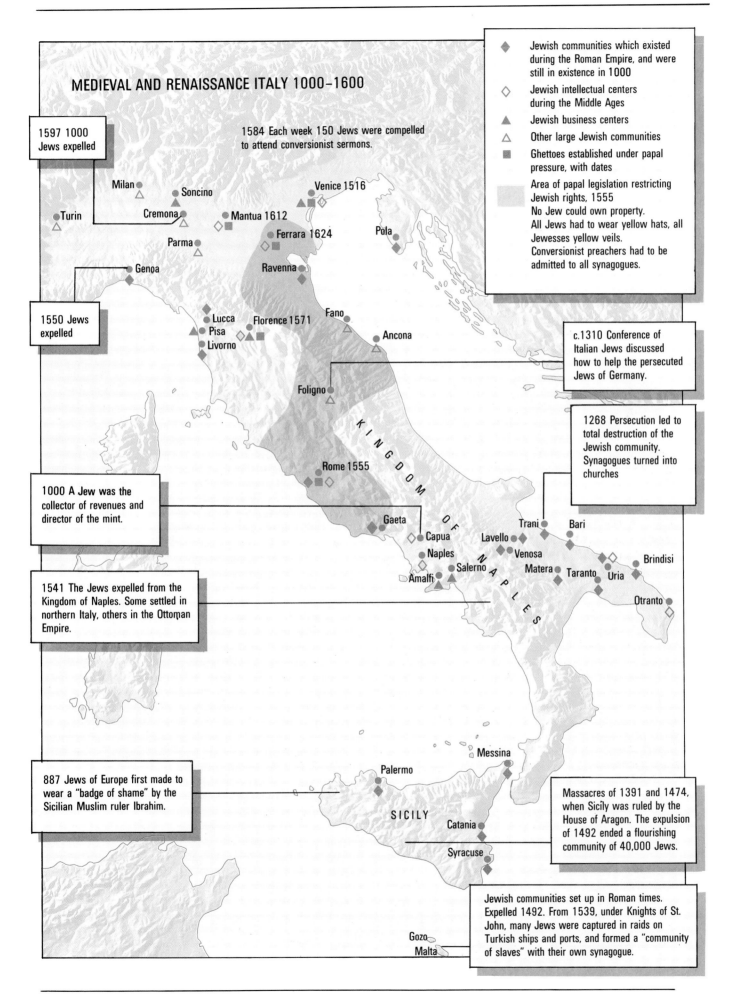

MEDIEVAL AND RENAISSANCE ITALY 1000–1600

Legend:
- ◆ Jewish communities which existed during the Roman Empire, and were still in existence in 1000
- ◇ Jewish intellectual centers during the Middle Ages
- ▲ Jewish business centers
- △ Other large Jewish communities
- ■ Ghettoes established under papal pressure, with dates
- Area of papal legislation restricting Jewish rights, 1555. No Jew could own property. All Jews had to wear yellow hats, all Jewesses yellow veils. Conversionist preachers had to be admitted to all synagogues.

1597 1000 Jews expelled

1584 Each week 150 Jews were compelled to attend conversionist sermons.

1550 Jews expelled

c.1310 Conference of Italian Jews discussed how to help the persecuted Jews of Germany.

1268 Persecution led to total destruction of the Jewish community. Synagogues turned into churches

1000 A Jew was the collector of revenues and director of the mint.

1541 The Jews expelled from the Kingdom of Naples. Some settled in northern Italy, others in the Ottoman Empire.

887 Jews of Europe first made to wear a "badge of shame" by the Sicilian Muslim ruler Ibrahim.

Massacres of 1391 and 1474, when Sicily was ruled by the House of Aragon. The expulsion of 1492 ended a flourishing community of 40,000 Jews.

Jewish communities set up in Roman times. Expelled 1492. From 1539, under Knights of St. John, many Jews were captured in raids on Turkish ships and ports, and formed a "community of slaves" with their own synagogue.

Place names:
Milan, Soncino, Turin, Cremona, Mantua 1612, Venice 1516, Parma, Ferrara 1624, Pola, Genoa, Ravenna, Lucca, Pisa, Livorno, Florence 1571, Fano, Ancona, Foligno, Rome 1555, Gaeta, Capua, Naples, Salerno, Amalfi, Trani, Bari, Lavello, Venosa, Matera, Taranto, Uria, Brindisi, Otranto, Messina, Palermo, Catania, Syracuse, SICILY, KINGDOM OF NAPLES, Gozo, Malta

communicate with each other using Hebrew as a *lingua franca* for business letters and transactions, secure in the knowledge that very few non-Jews would be able to understand or read their words. And in those troubled times, they were always sure of a hospitable reception by their co-religionists even in the most remote areas.

From the sixth to the tenth century, Jewish merchants known as Radanites traveled throughout Europe and Asia, trading in spices, silks, and jewels. They acted as middlemen between the Christian and Muslim worlds, and were a channel for re-introducing into Christian Europe the philosophical and scientific concepts of antiquity

RIGHT: *This map of the world, with Jerusalem as the center, was drawn in the fourteenth century. The crusaders hoped to establish a Christian state in the land where Jesus had lived. For a brief period they were successful.*

BELOW: *Italian bankers from a late fourteenth century treatise on the seven deadly sins. This illustrates avarice.*

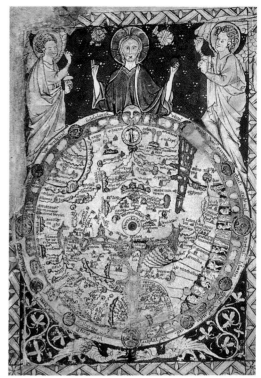

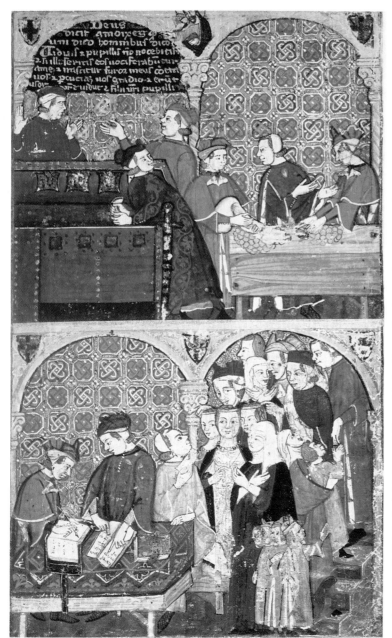

that had been kept alive by the Muslims. The rediscovery in the West of the sciences of mathematics, astronomy, and cartography prepared the ground for the Renaissance.

With their virtual monopoly of financial transactions, Jews rapidly became the bankers of Europe, winning themselves economic power. However, this was a two-edged sword. Although some monarchs showed their gratitude toward their Jewish financiers and rewarded them, most bled them with heavy taxes and levies. An extreme example was King John of England (reigned 1199–1216), who demanded a huge tribute from the Jews in 1210, ordering that any who could not or would not pay be tortured. Life in England became so unbearable that in 1254 Elias of London begged Henry III to allow the Jews to leave – but in vain: they had become far too useful as a source of funds.

However, whenever a monarch found himself too heavily in debt to his money-lenders, he merely expelled the Jews and confiscated all their property. This happened in England in 1290 under Edward I, as well as several times in France, culminating in the Jews' expulsion from all French territory in 1394. These expulsions were in addition to the numerous banishments from various cities and provinces that occurred sporadically throughout the Middle Ages.

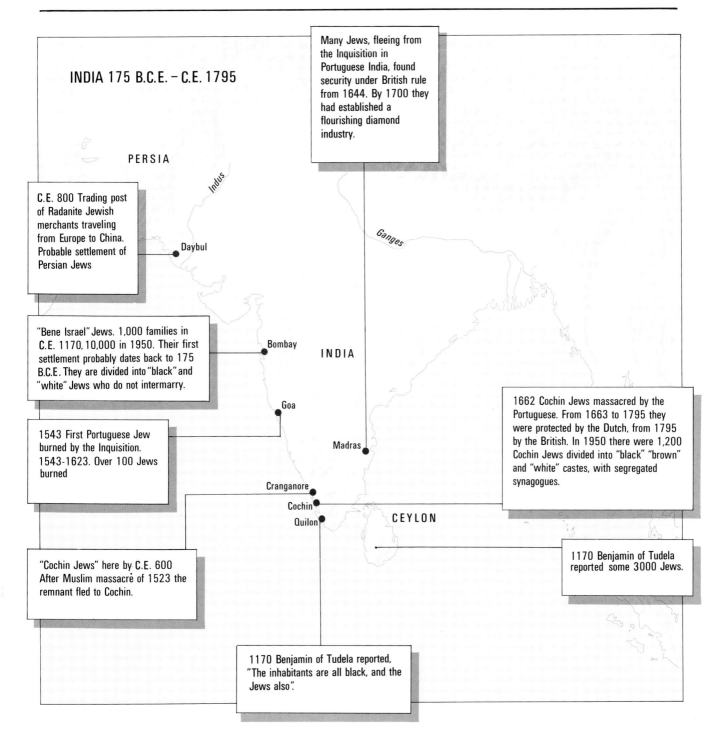

INDIA 175 B.C.E. – C.E. 1795

PERSIA

Many Jews, fleeing from the Inquisition in Portuguese India, found security under British rule from 1644. By 1700 they had established a flourishing diamond industry.

C.E. 800 Trading post of Radanite Jewish merchants traveling from Europe to China. Probable settlement of Persian Jews

Daybul

Indus

Ganges

"Bene Israel" Jews. 1,000 families in C.E. 1170, 10,000 in 1950. Their first settlement probably dates back to 175 B.C.E. They are divided into "black" and "white" Jews who do not intermarry.

Bombay

INDIA

1662 Cochin Jews massacred by the Portuguese. From 1663 to 1795 they were protected by the Dutch, from 1795 by the British. In 1950 there were 1,200 Cochin Jews divided into "black" "brown" and "white" castes, with segregated synagogues.

Goa

1543 First Portuguese Jew burned by the Inquisition. 1543-1623. Over 100 Jews burned

Madras

Cranganore

Cochin

Quilon

CEYLON

"Cochin Jews" here by C.E. 600 After Muslim massacre of 1523 the remnant fled to Cochin.

1170 Benjamin of Tudela reported some 3000 Jews.

1170 Benjamin of Tudela reported, "The inhabitants are all black, and the Jews also".

The Crusades

The worst catastrophe to befall European and Middle Eastern Jewry in the Middle Ages was the Crusades. The first call to win back the Holy Land for Christianity was made in 1095 at the Council of Clermont by Pope Urban II, who died in 1099, just before the news of the capture of Jerusalem arrived. No doubt the Pope expired believing that he had contrived a brilliant diversion for the energies of the numerous Christian princes who were warring against each other.

Ironically, the idea of a crusade may not have been thought up by Urban II but by his immediate predecessor, Pope Gregory VII (c. 1015–85), who was of Jewish descent. Gregory was the grandson of the banker Baruch, founder of the house of Pierleone, who became a Christian under the name of Benedictus Christianus. Another member of this prominent Jewish family was the "anti-pope", Anacletus II, in the following century. (The Borgias, who produced, among other notables, Pope Alexander VI and St. Francis Borgia, were descended from Spanish mar-ranos.) Gregory's papacy proved extremely

ABOVE: *Alexander the Great's conquests opened the way to India and where his armies led, Jewish migrants followed. The first Jewish settlers probably reached India around 175 B.C.E., traveling across Persia or via the Persian Gulf. Their first large settlement was in Bombay.*

important for the Church, for he rescued it from disrepute, following a succession of debauched popes, some of them teenagers, who were placed in power by ambitious relatives.

There were eight crusades in all, the last in 1270–2. Religion became the pretext for murder and looting. Only the First Crusade, ending with the capture of Jerusalem at a terrible cost in innocent lives, was in any way successful in achieving its supposed religious aims. After the capture and the massacre of the Muslim and Jewish populations (the Jews having been allowed back into the city when it had fallen into Arab hands), the knights gave thanks in the Church of the Holy Sepulchre, built by the mother of the emperor Constantine I. According to a contemporary account, "the stream of blood rose to the knees of the riders, up to the reins on the horses' necks." Less than a century later Jerusalem was recaptured. (The Crusades and their consequences for the Jews are dealt with in greater depth in Chapter 5.)

The Rise of the East European Communities

Despite the appalling sufferings of the European Jews, which lasted from the High Middle Ages until the late seventeenth century, they were still capable of notable

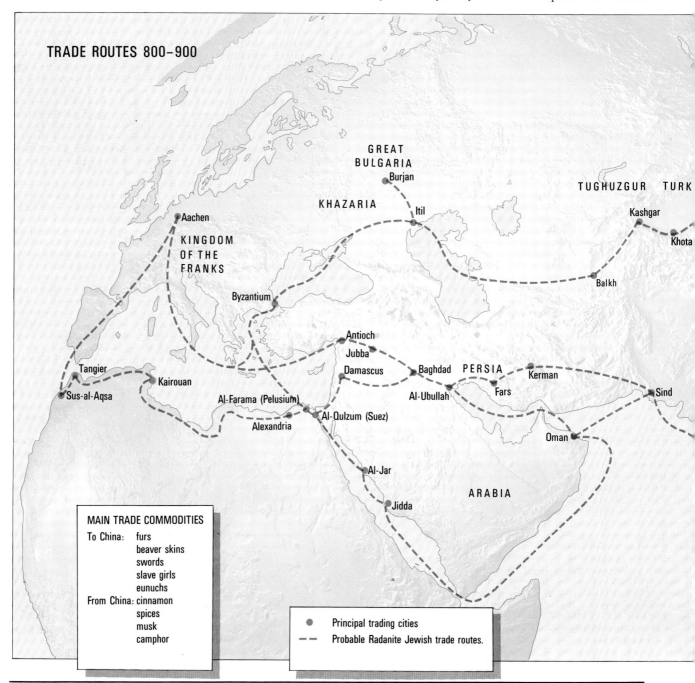

TRADE ROUTES 800–900

GREAT BULGARIA
Burjan

KHAZARIA

TUGHUZGUR TURK

Kashgar

Khota

Itil

Aachen

KINGDOM OF THE FRANKS

Balkh

Byzantium

Antioch
Jubba
Damascus

Baghdad   PERSIA

Kerman

Tangier

Kairouan

Al-Ubullah   Fars

Sind

Sus-al-Aqsa

Al-Farama (Pelusium)

Al-Qulzum (Suez)

Alexandria

Oman

Al-Jar

ARABIA

Jidda

MAIN TRADE COMMODITIES
To China: furs
           beaver skins
           swords
           slave girls
           eunuchs
From China: cinnamon
           spices
           musk
           camphor

●   Principal trading cities

‐ ‐ ‐   Probable Radanite Jewish trade routes.

achievement, and their contribution to world culture continued, albeit in a more indirect and circumspect way than before.

The codification and interpretation of the Talmud progressed, despite it being repeatedly condemned and publicly burned by Christians. Because of this persecution, the center of Jewish learning shifted for a time to Muslim Spain and to the Muslim lands conquered by the Mamelukes and the Seljuk Turks, successive conquerors of the Middle East. It was later centered in eastern Europe, especially in what is now Poland. In the tenth and eleventh centuries, Jews had emigrated eastward, setting up the famous Jewish community in Prague and then moving into

ABOVE: *The old town hall in the Jewish ghetto in Prague. Throughout Europe, the Jews were gradually herded into ghettoes as the Middle Ages progressed, the first compulsory ones being established in Spain and Portugal at the end of the fourteenth century. The Christian argument was that faith would be weakened by the presence of Jews, who, outside the ghettoes, were forced to wear identification badges.*

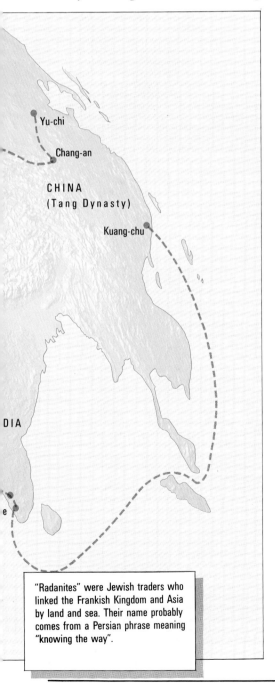

"Radanites" were Jewish traders who linked the Frankish Kingdom and Asia by land and sea. Their name probably comes from a Persian phrase meaning "knowing the way".

LEFT: *Long before Roman times, the Jews had established themselves as traders, and this continued after Rome's fall, particularly in the Islamic world, where their activities were encouraged. An adventurous group known as "Radanites" formed the trading link between Frankist Europe and China; their journeys were recorded by a Persian writer around C.E.850.*

Hungary and Poland. Here they lived in comparative peace, and were even welcomed in the lands that had been decimated by plague and especially in Hungary, where the Mongols had invaded in 1241–2.

In Poland, Grand Prince Boleslav V issued a charter of Jewish rights in 1264. King Casimir III the Great (reigned 1330–70) is reputed to have had a Jewish mistress, Esterka, whose daughters were raised as Jews but whose sons became the ancestors of many members of the Polish nobility. This spirit of tolerance continued under Sigismund I (reigned 1506–48) and Sigismund II (reigned 1548–72). Poland was the last major center of Jewish learning to emerge and one of the longest lived (*c.*1500–1939). It was also the largest. By the early seventeenth century Rabbi Nathan Hannover was able to write: "In every community, there is a *yeshiva* [religious academy]...in all the lands of the Polish king, there is scarcely a family in which the Torah is not studied." This happy state of affairs was to end scarcely a century later with the coming of the Cossacks (*see* Chapter 5), but in the meantime, Jewish life flourished.

The Kabbalah

The major innovation in Jewish learning in the Middle Ages was the mysticism of the *Kabbalah* ("a thing received"). Its source was the *Book of Splendor* (*Sefer ha-Zohar*, commonly called the *Zohar*), written by Moses de León (*c.*1240–1305) who lived in southern Spain. He claimed that it was a compilation of writings by the second-century Palestinian rabbi Simeon ben Yochai, although this has been disputed.

There had always been a mystical strain running through Jewish scholarship, alongside more rational and pragmatic thought. Now, in times of dire persecution and peril, Jews turned to the supernatural. The *Zohar* became a major object of study, and the number of Kabbalists multiplied. The center of Kabbalah study moved from Spain to the city of Safed in Lower Galilee, where Isaac Luria (1534–72) founded a new school. Another major Kabbalistic work was written by his disciple Hayim Vital (1543–1620), who entitled his book *Etz Hayim*, meaning "The Tree of Life" but also, of course, a pun

RIGHT: *A Kabbalist charm, drawn on parchment. The mystical Kabbalist movement spread throughout the Jewish world from Spain and France from the thirteenth century onward. Its adherents claimed that every letter, word, number, and even accent in the Bible contained hidden mysteries which they alone could interpret.*

BELOW: *For the Jews of central Europe, the Middle Ages were indeed a dark age, their fortunes waning as those of the Christian church rose.*

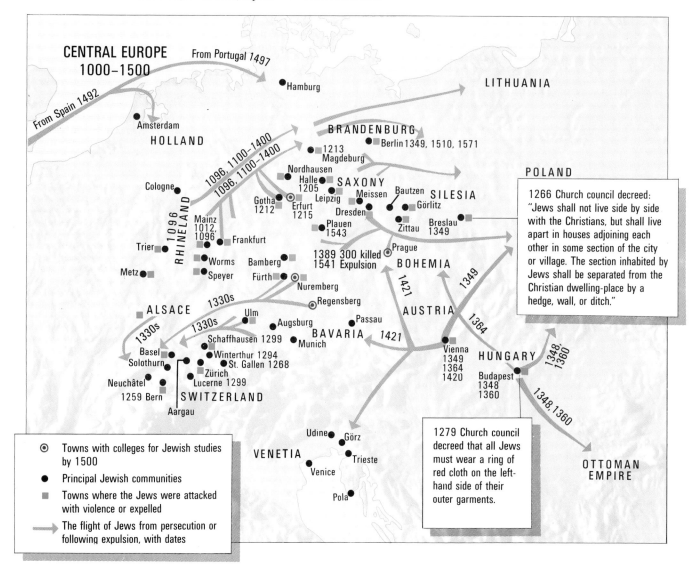

CENTRAL EUROPE 1000–1500

From Portugal 1497

From Spain 1492

LITHUANIA

Hamburg

Amsterdam

HOLLAND

1096, 1100–1400
1096, 1100–1400

BRANDENBURG

Berlin 1349, 1510, 1571

POLAND

1213
Magdeburg

Cologne

Nordhausen

Halle 1205

SAXONY

Meissen

Bautzen

SILESIA

Görlitz

Gotha 1212

Erfurt 1215

Leipzig

Dresden

Mainz 1012, 1096

RHINELAND

Frankfurt

Plauen 1543

Zittau

Breslau 1349

1096

Trier

Worms

Bamberg

1389 300 killed
1541 Expulsion

Prague

BOHEMIA

1266 Church council decreed: "Jews shall not live side by side with the Christians, but shall live apart in houses adjoining each other in some section of the city or village. The section inhabited by Jews shall be separated from the Christian dwelling-place by a hedge, wall, or ditch."

Metz

Speyer

Fürth

Nuremberg

1421

1349

ALSACE

1330s

Regensberg

1330s

Ulm

Augsburg

Passau

AUSTRIA

1364

1330s

1330s

Schaffhausen 1299

BAVARIA

1421

Basel

Winterthur 1294

Munich

St. Gallen 1268

Vienna 1349 1364 1420

HUNGARY

1348, 1360

Solothurn

Zürich

Neuchâtel

Lucerne 1299

Budapest 1348 1360

1259 Bern

SWITZERLAND

Aargau

1348, 1360

Udine

Görz

VENETIA

Trieste

1279 Church council decreed that all Jews must wear a ring of red cloth on the left-hand side of their outer garments.

OTTOMAN EMPIRE

Venice

Pola

⊙ Towns with colleges for Jewish studies by 1500

● Principal Jewish communities

■ Towns where the Jews were attacked with violence or expelled

→ The flight of Jews from persecution or following expulsion, with dates

on the author's name.

The Kabbalah spread throughout the Jewish world. Isaiah Horowitz (c.1565–1630) – who lived in Poland, Bohemia, and Germany, but eventually settled in Palestine – wrote another important Kabbalistic work, *The Two Tablets of the Covenant (Shnai Luhot ha-Brit)*. The two strands, Kabbalah and Talmud, were united by Joseph Caro and Moses Isserles. The mystic Joseph Caro, who resided in various parts of the Turkish Empire, compiled the greatest codification of the Talmud: *The Set Table (Shulkhan Arukh)*. To this, Moses Isserles (1520–72), a Polish rabbi, added glosses which he called *The Tablecloth (Mappah)*, and which are now incorporated in the *Shulkhan Arukh*. Isserles, whose synagogue in Cracow still stands, had his own *yeshiva*, as did the other two great scholars of that time: Shalom Shachna

of Lublin (1500–59) and Solomon Luria of Poznan (1510–73).

The Jewish thirst for learning was encouraged by the invention of printing in the mid-fifteenth century. The first Hebrew book to be printed was Rashi's commentary on the Talmud, produced in 1475 in Reggio di Calabria in Italy. At the time, Jews there were not banned from engaging in crafts, and Hebrew presses were opened in a few places where they felt themselves to be safe – in Cremona and in Venice, where a non-Jew, Daniel Bomberg, printed Hebrew Bibles.

To the Americas

As Europe became increasingly oppressive, newly discovered lands were opening up. Jews such as Abraham Cresques and his son Judah became famous mapmakers, Abraham producing (in 1375) the first world map,

BELOW: *From the tenth century onward, Jewish refugees fleeing from persecution in Germany found a welcome in the east, particularly in Poland, where a charter protecting Jewish rights was issued in 1264. Polish tolerance reached its height during the reign of Casimir the Great in the fourteenth century. Though there were sporadic anti-Semitic outbreaks after this, there were no full-scale persecutions until the Cossack incursions of the seventeenth century.*

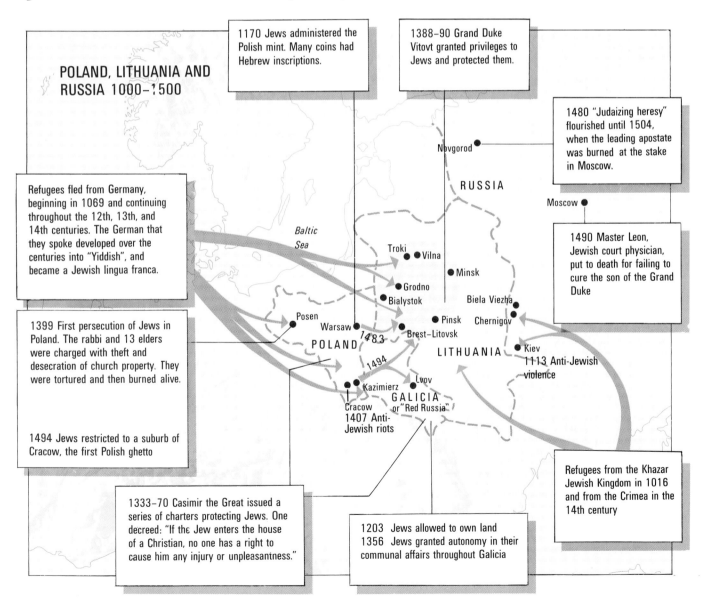

POLAND, LITHUANIA AND RUSSIA 1000–1500

1170 Jews administered the Polish mint. Many coins had Hebrew inscriptions.

1388–90 Grand Duke Vitovt granted privileges to Jews and protected them.

1480 "Judaizing heresy" flourished until 1504, when the leading apostate was burned at the stake in Moscow.

Refugees fled from Germany, beginning in 1069 and continuing throughout the 12th, 13th, and 14th centuries. The German that they spoke developed over the centuries into "Yiddish", and became a Jewish lingua franca.

1490 Master Leon, Jewish court physician, put to death for failing to cure the son of the Grand Duke

1399 First persecution of Jews in Poland. The rabbi and 13 elders were charged with theft and desecration of church property. They were tortured and then burned alive.

1494 Jews restricted to a suburb of Cracow, the first Polish ghetto

1333–70 Casimir the Great issued a series of charters protecting Jews. One decreed: "If the Jew enters the house of a Christian, no one has a right to cause him any injury or unpleasantness."

1203 Jews allowed to own land
1356 Jews granted autonomy in their communal affairs throughout Galicia

Refugees from the Khazar Jewish Kingdom in 1016 and from the Crimea in the 14th century

1407 Anti-Jewish riots

1113 Anti-Jewish violence

Baltic Sea

Novgorod

RUSSIA

Moscow

Troki · Vilna

Minsk

Grodno

Bialystok

Biela Viezha

Posen

Warsaw

Pinsk

Chernigov

Brest-Litovsk

POLAND

LITHUANIA

Kiev

Lvov

Kazimierz

GALICIA or "Red Russia"

Cracow

1483

1494

PRINTING AND LEARNING

These woodcuts come from three Jewish sacred texts and prayer books, printed between 1515 and 1695. Printing was quickly recognized by the Jews as the ideal tool to promote the spread of knowledge and learning. The first printed Jewish book was produced in 1475 in Italy; it was a commentary on the Talmud.

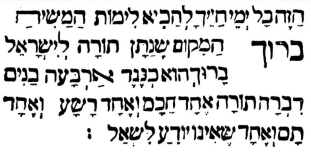

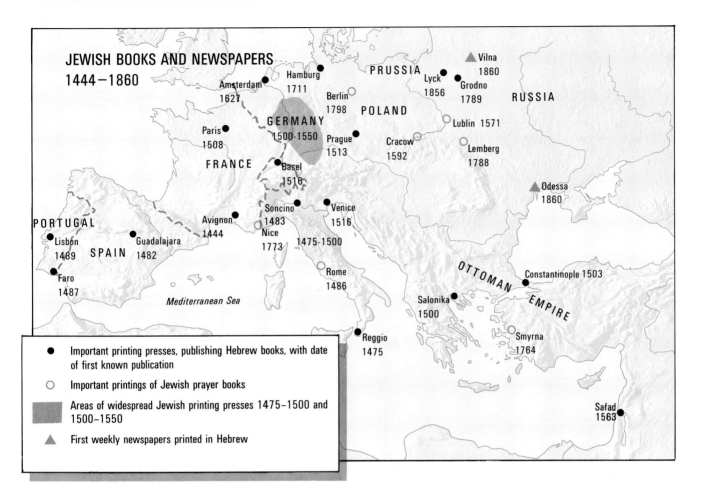

JEWISH BOOKS AND NEWSPAPERS
1444–1860

- ● Important printing presses, publishing Hebrew books, with date of first known publication
- ○ Important printings of Jewish prayer books
- � Areas of widespread Jewish printing presses 1475–1500 and 1500–1550
- ▲ First weekly newspapers printed in Hebrew

ABOVE: *Among Jews the printing trade tended to run in families, some of whom were extremely peripatetic. Gershom Soncino, for example, worked in some ten different towns in Italy between 1489 and 1527 before moving to Salonica and then Constantinople. He printed the first Jewish illustrated book in 1491 at Brescia.*

showing Marco Polo's travels; and Master Jacob – like Cresques *père et fils*, a Majorcan Jew – was the chief mapmaker to Portugal's Prince Henry the Navigator (1395–1460).

There is circumstantial evidence, but no absolute proof, that Christopher Columbus was himself a marrano. Little is known of his origins except that he was born in Genoa of Spanish parents and that "Colombo" and its variants "Palombo" and "Golomb" are Jewish names. In addition, Columbus placed a strange cipher at the top of all his letters, and enjoined his son always to do the same. This cipher bears a strong resemblance to the Hebrew initials for "In God's name," with which religious Jews would always preface a document. It is also known that Columbus mixed with Jews and marranos; that his expeditions were funded by marranos; and that he took several "New Christians" on his voyages, including the two physicians, Bernal and Marco. In the belief that he was going to India and that the Indians spoke Hebrew (then believed to be the oldest language), Columbus also took a Hebrew interpreter with him – Luis de Torres – who was hastily

baptized just before the *Niña*, the *Pinta*, and the *Santa Maria* set sail. Torres never returned but settled in Cuba, where he died in 1508, having become the first European tobacco grower.

Jews flocked to the New World to escape the horrors of the Old. They had settled on the west African island of São Tomé (then a Portuguese colony) as early as 1492, and later spread to the colonies and islands of the West Indies under Spanish rule, such as Trinidad and Jamaica. Having been the first to import sugar from Madeira (off the coast of Morocco), they made the West Indies into what eventually became the world's biggest sugar-producing region.

The Jews' hope that they had managed to escape the Inquisition by moving to the New World was shortlived. In 1515, the first marrano was arrested on the island of Hispaniola (now comprising Haiti and the Dominican Republic) and brought back to Spain to be put on trial for allegedly practicing Judaism in secret. There were successive inquisitions in Mexico, starting in 1571 and culminating in the *"auto general"* of

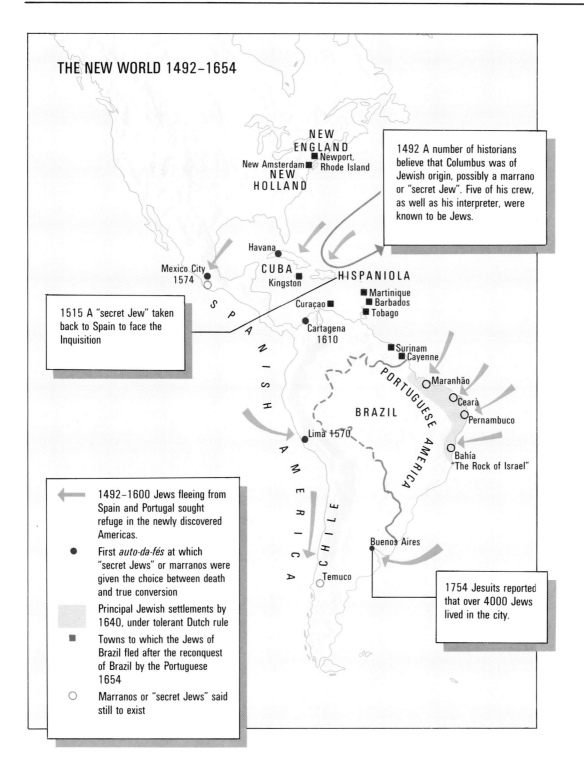

THE NEW WORLD 1492–1654

1492 A number of historians believe that Columbus was of Jewish origin, possibly a marrano or "secret Jew". Five of his crew, as well as his interpreter, were known to be Jews.

NEW ENGLAND
New Amsterdam ■ ■ Newport, Rhode Island
NEW HOLLAND

Havana
Mexico City 1574
CUBA
Kingston
HISPANIOLA
Curaçao ■ ■ Martinique ■ Barbados ■ Tobago
Cartagena 1610
Surinam ■ ■ Cayenne

1515 A "secret Jew" taken back to Spain to face the Inquisition

SPANISH AMERICA
CHILE

PORTUGUESE AMERICA
○ Maranhão
○ Ceará
○ Pernambuco
BRAZIL
Lima 1570
○ Bahía "The Rock of Israel"

Buenos Aires
○ Temuco

1754 Jesuits reported that over 4000 Jews lived in the city.

← **1492–1600** Jews fleeing from Spain and Portugal sought refuge in the newly discovered Americas.

● First *auto-da-fés* at which "secret Jews" or marranos were given the choice between death and true conversion

▨ Principal Jewish settlements by 1640, under tolerant Dutch rule

■ Towns to which the Jews of Brazil fled after the reconquest of Brazil by the Portuguese 1654

○ Marranos or "secret Jews" said still to exist

ABOVE: *Among the refuges for Jews fleeing from Spain and Portugal were the colonies in the newly-discovered New World. However, the Inquisition soon followed; by 1640, the only safe Jewish settlements were those under Dutch rule.*

1649 – the worst in the Americas – when hundreds of New Christians were burned to death.

Jews had at first voluntarily taken refuge in Brazil, discovered and claimed by the Portuguese in 1500. Then, from 1548, the Portuguese Inquisition actually condemned those found guilty to deportation to Brazil. However, in 1579, the Bishop of Salvador was ordered to install the Inquisition in Brazil and send the convicted back to Portugal for sentencing – a practice that lasted until 1624, the year that the Dutch West Indies Company began to make forays into the region.

Refuge in the Netherlands

The Jews of the Iberian peninsula had also found a haven in the Netherlands, part of which had recently rebelled against Spanish Catholic rule. In 1579, the Protestant northern Dutch provinces signed the Union of Utrecht, which established the Dutch Republic as well as complete freedom of worship. Although Spain did not formally recognize the Netherlands' independence until 1648, by the 1590s Jewish refugees were arriving from Portugal, which had been conquered by Spain in 1580, as well as from Spain itself.

Ironically, the newcomers at first aroused the suspicions of the Dutch, who thought they were Catholics and Spanish spies. However the Jewish community in the Netherlands soon flourished, producing famous physicians and financiers, some of whom – notably Manasseh ben Israel, rabbi of Amsterdam – were painted by Rembrandt.

Above all, this first taste of freedom and equality spawned two of the greatest of all Jewish philosophers, precursors of Jewish reform. Sadly, both were attacked by their co-religionists for their admittedly controversial views of Judaism. The first, Uriel d'Acosta, had been born a marrano and given the name of Gabriel, but he had reverted to Judaism. In his *Theses against the Tradition*, he attacked Jewish traditions and the rabbis, who became so enraged that they excommunicated him. D'Acosta's internal struggle between his Jewish identity and his Jewish faith became so unbearable that, after doing public penance for his condemnation

LEFT: *A detail from Rembrandt's* Jewish Bride. *The Netherlands was one of the first European nations officially to adopt policies of toleration toward the Jews and to offer them legal emancipation. As a result the Dutch Jewish community prospered greatly from the seventeenth century onward.*

ABOVE: *Baruch Spinoza's independent way of thought led to his excommunication by the Jews of Amsterdam in 1656. During much of his lifetime, his philosophy of pantheism was regarded as blasphemous by Jew and Christian alike.*

OPPOSITE PAGE: *The Jewish graveyard in Prague. The seventeenth and eighteenth centuries were a time of pogrom and persecution for the Jews of central Europe.*

of Judaism, he committed suicide.

Twenty years later, in 1656, the rabbis excommunicated another philosopher, Baruch Spinoza (1632–77), who would become even more famous. This brilliant thinker, who has been the inspiration of so many others, Jewish and non-Jewish, published only two works during his lifetime: *The Philosophical Principles of Descartes*, in which he explained the rationalist thinking of the French philosopher René Descartes (1596–1650), and *Treatise on Religious and Political Philosophy*, which contained the first modern historical interpretation of the Bible. The latter was published anonymously because of Spinoza's fear of his co-religionists. His greatest work – *Ethics*, in which he held that free will is an illusion – was found in its manuscript form after his death and published posthumously.

Thanks largely to the Jewish cartographers and astronomers who had fled from Portu-

gal, and the Jewish financiers who paid for the expeditions, Holland now became the greatest naval power in Europe. When the Dutch attacked Brazil in 1630, they were supported as potential liberators by both the marranos and the Jews who openly practiced their faith in the South American colony. Gradually, with Jewish assistance, the Dutch conquered a rich area along the northern coast, where the Jews were able at last – and for the first time in the Americas – to practice their faith without fear.

However, there was a mighty reversal in their fortunes when, in 1654, the Portuguese regained control of Brazil. In the peace negotiations, the Dutch insisted on an amnesty for the Jews, but as soon as the peace was signed in 1661, the Portuguese went back on their word and expelled the Jews. These deportees went to other parts of the Americas – to the English, Dutch, and French possessions where they could practice their religion and, in many cases, expand their sugar cultivation.

One group sailed north to New Amsterdam. There they were treated to a distinctly unfriendly reception by the Dutch governor, Peter Stuyvesant, who in a letter appealed to his masters in Holland, stating that he feared that the Jews might "infect the New Netherlands." However, the reply came back that those who had helped Holland conquer its former territory in Brazil should be accorded sanctuary. With this permission from the Dutch government, the Brazilian Jews stayed, they and their successors forming what would become the influential Jewish community of New York.

The Opening of England

The countries of northern Europe that had defied the Pope and were now ruled by Protestant monarchs gradually began to change their attitudes toward the Jews. As we have seen, the Dutch allowed them to practice their religion without hindrance from 1579, and this was followed by a change in government policy in England.

Here, a community of marranos, led by the Portuguese ambassador, was already flourishing, and many of its members were practicing their true religion in secret. In 1655, Manasseh ben Israel, the rabbi of the Amsterdam community who had been

RIGHT: *Protected by royal favor, Jews could rise in eighteenth-century Germany; Joseph Süss Oppenheimer, for example, was court treasurer to the Duke of Württemberg. However, they could also fall; after the death of his royal master, Oppenheimer was tried, imprisoned, and hanged. Two films based on his life were made in the early 1930s; the Hollywood version is a plea for greater toleration; the Nazi version casts Oppenheimer as the villain.*

immortalized by Rembrandt, traveled to England to present a petition to Oliver Cromwell, who was now Lord Protector following the execution of Charles I. Despite the objections of some of his advisers, Cromwell was well disposed toward the Jews, and gave his permission – albeit verbally – for more marranos to enter England.

These marranos arrived in a country deeply hostile to Catholicism and so were soon able to throw off their pretense of being Catholics. And although their lives would sometimes be made difficult by government policy and society's attitudes, Jews would never again be expelled from England.

The Court Jews

In Germany and Austria, it was not long before the emperors and princelings who had expelled the Jews in the early seventeenth century found that they wanted them back to bring in much-needed funds. They devised a new means of encouraging the backing of Jewish financiers by appointing them to the influential positions of "court factors."

This was the age of the "court jew," of which the best-known were Samson Wertheimer and Joseph Süss Oppenheimer. Wertheimer was chief court factor, banker, and financial agent for three Holy Roman emperors: Leopold I (from whom he received the title of "imperial factor" in 1674), Joseph I, and Charles VI. Financier to the Duke of

Württemberg, Oppenheimer provided the money for the Austrian defense against the Turks, whose armies stood at the very gates of Vienna in 1683. They were finally repulsed by a joint Austrian-Polish army, led by Prince Eugène of Savoy and King Jan Sobieski. (It is ironic that it was Prince Eugène who, mindful of the Jew's invaluable help, publicly embraced Oppenheimer at a reception "before the assembled generals and astonished courtiers," for it was this prince who was later to be held up as an example by the Austrian Nazis, and a crack Waffen SS brigade was named after him.)

The court factors were even more unpopular with the Christians of Germany and Austria than they were with their poorer – and envious – co-religionists. On one occasion Wertheimer's house was ransacked by rioters, and when he died, his royal creditors used his death as an excuse to default on their debts, bringing about numerous Jewish bankruptcies. An even worse fate awaited Oppenheimer. Despite the fact that Württemberg's economy had become profitable after his reorganization of it, his advanced ideas had made him thoroughly disliked by all classes of the population. After the death of his patron, the duke, he was imprisoned and sentenced to be hanged; on the gallows, he refused to convert to Christianity. His execution served as a pretext for the expulsion of the Jews from Stuttgart.

The privileges extended to these men and the wealth that they were able to amass became the foundations for the great German banking houses of Warburg, Ansbacher, Schiff, and Rothschild – and brought prosperity to their fellow Jews.

False Messiahs

It is hardly surprising that these troubled times were also the era of the most successful of the Jewish false messiahs: Sabbatai Zevi. There had been many before him. Just ten years after the death of Jesus, a man called Theudas had been proclaimed the Messiah; he was beheaded and all his followers executed. Simeon bar Kochba, who led the final revolt against the Romans in 132–5, had also been given the status of Messiah by his protector, the eminent Rabbi Akiva.

At Istria in northern Italy in 1502, Asher Lämmkin proclaimed himself the forerunner of a messiah and called on the Jews to do penance. Perhaps the messiah he was heralding was David Reubeni, who appeared in Venice in 1524. He claimed to be the brother of the king of the tribe of Reuben – one of the lost Tribes of Israel – who was at that moment waiting behind Turkish lines, ready to pounce on the infidel army which was then threatening Christian Europe. Reubeni was so convincing that even Pope Clement VII agreed to grant him an audience, and King João III of Portugal was persuaded to give him ships and weapons to fight the Turks and conquer the Holy Land. Reubeni had a

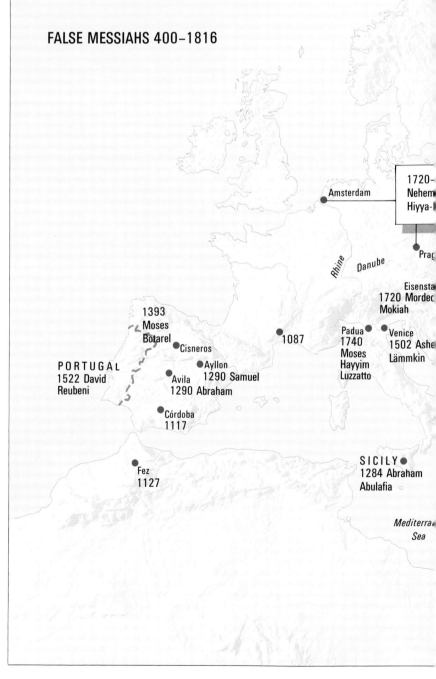

FALSE MESSIAHS 400–1816

Amsterdam

1720–
Nehem
Hiyya-

Rhine Danube

Prag

Eisensta
1720 Mordec
Mokiah

1393
Moses
Botarel

Cisneros

1087

Padua
1740
Moses
Hayyim
Luzzatto

Venice
1502 Ashe
Lämmkin

PORTUGAL
1522 David
Reubeni

Avila
1290 Abraham

Ayllon
1290 Samuel

Córdoba
1117

SICILY
1284 Abraham
Abulafia

Fez
1127

Mediterra
Sea

fervent spokesman in the former marrano Shlomo Molcho. However, Molcho was unsuccessful in his efforts to convince Yossl Rosheim, the leader of the German Jewish community in Vienna, who warned him not to attempt to speak to Emperor Charles V about Reubeni's latter-day crusade. Rosheim was right: in 1530, Molcho was taken by the emperor's men to Mantua and burned at the stake. David Reubeni ended his days in prison.

Sabbatai Zevi (1626–76), a Turkish Jew from Smyrna, made the greatest impact of any of the false messiahs. In 1665, two years after moving to Jerusalem and proclaiming his mission, he won over a young scholar of the Kabbalah, Nathan of Gaza. Nathan sent letters all over the Diaspora, announcing that a savior was nigh who would rescue the Jews from the hideous persecutions then taking place, particularly in Poland, where the era of toleration had ended with the death of Sigismund II.

Jews throughout the world began to make ready for Judgment Day. A Jewish woman, Glückl of Hamlin, witnessed the excitement that gripped her people. She recounts in her diary how many sold all their possessions in readiness for the event, and how her own father-in-law converted much of his wealth into goods and foodstuffs to take with him on the long journey to the Holy Land when the eventual call came.

However Sabbatai Zevi did not make a favourable impression on the rabbis of the Holy Land; in fact, they threatened to excommunicate him. He decided, in the light of this, to return to his adoring public in Constantinople, but made the mistake of also threatening to march on the sultan, Mehmet IV, and depose him. In 1666, as Zevi's ship sailed for the Bosporus, it was intercepted by the Turkish authorities, and he was taken in chains to Adrianople. There, the sultan gave him the choice of accepting Islam or being put to death. Zevi immediately chose Islam and accepted a royal pension. He declared that the Torah and all halacha was henceforth inverted; apostasy, not fidelity to God's word, was now the pathway to a redeemed world. He was eventually banished to a remote town in Albania, where he died. Some of his followers chose to convert with him, and to this day, a group of their descendants – known as the *Dönme*, the Turkish word for "converts" – live in the holy city of Mashhad in northeast Iran.

Another false messiah of a very different sort was Yankiev Frank (1726–91) from Podolia, the Polish province that suffered the worst excesses of Chmielnicki's Cossacks (*see* Chapter 5). When Frank's "prophet," Leib Krysa, proclaimed him the Messiah, Frank immediately announced that the Talmud had been abolished and that the Zohar, the book of the Kabbalah, was the new Bible. However, his main theme attracted the most followers: through vice, he said, one could

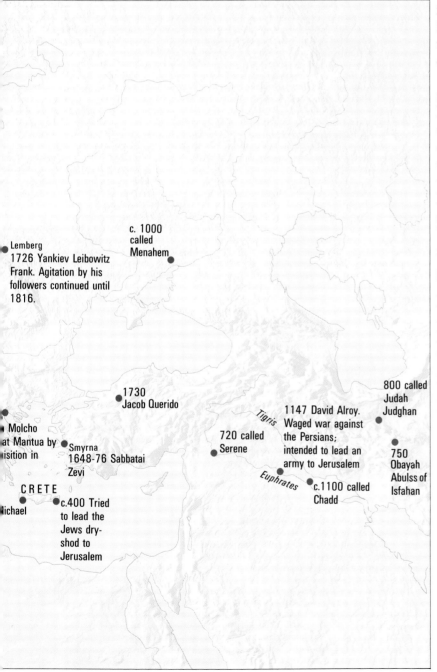

LEFT: *The nine-branched Menorah. On each of the eight days of the festival of the* Chanukah, *a separate candle is lit; the festival itself commemorates the liberation of the Temple in Jerusalem by the Maccabees.*

usage, it is loosely applied to all ultra-orthodox Jews, but in fact, there are ultra-orthodox Jews who are completely opposed to Hassidism.

The founder of Hassidism was an obscure figure named Israel ben Eliezer (*c.*1700–60) and known as the Baal Shem Tov ("Master of the Good Name") or "the Besht" for short. He left no written records, and what little is known about him may be fact, speculation, or legend. The Besht was allegedly born in Podolia (also the birthplace of his diametrical opposite, Yankiev Frank).

attain virtue, and it was only through performing all kinds of sexual acts that one attained purity. To give substance to this theory, he and his disciples held orgies, for which the horrified rabbis promptly excommunicated him.

Compared to those of the other false messiahs, Frank's fate was quite pleasant. He suddenly claimed that it had been revealed to him that he must convert to Christianity, and his followers – the Frankists – did the same. They did not, however, give up any of their other, more hedonistic beliefs, and when the Church in Poland discovered this, they imprisoned the "Messiah." He was freed by the Russians when they invaded Poland, and he lived out his days in luxury supported by his followers, although his daughter Eve, who carried on his mission after his death, died in poverty. Eventually all the Frankists assimilated into the Polish nobility.

Hassidism

Turning to false messiahs was one response to the unbearable persecutions suffered by the Jews in the seventeenth century. Another was the Hassidic movement. The word *Hassid* means "pious" or "observant." In modern

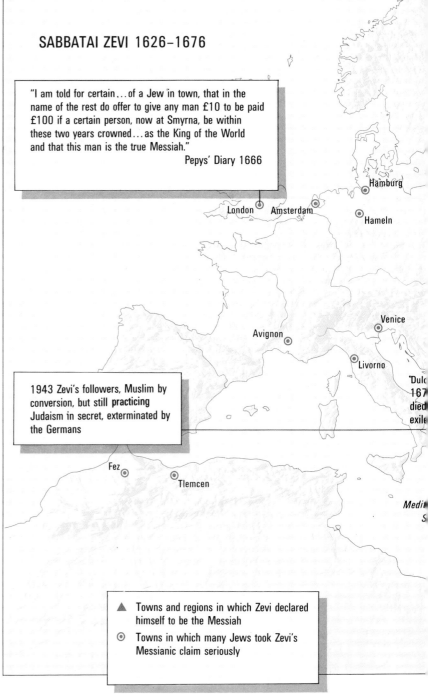

SABBATAI ZEVI 1626–1676

"I am told for certain...of a Jew in town, that in the name of the rest do offer to give any man £10 to be paid £100 if a certain person, now at Smyrna, be within these two years crowned...as the King of the World and that this man is the true Messiah."

Pepys' Diary 1666

1943 Zevi's followers, Muslim by conversion, but still practicing Judaism in secret, exterminated by the Germans

Hamburg

London   Amsterdam

Hameln

Venice

Avignon

Livorno

'Dulc
167
died
exile

Fez

Tlemcen

Medi
S

▲ Towns and regions in which Zevi declared himself to be the Messiah

◉ Towns in which many Jews took Zevi's Messianic claim seriously

Left an orphan after the horrific massacres of the Jews, the Besht held various jobs, including synagogue watchman and innkeeper. He had a great love of nature and would often steal away into the vast pine forests of the region to meditate and pray.

In his fortieth year, the Besht proclaimed himself a teacher, and what he taught had great appeal: even the simple and uneducated can "cleave to God," as he put it, through their actions and prayers; and God is to be found everywhere in nature, and should be worshiped with joy and dancing.

Scholars often contend that, although the mystical ideas of Hassidism include elements of the Kabbalah and traditional Jewish mysticism, they are closer to pantheism (i.e. God as the creator of nature) and similar pagan doctrines. Whatever their origins, his ideas, which had many erudite followers among his contemporaries, brought joy and hope to the Jews of eastern Europe, and comforted them in their sufferings for centuries to come.

The doctrine of Hassidism was spread by Rabbi Dov Baer (1710–72), known as the "Maggid of Mezericz," a great preacher (*maggid*) who spread the word throughout Poland, Byelorussia, and Lithuania. Despite the absence of writings by the Besht, there developed a wealth of Hassidic literature, much of it telling of the wonders worked by rabbis in various towns.

However, once the Besht was dead, Hassidism fragmented into several sects headed by *rebbes*, or "righteous ones." Among the most renowned of the Hassidic writers was Schneor Zalman of Lyady (1745–1813), who founded a successful branch known as the Chabad Movement. *Chabad* is a combination of three letters which stand for the Hebrew words for "wisdom," "understanding," and "knowledge." The greatest thinker of the movement was Rabbi Nachman of Bratslav (1772–1811), whose sayings were collected by his disciple Nathan Sternharz (1780–1845).

The early Hassidim had some very serious opposition from the great rabbis of their day, notably Elijah ben Solomon (1720–97) of Vilna in Lithuania, known as the Vilna Gaon. He collected a band of Talmudists around him who condemned the Hassidic movement, claiming that the only way to God was through deep study, reason, and thought. They were known as the *mitnagdim*, or opponents. The Vilna Gaon even went so far as to excommunicate the Hassidim.

Hassidism never died out, although it did go into a serious decline at the end of the nineteenth century. Significantly, its revival came after the Jews' darkest hour, following the Holocaust, and it still flourishes in various ultra-orthodox Jewish communities, chiefly in the United States, Britain, and Israel. The best-known part of the Chabad Movement is the particularly active Lubavitch Movement, under its hereditary leader, the Lubavitcher Rebbe, who lives in New

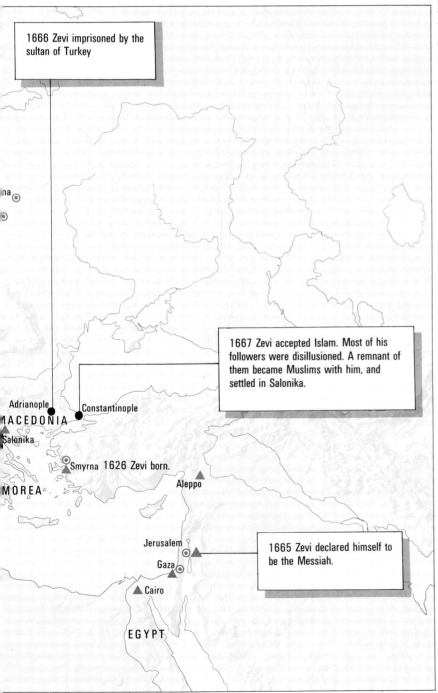

1666 Zevi imprisoned by the sultan of Turkey

1667 Zevi accepted Islam. Most of his followers were disillusioned. A remnant of them became Muslims with him, and settled in Salonika.

Adrianople
Constantinople
MACEDONIA
Salonika
Smyrna 1626 Zevi born.
MOREA
Aleppo

Jerusalem
Gaza
Cairo

1665 Zevi declared himself to be the Messiah.

EGYPT

LEFT: *This tapestry curtain, used to conceal the ark holding the sacred scrolls of the Torah, was woven in 1750. The central panel lists the ten commandments.*

York. The Lubavitch proselytize energetically among Jews, attempting to convert the non-orthodox to a more religious way of life.

Liberalization in the West

While the Jews of eastern Europe sought comfort and salvation within their own religion, the Jews of the West were looking outward. In Holland, Britain, and Scandina-

via, they dressed and behaved much as their compatriots, as many contemporary illustrations show.

In 1701 in London, the first synagogue in the British Isles opened (and still stands) in Bevis Marks, a small lane east of the present sites of the Bank of England and the Stock Exchange. The location was discreet, but the building and its accoutrements were opulent,

Le REPAS de PAQUES. chez les JUIFS PORTUGAIS.

attesting to the prosperity of the worshipers, many of whom were wealthy financiers and merchants, members of the Royal Exchange and the East India Company.

However, life did not always go smoothly for the Jews of Spanish and Portuguese origin – the former marranos – who at this time were the only representatives of their faith in Britain. The Jewish Naturalization Act of 1753, which gave these "foreign" Jews the right to become British subjects without having to swear a Christian oath of allegiance, was repealed due to the outcry from Christian merchants. However, it was not long before the Iberian Jews were joined by Jews from Germany, who were to make such an impact on finance in the next century. The two communities remained separate, although there was some intermarrying, notably by the Iberian Jew Sir Moses Montefiore, who married into the German-Jewish Rothschild family.

Jews had begun trickling back into France

as soon as the series of expulsions in the fourteenth century were over. However, their numbers were not significant until the mid-1500s, when they were joined by the New Christians, or "Portuguese," to whom the French king Henri II granted the right to live anywhere they pleased. Most of the newcomers, who did not necessarily revert to Judaism, settled in southwest France, some venturing as far north as La Rochelle on the Atlantic coast. One of them, a Señor Mendes, married Isabella da Francia, a member of the Bourbon family with a claim to the French throne. One of the couple's descendants was Pierre Mendès-France, who became prime minister of France in the mid-1950s.

In 1648, the Jews of Alsace and Lorraine – independent dukedoms that were not then part of France – were joined by co-religionists from Russia and Poland fleeing the Cossack hordes of Bogdan Chmielnicki (*see* Chapter 5), and three years later, Jews

ABOVE: *The Passover feast is celebrated in the home of an eighteenth-century Portuguese Jew. Persecution, and ultimately expulsion, meant that many Jews of Portuguese origin faced exile, notably to France and Britain.*

from Holland came to settle in the French town of Charleville, near the Belgian border. However, none moved into Paris for another century.

By the mid-eighteenth century, 84 per cent of French Jewry were Ashkenazi and, except for the ancient community at Nancy, were Yiddish speaking. The remaining 16 per cent were Sephardi and lived south of the Loire, with a few remnants of the medieval community who had their own dialect – Judéo-Provençal.

The American Revolution

The Jews benefited from the revolutions of the late eighteenth century. The hostility of Peter Stuyvesant to Jews in North America was the exception. Many people had fled from Europe to the New World to escape religious persecution, and several of the colonies – notably Pennsylvania and Rhode Island – proclaimed tolerance as their watch-word. Consequently, Jewish communities flourished soon after the beginning of European settlement in the Americas.

When Cromwell allowed Jews to enter England, they also became free to settle in any English colony, and they arrived at one of the earliest settlements – Newport, Rhode Island – in 1677. By 1763, they had built there the first synagogue in the New World, naming it after Judah Touro, who had left a bequest for its upkeep. Designed by a Quaker architect, it has a classical style, very similar to that of the Bevis Marks synagogue in London. It was here that the Rhode Island General Assembly met after the 14-month British occupation of the state had ended in 1779, and 11 years later, George Washington visited the synagogue in his official capacity as first President of the United States. There was a moving exchange of greetings between the president and Moses Seixas, leader of the Jewish community, during which Washington stated: "May the children of the Stock of Abraham who dwell in this land continue to merit and enjoy the good will of the other inhabitants, while every one shall sit in safety under his own vine and fig-tree, and there shall be none to make him afraid."

Jews began to settle throughout eastern North America. Savannah, Georgia, became home to a party of Jews who arrived in 1733, the year that the city was founded as a refuge for debtors and European Protestants by James Oglethorpe; shortly after, a Dr. Samuel Nuñes helped to quell an outbreak of yellow fever. Once the British had conquered the Dutch territories farther north, more Jews joined the small group that had managed to put down roots despite the anti-Semitism of the previous Dutch governor. They also moved into Canada, establishing the first Jewish settlement in Montreal in 1759.

Francis Salvador (1747–76) was the first Jew to die for the cause of American independence in the struggle against British rule. He served in the Revolutionary Congress of South Carolina, and when that colony proclaimed its independence in 1776, he was the first Jew to hold state office. He died at the hands of Indians while serving with the Revolutionary forces, and is commemorated on a plaque in Charleston's City Hall.

BELOW: *A member of the Assembly of Notables, founded by Napoleon in 1808 to provide French Jewry with a voice in national affairs. Though Napoleon's liberalizing process was by no means as thorough as some have claimed, he did much to better the lot of the Jews in Europe, sweeping away the ghettoes and giving them equal rights.*

RIGHT: *Napoleon's reshaping of the map of Europe in the name of liberty, equality, and fraternity was mirrored in his liberal attitude toward the Jews in the territories he conquered. In the wake of his armies, the ghettoes were swept away, only to be restored after his final defeat at Waterloo in 1815. Despite this, the freedom he gave the Jews spurred them on in their ambition to win political and social emancipation.*

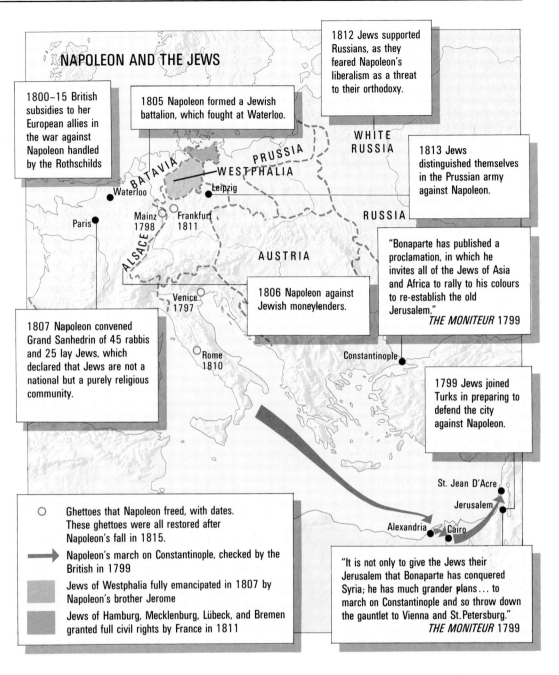

NAPOLEON AND THE JEWS

1800–15 British subsidies to her European allies in the war against Napoleon handled by the Rothschilds

1805 Napoleon formed a Jewish battalion, which fought at Waterloo.

1812 Jews supported Russians, as they feared Napoleon's liberalism as a threat to their orthodoxy.

1813 Jews distinguished themselves in the Prussian army against Napoleon.

"Bonaparte has published a proclamation, in which he invites all of the Jews of Asia and Africa to rally to his colours to re-establish the old Jerusalem."
THE MONITEUR 1799

1806 Napoleon against Jewish moneylenders.

1807 Napoleon convened Grand Sanhedrin of 45 rabbis and 25 lay Jews, which declared that Jews are not a national but a purely religious community.

1799 Jews joined Turks in preparing to defend the city against Napoleon.

"It is not only to give the Jews their Jerusalem that Bonaparte has conquered Syria; he has much grander plans... to march on Constantinople and so throw down the gauntlet to Vienna and St. Petersburg."
THE MONITEUR 1799

○ Ghettoes that Napoleon freed, with dates. These ghettoes were all restored after Napoleon's fall in 1815.

➤ Napoleon's march on Constantinople, checked by the British in 1799

▮ Jews of Westphalia fully emancipated in 1807 by Napoleon's brother Jerome

▮ Jews of Hamburg, Mecklenburg, Lübeck, and Bremen granted full civil rights by France in 1811

Map labels: BATAVIA, PRUSSIA, WHITE RUSSIA, WESTPHALIA, ALSACE, AUSTRIA, RUSSIA, Waterloo, Leipzig, Paris, Mainz 1798, Frankfurt 1811, Venice 1797, Rome 1810, Constantinople, St. Jean D'Acre, Jerusalem, Alexandria, Cairo

The French Revolution

The French Revolution marked a watershed for the Jews of Europe and eventually led to their emancipation throughout the Continent. Even before the events of 1789, there had been increasing tolerance toward Jews. For example, in 1784, after the Jews of Alsace (which had become part of France in the previous century) had addressed a petition to him, Louis XVI abolished the poll tax that had been imposed on them. However, any Jew entering Paris still had to report to the *Inspecteur des Escrocs et des Juifs* – the Inspector of Swindlers and Jews.

Among the leading advocates of Jewish emancipation were the Comte de Mirabeau (1749–91) and the Abbé Gregoire (1750–1831). In 1785, the Royal Academy for the Arts and Sciences invited essays answering the question "Is there a way to make the Jews of France happier and more useful?" In his, the Abbé Gregoire called for the nation to cease persecuting the Jews and to give them equal rights – sentiments that were echoed by the second-prize winner, a lawyer from Nancy named Adolphe Thierry. Much space was given in the French press to the essays and the issues they raised.

As for Mirabeau, after meeting Moses Mendelssohn of Dessau *(see below)* and being very impressed by him, he published, in 1787, the treatise *On Mendelssohn and*

MOSES MENDELSSOHN.

Dem Könige Friedrich Wilhelm II.
unterthänigst gewidmet
von der Jüdischen Freyschule zu Berlin 1787.

the Political Reform of the Jews. When representatives of the Jewish community appeared before the Constituent Assembly in 1791 to state their case for equal rights, Mirabeau supported them. On 27 September of that year, five months after Mirabeau's untimely death, three-quarters of the districts of Paris voted in favor of making the Jews equal citizens of France for the first time since the days of Roman rule.

Three years after crowning himself emperor, Napoleon decided to make a *grand geste* toward the Jews. To this end, he invented the "Grand Sanhedrin" (Jewish parliament), consisting of 45 rabbis and 26 laymen, which met in 1807 and deliberated for the required two days. In 1808, this was replaced by an Assembly of Notables. Although these assemblies were ineffective, they did lead to the founding of a national representative body of French Jewry, which, in the years that followed, ensured that their voice was heard.

Napoleon's attitude toward the Jews was mixed, for besides giving them a semi-official status, he was also intent on submitting them to intensive regulation and legislation. In 1808, the same year in which he abolished the Inquisition in Spain and Italy, he published a decree concerning the Jews. Although this contained some liberalizing clauses, it also included enough petty restrictions and coercion for the Jews to nickname it *"le decret infâme"* ("the infamous decree"). Yet, at the same time, Napoleon was tearing down the ghetto walls wherever he encountered them – at first in Italy, later in central Europe – and his proconsuls proclaimed Jewish equality throughout the French empire.

The reactionary forces that defeated Napoleon forced the Jews back into their ghettos, but not before both they and the common people in the countries that had been conquered by the French emperor had had a tantalizing glimpse of freedom.

The Beginning of the Jewish Enlightenment

In the mid-1700s changes were taking place even in Germany, and they can best be seen in the life of one remarkable man: a hunchback from the Dessau ghetto by the name of Moses Mendelssohn.

Mendelssohn (1729–86) was an avid scholar, and was particularly inspired by the combination of secular learning and Jewish erudition displayed in Maimonides' *Guide to the Perplexed*. At the age of 14, convinced that the ghetto teachers had taught him all they knew, the Yiddish-speaking young Moses walked to Berlin to study at the feet of the masters, learned Jews who taught him German language and literature and the sciences. He became – with the publication of *Dialogues* – the first Jew to write a book in German, a great achievement for one who

had not been able even to speak the language until a few years previously.

With this and other books, Mendelssohn began to win recognition in the literary world. In 1777, he met Immanuel Kant (1724–1804), the leading German philosopher of the day, who, extremely impressed by the little hunchbacked Jew, became his lifelong friend. Among the other Christian savants with whom he met and talked was the dramatist and philosopher Gotthold Ephraim Lessing (1729–81), who used Mendelssohn as the model for the protagonists of two of his plays – *Nathan the Wise* and *The Jew*. The latter play, the first to portray a Jew in a completely favorable light, caused a storm of controversy and awakened Mendelssohn to the depth and extent of German anti-Semitism.

Mendelssohn made it his mission to lead Judaism out of the ghetto and into the new Enlightenment, in which the practice of Judaism would not conflict with life in a non-Jewish world. He set about translating the Torah into German, thus opening up all of German literature to the Jews. However, when it appeared set in Hebrew characters – the holy language – the Jewish community, and especially its ultra-orthodox section, was shocked. His commentary on the Torah, containing as it did radical, modern ideas, was in their eyes just as bad.

Mendelssohn's descendants embraced Christianity, and his grandson, the composer Felix Mendelssohn-Bartholdy, was born a Christian, but Moses Mendelssohn's own contribution to the spread and continuation of Judaism was invaluable. He was the first figure of the Jewish Enlightenment, which would produce artists, writers, musicians, and scientists, the numbers of which were out of all proportion to the tiny percentage of Jews within the general population, and who would make perhaps the greatest contribution to world culture by any one people.

CHAPTER FOUR

THE JEWISH ENLIGHTENMENT TO THE EVE OF THE HOLOCAUST

I n countries such as Britain and Holland, the liberation of the Jews was lasting and complete. Elsewhere, it was shortlived, the forces of reaction rising against it, and in Russia the Jews did not acquire ostensibly full political rights until the 1917 revolution. However, as the Jewish people began to taste freedom – first, in Europe, and then farther afield in the Americas and Palestine – the influence of their thinking and their flourishing culture made an enormous impact on the Gentile world.

Emancipation

In Britain, the remaining restrictions on Jewish settlement in London were removed by act of Parliament in 1831, although bills of 1830 and 1833, which would have given Jews full voting rights, failed to pass successfully through both Houses of Parliament. However, in 1833, the first Jew was admitted to the bar; and two years later, Francis Goldsmid became the first to become a judge, and a Jew was elected a sheriff of the City of London for the first time.

Benjamin Disraeli, the baptized son of Isaac d'Israeli, entered Parliament in 1837, the same year as the accession to the throne of Queen Victoria, whose favorite prime minister he was to become. Although professing Jews were elected to Parliament from 1847, they could not serve because, to do so, they would have been forced to swear to take their seats "in the true faith of a Christian." It

was not until 1858 that an Act of Parliament removed the last vestiges of anti-Jewish legislation, and the first Jewish MP, Lionel de Rothschild, was able to take his seat without swearing the oath. The first Jewish mem-

ABOVE: *Benjamin Disraeli, a Jew by ancestry, overcame political and social prejudice to become prime minister.*

ber of a British government was Sir George Jessel, who became solicitor-general under Gladstone in 1871.

In the United States, Jews from Spain and Portugal were followed, in the eighteenth and nineteenth centuries, by those from Germany, who were in turn joined by large waves from eastern Europe in the late nineteenth and early twentieth centuries. An early settler was Hayim Solomon, who became one of George Washington's financiers. The U.S. Declaration of Independence of July 4, 1776 gave Jewish males equal status with their Christian counterparts (the words "all men are created equal...with certain inalienable rights" were deemed to apply only to all white males), and because of this and the Bill of Rights enshrined in the Constitution, Jews in America felt no need for self-government or their own law courts.

By 1870, the Jewish population of the United States had reached 250,000. Although many remained in New York and elsewhere on the east coast, large numbers

BELOW: Jews first entered the French cabinet in 1848 in the aftermath of the revolution that overthrew the Orleans monarchy; the same thing happened in Germany in 1918, following the enforced abdication of Kaiser Wilhelm II and the fall of the Hohenzollern dynasty.

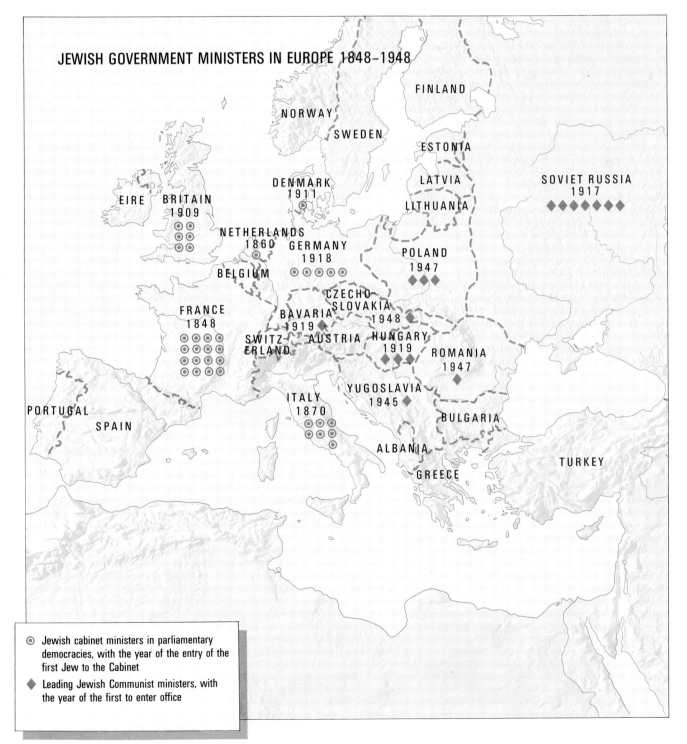

JEWISH GOVERNMENT MINISTERS IN EUROPE 1848–1948

⊙ Jewish cabinet ministers in parliamentary democracies, with the year of the entry of the first Jew to the Cabinet

◆ Leading Jewish Communist ministers, with the year of the first to enter office

had gone to seek their fortunes with other immigrants in the west, often serving the new communities as itinerant peddlers. Some had joined the California Gold Rush (1848–9): Adolph Sutro made his fortune from the Comstock Lode, later becoming a San Francisco philanthropist; and Levi Strauss made his by selling work clothes to the miners, inventing denim jeans that had pockets secured by rivets, which would not rip if stuffed with gold-bearing ore. During the Civil War, Jews were involved on both sides, and one – Judah Benjamin – served as Secretary of State in the Confederate govern-

ment, the first senior Jewish statesman in U.S. history.

Nineteenth-century American industrialization was in the hands of the Protestant élite. (An exception was Isaac Merritt Singer, whose father had been reared a Protestant. He became a millionaire 13 times over through the perfection and marketing of the sewing machine that bore his name.) The Jews pioneered retailing and banking. Sears Roebuck, Bloomingdales, and Neiman Marcus were all Jewish enterprises, and the families who made their fortunes in this way–the Belmonts, Guggenheims, Warburgs,

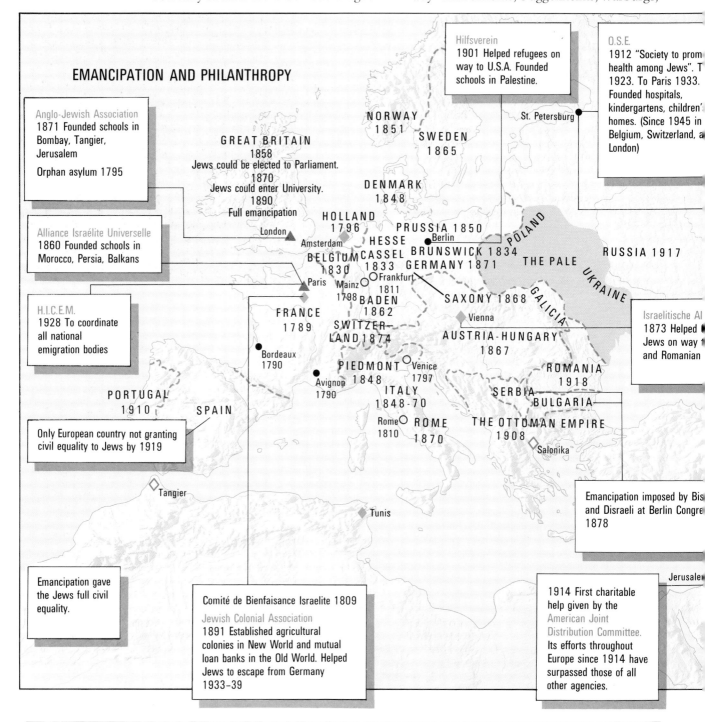

EMANCIPATION AND PHILANTHROPY

Anglo-Jewish Association
1871 Founded schools in Bombay, Tangier, Jerusalem

Orphan asylum 1795

Alliance Israélite Universelle
1860 Founded schools in Morocco, Persia, Balkans

H.I.C.E.M.
1928 To coordinate all national emigration bodies

Emancipation gave the Jews full civil equality.

Comité de Bienfaisance Israelite 1809
Jewish Colonial Association
1891 Established agricultural colonies in New World and mutual loan banks in the Old World. Helped Jews to escape from Germany 1933–39

Hilfsverein
1901 Helped refugees on way to U.S.A. Founded schools in Palestine.

O.S.E.
1912 "Society to prom health among Jews". T 1923. To Paris 1933. Founded hospitals, kindergartens, children' homes. (Since 1945 in Belgium, Switzerland, a London)

GREAT BRITAIN
1858
Jews could be elected to Parliament.
1870
Jews could enter University.
1890
Full emancipation

NORWAY 1851

SWEDEN 1865

St. Petersburg

DENMARK 1848

HOLLAND 1796

PRUSSIA 1850

London

Amsterdam

HESSE

CASSEL BRUNSWICK 1834

BELGIUM 1830 1833 GERMANY 1871

POLAND

RUSSIA 1917

Berlin

Frankfurt

THE PALE

Mainz 1811

UKRAINE

Paris

1798 BADEN 1862

SAXONY 1868

FRANCE 1789

SWITZER-LAND 1874

Vienna

GALICIA

Bordeaux 1790

AUSTRIA-HUNGARY 1867

Israelitische A
1873 Helped
Jews on way
and Romanian

PIEDMONT 1848 Venice 1797

ROMANIA 1918

Avignon 1790

ITALY 1848-70

SERBIA

PORTUGAL 1910

SPAIN

Rome 1810 ROME 1870

BULGARIA

THE OTTOMAN EMPIRE 1908

Salonika

Only European country not granting civil equality to Jews by 1919

Tangier

Tunis

Emancipation imposed by Bis and Disraeli at Berlin Congre 1878

Jerusale

1914 First charitable help given by the American Joint Distribution Committee. Its efforts throughout Europe since 1914 have surpassed those of all other agencies.

Schiffs, and Strausses – all made significant contributions to the cultural life of their home cities and states.

The Advent of the Enlightenment

The Jewish Enlightenment began in central and eastern Europe and flourished in spite of, rather than because of, the prevailing cultural climate, which was decidedly anti-Semitic. Strangely, the inspiration for this cultural flowering came not from those countries that already had an admirable record of tolerance for their resident Jewish populations – Denmark, the Netherlands,

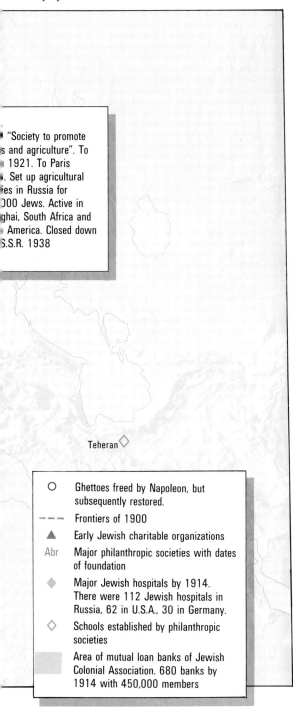

"Society to promote
s and agriculture". To
1921. To Paris
. Set up agricultural
es in Russia for
]00 Jews. Active in
ghai, South Africa and
America. Closed down
S.S.R. 1938

Teheran ◇

○	Ghettoes freed by Napoleon, but subsequently restored.
– – –	Frontiers of 1900
▲	Early Jewish charitable organizations
Abr	Major philanthropic societies with dates of foundation
◆	Major Jewish hospitals by 1914. There were 112 Jewish hospitals in Russia, 62 in U.S.A., 30 in Germany.
◇	Schools established by philanthropic societies
	Area of mutual loan banks of Jewish Colonial Association. 680 banks by 1914 with 450,000 members

ABOVE: *Jewish immigrants from eastern Europe arriving in New York in the late nineteenth century.*

LEFT: *During the nineteenth century, almost every major European country granted the Jews civil equality, the exceptions being Russia, where it took the 1917 revolution to bring about changes, and Spain, where it was not granted until the 1920s. At the same time, the Jews themselves actively promoted improvements within their communities with the widespread foundation of schools and hospitals.*

Britain, and the United States – but from the German-speaking nations, Poland, and Russia, where Jewish persecution was worse than in any other part of Europe. Anti-Semitic writers and pamphleteers were to prosper alongside Moses Mendelssohn and his contemporaries and successors.

While it cannot be denied that there was a movement among Christians to liberate the Jews, inspired largely by the principles of the French Revolution, it is one thing to abolish the ghetto and quite another to ensure that help is given to those who want to leave it. Jews had to force their way into institutions of higher education, many of which were still most reluctant to receive them, and improve themselves primarily through their own efforts.

In eastern Europe, the Enlightenment progressed more slowly than elsewhere. The feudal structure of Polish society had been

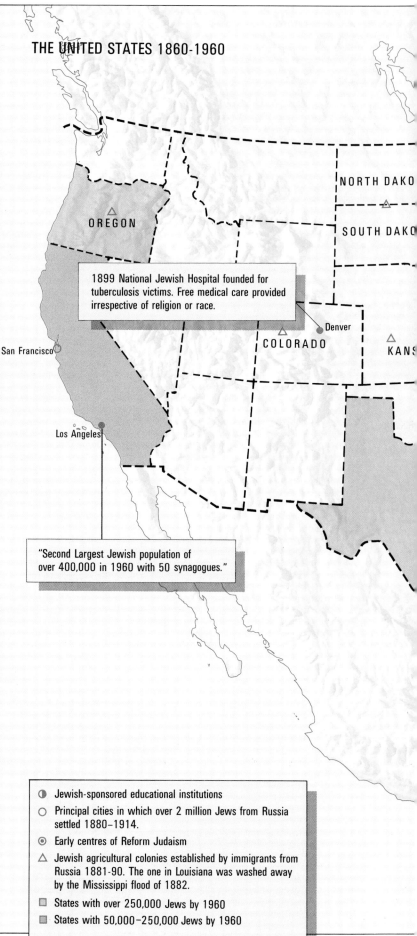

THE UNITED STATES 1860-1960

1899 National Jewish Hospital founded for tuberculosis victims. Free medical care provided irrespective of religion or race.

NORTH DAKO

SOUTH DAKO

OREGON

Denver

COLORADO

KANS

San Francisco

Los Angeles

"Second Largest Jewish population of over 400,000 in 1960 with 50 synagogues."

◐ Jewish-sponsored educational institutions

○ Principal cities in which over 2 million Jews from Russia settled 1880–1914.

◉ Early centres of Reform Judaism

△ Jewish agricultural colonies established by immigrants from Russia 1881-90. The one in Louisiana was washed away by the Mississippi flood of 1882.

▢ States with over 250,000 Jews by 1960

▢ States with 50,000–250,000 Jews by 1960

severely shaken by Napoleon, who had attempted to liberate the Jews from their ghettos, but his end had come too swiftly. In Russia, however, despite repressive, reactionary measures of successive tsars, Jews were influenced both by liberalization in the West and by their government's drive to "russify" them. At last – under certain conditions – they could study secular subjects such as law and medicine, often to the horror of their traditionally minded parents.

Economics played a major role in the emancipation of the Jews and their extraordinary emergence, seemingly overnight, at the forefront of philosophy, science, invention, and the arts. For centuries, the Jewish masses had lived in grinding poverty, with little chance of a secular education. The only way out of the ghetto was through making money, and especially in banking or finance. Nowhere more than among the Jews was the emergence of a middle class in the nineteenth century the key to a spiritual as well as an economic freedom.

The Reformers

As Jewish education began to open up to the rest of the Western world, a very new type of synagogue worship appeared in Germany. The first of what would come to be called

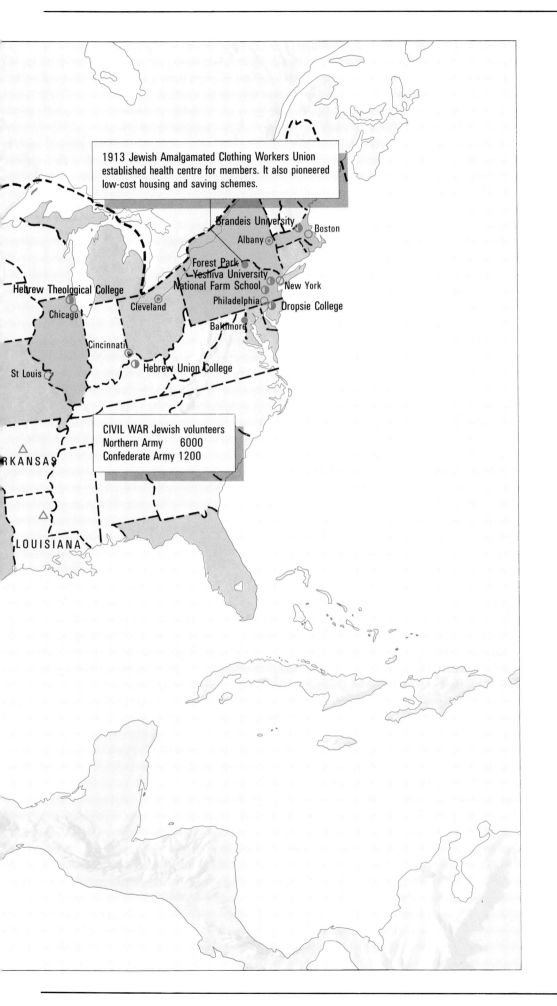

1913 Jewish Amalgamated Clothing Workers Union established health centre for members. It also pioneered low-cost housing and saving schemes.

Brandeis University

Albany

Boston

Forest Park
Yeshiva University
National Farm School

New York

Hebrew Theological College

Cleveland

Philadelphia

Dropsie College

Chicago

Cincinnati

Baltimore

St Louis

Hebrew Union College

CIVIL WAR Jewish volunteers
Northern Army   6000
Confederate Army 1200

RKANSAS

LOUISIANA

FAR LEFT: *A street in the Jewish ghetto in Prague. Though Napoleon had swept away the ghettos, they were restored after his final defeat in 1815. It was not until 1870 that the last ghetto in Western Europe in Rome was abolished, while, in Russia, the Pale remained in existence until the 1917 Revolution.*

LEFT: *From a population of around 100,000 in 1855, the number of Jews in the United States had reached a total of 5,720,000 by 1968. The first wave of immigrants – refugees from Germany and Poland – numbered some 150,000 and arrived between 1860 and 1870; between 1880 and 1914 they were joined by 2 million Russian and 125,000 Romanian Jews. The last great wave of immigration started in 1933, when Hitler's rise to supreme power led to the flight of 240,000 German and Austrian Jews from Nazi persecution.*

"reform" synagogues was opened by the philanthropist Israel Jacobson in the small town of Seesen in 1810. The services held there bore many of the trappings of German Lutheran practice, including an organ with a choir *(see below)* and prayers in the vernacular. After he moved to Berlin and established a reform temple in his home, Jacobson himself delivered a sermon in German at his

son's confirmation. Another reform synagogue was opened in Berlin in the home of the banker Jacob Beer, and in 1818 one was established in Hamburg. The following year a revised prayerbook appeared.

Also in 1819, a group of young Jews formed the Society for the Scientific Study of Judaism. Although this had no official links with the reform synagogue movement, its aims were very much in the same spirit, as evinced by its German (not Hebrew) name. The group's major contribution to Jewish knowledge was the publication of the first scholarly journal, devoted to the study of Judaism, edited by the historian Leopold Zunz: *Zeitschrift für die Wissenschaft des Judentums.*

The leading rabbi of the early reform movement was Abraham Geiger (1810–74), who came from a prominent Frankfurt family and received both a secular and a Jewish education. Following his appointment as rabbi at Wiesbaden in 1832, he edited a journal that, besides publishing Jewish historical essays, called for reform of the liturgy. Geiger's progressive ideas naturally aroused the ire of his orthodox colleagues, and the situation became acute when he was appointed assistant rabbi at Breslau in 1838. His superior, Rabbi Solomon Tiktin, would have nothing to do with him and, in 1842, issued a pamphlet condemning the new reforms and asserting that the only acceptable form of Judaism was one that adhered strictly to the laws and customs of the Talmud and of later commentaries.

Nothing, however, could stop a movement that was so much in keeping with the needs of the time. Reform rabbinical conferences were held in Brunswick in 1844, Frankfurt in 1845, and Breslau in 1846. Two years later, Solomon Tiktin died, and after his death, the

ABOVE: The Jewish Rabbi, *painted by Sir M. Archer Shee. The nineteenth century saw leading British Jews rise to considerable social prominence; this was particularly true of the banking families, such as the Rothschilds, Cassells, and Sassoons. They also gave generously to charitable works, particularly on Jewish education.*

LEFT: The Rothschild family at prayer, *painted by Moritz Daniel Oppenheim. In the course of two generations, the Rothschilds rose from being money changers in the Frankfurt ghetto to establish themselves as a banking dynasty, dominating European finance.*

LEFT: *Alphonse de Rothschild was head of the French branch of the Rothschild dynasty, following in the footsteps of his father, Jacob. The family were principal bankers to Napoleon III and heavily involved in the industrialization of France, particularly the building of the railroads.*

Breslau Jews divided into two camps, each with their own synagogue – one reform and the other orthodox. The Breslau practice was soon followed throughout Germany and Austria-Hungary.

Geiger's greatest opponent was Samson Raphael Hirsch (1808–88). Although most Jewish historians classify him as a reactionary, he was in his own way just as much a reformer as Geiger. Like Geiger, he came from Frankfurt, and in fact, the two had been friends and colleagues at the University of Bonn. Hirsch had also received a typical Enlightenment education, combining Judaism with secu-

lar studies, and he wrote fluently in German. Although bitterly opposed to the reform movement, he subtly introduced innovations into orthodox ritual – choral singing and sermons in the vernacular – which would have been unthinkable only a few years before (and still were outside Germany). His "reforms" paved the way for the type of orthodoxy practiced today by the united synagogues in Britain and the United States, an orthodoxy that suits the modern Jew or, as Hirsch would have expressed it, *"Torah im derekh-eretz"* ("Torah with a secular way of life"). A man no longer needed to wear a kaftan and grow side-curls to consider himself an orthodox Jew.

A third religious movement emerged under the influence of Rabbi Zacharias Frankel (1805–75), which was to be the forerunner of what is today known as "conservative" Judaism. Frankel was the first rabbi in Bohemia (now in Czechoslovakia) to have received a secular education. Attracted to reformist ideas, he nevertheless drew the line at some of that movement's more extreme innovations, and when he became principal of the Jewish Theological Seminary in Breslau, which had been established by

Geiger, he refused to have Geiger on the faculty. On the other hand, he also refused to give Hirsch an undertaking that the seminary would adhere strictly to the orthodox religious line.

The Development of Jewish Liturgical Music

Incessant persecution had reduced the majority of Jews to a penury that closed their minds and deeply prejudiced them against anything that smacked of Christian worship. This can be seen particularly clearly in the controversies surrounding the role of music

RIGHT: *Among the merchant princes of world Jewry, no family was more prominent than the Rothschilds. Their shrewd investments created a fortune; their philanthropic activities won them honor and renown. One of their principles was to refuse loans to governments supporting anti-Semitic policies; hence, unlike many gentile bankers, they escaped unscathed when the communists repudiated the loans made to Tsarist Russia following the 1917 revolution.*

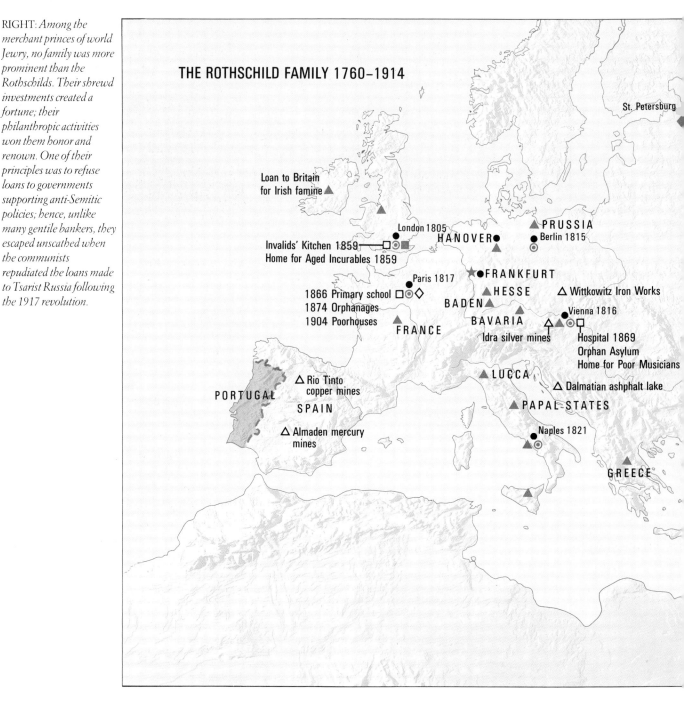

as a part of worship.

Instrumental music – *"the sounding brass and the tinkling cymbal"* of the Bible – had been an important part of Jewish religious life during the existence of the Temple. However, in the Middle Ages it was totally banned from the synagogue, largely because it had become increasingly important in the Christian Church. (In fact, some Gregorian chants were actually derived from Jewish melodies, which themselves may be based on Temple chants.) During the Jewish Enlightenment, however, secular music came to influence the synagogue liturgy.

RIGHT: *Mayer Amschel Rothschild's birthplace in the Frankfurt ghetto. He laid the foundations of his family's fortunes through his skillful manipulation of Elector William I's investments. His five sons set up banking houses in London, Paris, Vienna, and Naples.*

★ First Rothschild bank, about 1760

◉ Banking houses set up by the sons of Meyer Rothschild with dates of foundation

▲ Major loans to finance government expenditure for wars, industry, etc

△ Important investments by Rothschild banks

◆ Loan refused on account of Russia's anti-Semitic policies

◇ Rival Catholic bank established, but collapsed

▣ Rival London bank, Barings, collapsed, but was then sustained by Rothschilds 1893

▢ Portuguese government accepted loan from rival Jewish bankers, Sterns

☐ Major philanthropic activity of members of the Rothschild family

to Britain and e for Crimean against Russia

△ Baku oilfields

URKEY

ral colonies bought st settlers 1887
☐

▲ Loan to Britain for Suez Canal shares 1876

Synagogues, which had once been small places of worship where people gathered informally (horrifying many Christian observers by the lack of decorum), now modeled themselves on the formality of Christian worship. As magnificent synagogues were constructed throughout Germany, the Austro-Hungarian Empire, Britain, and the United States to reflect the new status and wealth of the congregants, it was considered fitting that suitable music should accompany the service.

The singing in larger synagogues, then as now, was led by a cantor (singer) who chanted the prayers, guided by the cantellation system of diacritical marks over the Hebrew letters to indicate how a word should be sung. Responses were then sung by the congregation. (In synagogues that could not afford a cantor, the congregation sang all the parts.) In addition, the most affluent synagogues in the West, in both the Ashkenazi and Sephardi traditions, had choirs, and this arrangement – soloist and chorus – was especially well adapted to operatic music. In particular, the Ashkenazi rite on "high holi-

SYNAGOGUES

With the gradual emancipation of the Jews throughout Western Europe and their rise to commercial, social, and political prominence, the money they lavished on their religion and their less-fortunate co-religionists also increased. Splendid synagogues arose – the ones illustrated here were built in London (below), Hanover (right) and New York (below right).

days" – the autumn festivals of the New Year and the Day of Atonement – has a very operatic feel to it.

Perhaps the man who did the most to change the Jewish liturgy was Solomon Sulzer (1804–90). A cantor who also wrote liturgical music, Sulzer was born in the Tyrol, but went, in 1826, to Vienna where he sang at the New Synagogue. His singing won him the admiration and friendship of Schubert and Liszt, and he adapted their music for performance in synagogues. It was his advocacy of the organ for use in synagogues, at least during festivals if not on the Sabbath, that led to his falling out with the orthodox authorities. However, today the playing of an organ or harmonium is a common sound in liberal and reform synagogues and even in a few conservative ones in the United States, although in some places it is omitted on the Sabbath. Other forms of instrumental music are, however, still rare.

The Trend toward Conversion

In the liberal climate of the nineteenth century, particularly in German-speaking countries, many "enlightened" Jews converted to Christianity – both the Lutheran and Catholic denominations. This was not a new phenomenon – as we have seen, Moses Mendelssohn's children had converted – but the number of converts grew throughout the century. Isaac d'Israeli (1766–1848), the literary historian and father of Benjamin Disraeli, allowed his children to be baptized after an argument with the elders of the Bevis Marks synagogue in London. The fact that a Jew disaffected from his community would even contemplate conversion, much less carry it out, throws an interesting sidelight on the psychology of nineteenth-century Jews, who generally did not take seriously the threat of assimilation and the loss of Jewish identity.

Between 1812 and 1845, more than 3,500 German-speaking Jews were baptized. Among those who succumbed were two of the founders of the *Wissenschaft* group – Eduard Gans and the great poet Heinrich Heine (1797–1856), who described conversion as "the entrance ticket to European culture" – as well as Heinrich Börne, a leading intellectual and friend of Heine, and Karl Marx's father, who took his whole family to the baptismal font in 1824. They

were later followed by the internationally renowned composer and conductor Gustav Mahler (1860–1911).

For women, conversion offered a double emancipation: release from the restrictions that Judaism imposed on women and the secular freedom of Christian society. This step was taken by a number of intellectual women moving in fashionable circles and holding their own "salons," including Rahel Varnhagen (*née* Levin, 1771–1832) and Dorothea Mendelssohn, Moses Mendelssohn's eldest daughter.

The rabbis naturally inveighed against the tendency, predicting the end of Judaism, and made accusations against the reform movement. The German-Jewish writers Gabriel Riesser and Berthold Auerbach argued strongly against conversion for another reason, seeing in it a danger that the "New Christians" might be persecuted as their counterparts had been 200 years earlier in Spain. In fact, it can be seen with hindsight that conversion was simply a fashion, limited to the top echelons of society; it had no influence on the vast majority of Jews in less exalted positions.

The Scientific and Industrial Advances of German Jews

Once the Jews were able to participate fully in the lives of their countries, they began to make significant contributions. While the new British and American industrialists were mostly self-made men from the Protestant working classes, a major role in Germany's industrialization was played by Jews, fascinated as ever by new ideas and processes.

Adolf von Bayer (1835–1917), whose mother was Jewish, produced the first synthetic indigo dye in 1878, and founded the chemical company that still bears his name; its success was based on the fact that, from 1899 to the outbreak of World War I, Bayer held the aspirin monopoly. Heinrich Caro headed the Baden Aniline and Soda Factory (BASF), the initials of which can still be seen on recording tapes worldwide. Rosenthal porcelain first emerged from a craft shop in Selb, Franconia; Philipp Rosenthal was to turn this small beginning into one of the biggest ceramics producers in the world.

The innovations of science and technology that, in the decades before World

War I, gave German manufacturing its momentum owed much to Jewish researchers. Among others, these include Fritz Haber (1868–1934), who perfected the conversion of atmospheric nitrogen into ammonia (and won the 1918 Nobel Prize for chemistry), and the physicist Heinrich Hertz (1857–94), who discovered radio waves (a unit of frequency is now called a "Hertz").

Leopold Ullstein, founder of a German publishing house that still carries his name, and Baron Paul Julius von Reuter (born Israel Beer Josaphat) – who started the Reuters news agency in Aachen in 1849 – were German-Jewish pioneers of the modern media.

The Rise of Yiddish and the Revival of Hebrew

The cultural achievement of Russian and Polish Jewry in the nineteenth century came almost exclusively through their writings – and, in particular, through their contribution to Yiddish and Hebrew literature.

Yiddish is basically a variety of German with the addition of many Hebrew and Slavic words, and is written using the Hebrew alphabet. Always the language of Jewish secular culture in eastern Europe, it was the first Jewish language in which secular literature was produced. The first great Yiddish writer was Mendele Mocher Sforim – "Mendel the Bookseller," the pseudonym of Shalom Jacob Abramowitz (1836–1917) – a master of the short story. Sholem Aleichem – "Peace be with you," the pseudonym of Salomon Rabinovitch (1859–1916) – was one of the few writers whose parents actually encouraged their son's secular ambitions. His earliest masterpiece was a Yiddish dictionary of his stepmother's curses. However, he is best known to people in the West through the characters of his book *Tevye and His Seven Daughters*, which was eventually transformed into the successful Broadway musical *Fiddler on the Roof*.

Concurrent with the flowering of Yiddish writing, a new, secular education movement pronounced Yiddish to be the "ghetto language" and acclaimed Hebrew as the language of "the new Jew." As a means of speech, Hebrew had been dead for 1,000 years for all but a handful of Jews still living in the Holy Land. However, it had been kept alive by the scholars of Babylonia and

Spain in the Golden Age, in the Jewish poetry of the Middle Ages, and it was still in use for prayer. Now, the Hebrew day-school movement, born in Russia, did much to disseminate Hebrew as a first, everyday, spoken language. Writers such as Ahad Ha'am (pseudonym of Asher Ginzberg, 1856–1927), who begged Jews to use their gifts to help their own people before others, produced works in the "holy tongue" – a blasphemy according to the ultra-orthodox, some of whom refuse to speak Hebrew, even in Israel, to this day.

By far the greatest contribution to the revival of Hebrew was made by the writer and lexicographer Eliezer ben Yehuda (1858–1922), who produced a Russian-Hebrew-Yiddish dictionary. He ingeniously invented a plethora of new words when the ancient

ABOVE: A Jewish cobbler on his rounds in the ghetto of the Lithuanian city Vilna. Though the Jews of Eastern Europe underwent a cultural revival in the nineteenth century, they still faced intolerance and persecution.

language lacked the means to express modern concepts and inventions. For example, his translation of "electricity" – *hashmal* – is a word whose original meaning is unclear but which is used in the Bible to describe the splendor around the throne of God. Some of Ben Yehuda's words, such as *orkester* for "orchestra," have since been replaced by others based on Hebrew roots: the modern word for orchestra is *tizmoret*, from the root *zmr*, "melody" or "song." Modern Hebrew now relies almost exclusively on Semitic roots, either Hebrew or Aramaic, for its newly invented words. *Ulpan*, meaning a studio or an intensive Hebrew course, comes from the Aramaic word for "teach," and *mehashev* – "computer" – is based on the Hebrew for "calculate." Almost all the vocabulary of electronics and medicine relies on these roots rather than on the more traditional (in the West), but also more alien, Latin or Greek, which do not fit comfortably into Semitic word patterns.

The two greatest Hebrew poets of the modern era – Hayyim Nahman Bialik (1873–1934) and Shaul Chernikhovsky (1875–1943) – ended their days in Palestine, as did Nathan Alterman (1910–70) and Abraham Shlonsky (1900–86). Perhaps the language received its ultimate accolade when the Hebrew and Yiddish writer Shmuel Yosef Agnon (1888–1970), was awarded the Nobel Prize for literature (jointly with the German-Jewish writer, Nelly Sachs) in 1966. However, Yiddish, too, received its due: in 1978, the Yiddish writer Isaac Bashevis Singer, who was born in Poland in 1904 and emigrated to the United States in 1935, was awarded the Nobel Prize for his work.

Yiddish and Hebrew Theater

There is a long tradition of theater among Jews, stretching back beyond Roman times. They were accustomed to performing plays,

BELOW: Jewish sugar peddlers in the market-place of the ghetto in Warsaw. At this time, much of Poland was part of the Russian empire and Polish Jews suffered accordingly. Many emigrated, while others turned to revolutionary politics and to Zionism.

THE JEWS AND THE THEATER

Jewish theater began in pre-Roman times: the tradition of performing plays on Biblical themes, particularly during the festival of Purim, dates back to this period. With the coming of emancipation in the nineteenth century, many Jewish actors and actresses emerged to win international acclaim on the stage; of them, Sarah Bernhardt (right) and Rachel (below) were among the most prominent. Both were great tragediennes and both were leading members of the Comédie Française. Among Rachel's triumphs were her performances in the major works of Racine and Corneille; Bernhardt starred in *Phèdre*, as Doña Sol in Victor Hugo's *Hernani*, and as Violette in *La Dame aux Camélias*. For Vincent Sardou, she created Fédora, Théodora, and La Tosca.

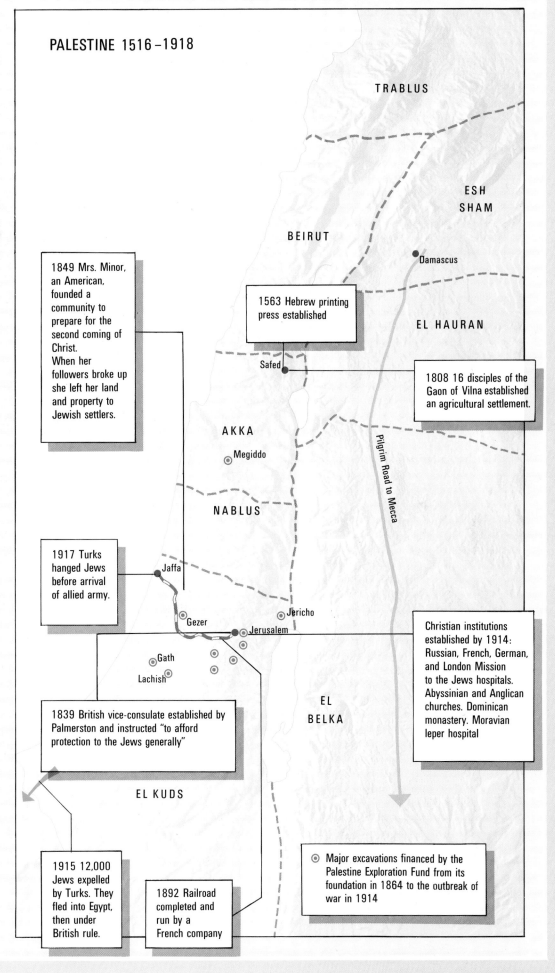

RIGHT: *Until the nineteenth century, Palestine itself remained quietly under Ottoman control; it was not until the birth of Zionism that pressure for the re-establishment of a Jewish state and a return to Israel gained ground among the Jews of the diaspora. For their part, the Turks tolerated the initial agricultural settlements, many of which were financed by rich Jewish philanthropists, such as the Rothschilds; it was only when faced with military defeat at the hands of Britain in the First World War that they responded with persecution.*

PALESTINE 1516–1918

TRABLUS

ESH SHAM

BEIRUT

Damascus

1849 Mrs. Minor, an American, founded a community to prepare for the second coming of Christ. When her followers broke up she left her land and property to Jewish settlers.

1563 Hebrew printing press established

EL HAURAN

Safed

1808 16 disciples of the Gaon of Vilna established an agricultural settlement.

AKKA

Megiddo

NABLUS

Pilgrim Road to Mecca

1917 Turks hanged Jews before arrival of allied army.

Jaffa

Jericho

Gezer

Jerusalem

Christian institutions established by 1914: Russian, French, German, and London Mission to the Jews hospitals. Abyssinian and Anglican churches. Dominican monastery. Moravian leper hospital

Gath

Lachish

EL BELKA

1839 British vice-consulate established by Palmerston and instructed "to afford protection to the Jews generally"

EL KUDS

1915 12,000 Jews expelled by Turks. They fled into Egypt, then under British rule.

1892 Railroad completed and run by a French company

⊚ Major excavations financed by the Palestine Exploration Fund from its foundation in 1864 to the outbreak of war in 1914

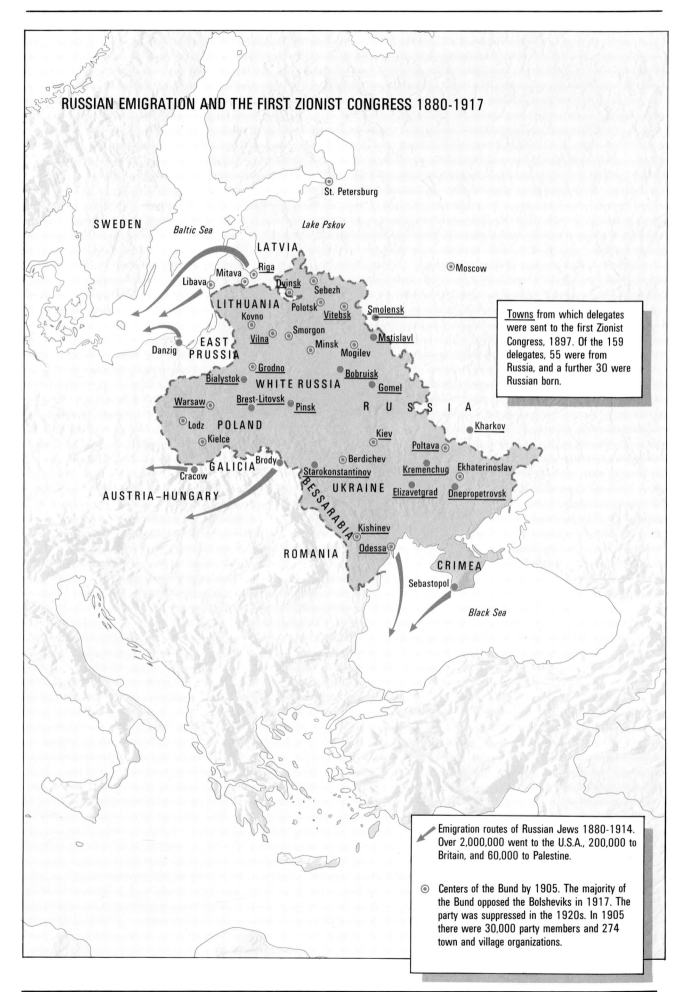

RUSSIAN EMIGRATION AND THE FIRST ZIONIST CONGRESS 1880-1917

SWEDEN

Baltic Sea

Lake Pskov

St. Petersburg

LATVIA

Moscow

Riga

Mitava

Libava

Dvinsk

Sebezh

LITHUANIA

Polotsk

Smolensk

Kovno

Vitebsk

Vilna

Smorgon

Mstislavl

EAST
PRUSSIA

Minsk

Danzig

Mogilev

Grodno

Bobruisk

Bialystok

WHITE RUSSIA

Gomel

Warsaw

Brest-Litovsk

Pinsk

R U S S I A

Lodz

POLAND

Kielce

Kiev

Kharkov

Brody

Berdichev

Poltava

Cracow

GALICIA

Starokonstantinov

Kremenchug

Ekhaterinoslav

UKRAINE

AUSTRIA-HUNGARY

BESSARABIA

Elizavetgrad

Dnepropetrovsk

Kishinev

Odessa

CRIMEA

ROMANIA

Sebastopol

Black Sea

Towns from which delegates
were sent to the first Zionist
Congress, 1897. Of the 159
delegates, 55 were from
Russia, and a further 30 were
Russian born.

Emigration routes of Russian Jews 1880-1914.
Over 2,000,000 went to the U.S.A., 200,000 to
Britain, and 60,000 to Palestine.

⊙ Centers of the Bund by 1905. The majority of
the Bund opposed the Bolsheviks in 1917. The
party was suppressed in the 1920s. In 1905
there were 30,000 party members and 274
town and village organizations.

RIGHT: *After the first major pogroms, 3,000 Russian Jews arrived in Palestine in 1882, to be followed by thousands of others from Russia, Galicia, and Romania. By 1914 there were over 60,000 Jews from these areas. Many of them settled on wasteland, sand-dunes, and malarial marsh, which they then drained, irrigated, and farmed.*

LEFT: *From 1881 onward, the "Lovers of Zion" movement urged Russian Jews to settle in Palestine, and by 1914, 60,000 of them had reached the promised land. Russian Jews played a prominent part in the birth of Zionism, when the first Zionist Congress was held in Basle in 1897, under the presidency of the founder of modern Zionism, Theodor Herzl. In the same year, the Jews of Russia founded their own Social Democratic party, the "Bund."*

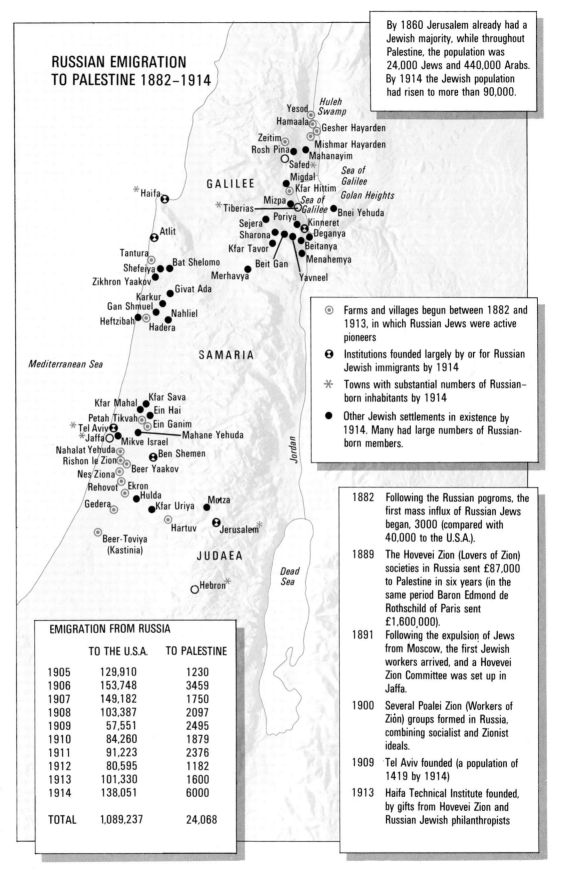

RUSSIAN EMIGRATION TO PALESTINE 1882–1914

By 1860 Jerusalem already had a Jewish majority, while throughout Palestine, the population was 24,000 Jews and 440,000 Arabs. By 1914 the Jewish population had risen to more than 90,000.

⊙ Farms and villages begun between 1882 and 1913, in which Russian Jews were active pioneers

☤ Institutions founded largely by or for Russian Jewish immigrants by 1914

✳ Towns with substantial numbers of Russian-born inhabitants by 1914

● Other Jewish settlements in existence by 1914. Many had large numbers of Russian-born members.

EMIGRATION FROM RUSSIA		
	TO THE U.S.A.	TO PALESTINE
1905	129,910	1230
1906	153,748	3459
1907	149,182	1750
1908	103,387	2097
1909	57,551	2495
1910	84,260	1879
1911	91,223	2376
1912	80,595	1182
1913	101,330	1600
1914	138,051	6000
TOTAL	1,089,237	24,068

1882	Following the Russian pogroms, the first mass influx of Russian Jews began, 3000 (compared with 40,000 to the U.S.A.).
1889	The Hovevei Zion (Lovers of Zion) societies in Russia sent £87,000 to Palestine in six years (in the same period Baron Edmond de Rothschild of Paris sent £1,600,000).
1891	Following the expulsion of Jews from Moscow, the first Jewish workers arrived, and a Hovevei Zion Committee was set up in Jaffa.
1900	Several Poalei Zion (Workers of Zion) groups formed in Russia, combining socialist and Zionist ideals.
1909	Tel Aviv founded (a population of 1419 by 1914)
1913	Haifa Technical Institute founded, by gifts from Hovevei Zion and Russian Jewish philanthropists

usually on biblical themes, and especially at the festival of Purim, which celebrates the story of Esther. During the Middle Ages, there was at least one Jewish *minnesinger* (minstrel), Süsskind of Trimberg, and in Italy, where the Catholic hierarchy forced the Jewish communities to present entertainments, the Jewish performers were very much admired. In seventeenth- and eighteenth-century Poland, Jewish clowns called *leitzim* and *marshalniks* presided over wedding festivities.

With emancipation, Jewish actors and actresses came to public attention. Many earned international reputations on the "legitimate" stage: Rachel (Eliza Felix, 1820–58); Sarah Bernhardt (Rosine Bernard, 1844–1923); and Hannah Norsa, who acted in the stage company of Henry Irving, the famous English actor-manager.

The founding father of Yiddish theater was the Ukrainian-born impresario-cum-playwright Abraham Goldfaden (1840–1908), who founded his first theatrical troupe in Jassy in Romania. Besides the classic Yiddish dramas *Shulamit*, *Bar Kokhba* and *Die Kishufmacherin*, he also wrote many popular Yiddish songs – including the well-known *"Rozhinkes und Mandeln"* ("Raisins and Almonds") – which were among the first pieces of music to be heard on the modern record player, patented in 1887 by the American inventor Emile Berliner (1851–1929). Goldfaden's mantle was inherited by Ida Kaminska (1899–1985), a member of a Polish theatrical family, whose parents were considered the greatest actors of their day. She took over her father's theatrical company, which after the war was given the name "The Jewish State Theater of Poland." In 1968, she left Poland and settled in Israel.

The greatest modern playwright whose works appeared in Hebrew was the learned ethnologist, folklorist, and fervent Russian revolutionary known as An-ski (1863–1920), whose real name was Solomon Zainvil Rapoport. His play *The Dibbuk* (in Jewish folklore, a ghost that gets into the soul of a living person), which he wrote in two versions, Russian and Yiddish, was translated into Hebrew by the poet Hayyim Nahman Bialik. When An-ski lost the original Yiddish version, he retranslated it back from Bialik's Hebrew edition, so recreating his original.

With the revival of Hebrew came the revival of the Hebrew theater. The first professional company performing in Hebrew – Ha-Bimah ("The Stage") – was founded in Moscow in 1917 by Nahum David Zemach, a disciple of the Stanislavski "Method." In 1926, the company went on tour abroad and, in view of the growing official Soviet hostility toward Jewish culture, never returned to the U.S.S.R. It eventually migrated to Palestine where, in 1971, it became the National Theater of Israel, with its own magnificent building in Tel-Aviv.

The Birth of Zionism

The most important intellectual development in the Jewish community of the nineteenth century was Zionism – the movement for the return of the Jews to the land of Israel, or Zion. Long before Theodor Herzl became its leading exponent, Zionism had had the support of a significant minority, comprising both Jews and non-Jews, as the ultimate Jewish emancipation.

After the Damascus Blood Libel trial in 1840 (*see* Chapter 5), the British consul in Syria wrote to the prominent Jewish statesman Sir Moses Montefiore, urging Jewish resettlement of Palestine as a viable response to anti-Semitism. Sir Moses was at first skeptical, but the following year, he was persuaded by Rabbi Zvi Hirsch Kalischer (1795–1874), the first orthodox religious Zionist, to buy an orange grove in Palestine, as a first step.

Moses Hess (1812–75), a German Jew, was a fervent socialist (he introduced Friedrich Engels to Karl Marx) and an advocate of the assimilation of the Jews into gentile society. He was also, however, strongly in favor of Jews having their own state, which, he thought, would enable them to achieve an equal status in society. In the context of nineteenth-century nationalism, these two seemingly contradictory beliefs – assimilation and separate nationhood – were seen as compatible.

In eastern Europe, the primary advocate of the Zionist ideal at this early stage was Peretz Smolenskin (1842–85), who edited and published the Hebrew newspaper *Ha-Shakhar* ("The Dawn") in the Pale of Settlement (*see* Chapter 5). Smolenskin began by attacking the restrictions of old-style orthodox Juda-

THE FIRST ZIONISTS

Concerted pressure for a Jewish return to Palestine started in the mid-nineteenth century, when the British Jewish philanthropist Sir Moses Montefiore (shown in a schoolroom, below right) was persuaded to finance a pioneer settlement; the windmill he had built in Jerusalem is shown (right). Theodor Herzl (bottom) founded the World Zionist Organization in 1897; he was its president until his death in 1904. Maurice de Hirsch, a German Jewish financier and philanthropist, also supported Jewish communities in Palestine; the photograph (below) shows the 1899 Passover celebration in the colony he founded outside Jerusalem.

ism, but the pogroms of the 1880s convinced him – and he then tried to convince his readers – that a Jewish homeland was the only solution to the age-old persecution.

These pogroms were the trigger for a mass movement throughout the Pale in favor of a Jewish homeland. However, at first this was limited to only the most enlightened circles in the big cities of the Ukraine, where there was a large, emergent Jewish middle class. An organization was formed called *Hibbat Zion* ("Love of Zion"), the members of which – *Hovevei Zion* ("Lovers of Zion") – promoted Jewish colonization in Palestine. In addition, a group of university students in Kharkov founded a society – named *Bilu*, the initial letters of a quotation from Isaiah 2:5: "*House of Jacob, let us arise and go*" – with the specific aim of emigrating to Palestine and establishing farms there.

The first important theoretician of the Ukrainian movement was a doctor from Odessa. In his book *Auto-Emancipation*, Leon (Yehuda Leib) Pinsker (1821–91) claimed (in an echo of Moses Hess) that anti-Semitism would be eradicated only when the Jews had their own state, and so were considered the equal of other nations in the eyes of the world. Dr. Pinsker eventually became the chairman of *Hibbat Zion*.

Just as anti-Semitism was the trigger for the Zionist movement in Poland and Russia, so it proved to be the catalyst among Jews in the affluent West, where Zionism gained even more currency. Theodor Herzl (1860–1904) was an assimilated Viennese journalist, born in Budapest. He became a correspondent of the important Vienna newspaper *Neue Freie Presse*, and, in that capacity, attended the trial of Alfred Dreyfus (*see* Chapter 5). What he witnessed shocked him deeply, and he became convinced that anti-Semitism was so ingrained that Jews would be able to survive only by abandoning gentile society completely and forming their own nation. His first essay on the subject – *"Der Judenstaat"* (*"The Jewish State"*) – appeared in 1896, and the following year, he organized the first Zionist conference, which was held in Basel, Switzerland, on August 29th. The World Zionist Organization, which was the result of the conference and of which Herzl became first president, eventually opened offices all over the world.

Herzl now began a round of visits to prominent Jews and non-Jews to persuade them to invest intellectually and financially in a new Jewish state. He met with a mixed reception. The majority of Jews – and especially the strongly assimilated communities of Germany and Britain – were very hostile toward Zionism, and in Britain this hostility lasted until well after the state of Israel was established. However, Herzl did find supporters. Among the earliest were such prominent men as the philanthropist Baron Edmond de Rothschild, of the French branch of the family, who had helped to finance the early settlements in Palestine of the 1880s, and Sir Moses Montefiore, who had by now become a convert to the new Jewish movement.

Among Zionism's opponents was the great Bavarian philanthropist Baron Maurice de Hirsch (1831–96), who considered the founding of a Jewish state in Palestine a foolish dream. Instead, he poured vast sums into his Jewish Colonization Association (JCA), which he founded in 1891 to finance the establishment of Jewish agricultural settlements in South America, primarily in Argentina and Brazil. Jewish farmers emigrated there from the Pale of Settlement, where the Russian authorities had rejected the Baron's offer of financial aid to the impoverished and persecuted resident Jewish population. (Some of de Hirsch's projects in South America are still in existence, although on a much reduced scale, and today most of the JCA's support for agriculture is invested in Israel.) Herzl was also eventually persuaded that a Jewish state could be established just about anywhere. For example, when the British offered the World Zionist Organization a tract of land in Uganda, he was all for taking it if Palestine was not available.

Jewish settlement in Palestine in the nineteenth century was largely financed by Jewish capitalists in Europe, who saw this mainly as a solution to the extreme poverty that was the lot of eastern European Jews. Their money helped to found villages based on traditional hierarchies. A new breed of Zionist was emerging, however. Committed socialists, they saw Palestine as the perfect "laboratory" to test their ideas. It was still part of the crumbling Ottoman Empire, and was remote from Western influence.

They decided on a communal form of agriculture as the only viable solution in such a barren land. One year after a group of tents had been erected on the sand dunes next to the port of Jaffa and named Tel-Aviv, their first communal settlement, or *Kibbutz* – which was owned by all its members – was established at Degania on the River Jordan near the Sea of Galilee. For those who found this type of life too restrictive, the first *moshav* – a village in which the land is divided into individual plots and only the major resources are shared communally – was established in 1921.

The Jewish Bund and Marxism

Even more powerful than the promise of Zionism was the desire of the Russian Jews for equality. This found its expression in socialism, and Jews figured prominently in the left-wing movements of the nineteenth and early twentieth centuries. Among the

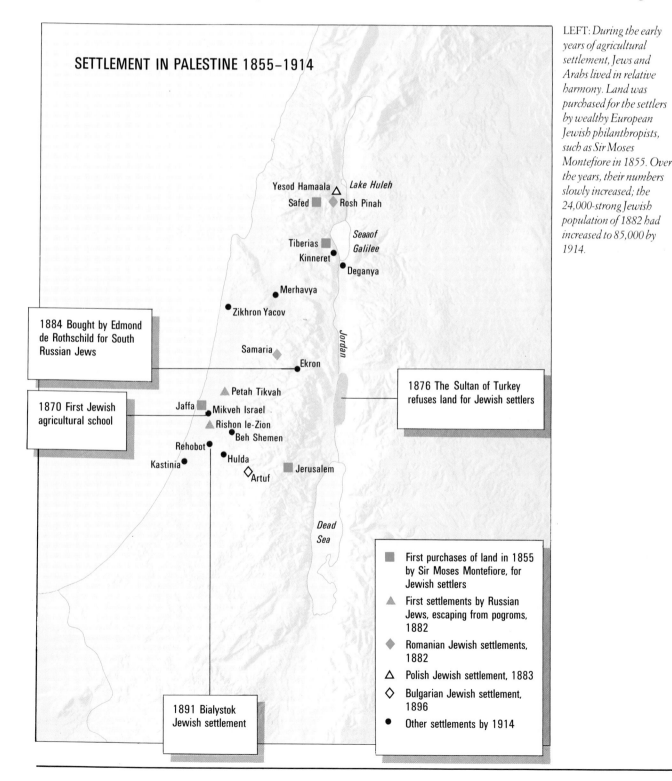

SETTLEMENT IN PALESTINE 1855–1914

Yesod Hamaala △ *Lake Huleh*
Safed ■ ◆ Rosh Pinah

Seaaof Galilee
Tiberias ■
Kinneret ●
● Deganya

● Merhavya

● Zikhron Yacov

Samaria ◆
● Ekron

▲ Petah Tikvah
Jaffa ■ ● Mikveh Israel
▲ Rishon le-Zion
● Beh Shemen
Rehobot ●
● Hulda
Kastinia ●
◇ Artuf ■ Jerusalem

Jordan

Dead Sea

1884 Bought by Edmond de Rothschild for South Russian Jews

1870 First Jewish agricultural school

1876 The Sultan of Turkey refuses land for Jewish settlers

1891 Bialystok Jewish settlement

■ First purchases of land in 1855 by Sir Moses Montefiore, for Jewish settlers

▲ First settlements by Russian Jews, escaping from pogroms, 1882

◆ Romanian Jewish settlements, 1882

△ Polish Jewish settlement, 1883

◇ Bulgarian Jewish settlement, 1896

● Other settlements by 1914

LEFT: *During the early years of agricultural settlement, Jews and Arabs lived in relative harmony. Land was purchased for the settlers by wealthy European Jewish philanthropists, such as Sir Moses Montefiore in 1855. Over the years, their numbers slowly increased; the 24,000-strong Jewish population of 1882 had increased to 85,000 by 1914.*

Jews, this socialism took two forms: the Jewish Bund and Marxism.

The Jewish Bund, founded in 1897 as a section within the Social Democratic (Marxist) party, insisted on equality with non-Jewish socialists. Nevertheless, it advocated secular Yiddish culture for its members, and organized defense groups to combat the Black Hundreds (*see* Chapter 5). The Bundists tended to look upon Zionists as middle class and elitist.

In 1903 the Bundists withdrew from the Social Democratic party after an argument and left the bolsheviks in control.

Karl Marx (1818–83) was the son of a baptized Jew and grandson of the rabbi of Trier. His writings formulated a new ideology of equality which inspired Jews all over the world: fiery Jewish revolutionaries Leon Jogiches (1867–1919) and Rosa Luxemburg (1870–1919) fought to bring Communism to Germany, but both were murdered by reactionaries. Another Jew, Béla Kun (1886–1937), briefly governed Hungary after the Communist revolution of 1919.

In Russia, many of the leading figures of the 1917 revolution were Jewish. The first Politburo was overwhelmingly Jewish, and

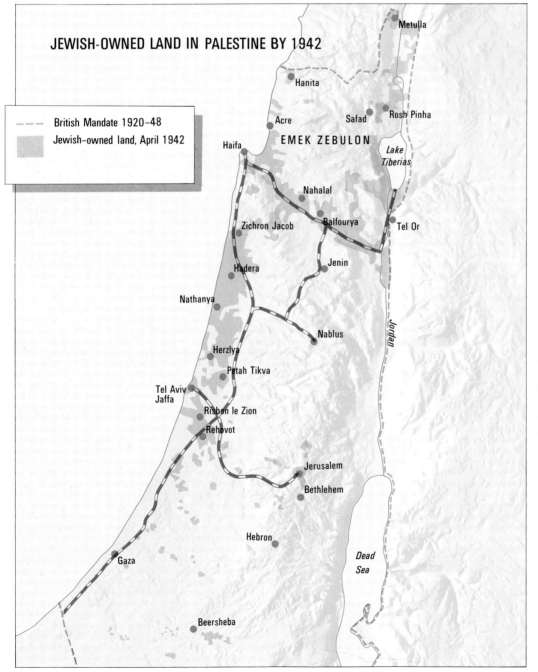

JEWISH-OWNED LAND IN PALESTINE BY 1942

- - - - British Mandate 1920–48
Jewish-owned land, April 1942

Metulla

Hanita

Acre · Safad · Rosh Pinha

Haifa · EMEK ZEBULON · Lake Tiberias

Nahalal

Zichron Jacob · Balfourya · Tel Or

Hadera · Jenin

Nathanya

Nablus

Herzlya

Petah Tikva

Tel Aviv Jaffa

Rishon le Zion

Rehovot

Jerusalem

Bethlehem

Hebron

Jordan

Dead Sea

Gaza

Beersheba

RIGHT: *Karl Marx's revolutionary socialist philosophy won a ready response from his fellow-Jews, particularly those of eastern Europe. Many of the leading figures of the early Communist party were Jewish.*

LEFT: *By 1942 the British government was struggling to hold the peace between Jew and Arab in Palestine, trying to deal with unrest in the country itself and, at the same time, coming under ever-increasing pressure to lift the immigration quotas it had imposed and open the gates to the Jews who could escape wartime Europe. One of the chief concerns of the Arabs was the substantial property holdings the Jews were building up, which gave them a legal right to the land they occupied.*

Austrian Ludwig Wittgenstein (1889–1951), who spent much of his working life teaching at Cambridge University in England. However, two Jewish theoreticians in fields allied to pure philosophy were to have an even greater effect on modern thought.

Sigmund Freud (1856–1939) began his work in Vienna with purely medical research initially into the condition then known as "hysteria," in which a patient is paralyzed but no physical cause can be found. Later he investigated other disturbances of the mind. This led him to develop a new therapy, psychoanalysis, which was to have far-reaching implications for the entire study of psychology. With the advent of Hitler, he was forced to flee to London. The German Jew Albert Einstein (1879–1955) conceived the Special Theory of Relativity (1905) and the General Theory (1916), contributing as much to modern physics as had Newton's

BELOW: An anti-Trotsky poster, produced in Russia in 1917. Though the revolution promised to end Jewish persecution, it was not long before anti-Semitism reared its head again. In Trotsky's case, his Jewish birth was used as a tool to defeat him in the struggle for power that followed the death of Lenin.

the first Soviet to be formed included an important delegation from the Jewish Bund. Jakov M. Sverdlov (1885–1919), allegedly the person who ordered the execution of the Russian royal family, became chairman of the All-Union Committee of the Communist Party. Lev Borisovich Kamenev (*né* Rosenfeld, 1883–1936) was editor of *Pravda* when the newspaper was published in exile. He returned to Russia for the revolution, and in 1922, following Lenin's stroke (which led to the leader's death two years later), he and his Jewish colleague Grigori Yevseyevich Zinoviev (*né* Rimysiski, 1883–1936) constituted two-thirds of the triumvirate that, with Stalin, led the party and the country. As commissar for foreign affairs, Leon Trotsky (*né* Lev Davidovitch Bronstein, 1879–1940) negotiated the Brest-Litovsk treaty which took the Soviet Union out of World War I; as commissar for war, he created the Red Army. (Kamenev and Zinoviev were both deposed by Stalin, who had them tried and executed in 1936; he had to wait another four years before he managed to have the Mexico-exiled Trotsky assassinated.)

The Influence of Jewish Thought
Nineteenth- and twentieth-century thought has been profoundly affected by the work of such Jewish philosophers as the Frenchman Henri Bergson (1859–1941) and the

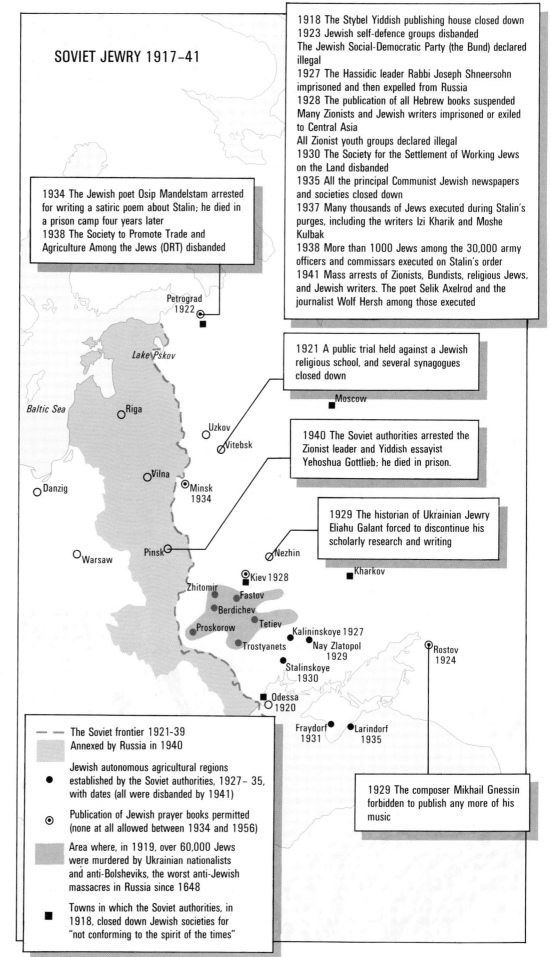

SOVIET JEWRY 1917–41

1918 The Stybel Yiddish publishing house closed down
1923 Jewish self-defence groups disbanded
The Jewish Social-Democratic Party (the Bund) declared illegal
1927 The Hassidic leader Rabbi Joseph Shneersohn imprisoned and then expelled from Russia
1928 The publication of all Hebrew books suspended
Many Zionists and Jewish writers imprisoned or exiled to Central Asia
All Zionist youth groups declared illegal
1930 The Society for the Settlement of Working Jews on the Land disbanded
1935 All the principal Communist Jewish newspapers and societies closed down
1937 Many thousands of Jews executed during Stalin's purges, including the writers Izi Kharik and Moshe Kulbak
1938 More than 1000 Jews among the 30,000 army officers and commissars executed on Stalin's order
1941 Mass arrests of Zionists, Bundists, religious Jews, and Jewish writers. The poet Selik Axelrod and the journalist Wolf Hersh among those executed

1934 The Jewish poet Osip Mandelstam arrested for writing a satiric poem about Stalin; he died in a prison camp four years later
1938 The Society to Promote Trade and Agriculture Among the Jews (ORT) disbanded

1921 A public trial held against a Jewish religious school, and several synagogues closed down

1940 The Soviet authorities arrested the Zionist leader and Yiddish essayist Yehoshua Gottlieb; he died in prison.

1929 The historian of Ukrainian Jewry Eliahu Galant forced to discontinue his scholarly research and writing

1929 The composer Mikhail Gnessin forbidden to publish any more of his music

Petrograd 1922

Lake Pskov

Baltic Sea

Riga

Uzkov
Vitebsk

Vilna

Danzig

Minsk 1934

Moscow

Nezhin

Kharkov

Warsaw

Pinsk

Kiev 1928

Zhitomir
Fastov
Berdichev
Proskorow
Tetiev
Trostyanets
Kalininskoye 1927
Nay Zlatopol 1929
Stalinskoye 1930

Rostov 1924

Odessa 1920

Fraydorf 1931
Larindorf 1935

Legend

- – – The Soviet frontier 1921-39
  Annexed by Russia in 1940

- ● Jewish autonomous agricultural regions established by the Soviet authorities, 1927– 35, with dates (all were disbanded by 1941)

- ⊙ Publication of Jewish prayer books permitted (none at all allowed between 1934 and 1956)

- Area where, in 1919, over 60,000 Jews were murdered by Ukrainian nationalists and anti-Bolsheviks, the worst anti-Jewish massacres in Russia since 1648

- ■ Towns in which the Soviet authorities, in 1918, closed down Jewish societies for "not conforming to the spirit of the times"

RIGHT: In 1917, with the fall of the Tsarist regime, all the repressive edicts that had governed Jewish life were repealed and the Pale of Settlement was abolished. This new spirit of tolerance was to be short-lived, however. As early as 1918, Jewish religious activity was under attack from the communists and by 1923 the government was suppressing all aspects of Zionist activity and of Hebrew self-expression. The great purges of the 1930s followed.

laws of motion and gravity, and paving the way for the atom bomb and nuclear power as well as for space exploration. He also had to leave his country when the Nazis came to power, first for Switzerland and then for the United States.

The first Jew to win a Nobel Prize was Albert Abraham Michelson (1852–1931), who received the prize for physics in 1907 for his studies on the velocity of light. Michelson was just the first in a long line: although Jews represent barely 0.3 percent of the world's population, they have won 10 percent of the Nobel Prizes.

It was not only in the library and the laboratory that Jews came to the fore. Many rapidly rose to political power in the new liberal climate of western Europe. In France,

BELOW: Right-wing anti-Semitic propaganda had frequently claimed that Europe's Jews felt no real loyalty to the countries in which they lived and could not be counted upon in time of war. First World War records should have dispelled this myth.

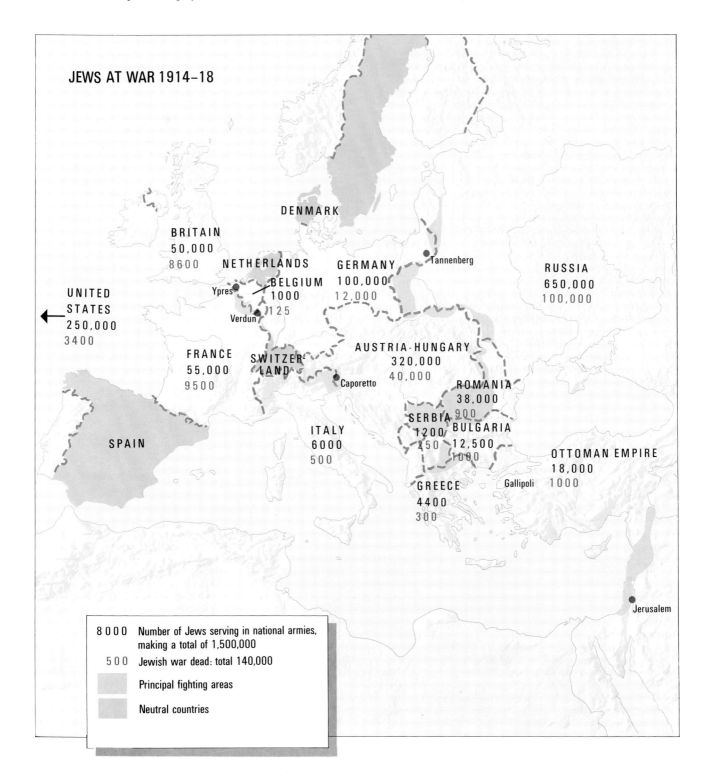

JEWS AT WAR 1914–18

DENMARK

BRITAIN
50,000
8600   NETHERLANDS   GERMANY
                       100,000   Tannenberg
UNITED   BELGIUM   12,000   RUSSIA
STATES   Ypres   1000   650,000
250,000   125   100,000
3400   Verdun

FRANCE   AUSTRIA-HUNGARY
55,000   SWITZER-   320,000
9500   LAND   40,000
                                  ROMANIA
                                  38,000
                        SERBIA 900
            ITALY   1200   BULGARIA
SPAIN   6000   450   12,500
            500   1000   OTTOMAN EMPIRE
                                                      18,000
                        GREECE   Gallipoli 1000
                        4400
                        300

                                                                Jerusalem

8000   Number of Jews serving in national armies,
       making a total of 1,500,000
500   Jewish war dead: total 140,000
       Principal fighting areas
       Neutral countries

ABOVE: *Albert Einstein and his wife. Einstein was one of the most prominent physicists of the twentieth century. He took refuge in the United States when Hitler came to power.*

RIGHT: *Sigmund Freud, founder of psychoanalysis. In pre-First World War Vienna, he was attacked as much for his Judaism as for the controversial nature of his revolutionary theories. He too fled into exile in the 1930s.*

OPPOSITE PAGE: *The U.S. Declaration of Independence gave all Jewish men equal status with their gentile fellow citizens, and in the next century, many Jews accordingly sought the freedom of the New World.*

during World War I. Other Jews flocked to fight in the new battles for liberation, in the revolution of 1848 in Austria and Germany and in the Italian campaigns of the Carbonari of the 1820s and the later "Young Italy" movement of Giuseppe Mazzini.

The Jewish Influence on Popular Culture

Popular culture in the twentieth century has been dominated by the United States, and it is not surprising that the most important Jewish contributors have been American citizens. One of the earliest was the theatrical impresario and director David Belasco (1854–1931), whose production of his own play *The Girl of the Golden West* was a smash hit on the Broadway stage in 1905. (It later formed the basis of the libretto for Puccini's opera of the same name.) Two years later, Florenz Ziegfeld (1869–1932) introduced the theatrical revue to the American stage in the form of the Ziegfield Follies, an imitation of the Parisian *Folies Bergère*. The Follies – with their glamorous showgirls, variety acts, and extravagant sets – were produced year after year until 1931, when Hollywood co-opted the style. Another Jewish impresario and master of lavish stage productions was Billy Rose (1899–1966).

Jews entered the film industry primarily as exhibitors, being quick to see that the "flickers" were not just peepshow attractions or a passing fad but could become theatrical events in their own right. By the 1930s, most of the Hollywood studios were in Jewish hands: Metro-Goldwyn-Mayer, Warner Bros., Universal, Twentieth Century-Fox, and Paramount. Even though the star and studio system has disappeared, Jews have continued to produce films, but there have been some major changes. The "Big Five" studios are no longer Jewish-owned (although Walt Disney now is), but new-style director-producers such as Mel Brooks, Steven Spielberg, and Woody Allen are making their own impact, with far more creative control over their pictures than they would have had under such studio bosses as Harry Cohn, Sam Goldwyn, and Louis B. Mayer.

The secular Yiddish songs written in the late nineteenth and early twentieth century provided much of the inspiration for such American-Jewish songwriters as Jerome Kern and George and Ira Gershwin, phenomen-

there were the politicians Adolphe (Isaac Moïse) Crémieux (1796–1880) and Léon Blum (1872–1950) and, in Germany, Ferdinand Lasalle (1825–64). In Italy, General Giuseppe Ottolenghi became minister of war

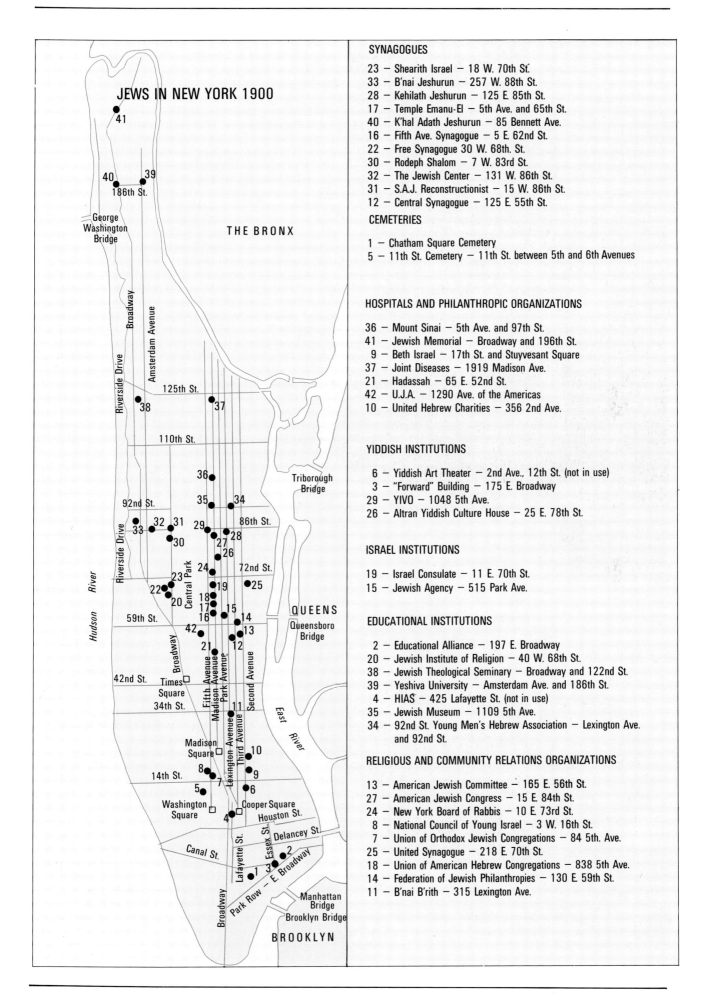

JEWS IN NEW YORK 1900

SYNAGOGUES

23 — Shearith Israel — 18 W. 70th St.
33 — B'nai Jeshurun — 257 W. 88th St.
28 — Kehilath Jeshurun — 125 E. 85th St.
17 — Temple Emanu-El — 5th Ave. and 65th St.
40 — K'hal Adath Jeshurun — 85 Bennett Ave.
16 — Fifth Ave. Synagogue — 5 E. 62nd St.
22 — Free Synagogue 30 W. 68th. St.
30 — Rodeph Shalom — 7 W. 83rd St.
32 — The Jewish Center — 131 W. 86th St.
31 — S.A.J. Reconstructionist — 15 W. 86th St.
12 — Central Synagogue — 125 E. 55th St.

CEMETERIES

1 — Chatham Square Cemetery
5 — 11th St. Cemetery — 11th St. between 5th and 6th Avenues

HOSPITALS AND PHILANTHROPIC ORGANIZATIONS

36 — Mount Sinai — 5th Ave. and 97th St.
41 — Jewish Memorial — Broadway and 196th St.
9 — Beth Israel — 17th St. and Stuyvesant Square
37 — Joint Diseases — 1919 Madison Ave.
21 — Hadassah — 65 E. 52nd St.
42 — U.J.A. — 1290 Ave. of the Americas
10 — United Hebrew Charities — 356 2nd Ave.

YIDDISH INSTITUTIONS

6 — Yiddish Art Theater — 2nd Ave., 12th St. (not in use)
3 — "Forward" Building — 175 E. Broadway
29 — YIVO — 1048 5th Ave.
26 — Altran Yiddish Culture House — 25 E. 78th St.

ISRAEL INSTITUTIONS

19 — Israel Consulate — 11 E. 70th St.
15 — Jewish Agency — 515 Park Ave.

EDUCATIONAL INSTITUTIONS

2 — Educational Alliance — 197 E. Broadway
20 — Jewish Institute of Religion — 40 W. 68th St.
38 — Jewish Theological Seminary — Broadway and 122nd St.
39 — Yeshiva University — Amsterdam Ave. and 186th St.
4 — HIAS — 425 Lafayette St. (not in use)
35 — Jewish Museum — 1109 5th Ave.
34 — 92nd St. Young Men's Hebrew Association — Lexington Ave. and 92nd St.

RELIGIOUS AND COMMUNITY RELATIONS ORGANIZATIONS

13 — American Jewish Committee — 165 E. 56th St.
27 — American Jewish Congress — 15 E. 84th St.
24 — New York Board of Rabbis — 10 E. 73rd St.
8 — National Council of Young Israel — 3 W. 16th St.
7 — Union of Orthodox Jewish Congregations — 84 5th. Ave.
25 — United Synagogue — 218 E. 70th St.
18 — Union of American Hebrew Congregations — 838 5th Ave.
14 — Federation of Jewish Philanthropies — 130 E. 59th St.
11 — B'nai B'rith — 315 Lexington Ave.

THE JEWS IN ART

Traditional Judaism bans the depiction of the human form in art, and this prohibition meant that until the nineteenth century, Jewish painters were largely isolated from mainstream European art movements and traditions. However, there were exceptions to the rule. Camille Pissarro, one of the most renowned Impressionists, painted *Women Haymaking* in 1889 (right); Amadeo Modigliani's *Nude* (below) is world-famous. Isidor Kaufmann's *Succoth* (detail, below right) takes a more conventional approach to its subject.

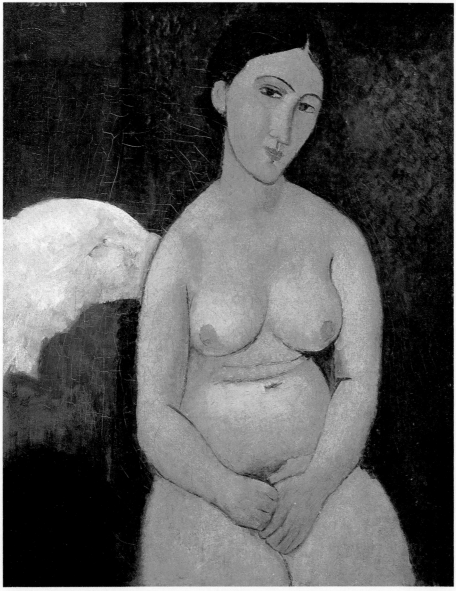

ally successful on the popular music scene until the 1950s. But the dominant figure in the music of Broadway and Hollywood during that period was Irving Berlin (*né* Israel Baline), who died in his 101st year in 1989. Other extremely influential songwriters were Oscar Hammerstein II (1895–1960) who, in partnership with Richard Rodgers, produced such hits as *Carousel, The King and I,* and *South Pacific,* and the team of Alan Jay Lerner (1918–86) and Frederick Loewe (1901–88), responsible for *My Fair Lady.* But for the Holocaust, Kurt Weill (1900–50) might have become the German Irving Berlin – before leaving for the United States in 1935, he wrote the music for the majority of Bertolt Brecht's musical plays, notably *The Three-penny Opera (Die Dreigroschenoper)* in 1928.

Jews have also featured prominently in American broadcasting and journalism. William Paley was the founder of the Columbia Broadcasting System (CBS) and Adolph Ochs of the *New York Times.* However, one of the best-known names in American newspaper publishing is that of Joseph Pulitzer (1847–1911), a Hungarian immigrant who came to the United States in 1868. Ten years later, he bought the *St. Louis Post Dispatch,* and then expanded his newspaper empire until it rivaled that of William Randolph Hearst. In particular, he made the *New York World* the largest circulation newspaper in the country by crusading for oppressed workers and against big business and government corruption. Unfortunately, Pulitzer and Hearst were jointly responsible for the decline in the standards of newspaper reporting that is known as "the gutter press" and "yellow journalism." In 1903, Pulitzer founded the world-famous Pulitzer School of Journalism at Columbia University, and to improve his image further, if only post-humously, he set up a trust fund in his will to provide the income for what would be the Pulitzer Prizes for journalism, letters, and music.

Some of the greatest authors and play-wrights of the modern era have been Jewish. They include, in Italy, Carlo Levi and Italo Svevo (pseudonym of Ettore Schmitz); in Austria, Franz Kafka, Stefan Zweig and Arthur Schnitzler; in France, Marcel Proust; and in Hungary, Ferenc Molnár. Despite centuries of isolation from European trends in art, due largely to the second command-ment's ban on the representation of the human form in Jewish art, great Jewish artists have emerged, including Pissarro, Modigliani, Soutine, and Chagall. The art historian and critic Bernard Berenson (1865–1959), strongly influenced contemporary taste.

All these individuals are just a few of the thousands of Jews who have contributed to modern culture, thought, and society. The impact of Jewish emancipation on nineteenth- and twentieth-century civiliza-tion as a whole has been incalculable and immensely enriching.

CHAPTER FIVE

THE DARK SIDE: ANTI-SEMITISM

E very era has found its own rationalizations for anti-Semitism, making it difficult to define. The definition in the *Concise Oxford Dictionary* – "hostility to Jews" – covers a vast range of sins. These include the polite refusal of a hotel clerk – with vacancies to offer – to accept a Jew's reservation, to restrictive laws, expulsions, executions, pogroms, and finally, the Holocaust. All these have been complicated by other factors in various societies at different times – class conflict, financial crisis, religious fanaticism, territorial encroachment, the ravages of disease – and the seemingly innate need of humans to find scapegoats.

The long catalogue of atrocities and banal, day-to-day adversities that make up the history of anti-Semitism turns the simple survival of the Jews into one of the most remarkable facets of the Jewish story.

Pre-Christian Anti-Semitism

The first manifestations of popular anti-Semitism may have occurred in ancient Egypt at the time of Moses. However, the first independently verified instances happened in the Holy Land among the mixture of races originally brought by the Babylonians to replace the Jews whom they had taken into captivity in 597 B.C.E. The descendants of these new residents, and other peoples who later joined them, enthusiastically embraced Hellenism (including the Greek pantheon of gods) following Alexander the Great's conquest of the Middle East. The Jews alone resisted attempts to divert them from their faith, causing resentment among the rest of the population.

This was exacerbated by the Jews' own social position. Those who returned from exile in Babylonia were granted a large measure of autonomy by successive rulers – above all, by the Persians. However, the

Seleucids (prior to Antiochus IV Epiphanes), the Ptolemies, and even the Romans, in the early days of their rule, all allowed the Jews privileges. To the pagans of the Holy Land, being Jewish came to mean belonging to a privileged, haughty, and élitist people with an incomprehensible religion. The New Testament story of the "Good Samaritan" clearly illustrates the contempt in which the Jews held even the Samaritans, despite the fact that these people were closest to them in religion and custom. The resent-

ABOVE: *The Wandering Jew is an archetypal figure in anti-Semitic mythology. There are various versions of the legend: according to one he was punished for mocking Christ on the way to the crucifixion by being condemned to wander the world until the Day of Judgment.*

ment of the non-Jews of the Holy Land expressed itself in the desecration of Jewish places of worship.

Anti-Semites down the centuries have sought legitimacy through literary or "historical" justification. The first of such propagandists was an Egyptian named Apion, who lived in Alexandria during the reign of the Roman emperor Tiberius (42 B.C.E.–C.E. 37). Among the claims that Apion made about the Jews and their history was the story that, once a year, Jews kidnapped a Greek and sacrificed his fattened body in the woods. This may be the origin of the myth of ritual murder, of which Jews have been accused through the ages, and which tells how the blood of the sacrificed gentile (often a child) is mixed with flour to make the unleavened bread eaten at Passover. Apion's writings have been lost, but the Jewish historian Josephus repeated the Egyptian's accusations in his own refutation of them, which he called *Against Apion*.

Apion was a great favorite of Tiberius, who called him *"cymbalum mundi,"* the "bell of the world." For his part, the Roman emperor, in what was the first persecution of the Jews in Rome, banished them from the city in C.E. 19 and even ordered the capital's synagogue to be stripped of its holy vessels.

Early Christian Anti-Semitism

Some parts of the Gospels were written at least 45 years after the death of Jesus, at a time when the Christians wished to placate the Romans. Responsibility for the crucifixion of Jesus is placed as much on "the Jews" – as on the Sanhedrin (the Jewish parliament which also acted as a court of law), or the high priest, or Judas the betrayer (his name, which means "Jew," is significant in this context), or the Romans themselves, as represented by Pontius Pilate. In fact historians have since shown that there was no custom of freeing a prisoner at Passover, as Pilate is alleged to have done to Barabbas (but not to Jesus). Nevertheless clerics, theologians, and Christian philosophers were able to find in the New Testament the clearcut "evidence" to hold the Jews collectively responsible for the death of their messiah.

As soon as Christianity became the official religion of the Roman Empire, its adherents were quick to show to others the intolerance

LEFT: *St. John Chrysostom, who became a priest in 386 and patriarch of Constantinople 12 years later, was the greatest of the Fathers of the Orthodox Church. Yet, despite his ascetic life and his noted charity, he, too, condemned the Jews, believing them to be responsible for the death of Christ, and so deserving of persecution.*

that had once been shown to them. Although in 313 the Emperor Constantine's Edict of Milan proclaimed Judaism to be, among others, a *religio licita* ("legal religion"), two years later he forbade conversion to Judaism and decreed that anyone found preaching Judaism to Christians would be burned alive. He restored the name of Jerusalem to the pagan city of Aelia Capitolina, but Jews were still forbidden entry except on one day a year – the 9th of Av, the anniversary of the destruction of the two Temples – when the Jews could come and mourn their loss. Constantine's son and successor, Constantius II, forbade all marriages between Jews and those of other religions.

The Roman Empire was divided into the eastern (or Byzantine) and western (or Latin) empires. The majority of Jews lived in the Byzantine Empire, where they suffered from the repressive measures of a number of emperors. In 414, the Christians of Alexandria rioted, breaking into and plundering synagogues and Jewish homes. The Jews were then banished from the city where they had lived for centuries. There were similar incidents in Minorca and in Syria, where synagogues were confiscated and turned into churches. This left the Jews without any places of worship for Theodosius II had issued a decree in 423 (renewed in 439) banning the building of synagogues. After the intercession of the prefect of Antioch, the emperor considered returning the confiscated synagogues to their rightful owners, but he was dissuaded by the hermit monk St. Simeon Stylites, who told him that he would be punished by God for assisting the "unbelieving Jews."

Other Church Fathers acted similarly. St. John Chrysostom, for example, wrote that in the synagogue "are gathered the murderers of Christ." St. Jerome described the Jews on their annual pilgrimage to Jerusalem as "hordes of wretches, not worthy of pity... their very exterior and clothing betraying the wrath of God" – this from a man who had asked the greatest of the contemporary Jewish sages, Bar Hanina, to teach him. (But, then, he did tell him to visit at night so that no one might see such a holy man consorting with a hated Jew.)

Christian theologians did not view the Jews as heretics or pagans, nor at this early stage did they advocate death for people in these categories. They did, however, see the Jews as the first people to reject Christ and considered them to be eternally damned for this and for their subsequent involvement in his execution. Only by accepting baptism could they be redeemed. At the same time, it was widely believed that all Jews would accept Christianity at the time of the Second Coming, and this is why the bishops often tried to halt the mob when it turned on the Jews. However, it was the hatred aroused by the writings of the Church Fathers that did much to incite laymen and the lower orders of the clergy to acts of anti-Semitic violence.

Christians were dismayed to find that the vast majority of Jews refused to convert to Christianity, unlike most of the pagans, who were subjected to the same restrictive measures and forced baptisms. Nevertheless, restrictions continued to be imposed. Whereas in 325 the Council of Nicaéa had forbidden Christians to celebrate their Easter at the same time as Passover, in 546 Justinian forbade the Jews to celebrate Passover at all if it fell before the Christian Easter. The reading aloud of translations of the Bible into Aramaic, Greek, or the vernacular – traditional since the time of Ezra and Nehemiah in the fourth century B.C.E. – was also forbidden, as was the study of the Talmud or any other commentaries on the Scriptures. Also under Justinian, Jews were even prevented from saying certain prayers that supposedly denied the Trinity: Imperial guards were posted in synagogues to make sure that they did not say, "The Lord is One," when intoning the Shema, their most solemn prayer, "Hear, O Israel."

Justinian has gone down in history as the great codifier of Roman law. The *Corpus Juris Civilis* authorized by the emperor was incorporated into the legal systems of most of the countries of Europe and, under Spanish influence, even farther afield in the New

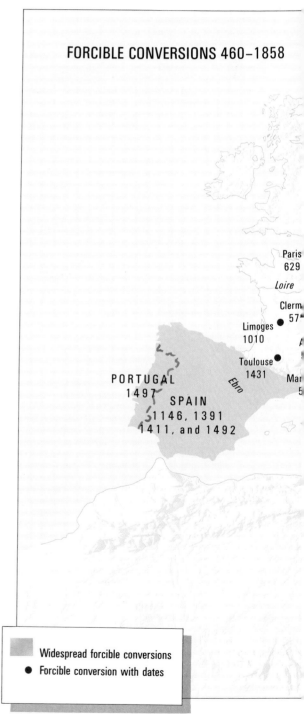

FORCIBLE CONVERSIONS 460–1858

Paris
629

Loire

Clerm
57

Limoges
1010

Toulouse
1431

Mar

PORTUGAL
1497

SPAIN
1146, 1391
1411, and 1492

Widespread forcible conversions
● Forcible conversion with dates

World. Unfortunately, it contained many anti-Jewish laws, some of which were not repealed until the nineteenth century.

New Rulers, New Perils

When the Roman Empire finally disintegrated in the fifth century, restrictions and prohibitions were lifted from many Jews. New rulers, in particular the Frankish kings who founded both France and the Holy Roman Empire in western Europe, proved more lenient. The Muslim caliphs of north Africa and the Middle East also treated them with the same tolerance that they extended to the Christians they had conquered.

The only exceptions to this Islamic tolerance were in Moorish Spain. The fanatical Almoravids, who conquered Morocco and Spain in the eleventh century, incited their fellow Muslims to attack anyone who would not convert to Islam. For instance, in 1066, a mob stormed through the Jewish quarter of Granada, pillaging and murdering; the situation became so bad that in 1090 the fam-

BELOW: With the accession of Constantine to the imperial throne and the subsequent establishment of Christianity as the official religion of the empire, anti-Jewish persecution grew, until, in the Eastern empire from 415 onward and later in medieval Europe, anti-Semitism had become inherent in Christian society.

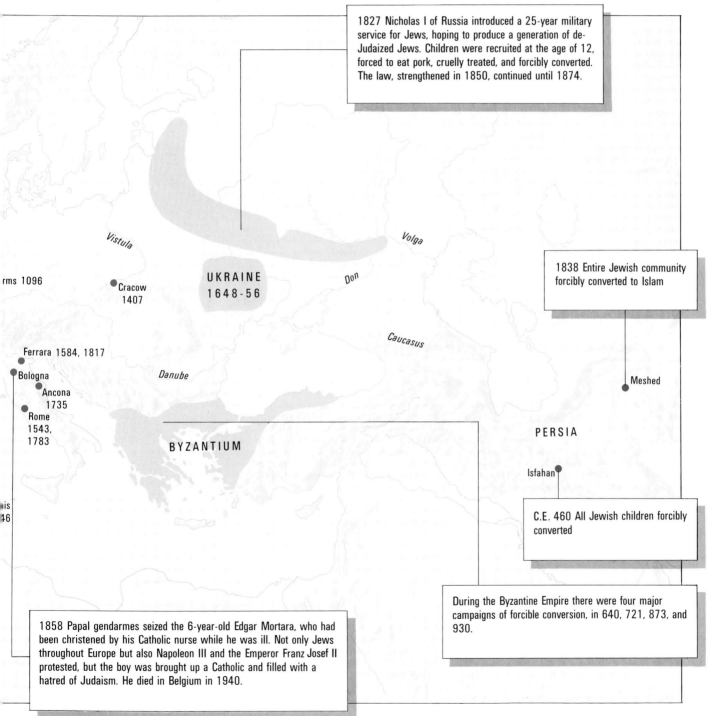

1827 Nicholas I of Russia introduced a 25-year military service for Jews, hoping to produce a generation of de-Judaized Jews. Children were recruited at the age of 12, forced to eat pork, cruelly treated, and forcibly converted. The law, strengthened in 1850, continued until 1874.

1838 Entire Jewish community forcibly converted to Islam

Meshed

rms 1096

Vistula

Cracow 1407

UKRAINE 1648-56

Volga

Don

Caucasus

Ferrara 1584, 1817

Bologna

Ancona 1735

Rome 1543, 1783

Danube

BYZANTIUM

PERSIA

Isfahan

C.E. 460 All Jewish children forcibly converted

During the Byzantine Empire there were four major campaigns of forcible conversion, in 640, 721, 873, and 930.

1858 Papal gendarmes seized the 6-year-old Edgar Mortara, who had been christened by his Catholic nurse while he was ill. Not only Jews throughout Europe but also Napoleon III and the Emperor Franz Josef II protested, but the boy was brought up a Catholic and filled with a hatred of Judaism. He died in Belgium in 1940.

ous Jewish philosopher and poet Moses ibn Ezra was forced to flee; he spent many years wandering in Christian Spain. The next wave of Muslim rulers from north Africa – the Almohads, who took over in Spain in the twelfth century – were equally intolerant. The family of the young Maimonides had to emigrate from Córdoba to Egypt as a result.

The Crusades and Mob Violence

Of all the hardships and tragedies that befell European Jewry during the Middle Ages, the worst occurred as the result of the Crusades. All over Europe, the armies ostensibly on their way to recapture the Holy Land from the infidel first turned on the infidels in their midst: the Jews. In this, they were inspired by clerics such as Peter of Cluny who wrote: "Why should we seek the enemies of Christ in distant lands when the blasphemous Jews live among us?" The bishops of Regensburg, Mainz, Worms, and other cities sheltered Jews in an attempt to maintain order and out of common humanity, but their efforts were sometimes in vain, for the mobs would occasionally storm the episcopal palaces. The flourishing Jewish communities of Mainz and Worms were destroyed, as were those of Trier, Cologne, and Strasbourg. Jews who did not submit to forced baptism were murdered; many others committed suicide.

The Jewish community of the Rhineland was the oldest in northern Europe, having been in existence since Roman times, and it had produced some of the greatest Jewish scholars. In 1146, for the first time in its history, the local Gentile population carried out a massacre of the Jews, incited by itinerants such as the monk Radulf who went from city to city preaching vengeance for "the Crucified One upon those of His enemies who live here in our midst." In the following year, the killings spread to northern France: the home of the leader of the French-Jewish community, Jacob Tam, was looted and he was attacked, his life being spared only through the intercession of a Crusader knight.

There were similar incidents in England, the first provoked by the Third Crusade (1189–92). The initial outbreak took place during the coronation of King Richard I in September 1189; then, on March 17, and, 1190, the Jews of York were herded into a

castle, where they were held prisoner by the mob. Rather than wait to be massacred, all 150 prisoners – men, women, and children – committed suicide.

The Eighth Crusade of 1270–2 was the last and least successful attempt to retain a foothold in the Holy Land. All hope for this died in 1291 with the loss of Acre, the only stronghold remaining of the so-called Latin kingdoms established by the Crusaders. Frustration about this may have been at the root of the Rindfleisch massacres.

The pretext for these attacks was the Jews' alleged desecration of the Host (the blessed bread distributed during the Eucharist). In 1243, this had been used for the first time as an excuse for an anti-Semitic massacre – all the Jews of Belitz near Berlin were burned to death. However, it is now known that when the starch in bread deteriorates, it can be attacked by a red mold, giving the consecrated bread the appearance of exuding blood.

ABOVE: *A fifteenth-century German broadsheet reports, in comic-strip style, how Jews allegedly stole and desecrated the Host. After using the Host as part of a ritual (top right), they return it to the church. However, their interference is detected, and in the third row of pictures they are tortured and executed. The Jews were repeatedly accused of this particular blasphemy. In the late thirteenth century it sparked off the Rindfleisch massacres, which took place in southern Germany and Austria between 1281 and 1298.*

JEWISH DRESS

Outside their ghettoes, Jews were forced to wear distinctive articles of clothing so they could be instantly identified. One such example was the conical hat, known as the *cornutus pileus* (below right); the group of Jews pictured here is receiving a letter of safe conduct from the Holy Roman Emperor Henry VII after his coronation in 1312. Judaism, too, has its own distinctive dress regulation. A man's head must always be covered – either by a hat or a skull-cap and a woman's by a headscarf. These examples show an eighteenth-century Jew from Berlin (below left) and nineteenth-century Jews in Odessa (bottom). There is also a Biblical prohibition on shaving, which meant that, for centuries, Jewish males and beards were inseparable. Today, however, the Orthodox can use a special razor.

JEWISH DRESS

RIGHT: *The sack of Jerusalem in 1099 by the Crusaders. The Muslim rulers of Palestine had allowed the Jews to live in peace, but the Crusaders showed no such toleration, exterminating Jew and Muslim alike during their campaigns.*

BELOW: *During the Middle Ages a series of disputations between Christians and Jews took place. Some were serious theological debates, but others were intended to provoke anti-Jewish violence. An example of the former is the disputation held at Tortosa in 1413-14 on the orders of Pope Benedict XIII, which used Talmudic evidence in an attempt to prove that Jesus was, in fact, the true Messiah.*

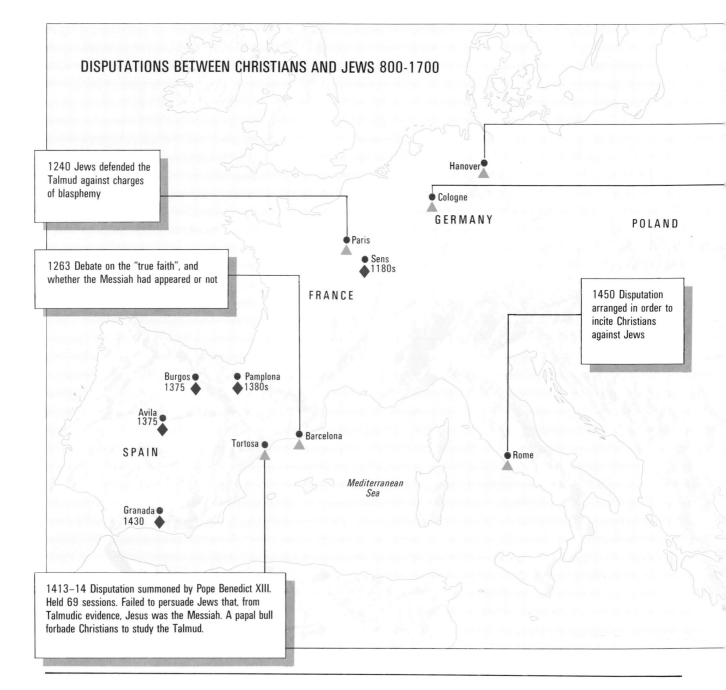

DISPUTATIONS BETWEEN CHRISTIANS AND JEWS 800-1700

1240 Jews defended the Talmud against charges of blasphemy

1263 Debate on the "true faith", and whether the Messiah had appeared or not

1450 Disputation arranged in order to incite Christians against Jews

Hanover

Cologne

GERMANY

POLAND

Paris

Sens
1180s

FRANCE

Burgos
1375

Pamplona
1380s

Avila
1375

Tortosa

Barcelona

SPAIN

Rome

Mediterranean Sea

Granada
1430

1413–14 Disputation summoned by Pope Benedict XIII. Held 69 sessions. Failed to persuade Jews that, from Talmudic evidence, Jesus was the Messiah. A papal bull forbade Christians to study the Talmud.

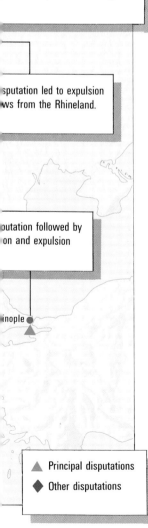

700 Christians failed to convert the Jews. The Jews said: "We believe what we have been taught; let the Christians adhere to what they have been taught."

sputation led to expulsion ws from the Rhineland.

putation followed by on and expulsion

nople

▲ Principal disputations
◆ Other disputations

RIGHT: *A dispute between Christians and Jews (the Jews can be identified by their distinctive conical hats). Sometimes, these were serious theological debates; at other times they served as a deliberate catalyst to stir up latent Christian anti-Semitism.*

This may have been what happened in southern Germany in the latter part of the thirteenth century. Rindfleisch, a knight of the Teutonic order, claimed that God had chosen him to avenge this desecration, and he and his band massacred Jews throughout Franconia, Bavaria, and Austria between 1281 and 1298, attacking 140 Jewish communities in the last year alone. Those who did not die at the hands of Rindfleisch and his men, killed themselves rather than be caught.

Discrimination, Ridicule, and Book Burning

The "danger" of the unconverted Jews was one of the major items on the agenda at the Fourth Lateran Council, convened in 1215 by Pope Innocent III. Besides reforming the Benedictines and Augustines, the council decreed that Jews should wear special dress to distinguish them from other people. Contemporary illustrations show them wearing badges consisting of a yellow circle, as well as other distinctive items of clothing such as the strange conical hat – the *cornutus pileus* – which, in Bohemia, had to be green. (In the mid-sixteenth century, Pope Paul IV would make the Jews wear a yellow hat.) All these items certainly made the Jews stand out in a crowd – and made them easy targets for Christians who, at Easter, were permitted by the clergy to throw stones and generally abuse the Jews.

Christian and Jewish theologians had traditionally engaged in religious disputations, during which, the Church reckoned, the public who assembled to listen would perceive the clear supremacy of Christianity in any argument. In fact, from the Church's point of view, the disputations were usually a dismal failure since the rabbis were, in general, much more learned than their Christian opponents – hardly surprising when it is remembered that Judaism places a high value on learning and that this was an age when the vast majority of Christians, including many of the lower clergy, were illiterate. In fact, precisely because of this, uneducated priests in the Rhineland and elsewhere in Germany were specifically forbidden to challenge rabbis to an argument. Finally, in 1233, Pope Gregory IX issued a total ban on such debates.

Many important anti-Semitic images and

symbols date from this period. On the portals of churches and on Bible covers in France and Germany, there appeared carvings or reliefs showing two women – *Ecclesia et Synagoga* – the one triumphant, the other blindfolded and carrying a broken lance. Another popular symbol was the "Jews' sow": Jews were often portrayed suckling the teats of sows or even eating their excrement. This specifically German motif began to appear in drawings and sculptures in the fourteenth century.

Throughout the Middle Ages, various prohibitions on the study or public reading by Jews of the Talmud and other interpretations of the Old Testament were introduced by the Christian clergy, as well as public burnings of these books. In 1240, the Talmud was actually put on trial in Paris by a panel of judges comprising Christian clerics (the result, a foregone conclusion). The Jews managed to obtain a stay of execution for two years, but in 1242 time ran out and all copies of the Talmud that could be found were publicly burned.

Attacks on Jewish religious literature continued. In 1559, in compliance with the instructions of Pope Paul IV, the inquisitor-general of Milan, Cardinal Ghislieri (the future Pius V), ordered the Talmud to be

RIGHT: *This fifteenth-century illustration comes from a life of St. Simon of Trent, who, it was alleged, was ritually murdered by Jews in 1475 while still a child.*

OPPOSITE PAGE: *St. Bernardino of Siena and a female saint presenting a donor to the Virgin and Child. Along with other Franciscan and Dominican friars he preached conversion sermons to the Jews.*

BELOW: *Throughout the Middle Ages, rabbinical councils were held to refine and codify Talmudic law. The result was a complex, but clearly defined, legal system that not only became binding on all Jews, but had a major impact on the development of gentile law of the period. One of the most important of these councils was held at Mainz in 1000 under the chairmanship of Rabbi Gershom ben Judah.*

burned at Cremona, the Italian center of Jewish learning, which had an early Hebrew printing press. Some 12,000 copies of the Talmud and other religious works were burned in the marketplace.

Plague and Panic

During the Middle Ages Jews were frequently accused of the ritual murder of Christian children. Such accusations were made in England, at Norwich in 1146 and at Lincoln in 1225; in France at Blois in 1171; and in northern Italy at Trent in 1475. All these supposed "victims" of the Jews were eventually canonized. Statues to one of them – St. Simon of Trent – were erected in various parts of Europe; in Frankfurt, the statue depicted the Jews with the Devil.

In 1320, a group of impoverished peasants and shepherds left their homes in northern France on what became known as the "Shepherds' Crusade." Urged on by mystics and preachers, they marched southward into the province of Aquitaine, massacring any Jews in their path. In the small town of Moissac, just north of Toulouse, there is a place today known as *Trou-aux-Juifs* ("Jews' Hole") because it was the site of one of these massacres. The mob marched into Spain, committing further atrocities. They eventually turned on the Christian clergy: they were soon captured and put to death.

The Aquitanian Jews' problems were not yet over. In 1321 the story was spread that, in revenge for their treatment by the Shepherds' Crusade and by those of the local population who had helped them, Jews and lepers had conspired together to poison the

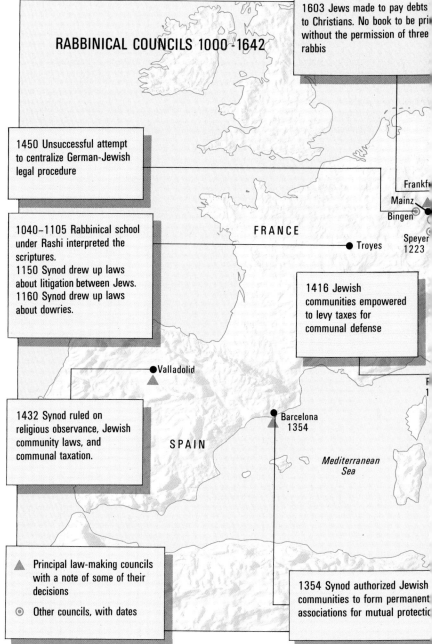

RABBINICAL COUNCILS 1000-1642

1603 Jews made to pay debts to Christians. No book to be pri[nted] without the permission of three rabbis

1450 Unsuccessful attempt to centralize German-Jewish legal procedure

1040–1105 Rabbinical school under Rashi interpreted the scriptures.
1150 Synod drew up laws about litigation between Jews.
1160 Synod drew up laws about dowries.

FRANCE

Troyes

Frankf[urt]
Mainz
Bingen
Speyer 1223

1416 Jewish communities empowered to levy taxes for communal defense

Valladolid

1432 Synod ruled on religious observance, Jewish community laws, and communal taxation.

Barcelona 1354

SPAIN

Mediterranean Sea

▲ Principal law-making councils with a note of some of their decisions

◉ Other councils, with dates

1354 Synod authorized Jewish communities to form permanent associations for mutual protecti[on]

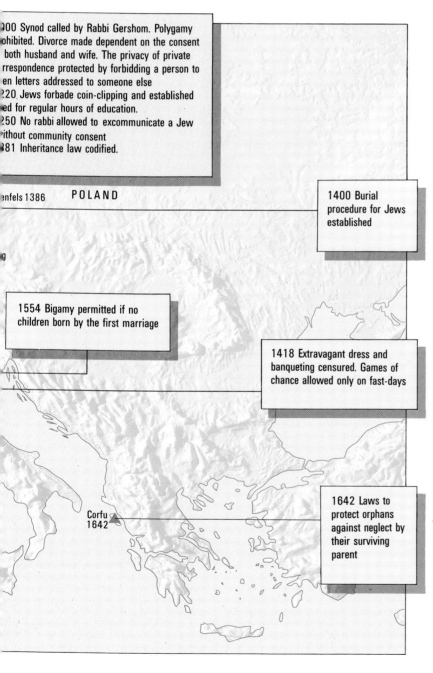

)00 Synod called by Rabbi Gershom. Polygamy
ohibited. Divorce made dependent on the consent
both husband and wife. The privacy of private
rrespondence protected by forbidding a person to
en letters addressed to someone else
!20. Jews forbade coin-clipping and established
ed for regular hours of education.
!50 No rabbi allowed to excommunicate a Jew
rithout community consent
!81 Inheritance law codified.

enfels 1386

1400 Burial
procedure for Jews
established

1554 Bigamy permitted if no
children born by the first marriage

1418 Extravagant dress and
banqueting censured. Games of
chance allowed only on fast-days

1642 Laws to
protect orphans
against neglect by
their surviving
parent

Corfu
1642

wells, using a concoction composed of human blood, urine, powdered consecrated bread, and three secret herbs. There were many arrests, trials, and executions for such alleged poisonings, including the famous burning of 160 Jews at Chinon in the Loire valley. The King, Philip V (reigned 1317–22), taking advantage of the situation, imposed huge fines on the Jews of Paris.

During the fourteenth century Europe was devastated by a series of disastrous harvests and subsequent famine, followed, in 1347–50 and after, by the Black Death. As catastrophe piled on catastrophe, the continent became a breeding ground for fantastic superstitions and prejudice. Life for the Jews was bound to get worse. The Black Death first raged through Europe in 1347–50, eventually killing 25–50 percent of the entire population. According to the contemporary account of the Italian poet Giovanni Boccaccio, "Men fell sick by their thousands, and lacking care and help, almost all of them died." All over Europe – in Switzerland, Italy, Germany, and France – the Jews were held responsible. It was in vain that Pope Clement VI published a papal bull in 1348 in which he reminded the faithful that Jews were dying of the plague just like the Christians, and that there had been outbreaks of the Black Death where there were no Jews at all. In parts of Alsace and western Germany, there are today places with names such as *Judenloch* ("Jews' Hole") and *Judenbühl* ("Jews' Mound") – evidence that here Jews were massacred for their alleged spreading of the plague.

Failed Conversion and Expulsion

The Council of Basel (1431–49) decreed that if Jews wanted to be admitted to universities, they would be compelled (by force if necessary) to listen to conversion sermons. Franciscan and Dominican friars, such as St. Bernardino of Siena and Bernardino de Feltre, enthusiastically began to preach to the Jews. The conversion sermons proved ineffective: in most parts of Europe Jews would rather die than convert.

As a result, there was a new wave of expulsions. During the first half of the fifteenth century, Jews were expelled from Mainz, Speyer, Augsburg, and Zurich and from Saxony, Moldavia, and Poland. Accompanied by violence and looting, these expul-

The Origins of the Ghetto

The requirements of the Jewish religion – for instance, there must be a minimum of ten men present before any act of public worship can take place – as well as the desirability of mutual protection had meant that Jews gathered together in particular neighborhoods. However, in most places, not all Jews lived in these, and there was no restriction on their size. The sixteenth-century Jewish quarters of such cities as Cologne might even contain Christian homes and public buildings, just as mainly Jewish neighborhoods in London, Paris, and New York do today.

However, the Jews were now forced to live

ABOVE: *The "Jewish sow" was a potent anti-Semitic symbol in Germany from the fourteenth century onward.*

RIGHT: *Martin Luther, the founding father of Protestantism. Though accused by his Catholic opponents of Judaic sympathies, Luther was quick to condemn Jews for refusing to turn to the new religion. Among the pamphlets he published was* The Jews and Their Lies, *in which he parroted current anti-Semitic calumnies.*

OPPOSITE PAGE: *The drive to confine the Jews of western Europe to specially designated ghettoes was given full Papal sanction in 1555, when Pope Paul IV called for their creation throughout Catholic Europe; in North Africa, Muslim rulers created their own equivalent – the Mellah. The Russian solution was the most extreme; from 1835 until the 1917 Revolution, the majority of Russian Jews were forced to live in an area known as the "Pale," where they faced the continual threat of pogrom.*

sions were mainly inspired by the fanatical inquisitor Friar John of Capistrano (1386–1456), who was later canonized.

Sigismund – king of Hungary from 1386 and of Bohemia from 1419 and Holy Roman emperor from 1433 to 1437 – confiscated one third of Jewish wealth, and gave his blessing to a massacre of Jews by his troops. They had been on their way to yet another "holy war" – this time against the followers of the Protestant reformer Jan Hus of Bohemia, who had been burned as a heretic in 1415.

Duke Albrecht of Austria, claiming that Austrian Jews were supporting the Hussites, stole their children and forcibly baptized them and, in 1421, burned 200 Jews at the stake at Vienna; the rest were expelled from Austria and their property confiscated. Albrecht succeeded Sigismund as Holy Roman emperor in 1438, and before he died the following year, he insisted that his burning of the Jews be recorded on his tombstone.

The great Protestant reformers – Calvin, Hus, Zwingli, and Luther – were all accused of being Jewish sympathizers, or "judaizers." This is especially ironic in Luther's case. Like many Christian reformers before him, he had assumed that, when the corruption of the Catholic Church had been exposed and a new church founded, Jews would flock to the baptismal font. His frustration at their refusal to do so was first expressed in 1538 in a pamphlet entitled *Letter against the Sabbathists*, which was followed by *The Jews and Their Lies*, in which he repeated all the calumnies leveled against the Jews throughout the Middle Ages: the poisoning of wells, ritual murder, the desecration of the Host.

in specially designated areas. In his papal bull of 1555 entitled *Cum nimis absurdum*, Pope Paul IV (reigned 1555–59) directed the erection of ghettos throughout Catholic Europe, especially in German-speaking countries.

The origin of the word "ghetto" is obscure. One explanation is that it derives from *borghetto*, the Italian word for "little town" or "suburb." Another is that it is derived from La Gheta, the name of the gun foundry that stood near the Venice Ghetto – the first compulsory Jewish quarter in Italy, established in 1516.

Gradually, every city in Italy that had not already expelled its Jews erected a ghetto to pen them in. After Cardinal Ghislieri be-

THE GHETTO AND THE PALE
1215–1870

Areas within which anti-Jewish riots took place, 1347–50

Some of the towns in which Jews were murdered, 1347–50

Principal ghettoes established by order of the city or state authorities, within which the Jews were forced to live

Countries in which the Jews lived in close-knit communities, subject to legal penalties if they moved outside their part of the town

The Pale of Settlement within which the majority of Russian Jews were forced to live 1835-1917

Muslim North Africa, where Jews lived in a special quarter, the Mellah, but were not subjected to the same restrictions and indignities as in Christian Europe

Church Councils that decreed that Jews must wear a special badge on their clothes. Sometimes this took the form of a yellow Star of David.

1662 Jews compelled to move to "swine's dungheap"

Jews lived in parts of towns called the "Juderia".

Before 1497 Jews lived in "Judiaria". If found outside the ghetto during the night, they were whipped through the streets.

came pope as Pius V (reigned 1566–72), he ordered the expulsion of the Jews from the Papal states. However, for commercial reasons, they were allowed to remain, under humiliating conditions, in Ancona (where the many marrano refugees had already been subjected to the Inquisition by Paul IV, and 25 had been burned at the stake) and in Rome, where they were forced into a small area near Trastevere – for many centuries a poor Jewish quarter. The Jews were allowed to return to the Papal states after the death of Pius V, and were also to be found in the French territories of Carpentras and Avignon, which at that time were still part of papal lands. The ghettos that were built to hold them were surrounded by their own walls, with only one gate, which was locked from dusk to dawn. In Italy, they were to remain in existence until the nineteenth century, the last ghetto, located in Rome, not being abolished until 1870.

Fettmilch and the Thirty Years' War

Just prior to the Thirty Years' War (1618–48), a new wave of anti-Semitism swept over central Europe, instigated by the burghers of Frankfurt-on-Main and led by a baker, one Vincenz Fettmilch. Rioters stormed the Jewish quarter there, murdering and robbing; then Fettmilch and his men assembled the remaining 1380 Jews in the cemetery, robbed them of all their possessions and turned them naked out of the city. (In 1615, a similar incident occurred in the Rhineland, at Worms, one of the oldest Jewish settlements outside the Holy Land.)

However, this time the Jews of Frankfurt received justice. Ferdinand, the archduke of Styria and later (1619–37) Holy Roman emperor, needed the Jews to raise money for the conflict that was on the horizon. He had Fettmilch executed and the Jews were allowed to return to their homes.

European Jews had a brief respite from persecution during the Thirty Years' War: their financial contribution to the economies of the warring states was too valuable. However, shortly after peace returned in 1648, it was the turn of the Jews of eastern Europe to suffer renewed and savage persecution.

Bogdan Chmielnicki and the Cossacks

Over the years, the Jews had found sanctuary in Poland – first, from the persecutions in France and Germany and, later, from the Spanish Inquisition.

In 1648, a band of Ukrainian Cossacks, under their leader Bogdan Chmielnicki, rampaged through the countryside. Although their grudge was against the Polish-Catholic estate owners, whom they claimed had ruthlessly exploited the Orthodox peasantry, they spared their lives and those of the Orthodox priests. Instead, their victims were Jewish men, women and children and, to a lesser extent, Catholic priests.

Chmielnicki's hordes – joined by Tatars from the Crimea as well as by Russians living in Poland – raged through Volhynia and Podolia, laying waste every city they came to and sparing only those of the Jews who had converted to Christianity. The carnage spread well beyond Poland and the Ukraine to Lithuania and Byelorussia. In the latter, in the city of Gomel, the Cossacks bribed the city prefect to hand over the Jews to them; all

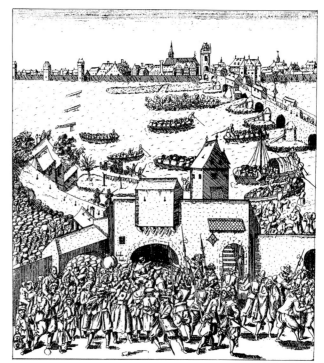

died rather than convert. It was only when a Polish army finally managed to defeat the Cossacks in 1651 that the atrocities ceased, at least temporarily.

In the meantime, Chmielnicki had concluded an alliance with the Russian tsar, Alexei Mikhailovich (reigned 1645–76), who saw in this an opportunity to seize Poland. Under Alexei's protection, the Cossacks murdered or drove out the Jews from all the major cities of Byelorussia and Lithuania – Polotsk, Vitebsk, Minsk and Vilna – and in 1655, they massacred the Jews of Lvov in the Ukraine. In a period of eight years – from 1648 to 1656 – as many as 500,000 Jews died in Poland and the western Russian Empire. It was the Jews' greatest catastrophe since the fall of the Second Temple, and the numbers of those who died were not to be exceeded until the Holocaust.

Jews flocked westward out of Poland, but late emigrants found their way barred. In 1669, the emperor, Leopold I, banned the Jews from Austria – both those who had come as refugees and those who had returned following the expulsion of 1421. The Jewish quarter of Vienna was renamed Leopoldstadt, and a church was erected over the site of the synagogue, with a foundation stone that claimed that it stood over what once had been a "den of thieves".

LEFT: *Bogdan Chmielnicki.*

FAR LEFT: *The exodus of the Jews from Frankfurt in 1614.*

BELOW: *Led by Bogdan Chmielnicki, the Cossacks rose against the Polish nobility in 1648 and, after defeating the Polish army, joined with the peasantry to turn on the Jews. The violence that followed lasted off and on for eight years; over 100,000 Jews were killed in Poland alone, while hundreds of thousands more were slaughtered in Russia after Chmielnicki allied himself with Tsar Alexei Mikhailovich.*

It is perhaps not surprising that it was now that the legend of the "Wandering Jew" was born, one version of which said that a Jew who had laughed at Jesus on the cross was condemned to wander the earth for ever.

Persecution in the "Age of Reason"

As the so-called Age of Reason dawned in the eighteenth century, anti-Semitism took on a more "rational" guise. The century saw the emergence of major anti-Jewish writings, most of them claiming scholarly and ancient foundations for their theories.

The most influential was a weighty tome written by a Protestant theologian of Frankfurt-on-Main. Johann Andreas Eisenmenger (1654–1704), who was also a professor of Oriental languages at Heidelberg University, scoured the Talmud for anything that could be construed as anti-Christian. The result of his labors was a book whose lengthy

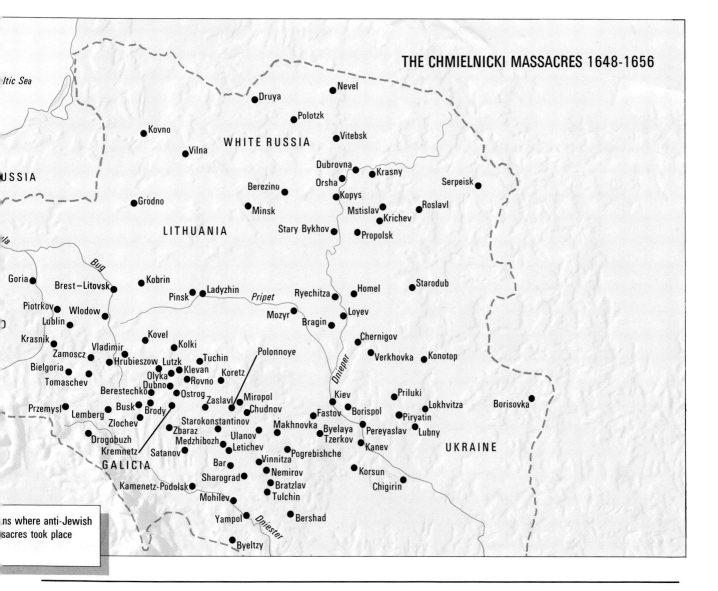

THE CHMIELNICKI MASSACRES 1648-1656

ns where anti-Jewish
sacres took place

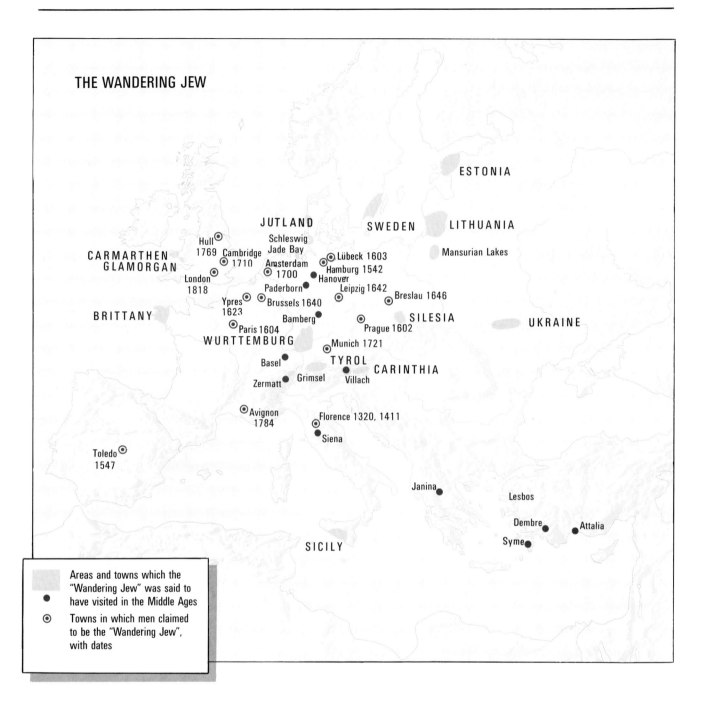

THE WANDERING JEW

ESTONIA

JUTLAND

SWEDEN LITHUANIA

Hull
1769 Schleswig
Cambridge Jade Bay
1710
CARMARTHEN
GLAMORGAN

Mansurian Lakes

Lübeck 1603

Amsterdam
London 1700 Hamburg 1542
1818 Hanover
Paderborn Leipzig 1642
Ypres Breslau 1646
1623 Brussels 1640
Bamberg SILESIA UKRAINE
BRITTANY Prague 1602
Paris 1604
WURTTEMBURG
Munich 1721

Basel TYROL CARINTHIA
Grimsel
Zermatt Villach

Avignon
1784 Florence 1320, 1411

Siena

Toledo
1547

Janina
Lesbos

Dembre Attalia
Syme
SICILY

Areas and towns which the
"Wandering Jew" was said to
have visited in the Middle Ages

Towns in which men claimed
to be the "Wandering Jew",
with dates

title begins *Judaism Unmasked...(Entdecktes Judenthum...)*.

The Jewish community of Frankfurt, hearing that this was about to be published and worried that it might incite violence when feelings were already running high, begged the Court Jews Samson Wertheimer and Joseph Süss Oppenheimer (*see* Chapter 3) to use their influence to get the book banned by the imperial authorities in Vienna. They were partially successful: publication was stopped in the Austrian territories, but it was allowed

in Prussia. First published there in 1699, *Judaism Unmasked...* became a bestseller, running into many editions and fueling the fires of anti-Semitism for decades to come.

The Court Jews were soon called upon for more help, and again, Frankfurt-on-Main was the center of the trouble. In early 1711, after fire broke out in the home of Rabbi Naphthali Cohen, the blaze spread rapidly and destroyed most of the tightly packed houses in the ghetto. It was the depths of winter and not only were the homeless re-

fused shelter by Christians outside the ghetto walls, but the town council also refused to allow the Jews to rebuild their homes. The Court Jews appealed to the emperor, Joseph I, who ordered "the rebuilding of the Jews' Street, so that the Jewry may as soon as possible once again be able to return to their former dwellings."

With Joseph's death in April of 1711, the fortunes of the Jews in the Habsburg Empire worsened considerably. In 1712, his successor, Charles VI, acceded to a petition presented by Christian merchants in Vienna. They asked for yet another expulsion of the Jews – those who had returned following the previous banning in 1669 – claiming that "unless the Jewry is entirely removed from the city, the citizens will be reduced to beggary." Most were expelled. Of those who remained, only the eldest son was permitted to marry, and those who were employed by a Jew could not have their wives and children resident in the city. Jews were also subject to what was then termed "separation": they were not allowed to move about in any part of the city that was inhabited by Christians, or to loiter in the vicinity of churches. By 1727, these measures had been extended to Bohemia by the Habsburgs.

The fortunes of the few privileged Court Jews were in decline, as their royal masters discovered more pressing claims on their purses than honoring their debts to their factors and financiers, and in 1738 Joseph Süss Oppenheimer, who had had a brilliant career at the court of the duke of Württemberg, was tried and executed (*see* Chapter 3). After his death, his story went through a series of strange changes: it was told in the 1917 novel *Jew Süss* by Lion Feuchtwanger, but Feuchtwanger's highly sympathetic portrait was later twisted into an anti-Semitic tract in the Nazi propaganda film of the same name, released under the patronage of Josef Goebbels in 1940.

The rule of the Austrian empress Maria Theresa, Charles VI's daughter, from 1740 to 1780 was, in many ways, even worse than her father's. In the disastrous wars with the Prussians, Bavarians, and French (all of whom disputed Maria Theresa's right to the Habsburg throne), Jews were accused of conspiring with the enemy and thus losing

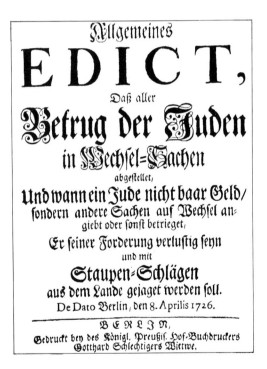

battles for her. Terrible revenge was taken on the Prague Ghetto in 1744, after Frederick II of Prussia captured and then was driven out of the city. Informed of the Jews' "treason" – one accusation being that, during the long-distance bombardments by the Prussians, not a single shell had fallen into the ghetto – Maria Theresa ordered them to be banished from Bohemia. The authorities there sent a letter to the empress pointing out that the Jews had done nothing to merit expulsion, but they did not even receive a reply. More than 10,000 Jews found it necessary to leave Prague. Only 2,000 remained – hostages until 120,000 *guilders* had been raised to ransom them. The empress then issued a similar order expelling the Jews from Moravia.

Maria Theresa's British and Dutch allies intervened on the Jews' behalf. The empress relented and, in 1748, allowed the Jews to return to the provinces of what is now Czechoslovakia. However, in 1753 and 1764, she issued decrees against the few Jews remaining in her own capital, Vienna, ordering them to wear a yellow ribbon in their hats and forbidding them to shave their beards or to employ fellow Jews in factories. She once wrote, "I know of no worse plague than this nation. Therefore as far as possible, they are to be kept away from here and their numbers kept down," yet she was as eager as the rulers of the German states to employ Jewish bankers and financiers.

Two kings of Prussia, Frederick William (reigned 1713–40) and his son, Frederick the Great (reigned 1740–86), both imposed severe restrictions on the Jews. As soon as he came to the throne, Frederick William decreed that only Jews who could prove that they were worth at least 10,000 *thalers* were permitted to live in Berlin, and that only the oldest child in every Jewish family could marry; a heavy marriage tax on Jews was also introduced. Jews could practice only a limited number of crafts, and all professions were forbidden to them.

Both Frederick the Great and his contemporary Maria Theresa acquired great numbers of Jewish subjects through the conquest of foreign lands. In 1772 Maria Theresa annexed Galicia in southern Poland, which had a Jewish community, as did the province of Silesia, which Frederick won at the start of the War of the Austrian Succession in 1741. He immediately ordered the expulsion of "excessive, unnecessary Jews" from the largest city – Breslau (Wroclaw) – allowing only 12 families to remain. Similarly when he acquired the Polish city of Posen (now Poznan) in 1772, he restricted the freedom of its large Jewish community.

Frederick William's prohibitions on marriage and on practicing trades were exten-

Is oufgezogen das ganze Regiment.

ded by his son in 1750, although from 1763 Frederick the Great agreed, in exchange for a huge bribe, to allow second-born Jewish children to marry. Like his father, he still needed his Jewish bankers and financiers, however. He ordered the most powerful of them – Veitel Ephraim, owner of the only mint in Prussia – to strike debased foreign coins, to be used, he said, to undermine the trading abilities of his adversaries. However, the coins were in fact used by the king in his own country to amass a fortune. The Prussians held the Jews responsible for the resulting economic crisis.

ABOVE: *The new German nationalism had little sympathy with the Jews, as this satirical print demonstrates. The Jews were seen as protecting their own self-interest, rather than rallying to the banner of a united Germany.*

Persecution in Nineteenth-century Germany

German Jews enjoyed a brief period of emancipation in those states that had been conquered by Napoleon. In addition, the king of Prussia, Frederick William III (reigned 1797–1840), was forced by his ministers to agree to liberalization since Jewish finance and enterprise were needed: the Jews were granted equal rights, although they continued to be barred from holding public office. The grand duke of Baden also granted equal rights, but as soon as Napoleon fell, and despite the fact that they had flocked to Baden's colors to defend the territory against the French, the Jews were sent back to the ghetto. The excuse was that the Jews had refused to abandon certain tenets of their religion in exchange for the dubious honor of offering their lives in battle.

BELOW: *Throughout the nineteenth century, anti-Semitism was a prevalent and powerful political and social force in Continental Europe.*

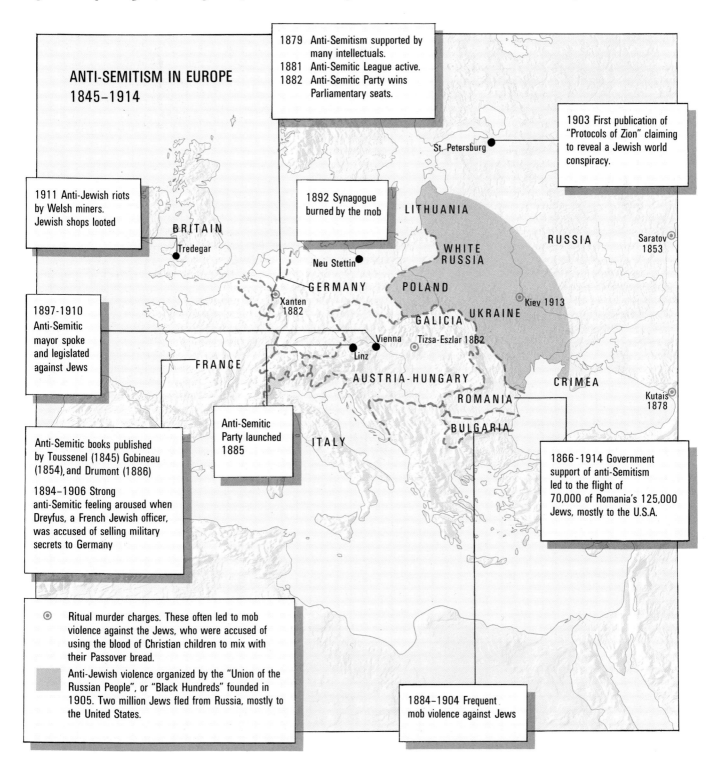

ANTI-SEMITISM IN EUROPE
1845–1914

1879 Anti-Semitism supported by many intellectuals.
1881 Anti-Semitic League active.
1882 Anti-Semitic Party wins Parliamentary seats.

1903 First publication of "Protocols of Zion" claiming to reveal a Jewish world conspiracy.

1911 Anti-Jewish riots by Welsh miners. Jewish shops looted

1892 Synagogue burned by the mob

1897-1910 Anti-Semitic mayor spoke and legislated against Jews

Anti-Semitic books published by Toussenel (1845) Gobineau (1854), and Drumont (1886)

1894–1906 Strong anti-Semitic feeling aroused when Dreyfus, a French Jewish officer, was accused of selling military secrets to Germany

Anti-Semitic Party launched 1885

1866-1914 Government support of anti-Semitism led to the flight of 70,000 of Romania's 125,000 Jews, mostly to the U.S.A.

⊙ Ritual murder charges. These often led to mob violence against the Jews, who were accused of using the blood of Christian children to mix with their Passover bread.

Anti-Jewish violence organized by the "Union of the Russian People", or "Black Hundreds" founded in 1905. Two million Jews fled from Russia, mostly to the United States.

1884–1904 Frequent mob violence against Jews

St. Petersburg

LITHUANIA

WHITE RUSSIA

RUSSIA

Saratov 1853

Tredegar

BRITAIN

Neu Stettin

GERMANY

POLAND

Kiev 1913

Xanten 1882

GALICIA

UKRAINE

FRANCE

Vienna

Tizsa-Eszlar 1882

Linz

AUSTRIA-HUNGARY

CRIMEA

Kutais 1878

ROMANIA

ITALY

BULGARIA

A draft constitution for the whole of Germany (then a loose alliance of various states), approved by the Austrian Prince Metternich, contained a clause granting equal rights to Jews, but the majority of delegates to the Congress of Vienna (1814–15) opposed it. Finally, a clause was agreed giving Jews equal rights only in those states that had been included in Napoleon's Confederation of the Rhine. However, in Frankfurt-on-Main in the Grand Duchy of Hesse, where the Jews had ostensibly been emancipated in 1806, they were again subjected to every kind of harassment by the local authorities. The Jews took legal action, ending in 1816 in an address by the Jewish community of Frankfurt to the Diet of the German Confederation then sitting in their city.

But the harshest German state was Prussia. In 1846 more than one third of the Jews had no civil rights at all, and the Prussian Jew Laws, enacted the following year, continued to exclude Jews from positions of authority. However, there were exceptions, such as in the city of Posen, where they had a larger measure of autonomy.

German Nationalism and the "Hep! Hep!" Riots

Throughout the nineteenth century the rise of German nationalism was tainted with anti-Semitism. Johann Gottlieb Fichte (1762–1814), who became the first rector of the new Berlin University in 1810, attacked the Jews in his 1793 essay on the French Revolution, claiming that it was dangerous to grant them equal rights as the French had done. In his *Addresses to the German Nation*, he wrote:

> **Throughout almost all the countries of Europe, there is spreading a mighty, hostilely minded state that is engaged in constant warfare with all others and that in many a country exerts a terrible pressure upon the citizenry. I speak of Jewry. I do not think it so fearsome because it forms a cohesive body that holds itself aloof from its fellow citizens, but because this cohesiveness is built upon hatred for the entire human race.**

Two other university professors published anti-Semitic diatribes. In his *On the Claims of the Jews to German Citizenship* (1815), Friedrich Rühs of Berlin advocated leading the Jews "gently" to embrace Christianity by imposing punitive taxes and restrictions on them. The philosopher Jakob Friedrich Fries of Heidelberg published his *On the Endangering of the Welfare and Character of the Germans by the Jews*, a year after Rühs' work, and called for a "war on Jewry," suggesting that the Jews should be exterminated "root and branch." These two works gave rise to a host of imitators.

In 1819, inspired by anti-Semitic literature of this kind, now popular throughout the German-speaking states, and no doubt influenced by the prevailing reactionary trend of the governments following Napoleon's defeat at Waterloo, a new wave of persecutions broke out. These were called the "Hep! Hep!" riots, from the war cry of the rioters, *"Hep! Hep! Jude verrecke!"* ("Hep! Hep! Perish Jew!" – *"Hep"* representing the initials of *Hierosolyma Est Perdita* meaning "Jerusalem is lost").

The rioting started among university students in Würzburg: Jewish shops were looted and several Jews were killed before order was restored. The unrest soon spread throughout Germany, to Bamberg, Darmstadt, Baden-Baden, Mannheim, Bayreuth, Karlsruhe, Hamburg, and Frankfurt. In Frankfurt, however, the authorities intervened when Amschel Rothschild's house in the ghetto was attacked – it was known that the German parliament had deposited large sums with the Frankfurt branch of the family bank.

The most popular and scurrilous pamphlet of all – *Der Judenspiegel ("Mirror of the Jews")* by Hartwig von Hundt-Radowski – was a justification of the "Hep! Hep!" riots. It claimed that killing a Jew was neither a sin nor a crime but, rather, a "police action." As for the Jews of Frankfurt, five years after the riots they were again denied autonomy in their communal affairs, and were subjected to restrictions on movement and marriage.

Many Jews took part in the 1848 revolutionary uprisings in Germany and elsewhere. However, there were also attacks on the Jewish communities of Hamburg and Prague by rioters who viewed the Jews simply as part of the property-owning class. Then, after the rebellions had been put down, restrictions – such as the ban on holding public office – stayed in place.

ABOVE: *Jewish emancipation in Bavaria, as seen in a satirical magazine of 1848. Though many German Jews took part in the liberal revolution of that year, they found themselves little better off as a result. Even though Bavaria had a relatively liberal constitution, innate conservatism and the influence of the Catholic Church kept the Jews firmly in their place.*

RIGHT: *Richard Wagner, Germany's leading operatic composer and founder of a whole new school of music, was virulently opposed to the influence of the Jews, which he saw as incompatible with the survival of true Aryan culture.*

In the 1860s Jews in the German states and Austria did gain some of the freedoms that they had been denied. However, throughout their history, the Jews had been on a proverbial see-saw under the control of the authorities – first, freedom and tolerance; then, restrictions and persecution – and so it was to prove in the following decade: in 1873, the financial crisis in Germany was immediately blamed on them, and the level of anti-Semitism rose dramatically.

In that year, *Gartenlaube*, a middle-class family magazine, ran a series of articles that held the Jews responsible for all sorts of financial swindles, and the term "anti-Semitism" *(Antisemitismus)* was actually coined by the virulently anti-Semitic journalist

Wilhelm Marr, whose father was Jewish. His highly successful pamphlet *The Victory of Judaism over Germanism* was reprinted 12 times between 1873 and 1879.

Another intellectual advocate of anti-Semitism was Adolf Stöcker, court chaplain to Kaiser Wilhelm I and founder (in 1878) of the Christian Social Party, who inveighed against the "Jewish menace" from the pulpit. The theme of Jewish world domination – as described in *The Protocols of the Learned Elders of Zion (see below)* – gradually supplanted the desecration of the Host and ritual murder in modern political demonology. In 1881, a petition bearing more than 250,000 signatures was presented to the Reichstag, those who had signed demanding that further Jewish immigration into Germany should be halted. In the same year, the composer Richard Wagner (1813–83) wrote to King Ludwig II of Bavaria: "I regard the Jewish race as the born enemy of humanity." And in 1899, Wagner's son-in-law – the English-born, naturalized-German, Houston Stewart Chamberlain – published *The Foundations of the Nineteenth Century*, in which he claimed that the Jews had destroyed the ancient world and were even now corrupting Europe, tainting the Aryan races with their Semitic blood.

From the late nineteenth century until the Holocaust, anti-Semitism became a convenient bandwagon from which unscrupulous politicians could win the support of the more unenlightened elements of the population. In 1893 overtly anti-Semitic German political parties elected 16 representatives to the Reichstag. In Austria, the populist demagogue Karl Lueger employed anti-Semitism to get himself elected mayor of Vienna in 1895. This did not, afterward, prevent him from having dealings with the most prominent of the city's 125,000 Jews, for, as he admitted, his anti-Semitism had just been a way of ingratiating himself with the working class.

The Damascus Blood Libel
In the mid-nineteenth century, anti-Semitism suddenly emerged in a part of the world

where it had been virtually unknown – the Ottoman Empire, which by the sixteenth century had absorbed the Byzantine Empire, Egypt, and Syria. Jews fleeing from Spain and Portugal had found refuge there under the Turks and had lived for centuries as one of the minorities officially recognized by the Ottoman sultans.

In 1840, however, this happy state of affairs came to an abrupt end when a Capuchin friar named Father Thomas, then living in Damascus, mysteriously disappeared with his servant. Because they had apparently been last seen in the Jewish quarter, Father Thomas's fellow friars immediately began

BELOW: As the empire expanded across the Mediterranean and into the Balkans, the Ottoman sultans welcomed a tide of European Jews, fleeing from persecution. As the empire declined and its borders contracted, so did the number of Jews under its control; by 1900, some 500,000 of the Sultanate's subjects were Jewish.

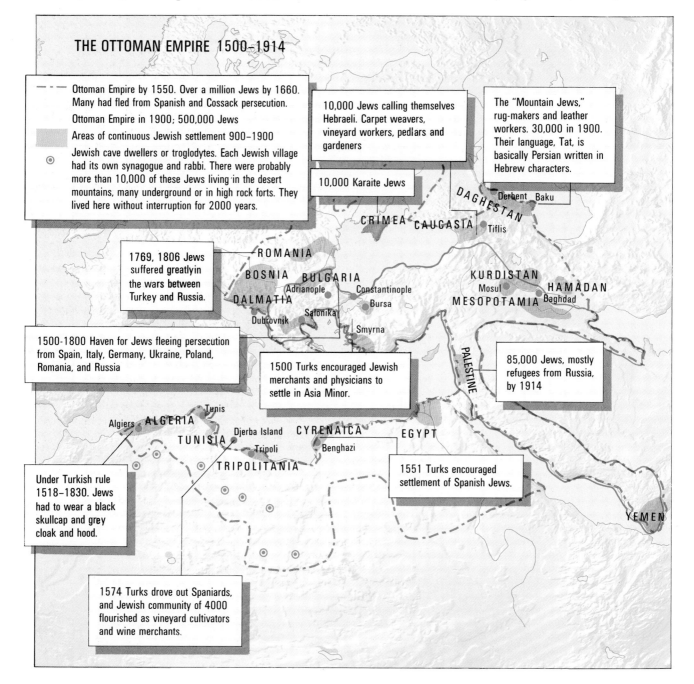

THE OTTOMAN EMPIRE 1500–1914

Ottoman Empire by 1550. Over a million Jews by 1660. Many had fled from Spanish and Cossack persecution.

Ottoman Empire in 1900; 500,000 Jews

Areas of continuous Jewish settlement 900–1900

Jewish cave dwellers or troglodytes. Each Jewish village had its own synagogue and rabbi. There were probably more than 10,000 of these Jews living in the desert mountains, many underground or in high rock forts. They lived here without interruption for 2000 years.

10,000 Jews calling themselves Hebraeli. Carpet weavers, vineyard workers, pedlars and gardeners

10,000 Karaite Jews

The "Mountain Jews," rug-makers and leather workers. 30,000 in 1900. Their language, Tat, is basically Persian written in Hebrew characters.

1769, 1806 Jews suffered greatly in the wars between Turkey and Russia.

1500-1800 Haven for Jews fleeing persecution from Spain, Italy, Germany, Ukraine, Poland, Romania, and Russia

1500 Turks encouraged Jewish merchants and physicians to settle in Asia Minor.

85,000 Jews, mostly refugees from Russia, by 1914

Under Turkish rule 1518–1830. Jews had to wear a black skullcap and grey cloak and hood.

1551 Turks encouraged settlement of Spanish Jews.

1574 Turks drove out Spaniards, and Jewish community of 4000 flourished as vineyard cultivators and wine merchants.

DAGHESTAN — Derbent — Baku

CRIMEA — CAUCASIA — Tiflis

ROMANIA

BOSNIA — BULGARIA
DALMATIA — Adrianople — Constantinople
Dubrovnik — Salonika — Bursa
Smyrna

KURDISTAN
Mosul — HAMADAN
MESOPOTAMIA — Baghdad

PALESTINE

Tunis
Algiers — ALGERIA
TUNISIA — Djerba Island — CYRENAICA — EGYPT
Tripoli — Benghazi
TRIPOLITANIA

YEMEN

accusing the Jews of kidnapping him for the purposes of ritual murder. They went to the French consul with their claims, and upon his intercession, Sharif Pasha, the local governor, made a random search of the Jewish quarter and arbitrarily imprisoned seven members of the most prominent families. When they refused to confess, even under torture, 63 Jewish children between the ages of three and ten were seized, locked up, and denied food. For a time, the adult prisoners continued to proclaim their innocence, but finally, five of them broke under torture and "confessed."

International Jewry was stirred into action. Prominent French Jews who tried to intervene received no support from their government, whose policy it was to prop up the

BELOW: *Damascus became the headquarters of anti-Jewish Arab propaganda in 1936; this was intensified after a Nazi delegation visited the city. Unrest increased until 1941, when British and Free French troops intervened to overthrow the Vichy administration.*

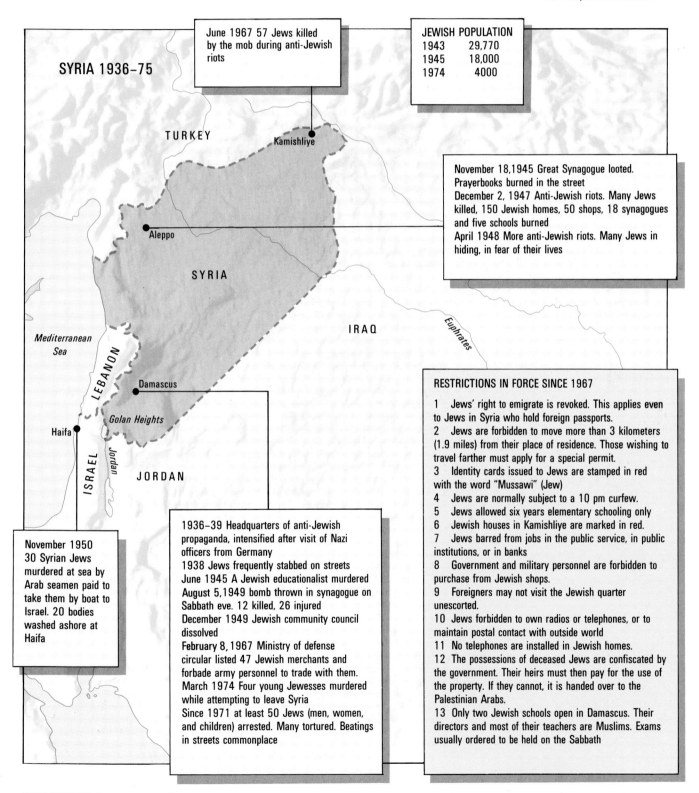

SYRIA 1936–75

June 1967 57 Jews killed by the mob during anti-Jewish riots

JEWISH POPULATION
1943   29,770
1945   18,000
1974   4000

TURKEY
Kamishliye

November 18, 1945 Great Synagogue looted. Prayerbooks burned in the street
December 2, 1947 Anti-Jewish riots. Many Jews killed, 150 Jewish homes, 50 shops, 18 synagogues and five schools burned
April 1948 More anti-Jewish riots. Many Jews in hiding, in fear of their lives

Aleppo

SYRIA

IRAQ

Euphrates

Mediterranean Sea

LEBANON

Damascus

Golan Heights

Haifa

ISRAEL   Jordan

JORDAN

November 1950 30 Syrian Jews murdered at sea by Arab seamen paid to take them by boat to Israel. 20 bodies washed ashore at Haifa

1936–39 Headquarters of anti-Jewish propaganda, intensified after visit of Nazi officers from Germany
1938 Jews frequently stabbed on streets
June 1945 A Jewish educationalist murdered
August 5, 1949 bomb thrown in synagogue on Sabbath eve. 12 killed, 26 injured
December 1949 Jewish community council dissolved
February 8, 1967 Ministry of defense circular listed 47 Jewish merchants and forbade army personnel to trade with them.
March 1974 Four young Jewesses murdered while attempting to leave Syria
Since 1971 at least 50 Jews (men, women, and children) arrested. Many tortured. Beatings in streets commonplace

RESTRICTIONS IN FORCE SINCE 1967

1   Jews' right to emigrate is revoked. This applies even to Jews in Syria who hold foreign passports.
2   Jews are forbidden to move more than 3 kilometers (1.9 miles) from their place of residence. Those wishing to travel farther must apply for a special permit.
3   Identity cards issued to Jews are stamped in red with the word "Mussawi" (Jew)
4   Jews are normally subject to a 10 pm curfew.
5   Jews allowed six years elementary schooling only
6   Jewish houses in Kamishliye are marked in red.
7   Jews barred from jobs in the public service, in public institutions, or in banks
8   Government and military personnel are forbidden to purchase from Jewish shops.
9   Foreigners may not visit the Jewish quarter unescorted.
10 Jews forbidden to own radios or telephones, or to maintain postal contact with outside world
11 No telephones are installed in Jewish homes.
12 The possessions of deceased Jews are confiscated by the government. Their heirs must then pay for the use of the property. If they cannot, it is handed over to the Palestinian Arabs.
13 Only two Jewish schools open in Damascus. Their directors and most of their teachers are Muslims. Exams usually ordered to be held on the Sabbath

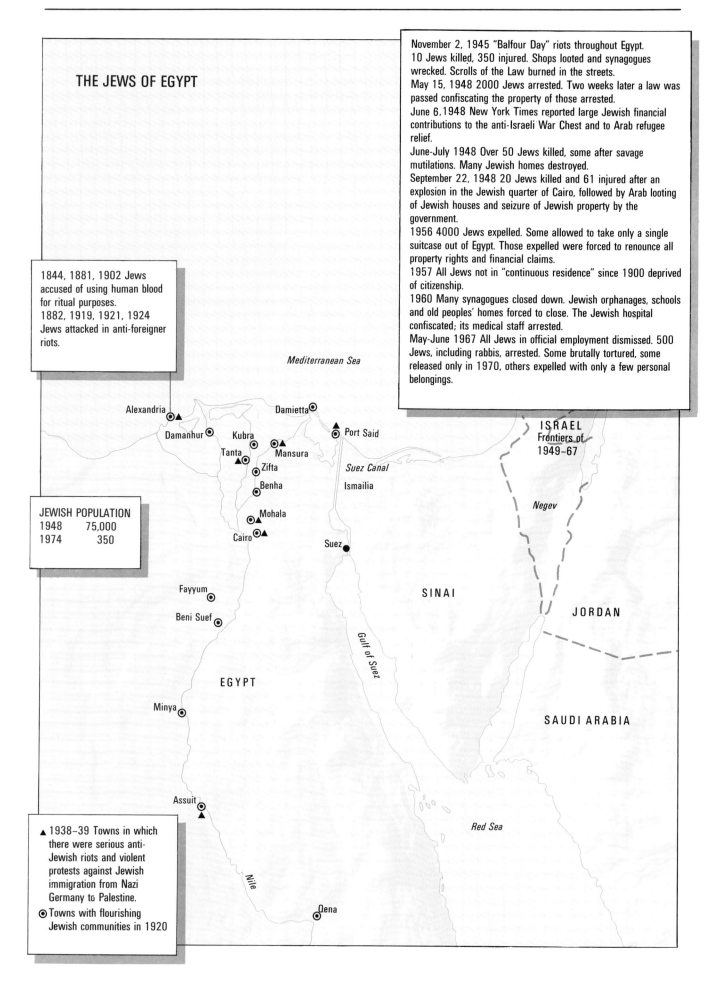

THE JEWS OF EGYPT

November 2, 1945 "Balfour Day" riots throughout Egypt.
10 Jews killed, 350 injured. Shops looted and synagogues
wrecked. Scrolls of the Law burned in the streets.
May 15, 1948 2000 Jews arrested. Two weeks later a law was
passed confiscating the property of those arrested.
June 6,1948 New York Times reported large Jewish financial
contributions to the anti-Israeli War Chest and to Arab refugee
relief.
June-July 1948 Over 50 Jews killed, some after savage
mutilations. Many Jewish homes destroyed.
September 22, 1948 20 Jews killed and 61 injured after an
explosion in the Jewish quarter of Cairo, followed by Arab looting
of Jewish houses and seizure of Jewish property by the
government.
1956 4000 Jews expelled. Some allowed to take only a single
suitcase out of Egypt. Those expelled were forced to renounce all
property rights and financial claims.
1957 All Jews not in "continuous residence" since 1900 deprived
of citizenship.
1960 Many synagogues closed down. Jewish orphanages, schools
and old peoples' homes forced to close. The Jewish hospital
confiscated; its medical staff arrested.
May-June 1967 All Jews in official employment dismissed. 500
Jews, including rabbis, arrested. Some brutally tortured, some
released only in 1970, others expelled with only a few personal
belongings.

1844, 1881, 1902 Jews
accused of using human blood
for ritual purposes.
1882, 1919, 1921, 1924
Jews attacked in anti-foreigner
riots.

Mediterranean Sea

ISRAEL
Frontiers of
1949–67

JEWISH POPULATION
1948   75,000
1974   350

Alexandria
Damietta
Damanhur
Kubra
Tanta   Mansura
Zifta   Port Said
Benha   Suez Canal
Ismailia
Mohala
Cairo
Suez

Negev

Fayyum

Beni Suef

SINAI

JORDAN

EGYPT

Minya

SAUDI ARABIA

Gulf of Suez

Assuit

Red Sea

▲ 1938–39 Towns in which
there were serious anti-
Jewish riots and violent
protests against Jewish
immigration from Nazi
Germany to Palestine.
◉ Towns with flourishing
Jewish communities in 1920

Nile

Qena

Turkish sultan against Russian incursions. However, the millionaire philanthropist Sir Moses Montefiore, who enjoyed the esteem and backing of his government, was able to form a delegation including the orientalist Solomon Munk and Adolphe Crémieux, a member of the Consistoire (the French Jewish representative council which was the descendant of Napoleon's Sanhedrin) and later twice prime minister of France. These men met with Pasha Mehmet Ali, viceroy of Egypt and Syria. As a result, the prisoners were freed, though they had been crippled for life by the tortures they had suffered.

The Jewish delegation was finally granted an audience with the boy sultan of Turkey, Abdul-Mejid I. After some persuasion, he issued a decree announcing that the accusation of ritual murder was a crude slander. It also promised the Jews within the Ottoman Empire full rights, including the right to practice their religion freely, as well as protection of their property.

The "Damascus affair" led, in 1860, to the founding of the Alliance Israélite Universelle, an organization with the aim of spreading Jewish culture to long-neglected communities of the Middle East, and fostering Jewish culture and solidarity everywhere. (Similar associations were later founded: the Israelitische Allianz in Vienna in 1873; and the Hilfsverein der Deutschen Juden in 1901.) Among other things, the Alliance, whose first president was Adolphe Crémieux, founded a network of excellent schools which gave the Jews possibly the best education in the Ottoman Empire.

Despite the greater Jewish solidarity that resulted from the Damascus Blood Libel, anti-Semitism was still rife in Europe. In

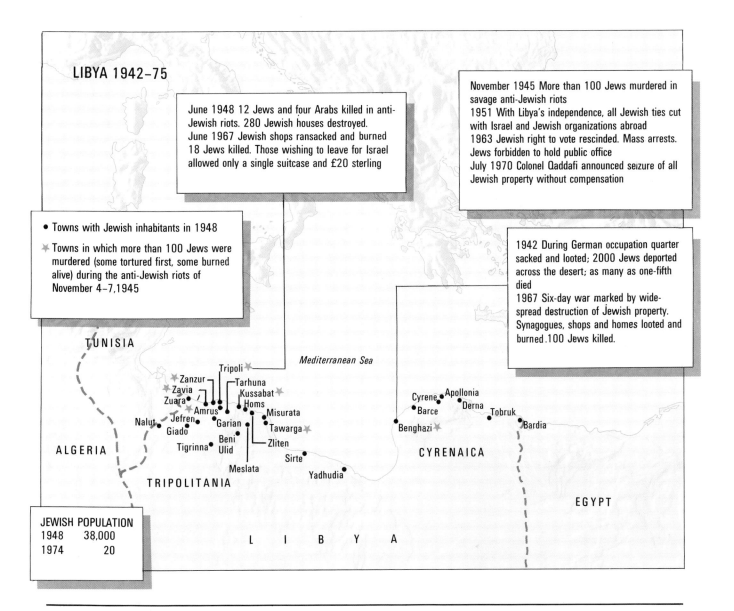

LIBYA 1942-75

June 1948 12 Jews and four Arabs killed in anti-Jewish riots. 280 Jewish houses destroyed.
June 1967 Jewish shops ransacked and burned 18 Jews killed. Those wishing to leave for Israel allowed only a single suitcase and £20 sterling

November 1945 More than 100 Jews murdered in savage anti-Jewish riots
1951 With Libya's independence, all Jewish ties cut with Israel and Jewish organizations abroad
1963 Jewish right to vote rescinded. Mass arrests. Jews forbidden to hold public office
July 1970 Colonel Qaddafi announced seizure of all Jewish property without compensation

• Towns with Jewish inhabitants in 1948

✳ Towns in which more than 100 Jews were murdered (some tortured first, some burned alive) during the anti-Jewish riots of November 4–7, 1945

1942 During German occupation quarter sacked and looted; 2000 Jews deported across the desert; as many as one-fifth died
1967 Six-day war marked by widespread destruction of Jewish property. Synagogues, shops and homes looted and burned. 100 Jews killed.

TUNISIA

Mediterranean Sea

Tripoli
Zanzur
Zavia   Tarhuna
Zuara   Kussabat
               Homs
Amrus
Nalut   Jefren   Misurata
        Giado   Garian
                Tawarga
        Beni   Zliten
Tigrinna Ulid

ALGERIA   Sirte
        Meslata
                Yadhudia

Cyrene Apollonia
        Derna
Barce   Tobruk
Benghazi   Bardia

CYRENAICA

TRIPOLITANIA

EGYPT

L   I   B   Y   A

JEWISH POPULATION
1948   38,000
1974   20

1858, one notorious incident was the kidnapping in Bologna (in the Papal states) of the Jewish child Edgardo Mortara by the family maid. She sent him to a Catholic seminary, and despite the efforts of Jewish leaders and of his own family, he was not returned, even after Bologna gained its independence from the papacy and became part of the Italian kingdom in 1860. Mortara eventually became a Catholic priest.

The Jews of Russia and the Pale of Settlement

Prior to 1500, Jews were allowed to live nearly anywhere in Russia, but then a strange phenomenon occurred in the city of Novgorod. The local Russian Orthodox clergy began preaching a quasi-Judaic concept: the true Christ had not visited the earth, but only his image; when the true Christ did arrive, they said, Mosaic law would be proclaimed on earth. Eventually, the members of this

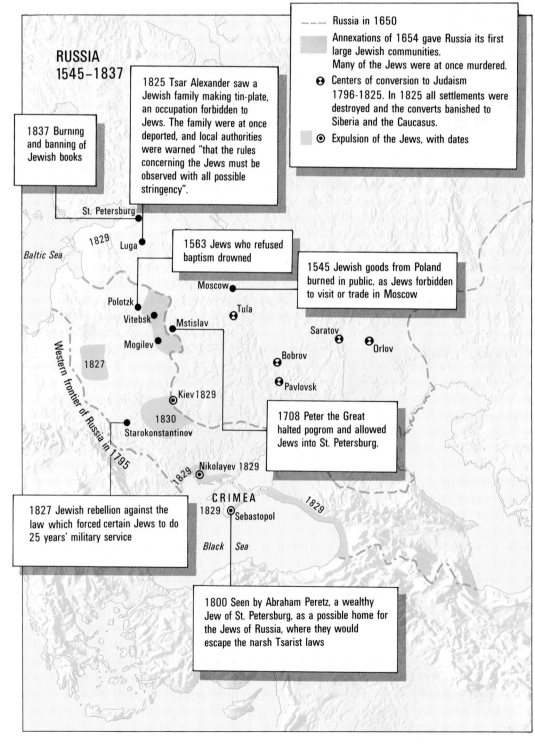

RUSSIA 1545–1837

1837 Burning and banning of Jewish books

1825 Tsar Alexander saw a Jewish family making tin-plate, an occupation forbidden to Jews. The family were at once deported, and local authorities were warned "that the rules concerning the Jews must be observed with all possible stringency".

- – – – Russia in 1650
- Annexations of 1654 gave Russia its first large Jewish communities. Many of the Jews were at once murdered.
- ❷ Centers of conversion to Judaism 1796-1825. In 1825 all settlements were destroyed and the converts banished to Siberia and the Caucasus.
- ⊙ Expulsion of the Jews, with dates

St. Petersburg

1829 Luga

Baltic Sea

1563 Jews who refused baptism drowned

1545 Jewish goods from Poland burned in public, as Jews forbidden to visit or trade in Moscow

Moscow

Polotzk
Vitebsk
Mstislav
Mogilev

Tula

Saratov ❷
Orlov ❷
Bobrov
Pavlovsk ❷

1827

Western frontier of Russia in 1795

Kiev 1829 ⊙

1830
Starokonstantinov

1708 Peter the Great halted pogrom and allowed Jews into St. Petersburg.

1829 Nikolayev 1829 ⊙

CRIMEA
1829 ⊙ Sebastopol

1829

1827 Jewish rebellion against the law which forced certain Jews to do 25 years' military service

Black Sea

1800 Seen by Abraham Peretz, a wealthy Jew of St. Petersburg, as a possible home for the Jews of Russia, where they would escape the narsh Tsarist laws

LEFT: *Originally, the Russians had little contact with the Jews; it was only with the expansion of Tsarist rule, particularly with the territorial annexations of 1654, that large Jewish communities first came under their control. The response was immediate persecution; by 1656, as many as 500,000 Jews had been killed in the western Russian empire and as a result of Cossack incursions into Poland. The pattern continued over the succeeding centuries, culminating in the creation of the Pale of Settlement in 1772.*

LEFT: *The Jewish calendar for 5613, from the Berlin satirical magazine* Kladderadatsch. *German anti-Semitism continued after national unity was achieved; this was the reason for Rothschild's refusal to re-found a German branch of his bank, even when requested to do so by William II.*

RIGHT: *The true face of social democracy, as depicted in an anti-Semitic Viennese magazine. The links between Judaism and capitalism were clear, at least in anti-Semitic eyes.*

sect openly denounced the official Church.

The Church authorities began to harbor fears of Jewish influence. As a result, while the heretics were burned at the stake, the Jews were banned from the whole of Russia. A few Jews did eventually return from Byelorussia and the Baltic provinces whence they had fled, but then Ivan the Terrible (reigned 1533–84) threatened all those Jews who would not accept Russian Orthodox Christianity with death by drowning in the River Dvina.

Peter the Great, like his German-speaking counterparts Frederick the Great and Maria Theresa, unwillingly acquired a large number of Jewish subjects when he conquered the Baltic provinces in his wars with the Swedes, which ended in 1721. The Empress Elizabeth (reigned 1741–62) again banned Jews from the heart of Russia in 1742. Thirty years later, Catherine the Great suddenly acquired 900,000 more Jews when, in the First Partition of Poland, she annexed most of eastern Poland and the Ukraine. In the same year, 1772, she issued a *ukase* (decree) allowing all her new Christian subjects the same rights as they had had before, but restricting the Jewish ones to areas where they had lived before partition. In 1791 Jews were also allowed to reside in some districts east of the River Dneiper and in others on the Black Sea.

The region into which the Jews were confined was known as the "Pale of Settlement." Successive tsars actually reduced the area of the Pale, increasing the economic difficulties of residents – both Jewish and Christian – and causing terrible hardship. Jewish writers of the nineteenth century provide many portraits of the appalling poverty of the typical Jewish township – the *shtetl*, as it is known in Yiddish – while the Christian peasants fared little better.

In 1804, Tsar Alexander I issued his "Statutes concerning the organization of the Jews." No longer were they to have the large measure of autonomy and self-government that they had previously enjoyed, but were to be forcibly assimilated into local Christian communities by a ban on their mother tongue – Yiddish: from now on they must speak the Christian vernacular. From 1807 only documents written in Russian, German, or Polish were valid in the eyes of the secular authorities within the Pale (outside the Pale, no Hebrew or Yiddish document had ever been valid), and no Jew could hold public office – not even as a rabbi within his own community – unless he had perfect command of whichever of these languages was the vernacular of the district in question.

This decree had a very limited effect. The Jews' hostility toward it was increased by

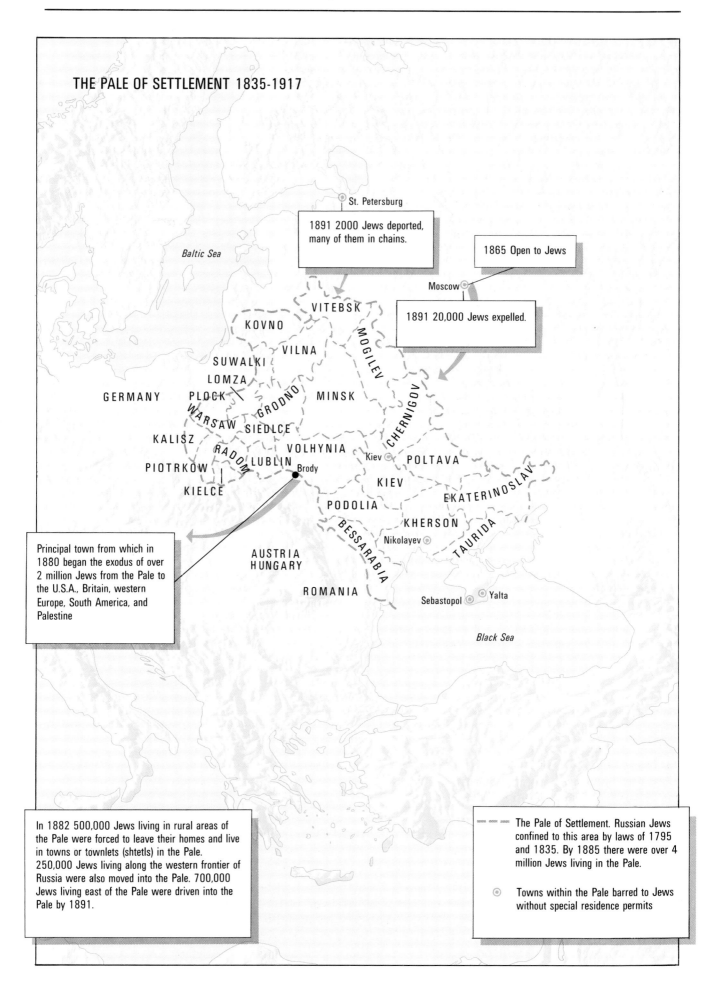

THE PALE OF SETTLEMENT 1835-1917

Baltic Sea

St. Petersburg

1891 2000 Jews deported, many of them in chains.

1865 Open to Jews

Moscow

1891 20,000 Jews expelled.

VITEBSK

KOVNO

MOGILEV

VILNA

SUWALKI

LOMZA

GERMANY

PLOCK

GRODNO

MINSK

CHERNIGOV

WARSAW

SIEDLCE

KALISZ

RADOM

VOLHYNIA

Kiev

POLTAVA

PIOTRKOW

LUBLIN

Brody

KIEV

KIELCE

PODOLIA

EKATERINOSLAV

KHERSON

BESSARABIA

Nikolayev

TAURIDA

AUSTRIA
HUNGARY

ROMANIA

Sebastopol

Yalta

Black Sea

Principal town from which in 1880 began the exodus of over 2 million Jews from the Pale to the U.S.A., Britain, western Europe, South America, and Palestine

In 1882 500,000 Jews living in rural areas of the Pale were forced to leave their homes and live in towns or townlets (shtetls) in the Pale. 250,000 Jews living along the western frontier of Russia were also moved into the Pale. 700,000 Jews living east of the Pale were driven into the Pale by 1891.

The Pale of Settlement. Russian Jews confined to this area by laws of 1795 and 1835. By 1885 there were over 4 million Jews living in the Pale.

Towns within the Pale barred to Jews without special residence permits

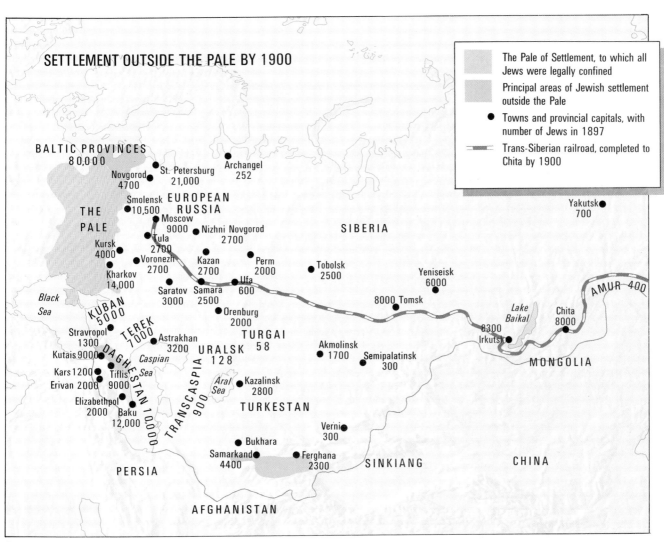

SETTLEMENT OUTSIDE THE PALE BY 1900

The Pale of Settlement, to which all Jews were legally confined

Principal areas of Jewish settlement outside the Pale

● Towns and provincial capitals, with number of Jews in 1897

Trans-Siberian railroad, completed to Chita by 1900

BALTIC PROVINCES 80,000

Archangel 252

St. Petersburg 21,000

Novgorod 4700

Smolensk 10,500

EUROPEAN RUSSIA

THE PALE

Moscow 9000

Nizhni Novgorod 2700

SIBERIA

Yakutsk 700

Tula 2700

Kursk 4000

Voronezh 2700

Kazan 2700

Perm 2000

Tobolsk 2500

Yeniseisk 6000

Kharkov 14,000

Saratov 3000

Samara 2500

Ufa 600

Black Sea

KUBAN 5000

Orenburg 2000

8000 Tomsk

Lake Baikal

Chita 8000

AMUR 400

Stravropol 1300

TEREK 7000

Astrakhan 3200

URALSK 128

TURGAI 58

Akmolinsk 1700

8300 Irkutsk

MONGOLIA

Kutais 9000

DAGHESTAN 10,000

Caspian Sea

Semipalatinsk 300

Kars 1200

Tiflis 9000

TRANSCASPIA 900

Aral Sea

Kazalinsk 2800

Erivan 2000

Elizabethpol 2000

Baku 12,000

TURKESTAN

Verni 300

CHINA

Bukhara

SINKIANG

Samarkand 4400

Ferghana 2300

PERSIA

AFGHANISTAN

their suspicions about the tsar's motives. After all, the scheme had been suggested to him by the English eccentric Lewis Way, who had founded a missionary organization called the London Society to Disseminate Christian Faith among the Jews. Similar attempts at converting the Jews were made. In 1841, Dr. Max Lilienthal, a Jewish educator, was invited from Germany to establish a network of Jewish schools that would teach secular subjects in Russian. However, the local Jewish population's fears that the schools would be used to enforce conversion proved to be well-founded, and Dr. Lilenthal left for the United States.

Tsar Alexander's decree was warmly embraced by the wealthy Jews who had been allowed to assimilate and had already become acculturated to German, Russian, or Polish life. However, they were simply a tiny élite. A survey of 1897 revealed that – 90 years after the decree had come into force – 97.6 per cent of Jews in the Pale of Settlement

still spoke Yiddish as their mother tongue.

The Jewish population maintained their cultural identity and separateness largely because they were denied access to state education. In 1887, the Ministry of Education introduced a quota system in the Pale, restricting Jewish enrollment in secondary education to 10 per cent. Given the huge numerical superiority of Jews over Gentiles seeking secondary education, the result was that most Jews were virtually barred from the high schools. Outside the Pale, the quota was 5 per cent in the larger cities and, in St. Petersburg and Moscow, only 3 per cent. This should be compared with Jewish enrollment in secondary and further education in central Europe: in some cities – for example, Vienna and Berlin – it was as high as 11 per cent, even though Jews made up only 3 per cent or less of the general population.

Nicholas I (reigned 1825–55) promulgated as many as 600 decrees affecting the Jews. In 1827, for example, he ordered them

ABOVE: Tsarist success in enforcing Jewish resettlement within the Pale is amply demonstrated in this map. By 1897, only 345,000 Jews were living outside the Pale, the majority being there illegally and, if discovered, liable to expulsion.

FAR LEFT: The first edicts confining the Jews of the Russian Empire to the Pale of Settlement were issued by the Tsarist regime in 1795; these were reinforced by further decrees, issued in 1835 on the orders of Tsar Nicholas I. By 1885, there were over 4 million Jews living in the Pale, their numbers increasing by a further 700,000 by 1891.

to be conscripted into the Russian army for the first time. The period of service was to be the customary 25 years, but in the case of the Jews, this was to be preceded by six years' training. The Jewish authorities were charged with filling the quota of conscripts from among the poor; no Jew could be commissioned an officer. The Russian revolutionary Alexander Hertzen describes in his autobiography how he saw Jewish child conscripts, some as young as eight years old, being herded by Russian officers, a sight that moved him to tears.

Also in 1827 the Jews were expelled from Kiev, the capital of the Ukraine, and forbidden to live less than 33 miles from the western border of the empire. A year later, censorship was imposed on all Jewish books. In 1850 traditional male Jewish dress was banned, but this decree had little success: orthodox Jews continued to wear their kaftans and side-locks (*peyos*) throughout the Russian empire.

Following Russia's defeat in the Crimean War, Alexander II (reigned 1855–81) initiated a number of attempts at modernization. To this end he permitted certain privileged classes of Jews – merchants, university graduates, registered craftsmen, and physicians – to live outside the Pale. For the first time Jewish communities were established in St. Petersburg and Moscow.

The Black Hundreds and the Pogroms

Unfortunately, Alexander II was assassinated in 1881, to be succeeded by Alexander III. He authorized bands of Cossacks – known as the Black Hundreds – to sweep through Jewish settlements in the Ukraine, slaughtering, raping, looting, and burning. The authorities were instructed not to intervene until the third day of each incident.

Reports of these atrocities began to appear in the Western press, and the word *pogrom* entered the English language. It derives from two Russian words that mean "like thunder" and is defined in the *American Heritage Dictionary* as "an organized and often officially encouraged massacre or persecution of a minority group, especially...the Jews." Official Russian sources immediately dismissed the reports of organized destruction, claiming that this was the spontaneous anger of the Russian peasants in retaliation for Jewish exploitation. The only government response to the pogroms was an edict further restricting the area of the Pale of Settlement and limiting the leasing or purchase of property by Jews.

In 1891 most of the Jewish population of Moscow was expelled on the pretext that the tsar was transferring his capital to that city. (This did not actually happen until after the revolution in 1918.) The following year, Jews were no longer allowed to hold office, and in 1893, Yalta was placed out of bounds, on the grounds that the tsar had a villa nearby. As the imperial train took the tsar to the Crimea for a holiday, it passed a train carrying deportees from Yalta.

The pogroms reached their height in the town of Kishinev, the capital of the province of Bessarabia (now in Moldavia), near the Romanian border. On the eve of Passover 1903, 45 Jews were murdered, nearly 600 injured, and 1500 homes destroyed. It caused an outcry in the foreign press, and despite censorship, Russian liberals – including Leo Tolstoy – learned of it and roundly condemned the authorities.

That same year, a Russian newspaper published what is generally considered to be the most famous piece of anti-Semitic literature in the world. *The Protocols of the Learned Elders of Zion*, which has been translated into many languages, has been claimed to be of great antiquity, but while this is certainly untrue, its authorship is uncertain. It may have been produced in Paris by an anonymous agent of the Okhrana, the tsarist secret police, or it may be the work of a Russian monk named Sergei Nilus. In either case, it seems to have been based on an attack on Napoleon III written in 1864. This satire, for which its author was imprisoned for libel, claimed that Napoleon III sought world domination, and it made no mention of the Jews. In the *Protocols*, however, he was replaced by the "Elders of Zion," a mythical council of Jews who were supposedly plotting to take over the world. The work was submitted for approval to the last tsar, Nicholas II (reigned 1894–1917) – who may, indeed, have commissioned it – but he rejected it as too obvious a fabrication. However, when it was published in Russia in 1903, it gained a great deal of public credence.

After Russia's disastrous war with Japan in

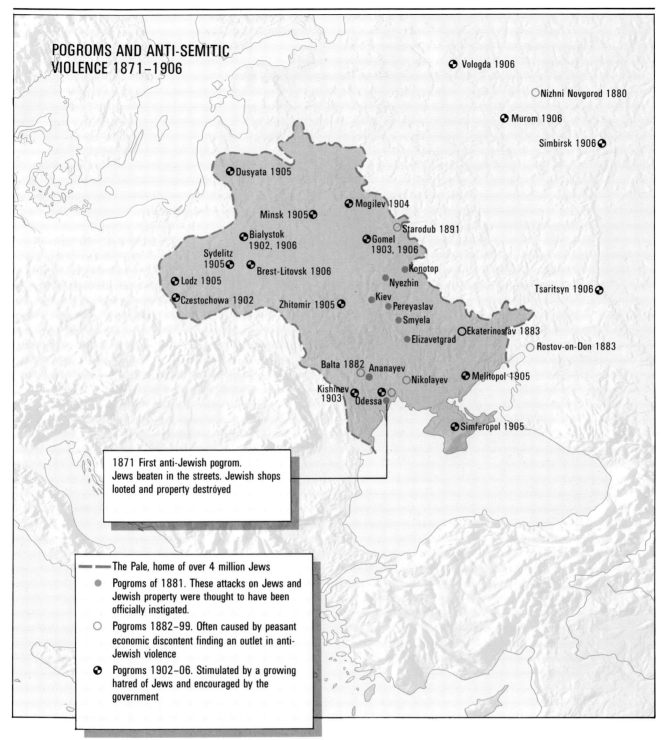

POGROMS AND ANTI-SEMITIC VIOLENCE 1871–1906

Vologda 1906

Nizhni Novgorod 1880

Murom 1906

Simbirsk 1906

Dusyata 1905

Mogilev 1904

Minsk 1905

Starodub 1891

Bialystok 1902, 1906

Gomel 1903, 1906

Sydelitz 1905

Brest-Litovsk 1906

Konotop

Lodz 1905

Nyezhin

Kiev

Tsaritsyn 1906

Czestochowa 1902

Zhitomir 1905

Pereyaslav

Smyela

Ekaterinoslav 1883

Elizavetgrad

Rostov-on-Don 1883

Balta 1882

Ananayev

Nikolayev

Melitopol 1905

Kishinev 1903

Odessa

Simferopol 1905

1871 First anti-Jewish pogrom. Jews beaten in the streets. Jewish shops looted and property destroyed

▬ ▬ The Pale, home of over 4 million Jews

● Pogroms of 1881. These attacks on Jews and Jewish property were thought to have been officially instigated.

○ Pogroms 1882–99. Often caused by peasant economic discontent finding an outlet in anti-Jewish violence

✪ Pogroms 1902–06. Stimulated by a growing hatred of Jews and encouraged by the government

---

ABOVE: *The first pogrom took place in Odessa in 1871; a decade later, the first extensive attacks on Jews and their property took place. It is likely that these were inspired by the reactionary regime of Tsar Alexander III. He encouraged the formation of the infamous Black Hundreds: in 1891, he expelled the Jews from Moscow.*

1904–5, the Black Hundreds struck again, causing devastation in Jewish settlements throughout the Pale. In one instance 300 Jews were killed in Odessa. Now, however, the Jews sometimes organized themselves into paramilitary units to repel the mob.

In 1911 Mendel Baylis was tried for ritual murder in Kiev. He was eventually acquitted, but not before the outraged Western press had presented Russia as the most backward and superstitious country in Europe. However, this bad publicity did nothing to curb the pogroms, nor did the fact that those carrying them out and those authorizing them were now subject to world scrutiny as Western journalists continued to champion the cause of the oppressed Russian Jews. Four years after the Baylis trial, in 1915, the worst anti-Jewish excesses of the twentieth century prior to the Holocaust took place in Russia and Russian-held Poland. It was not until the revolution of 1917 that Russian Jews were finally emancipated and granted equal rights, at least on paper.

Between 1881 and 1917, over two million Jews left Russia to find a better life. Two million of them went to the United States, 200,000 to Britain, 100,000 to Canada, and 40,000 to South Africa (mostly from Lithuania). Both Britain and the United States tried to bring in legislation to reduce the numbers, but they were too late. About 300,000 Jews resettled elsewhere in Europe, although their fellow Jews, to their shame, did not always welcome these *Ostjuden*.

The Dreyfus Affair

In 1894 Captain Alfred Dreyfus (1859–1935) was one of the very few Jewish officers in the French army and the only Jew on the army staff. In the summer of that year, it came to light that someone was leaking military secrets to Germany's military attaché in Paris, and flimsy handwritten evidence linked an incriminating document to Dreyfus. Because he was a Jew, the prejudiced French military establishment focused suspicion on him

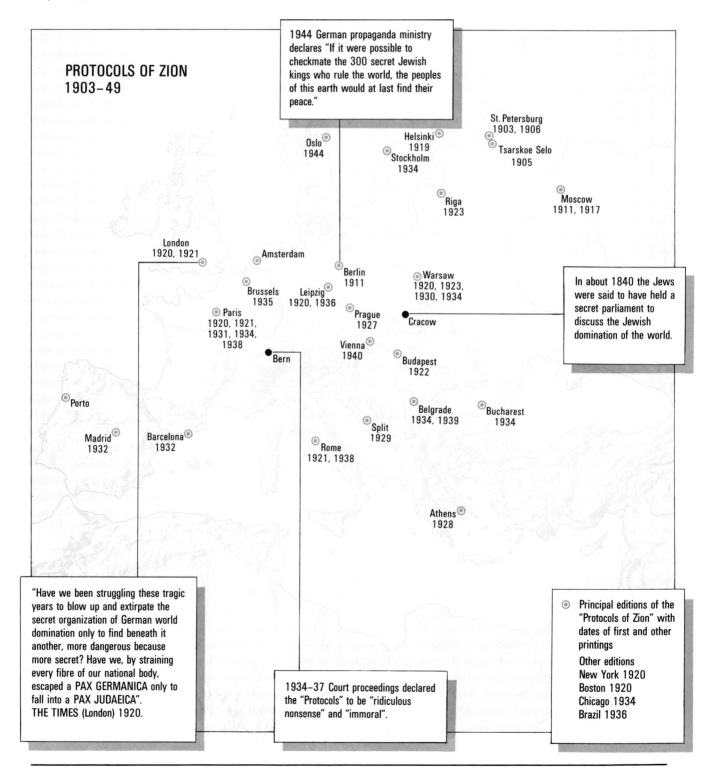

**PROTOCOLS OF ZION
1903–49**

1944 German propaganda ministry declares "If it were possible to checkmate the 300 secret Jewish kings who rule the world, the peoples of this earth would at last find their peace."

Oslo 1944

Helsinki 1919
Stockholm 1934

St. Petersburg 1903, 1906
Tsarskoe Selo 1905

Riga 1923

Moscow 1911, 1917

London 1920, 1921

Amsterdam

Berlin 1911

Warsaw 1920, 1923, 1930, 1934

Brussels 1935
Leipzig 1920, 1936

Prague 1927

Cracow

In about 1840 the Jews were said to have held a secret parliament to discuss the Jewish domination of the world.

Paris 1920, 1921, 1931, 1934, 1938

Vienna 1940

Bern

Budapest 1922

Porto

Belgrade 1934, 1939

Bucharest 1934

Split 1929

Madrid 1932

Barcelona 1932

Rome 1921, 1938

Athens 1928

"Have we been struggling these tragic years to blow up and extirpate the secret organization of German world domination only to find beneath it another, more dangerous because more secret? Have we, by straining every fibre of our national body, escaped a PAX GERMANICA only to fall into a PAX JUDAEICA".
THE TIMES (London) 1920.

1934–37 Court proceedings declared the "Protocols" to be "ridiculous nonsense" and "immoral".

⊙ Principal editions of the "Protocols of Zion" with dates of first and other printings

Other editions
New York 1920
Boston 1920
Chicago 1934
Brazil 1936

despite the fact that there were others – non-Jews – against whom there was more evidence. Dreyfus was arrested in October, and following his court martial two months later, French society was divided into two passionately opposed camps: those who believed in the Jew's treason; and those who saw the affair as an infamous persecution of an innocent man by the anti-republican, militaristic, and Catholic aristocracy and bourgeoisie.

Dreyfus was sentenced – *in camera* – to life imprisonment and dispatched to the notorious prison of Devil's Island, off the coast of French Guiana in South America. Then, in 1896, new evidence came into the hands of the head of French military intelligence, Colonel Picquart, proving that a dissipated aristocrat, Major Ferdinand Esterhazy, had been selling secrets to the Germans. The chiefs of the army general staff would not listen to Picquart; instead, they transferred him to a remote outpost in Tunisia.

In the meantime, a campaign demanding a retrial was gathering momentum among liberal lawyers, politicians (including Georges Clemenceau, the future prime minister), journalists, and intellectuals. The general staff, rattled, had Picquart locked up on a charge of breaching security. Esterhazy was tried at a court martial, which, on January 11, 1898, cleared him.

The fury of the *Dreyfusards* exploded. Two days after Esterhazy's acquittal, the journalist and novelist Emile Zola published, in the newspaper *L'Aurore*, his famous broadside *"J'accuse"* ("I Accuse") – an open letter to the president of the republic – in which he dubbed the Dreyfus trial a "crime of high treason against humanity." For this, Zola was arrested a month later on a charge of libel and condemned to a year's imprisonment. (However, instead, he spent the next 11 months in exile in England.)

The French government, risking unpopularity with the anti-*Dreyfusard* section of the public, allowed Dreyfus's case to go to appeal. In June 1899, the original sentence was annulled and a new court martial ordered. Dreyfus was brought back from Devil's Island and, in September, was tried at Rennes. He was again convicted – this time, "with extenuating circumstances" – and, to the amazement of the *Dreyfusards* and the

world's press, was sentenced to ten years' imprisonment. Ten days later, however, the government pardoned him and he was immediately released. Esterhazy killed himself.

Reinstated in the army and promoted to major, Dreyfus took up his duties again, but it was not until 1906, after long inquiries, that he was completely exonerated. By then he had become a symbol of injustice, but one that had been righted by the determination of liberals. The bitterness of the opposing sides in the affair was to poison French politics for decades. Indeed, the collaboration of certain Frenchmen with the Nazis during World War II can be traced back to their anti-Semitic stand over Dreyfus.

Two leading anti-*Dreyfusards* were Edouard Drumont and Charles Maurras. Drumont, a notorious anti-Semite, was already the author of *La France Juive* ("*Jewish France*", 1886). In the newspaper he published called *Libre Parole* ("*Free Speech*"), he used the Dreyfus affair to try to demonstrate how the Jews were working to "take over France."

Maurras (1868–1952) founded the fascistic *Action Française* movement and the newspaper of the same name. A Catholic reactionary, he was obsessed with the monarchical concept of a mythical "authentic Old France," and he encouraged the use of the offensive tag *métèque* (a word of Greek origin meaning "foreign non-citizens") not only for Jews but for all foreigners resident in France. However, Maurras managed to overcome his dislike of foreigners sufficiently to salute Hitler as a "heavenly surprise." He was sentenced to life imprisonment as a collaborator in 1945.

The Rise of Anti-Semitism between the World Wars

Jews all over the world were made the scapegoats for the inflation of the 1920s, the Wall Street crash of 1929, and the ensuing worldwide depression. However, there was another dimension to anti-Semitism, which could be described as "fashionable prejudice," a part of the *Zeitgeist* of the 1920s and 1930s. Racism was blatant and radical right-wing politics were in vogue. New movements claimed to be shaping a better future for their nations – an aspect of fascism and, eventually, of Nazism that attracted thousands at

Gli strani funerali di un membro del "Ku-Klux-Klan", negli Stati Uniti - In occasione della morte di uno dei suoi adepti più influenti questa grande società segreta americana ha fatto una pubblica apparizione in una città della Pensilvania. Una numerosa rappresentanza ha preso parte al corteo funebre indossando il bizzarro costume della setta   *(Dis. di A. Orlolli)*

ABOVE: *The funeral of a prominent member of the Ku Klux Klan in Pennsylvania. The Klan's demands for a "white America" in the 1920s embraced anti-Semitic as well as anti-black prejudices.*

eastern seaboard and especially in Boston and New York. Father Coughlin's popular radio broadcasts were heard all over the northern United States and were supported by official Catholic publications, and he had some success in persuading Americans of the supposed pernicious influence of the Jews.

So did his contemporary, the aviator and national hero Charles Lindbergh (1902–74), an isolationist who was a leading light in the Fascist "America First" Committee. However, the most powerful individual anti-Semite in the United States was the automobile manufacturer Henry Ford (1863–1947). In 1920 he launched a newspaper – the *Dearborn Independent* – specifically to publish an English translation of the *Protocols of the Learned Elders of Zion* and other anti-Semitic literature.

In addition to such overt anti-Semitism, unofficial discrimination was rife within the United States, aimed at both non-whites and Jews. City planners and town hall functionaries ensured that Jews could not live or build in certain areas. (When the Israeli embassy was opened in Washington in 1948, it was discovered that it stood in an area "zoned" to exclude Jews!) Jews, like blacks, were refused entry by many fashionable clubs and hotels right across the United States. It was not until the passing of the Civil Rights Acts of 1964 and 1968 that such discrimination was officially outlawed.

In Britain the anti-Semitism of such writers as Hilaire Belloc, G. K. Chesterton, and the American-born poet T. S. Eliot is well documented. In politics Sir Oswald Mosley – who, in 1924, had been Chancellor of the Duchy of Lancaster as a member of the Labour government – formed the British Union of Fascists in 1932. Four years later, he and his Blackshirts deliberately marched through Jewish neighborhoods in the East End of London. The combined efforts of Jews and the local working-class population – under their slogan "They shall not pass" – halted the marches, despite the fact that a large contingent of police had been brought in to ensure that Mosley's marchers could demonstrate without hindrance. Mosley – married to Diana Mitford, daughter of Lord and Lady Redesdale – had the tacit support of some of the most influential members of the British aristocracy, many of whom were

the time.

In the United States, widespread overt anti-Semitism surfaced for the first time as the Ku Klux Klan gained supporters all over the country. Although originally an anti-black racist movement founded in the southern states after their defeat in the Civil War in 1865, it now extended its prejudices to Jews and even to Catholics. In the 1920s – when its membership had reached about 5 million – hooded Klan members staged marches demanding a "white America" and denouncing Catholics, Jews, and blacks.

Another phenomenon of 1930s America was Father Charles Coughlin, a priest from Detroit. His Christian Front movement, with anti-Semitism as its main platform, found powerful support among the Catholics of the

JEWS IN POLAND 1935–37

LITHUANIA

EAST PRUSSIA

DANZIG

Danzig

Suwalki

Grodno

Jasionowka

Lomza

Bialystok

Bydgoszcz

Wysokie Mazowieckie

Dybek

Suraz

Raciaz

Stok

Bransk

Wloclawek

Plonsk

Vistula

Serock

Sterdyn

Stoczek

Warsaw

Kaluszyn

Brest-Litovsk

Zyrardow

Otwock

Minsk Mazowiecki

Lukow

Warka

P O L A N D

Nowe Miasto

Odrzywol

Piotrkow

Opoczno

Przytyk

Lublin

Kleszcow

Kamiensk

Bug

Przedborz

Dzialoszyn

Radomsko

Czestochowa

Koniecpol

Jedrzejow

Stawiany

SILESIA

Zarki

Stawy

Imielno

Mierzwin

Vistula

Katowice

Lvov

Myslenice

Attacks on Jews 1935–37
Instances of Jewish self-defence
79 Jews killed throughout Poland between 1935 and 1937

part of what was called the "Cliveden Set," after the home of Viscountess Nancy Astor, who had been the first woman to sit in Parliament.

The rise of state-sponsored anti-Semitism in Nazi Germany encouraged the parallel growth of similar movements in other countries where there was some endemic anti-Jewish prejudice to exploit. For instance, the "Iron Guard" in Romania and the "Arrow Cross" party in Hungary – both nations that were soon to become Hitler's allies – matched the German Nazis in their extreme anti-Semitic propaganda as they gained

strength in the late 1930s. Poland, soon to be Hitler's first victim in World War II, was run by a feudal, anti-Semitic caste which was happy to emulate Hitler in depriving its Jewish citizens of their rights. Norway had a tiny but vociferous Nazi movement – the *Nasjonal Samling* – led by Vidkun Quisling, whose name would soon be synonymous with "traitor."

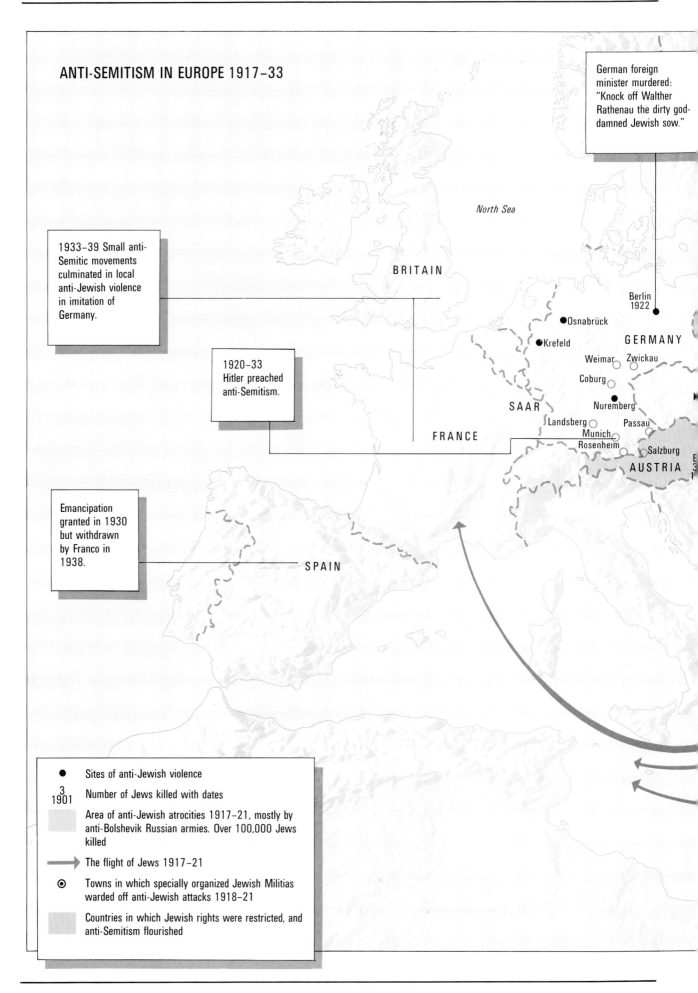

ANTI-SEMITISM IN EUROPE 1917–33

German foreign minister murdered: "Knock off Walther Rathenau the dirty god-damned Jewish sow."

1933–39 Small anti-Semitic movements culminated in local anti-Jewish violence in imitation of Germany.

1920–33 Hitler preached anti-Semitism.

Emancipation granted in 1930 but withdrawn by Franco in 1938.

North Sea

BRITAIN

FRANCE

SAAR

SPAIN

Berlin 1922

●Osnabrück

●Krefeld

GERMANY

Weimar○ Zwickau○

Coburg○

Nuremberg○

Landsberg○ Passau○

Munich○

Rosenheim○ Salzburg○

AUSTRIA

Legend:

● Sites of anti-Jewish violence

3
1901   Number of Jews killed with dates

Area of anti-Jewish atrocities 1917–21, mostly by anti-Bolshevik Russian armies. Over 100,000 Jews killed

➤ The flight of Jews 1917–21

⊙ Towns in which specially organized Jewish Militias warded off anti-Jewish attacks 1918–21

Countries in which Jewish rights were restricted, and anti-Semitism flourished

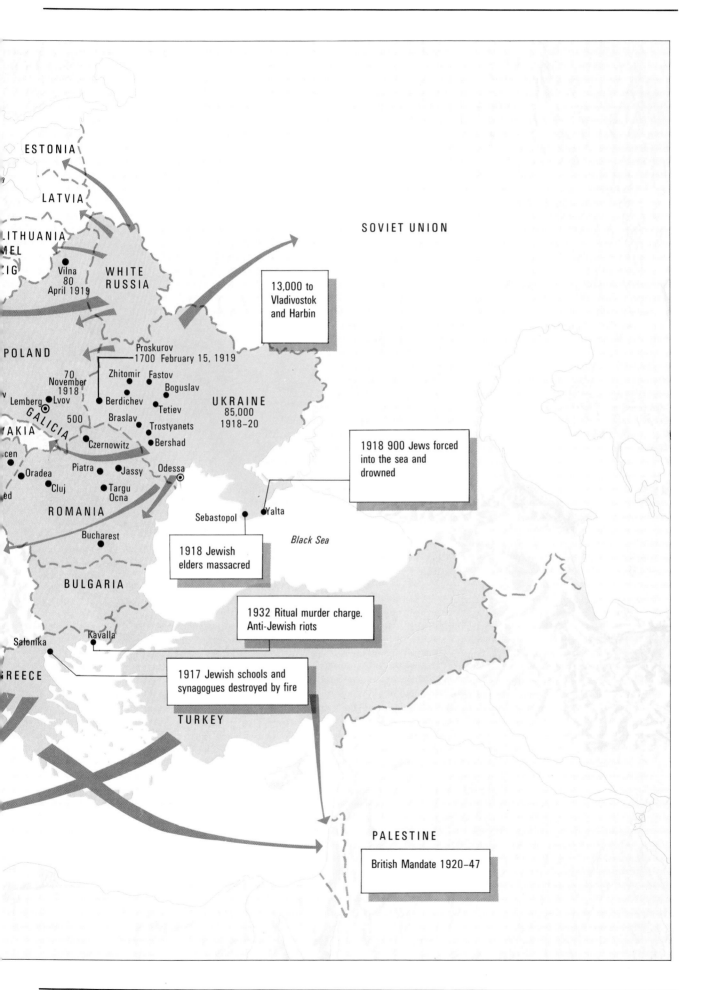

ESTONIA

LATVIA

LITHUANIA
MEL
IG

Vilna
80
April 1919

WHITE
RUSSIA

SOVIET UNION

13,000 to
Vladivostok
and Harbin

POLAND

Proskurov
1700 February 15, 1919

70
November
1918
Lemberg Lvov

Zhitomir Fastov

Boguslav

Berdichev

Tetiev

UKRAINE
85,000
1918–20

GALICIA
500

Braslav

Trostyanets

AKIA

Czernowitz

Bershad

1918 900 Jews forced
into the sea and
drowned

cen

Oradea

Piatra

Jassy

Odessa

Cluj

Targu
Ocna

Sebastopol

Yalta

ROMANIA

1918 Jewish
elders massacred

Black Sea

Bucharest

BULGARIA

1932 Ritual murder charge.
Anti-Jewish riots

Salonika

Kavalla

1917 Jewish schools and
synagogues destroyed by fire

REECE

TURKEY

PALESTINE

British Mandate 1920–47

CHAPTER SIX

THE HOLOCAUST

T he seeds for the Holocaust were sown in nineteenth-century central Europe. It seems paradoxical that the German-speaking nations, which produced Kant, Goethe, Schiller, and most of the greatest classical composers, could be guilty of the unparalleled atrocities of the mid-twentieth century. But, in fact, throughout history Jewish communities in German or Austrian towns and villages had suffered at the hands of their Gentile neighbours.

When Hitler came to power in 1933, Jewish emancipation in all of Germany was only 66 years old, and nowhere had the theory of racial superiority over the Jews gained such widespread acceptance. Hitler merely took advantage of the renewed anti-Semitism that enveloped Europe and America in the wake of World War I – especially after Germany was hit by colossal inflation in 1923. Hitler and his immediate circle were extremely adept at exploiting prejudice and fear, adopting the most advanced techniques in the fields of public relations and propaganda to win over the German people.

Since their emancipation, the Jews had prospered greatly in Germany and in its eastern and southeastern neighboring states (Austria, Hungary, Czechoslovakia, Romania, Yugoslavia). Even in Poland the lot of the Jews was beginning to improve. A significant percentage of the middle classes – and particularly doctors and lawyers – comprised partially or totally assimilated Jews. They opened department stores and factories; they revolutionized industry by introducing modern techniques in cotton spinning, chemical production, and heavy industry. Although many thousands still lived in poverty or near-poverty as small craftsmen and traders, the Jews were nevertheless a very visible and influential minority with a flourishing Yiddish culture.

Hitler and the Road to Power

Adolf Hitler, born in 1889 at Braunau in Austria, near the German border, was the son of a petty official originally named Schicklgruber. As a down-and-out teenager and failed art student in Vienna and then as an ex-corporal in Munich after Germany's defeat in World War I, Hitler learned his anti-Semitism in the streets.

He first attempted to seize power in Germany in 1923 in an abortive coup organized in a Munich beer hall. For this, he was sentenced to five years' imprisonment, but in the end served only nine months. While in prison, he wrote (and had pub-

ABOVE: *Slowly but surely, a web of legal restrictions tightened around the Jews. They were forbidden, for example, to go to cinemas, theaters, and concerts, denied a tobacco ration, and banned from public transport. Here, the North Sea bathing resort of Norderney proudly proclaims it is "Jew free."*

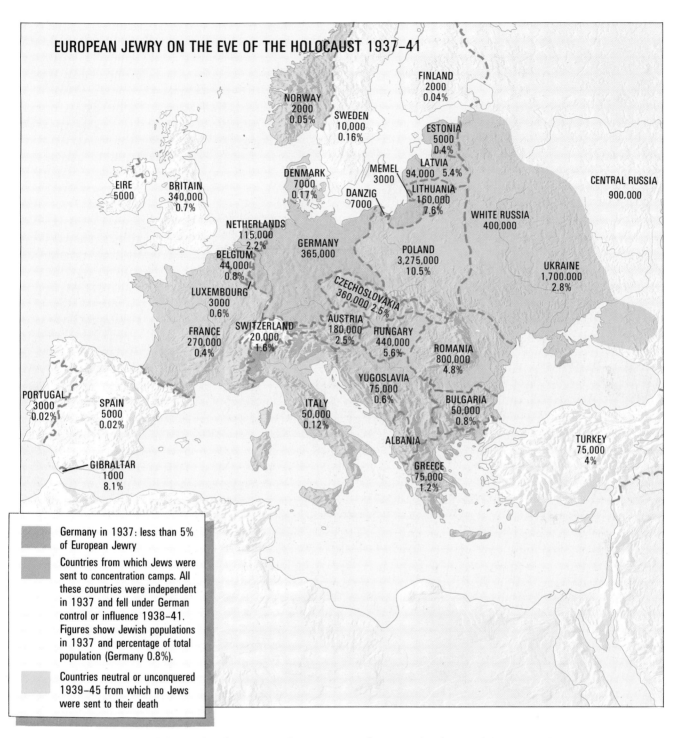

EUROPEAN JEWRY ON THE EVE OF THE HOLOCAUST 1937–41

FINLAND
2000
0.04%

NORWAY
2000
0.05%

SWEDEN
10,000
0.16%

ESTONIA
5000
0.4%

MEMEL
3000

LATVIA
94,000 5.4%

DENMARK
7000
0.17%

DANZIG
7000

LITHUANIA
160,000
7.6%

WHITE RUSSIA
400,000

CENTRAL RUSSIA
900,000

EIRE
5000

BRITAIN
340,000
0.7%

NETHERLANDS
115,000
2.2%

GERMANY
365,000

POLAND
3,275,000
10.5%

UKRAINE
1,700,000
2.8%

BELGIUM
44,000
0.8%

CZECHOSLOVAKIA
360,000 2.5%

LUXEMBOURG
3000
0.6%

AUSTRIA
180,000
2.5%

HUNGARY
440,000
5.6%

FRANCE
270,000
0.4%

SWITZERLAND
20,000
1.6%

ROMANIA
800,000
4.8%

YUGOSLAVIA
75,000
0.6%

BULGARIA
50,000
0.8%

PORTUGAL
3000
0.02%

SPAIN
5000
0.02%

ITALY
50,000
0.12%

ALBANIA

TURKEY
75,000
4%

GIBRALTAR
1000
8.1%

GREECE
75,000
1.2%

Germany in 1937: less than 5% of European Jewry

Countries from which Jews were sent to concentration camps. All these countries were independent in 1937 and fell under German control or influence 1938–41. Figures show Jewish populations in 1937 and percentage of total population (Germany 0.8%).

Countries neutral or unconquered 1939–45 from which no Jews were sent to their death

ABOVE: *In 1937 Hitler controlled less than five percent of European Jewry; the Anschluss with Austria and the sacking of Czechoslovakia brought the fear of persecution and the concentration camps in their train. As Hitler's Reich expanded, ever-increasing numbers of European Jews came under Nazi rule.*

lished) the first part of *Mein Kampf ("My Struggle"),* a long, detailed personal testament explaining his life and attitudes which is filled with his pathological hatred of the Jews.

Hitler's National Socialist German Workers' Party – *National-sozialistische Deutsche Arbeiterpartei,* from the first two syllables of which is derived the better-known name: Nazi – gained in popularity from the late 1920s. In 1928, after Hitler had modified the "socialist" element in return for the financial backing of German industrialists, the party polled 810,000 votes. In 1930 it garnered over 6 million, and by 1932 it had reached its electoral zenith, with 14 million votes and 230 seats in the Reichstag.

However, these made up only 42 percent of the total, not enough for the Nazis to take power, and there were signs of the German public's growing disaffection with the excesses of Hitler's Brownshirts. Hitler quickly made a secret deal with the former chancellor, Franz von Papen, and in Janu-

THE JEWS OF GERMANY AND THE
TRIUMPH OF NAZISM 1933–38

RIGHT: *One of the first Nazi moves on coming to power in 1933 was to urge all loyal Aryan Germans to boycott Jewish stores and goods. Here, two Brownshirts are sticking posters on a large Berlin department store.*

Concentration camps and dates when established

10,068   Number of Jews in major cities

RIGHT: *For those members of the Jewish community who could afford to do so, the answer to Nazi persecution was flight. Paradoxically, in the 1930s, this was encouraged by the Nazi authorities, who were not at that time committed to a policy of extermination. Even so, many Jews remained, convinced that Nazi anti-Semitism was a temporary aberration, introduced for reasons of political expediency.*

ABOVE: *Systematic persecution of Germany's Jewish community started immediately after Hitler's accession to power in 1933; the same year saw the establishment of the first concentration camps, the most notorious of which were Dachau and Sachsenhausen. The persecution gathered pace with the introduction of the notorious Nuremberg racial laws in 1935.*

ary 1933 the president – 85-year-old Field Marshal Paul von Hindenburg – appointed Hitler Chancellor. Two months later laws were passed granting him dictatorial powers – hardly surprising, then, that, in November, the Nazis dominated the elections, with 92 percent of the electorate voting for their candidates. In 1934, following the death of Hindenburg, Hitler elevated himself to the position of *Führer* ("leader") of what he claimed would be a "Thousand-Year Reich."

Persecution in Germany

Anti-Jewish measures had already begun in earnest. Initially, the Nazis acted cautiously. The first concentration camps were set up, primarily (at this stage) with the object of detaining political opponents such as the Communists and Socialists, and to punish dissenters such as the non-Jewish comedian Karl Valentin, whose nightclub act made fun of Hitler and his mannerisms.

Then, on April 1, 1933, Hitler's Brown-

shirts, or "stormtroopers" (*Sturmabteilung*), organized a national boycott of Jewish businesses and professional people, daubing Jewish shops all over Germany with swastikas, stars of David, and slogans such as *"Kauff nicht bei Juden"* ("Don't buy from Jews"). Less than a week later, the "Law for the restoration of a professional civil service" was passed, which compulsorily retired civil servants of "non-Aryan descent."

A succession of petty anti-Jewish measures followed, culminating in the Nuremberg Laws of 1935, which reduced Jews to the status of second-class citizens. It was now illegal for them to visit cafés and places of entertainment or to frequent public baths or swimming pools, and marriages and extramarital sexual relations between Jews and non-Jews were prohibited. (Some who had been caught engaging in the latter were publicly paraded with placards around their necks proclaiming: "I slept with a Jew"). Jews were also barred from voting and hold-

ing public office, and books and paintings by and about them were burned under the personal supervision of Josef Goebbels, the propaganda minister, who screamed at the flames: "The soul of the German people can once again express itself! These flames...light up a new age!" Soon Jews were also officially barred from the professions.

In 1936, when Germany hosted the Olympic Games, no German Jews were allowed to participate (although those from abroad could and did), and anti-Semitic posters were prominently displayed. This received scant attention from the Western media.

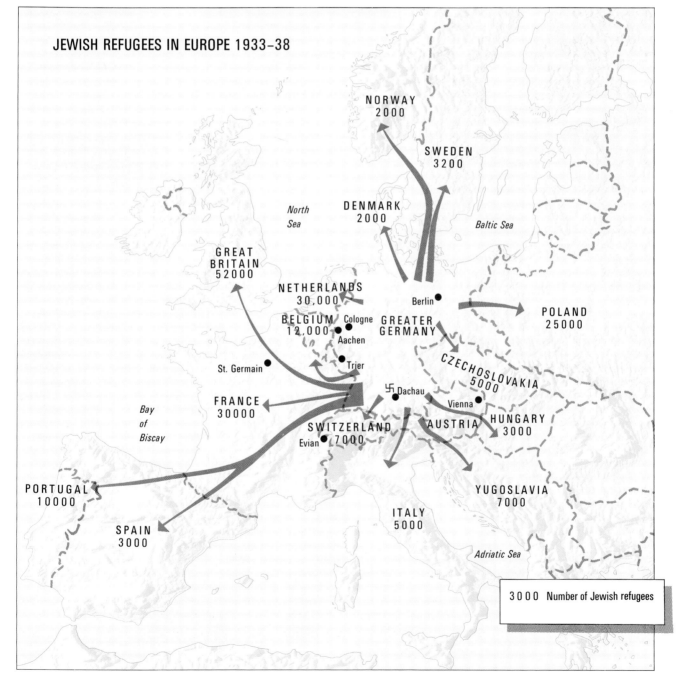

JEWISH REFUGEES IN EUROPE 1933–38

NORWAY
2000

SWEDEN
3200

North
Sea

DENMARK
2000

Baltic Sea

GREAT
BRITAIN
52000

NETHERLANDS
30,000

Berlin

BELGIUM
12,000

Cologne

GREATER
GERMANY

POLAND
25000

Aachen

Trier

St. Germain

CZECHOSLOVAKIA
5000

Dachau

Vienna

FRANCE
30000

Bay
of
Biscay

SWITZERLAND
7000

AUSTRIA

HUNGARY
3000

Evian

PORTUGAL
10000

YUGOSLAVIA
7000

ITALY
5000

SPAIN
3000

Adriatic Sea

3000   Number of Jewish refugees

In March of the same year, the German army marched back into the Rhineland, which had been demilitarized under the Treaty of Versailles after World War I. Hitler was now sure that he would encounter little or no opposition to his plans for the Jews or for world domination.

On March 11, 1938, German troops marched into Austria. The Austrian Nazi party was well prepared and welcomed the soldiers – with Hitler at their head – with open arms. Anti-Semitic policies were immediately put into action: Jews, including elderly men, were forced to clean the streets with corrosives that damaged their skin; Jewish shops were looted and synagogues stoned and burned; mass arrests also began.

The Refugees

As a result of Hitler's anti-Semitic measures, there was a mass exodus of skilled and gifted Jews, and by 1938 118,000 had left Germany. Most fled to parts of western Europe or to America; more than 50,000 entered Britain, including many children; 15,000 went to the United States; and many, unfortunately, simply moved elsewhere in Europe, where the Nazis would eventually catch up with them. Approximately 47,000 went to Palestine, then under British control.

As Jewish emigration increased, encouraged by the Nazis, the presence of refugees caused crises in other countries. In July 1938 President Roosevelt called an international conference on the refugee question at Evian-les-Bains on Lake Geneva. Those attending claimed that their countries could not take in more than a trickle. (In 1940, an American correspondent in Berlin, William Shirer, discovered that although the quota of Germans allowed entrance into the United States was only 27,000 annually, there was a

RIGHT: *Jews in Paris wearing the yellow Star of David. Though this symbol of humiliation is now associated with the years of the Holocaust, its origins date back to the Middle Ages, when Jews in many communities were forced to wear distinguishing articles of clothing.*

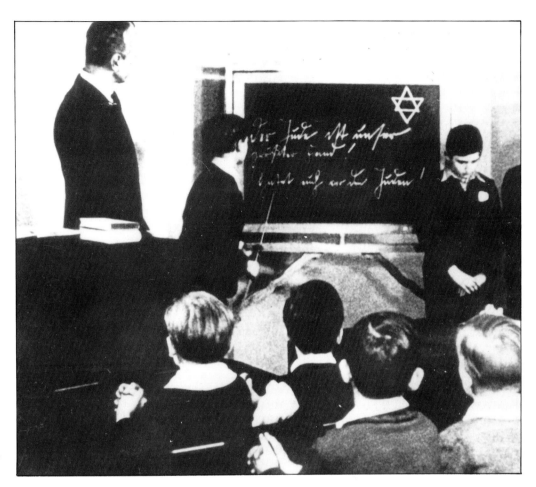

RIGHT: *Anti-Jewish propaganda started in the schools under the Nazi regime. This still photograph from the U.S. documentary.* The March of Time *is an accurate reconstruction of a typical classroom scene, in which Jewish schoolboys are humiliated by their teacher and their fellows. The slogan on the blackboard reads "The Jew is our worst enemy."*

waiting list of 248,000 names, 98 per cent of them Jewish – which he estimated to be about half the Jewish population left in Germany at the time.)

The British, who agreed with these sentiments, were there to speak not only for themselves but also for Palestine. They had controlled the territory under the terms of a League of Nations mandate since 1922, and had gone to great lengths to placate the region's Arab majority.

It is a bitter irony that the Arab population of this once-neglected and barren land had swollen considerably with the promise of new jobs created by Jewish immigrants who, in the "national home" promised to them by the British Foreign Secretary Arthur Balfour, in 1917, had revitalized its agriculture and trade. However, the Arabs, so recently granted a measure of self-government by the Allies after the fall of the Ottoman Empire following World War I, also considered Palestine their own. Many greatly resented the prosperous Jewish settlements in their midst, and this resentment increasingly boiled over into riots and bloodshed,

notably the massacre of Jews at Hebron in 1928 and the attacks on Jews in August 1929 following disputes over the latter's access to the Western Wall in Jerusalem.

The Grand Mufti of Jerusalem, Haj Amin al-Husseini, had strong Nazi sympathies, and the Nazis forged a secret alliance with him as soon as they took office in Germany. Arms and money reached the Arabs via the Templars, a German religious fraternity which had several colonies in Palestine. When letters were discovered proving how close were the links between the Templars and Nazi Germany and how they helped to foment the unrest, the British expelled the Templars from Palestine in 1939.

While trying to keep the peace, the British were loath to act against the Palestinian Arabs, hoping to win the support of Arabs throughout the Middle East for their fight against Germany (they knew they could rely on the Jews' support). When increasing Jewish emigration to Palestine became an issue, the British appointed a commission of inquiry. The Peel Commission took over a year to reach its decision, but when this was announced, in July 1937, it was greeted with an outcry by the Jews. Jewish immigration into Palestine, said the Commission, was to be limited to 12,000 a year for five years, with a further 25,000 certificates available for issue in the event of an emergency.

Although the British were fully aware of Hitler's policy toward the Jews, they had no way of knowing that this would lead to mass murder. The moment that they learned the true fate of the Jews of Europe, in 1942 *(see below)*, all barriers to Jewish immigration into Palestine were lifted.

Increasing Nazi Persecution and Incursions
Following Benito Mussolini's proclamation of the Rome-Berlin Axis in November 1936, Nuremberg-style laws were introduced into Italy, as they had already been in Hungary.

In October 1938, Jews of Polish origin were expelled from German soil. Many lived in Austria (now part of the Reich), descendants of those who had resided in the part of Poland taken by the Habsburgs after the partitions of the eighteenth century. However, when these Austrian-Polish Jews attempted to leave, 5,000 were stranded in a no-man's-land on the Polish border because the Poles at first refused to admit them. At

RIGHT: *Orchestrated by propaganda minister Josef Goebbels, the night of November 9, 1938, saw the destruction of 191 synagogues throughout Germany. This act of mass-vandalism and violence was supposedly a spontaneous national reaction to the assassination of a German diplomat by a young Jew named Herschel Grynszpan in Paris. Jewish businesses and shops were also attacked in what became known as* Kristallnacht, *"the night of broken glass."*

ABOVE: *The wrecked and pillaged windows of a Jewish store in Berlin's fashionable Friedrichstrasse, photographed in the wake of the* Kristallnacht *destruction of November 1938.*

DESTRUCTION OF THE SYNAGOGUES
NOVEMBER 9, 1938

Baltic Sea

North Sea

Kiel

NETHERLANDS Emden

Lübeck
Hamburg

Bremen

Hanover

Munster   Brunswick   Berlin

Essen   Magdeburg

Düsseldorf   GREATER
Cologne   GERMANY

Bonn   Leipzig

Coblenz   Chemnitz   Dresden

Frankfurt   Plauen
Darmstadt

Mannheim   Würzburg   Karlsbad

Saarbrücken   Furth

LUXEMBOURG   Karlsrühe   Nuremberg

FRANCE

Freiburg   Ulm   Augsburg
Constance   Munich

Stettin

Danzig   Königsberg

FREE
CITY
OF
DANZIG   Allenstein

POLAND

Glogau

Liegnitz

Breslau   Oppeln

Hindenburg

Gleiwitz

SUDETENLAND

CZECHOSLOVAKIA

Linz

Baden
Bad Vöslau   Eisenstadt

Salzburg   Wiener Neustadt

Innsbruck   AUSTRIA

SWITZERLAND   Graz

Klagenfurt   HUNGARY

BELGIUM

● Towns where
synagogues
destroyed

this point a young Polish Jew living in Paris, whose parents were waiting at one of these border transit camps, went to the German embassy and shot one of the diplomats, Ernst von Rath.

This was just the excuse the Nazis needed. On the night of 9–10 November 1938, they staged the *Kristallnacht* purge (the "night of [the broken] glass"). This carefully targeted attack on Jewish homes, shops, offices, and synagogues in Germany and Austria was designed to do as much damage as possible – the name of this pogrom derives from the fragments of glass from the thousands of broken windows which littered the streets. The non-Jewish populace was involved: in Hanover and elsewhere, people were encouraged to stone, loot, and burn the local synagogues. In recently annexed Austria, more than 40 were destroyed. In addition, some 35,000 Jews were arrested throughout the Reich.

Jews began to be transported *en masse* to

ABOVE: *A burning synagogue in Baden-Baden, photographed on November 10, 1938, the morning after the nationwide attack on Jewish property, named "the night of broken glass." The fire fighters are not there to save the synagogue, but to prevent the fire spreading to neighboring Aryan property.*

RIGHT: *The expulsion of 15,000 Polish-born Jews over the border to Poland was the spark that led Herschel Grynszpan, who was related to one of the expelled families, to assassinate Ernst von Rath in Paris. The consequences were immediate and terrible; forced deportations to Germany's main concentration camps began the day after "the night of broken glass." This savage pogrom led to substantial international protest, notably in the United States and Britain.*

GERMANY
OCTOBER–NOVEMBER 1938

Areas from which Jews were sent to concentration camps November 10, 1938

20,000 Number of Jews in each camp after November 10, 1938

Concentration camps

Expulsion of Polish-born Jews from Germany October 28, 1938

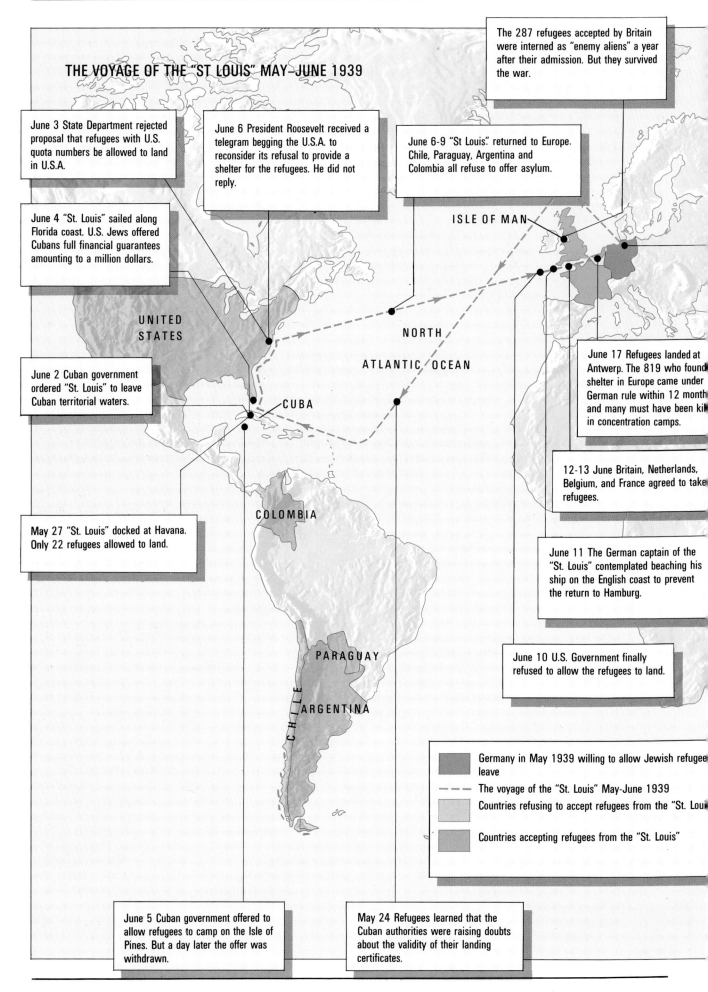

THE VOYAGE OF THE "ST LOUIS" MAY–JUNE 1939

The 287 refugees accepted by Britain were interned as "enemy aliens" a year after their admission. But they survived the war.

June 3 State Department rejected proposal that refugees with U.S. quota numbers be allowed to land in U.S.A.

June 6 President Roosevelt received a telegram begging the U.S.A. to reconsider its refusal to provide a shelter for the refugees. He did not reply.

June 6-9 "St Louis" returned to Europe. Chile, Paraguay, Argentina and Colombia all refuse to offer asylum.

June 4 "St. Louis" sailed along Florida coast. U.S. Jews offered Cubans full financial guarantees amounting to a million dollars.

ISLE OF MAN

UNITED STATES

NORTH

ATLANTIC OCEAN

June 17 Refugees landed at Antwerp. The 819 who found shelter in Europe came under German rule within 12 months and many must have been killed in concentration camps.

June 2 Cuban government ordered "St. Louis" to leave Cuban territorial waters.

CUBA

12-13 June Britain, Netherlands, Belgium, and France agreed to take refugees.

May 27 "St. Louis" docked at Havana. Only 22 refugees allowed to land.

COLOMBIA

June 11 The German captain of the "St. Louis" contemplated beaching his ship on the English coast to prevent the return to Hamburg.

PARAGUAY

CHILE

ARGENTINA

June 10 U.S. Government finally refused to allow the refugees to land.

Germany in May 1939 willing to allow Jewish refugees leave

The voyage of the "St. Louis" May-June 1939

Countries refusing to accept refugees from the "St. Louis"

Countries accepting refugees from the "St. Louis"

June 5 Cuban government offered to allow refugees to camp on the Isle of Pines. But a day later the offer was withdrawn.

May 24 Refugees learned that the Cuban authorities were raising doubts about the validity of their landing certificates.

concentration camps: 20,000 were deported and several thousand died before the survivors were released in early 1939. The Jewish community of Vienna was dissolved. Those Jews who wanted to emigrate now had to hand over their entire wealth to the Germans, instead of just a large ransom as before. The Nazis considered demanding a huge sum from world Jewry as a ransom for the release of the Jews still remaining in Germany but abandoned the idea on the outbreak of war. Some 300,000 Jews had already been deported and 8,000 had committed suicide. In Austria, 400,000 had not been able to get away. The reaction of the world's press was amazement and outrage at Germany's treatment of the Jews.

The Beginning of War

Hitler continued with his expansionist plans, confident that no concerted action would be taken against him if he marched into ill-protected neighboring countries. On October 1, 1938, as a consequence of the Munich agreement made between Germany, Britain, France, and Italy at the end of September, his army occupied the Sudetenland, the German-speaking part of Czechoslovakia. As elsewhere, the ground had been well prepared and the local Nazis greeted him enthusiastically.

At Munich, Hitler had given Britain's Prime Minister, Neville Chamberlain, assurances that there would be "peace in our time," but on March 15, 1939, the rest of Czechoslovakia was annexed. Bohemia and Moravia became part of the Reich, and Slovakia was turned into a puppet state, ruled by a priest, Father Joseph Tiso. Once again, Western opinion was outraged at the treatment of Jews by Hitler and this became part of the wider indictment against Nazism.

When Poland was threatened, Britain and France no longer felt able to ignore Nazi ambitions for world domination. That this

LEFT: *Hitler claimed in his own defense that nations that protested against Nazi policies against the Jews were deeply reluctant to provide the Jews with practical help, and the voyage of the "St. Louis" seemed to support his point. Even the U.S. refused to admit the refugees; it was not until after the "St. Louis" captain threatened to beach his ship rather than return to Germany that Britain, France, Holland, and Belgium each agreed to accept a quota of the refugees.*

was what they planned was already clear to Stalin: on August 23, and, 1939, he signed a non-aggression pact with the German Foreign Minister, Joachim von Ribbentrop, in order to gain much-needed time for the Soviet Union to prepare itself (and at the same time to carve out a piece of Poland).

The German invasion of Poland on September 1, 1939 at last drew a response from the West: two days later, Britain and France declared war on Germany.

The Massacres Begin

As soon as the German troops had conquered Poland, there were mass executions of Polish Jews. Those who escaped death were forcibly expelled from the smaller Polish cities into specially built ghettos, such as the one in Lublin.

For the first time since Maria Theresa's decree of the eighteenth century, Jews were forced to wear a distinguishing mark – often a yellow star of David, emblazoned with the word "Jüde" – initially in Poland and then, in 1941, in Germany, Bohemia, and Moravia. In 1942, all the other countries under Nazi occupation received similar orders.

The Nazis now had under their direct control – or under their influence, in countries sympathetic to their regime, such as Italy, Hungary, and Romania – most of the Jewish population of Europe. They had also failed to make Germany and Austria *judenrein* ("cleansed of Jews") and between 1939 and 1941, they continued to deport German and Austrian Jews to the ghettos they had created in Poland and, later, in Lithuania and Latvia.

It is not known exactly when the mass murder of the Jews – the "final solution" – was decided upon. However historians now concur that Hitler and Himmler must have agreed upon it between December 1940 and February 1941, while the invasion of the Soviet Union was being planned.

The mass killings began in the areas of the Soviet Union occupied by the Germans from June 1941. *Einsatzgruppen* ("task forces") of the SS mobilized local collaborators to help them round up Jews, take them to prepared trenches and pits, and force them to strip naked at gunpoint. The Germans then shot them. Within a three-day period in September 1941, 34,000 Jews were shot at Babi-Yar near Kiev in the Ukraine. (Over 100,000

LEFT: *The Jewish world conspiracy through Nazi eyes. Supported by a suffering proletariat and the bayonets of their armies, Roosevelt, Stalin, Churchill, and their cronies plot the downfall of the Aryan race.*

RIGHT: *On the way to the gas chambers.*

BELOW RIGHT: *In the Warsaw Ghetto. Here, as crack SS troops sought to deport the Jews, the inhabitants rose in open revolt in February 1943.*

were to die in the city before the Soviet army liberated it in 1944.)

The Germans seem to have found such collaborators wherever they decided to eliminate the Jews – especially in Latvia, Lithuania, Byelorussia, and, as we have seen, the Ukraine. In the large Ukrainian city of Odessa, local ethnic Romanians, given machine-guns by the Germans, slaughtered 25,000 Jews.

"The Final Solution of the Jewish Question"

On January 20, 1942 *Gruppenführer* Reinhard Heydrich, deputy commander of the Gestapo, announced at a conference at Wannsee, a lakeside suburb of Berlin, Hitler's plans for the extermination of the Jews.

The "final solution" was horrific in its simplicity: all Jews would be deported to camps; those unfit would be exterminated immediately; those still capable of work would be forced to work to death. Five special "death camps" were set up in remote areas of Poland with the sole purpose of murdering Jews: Chelmno, Belzec, Maidanek, Sobibór, Treblinka. These had only extermination facilities, so even able-bodied people were murdered (apart from the small band of Jews who carried out the menial work within the camps). There was, however,

BELOW: *Soviet Jews and gentiles found a common cause in the face of the Nazi onslaught on the U.S.S.R. in 1941. More than 500,000 Jews served in the Soviet army; at least 200,000 were killed.*

a sixth camp, Auschwitz, where able-bodied deportees – arriving through gates bearing the sinister motto *"ARBEIT MACH FREI"* ("WORK MAKES FREE") – were sent to nearby slave labor camps, while women, children, the old and the sick were sent to the gas chambers at a rate of 12,000 a day. Here, between 1941 and 1944, more than 2 million Jews were murdered (together with 2 million non-Jews); another 2 million Jews were murdered at the other four death camps. In addition, there were the already established camps in Germany (including Bergen-Belsen, Ravensbrück, Buchenwald, Dachau),

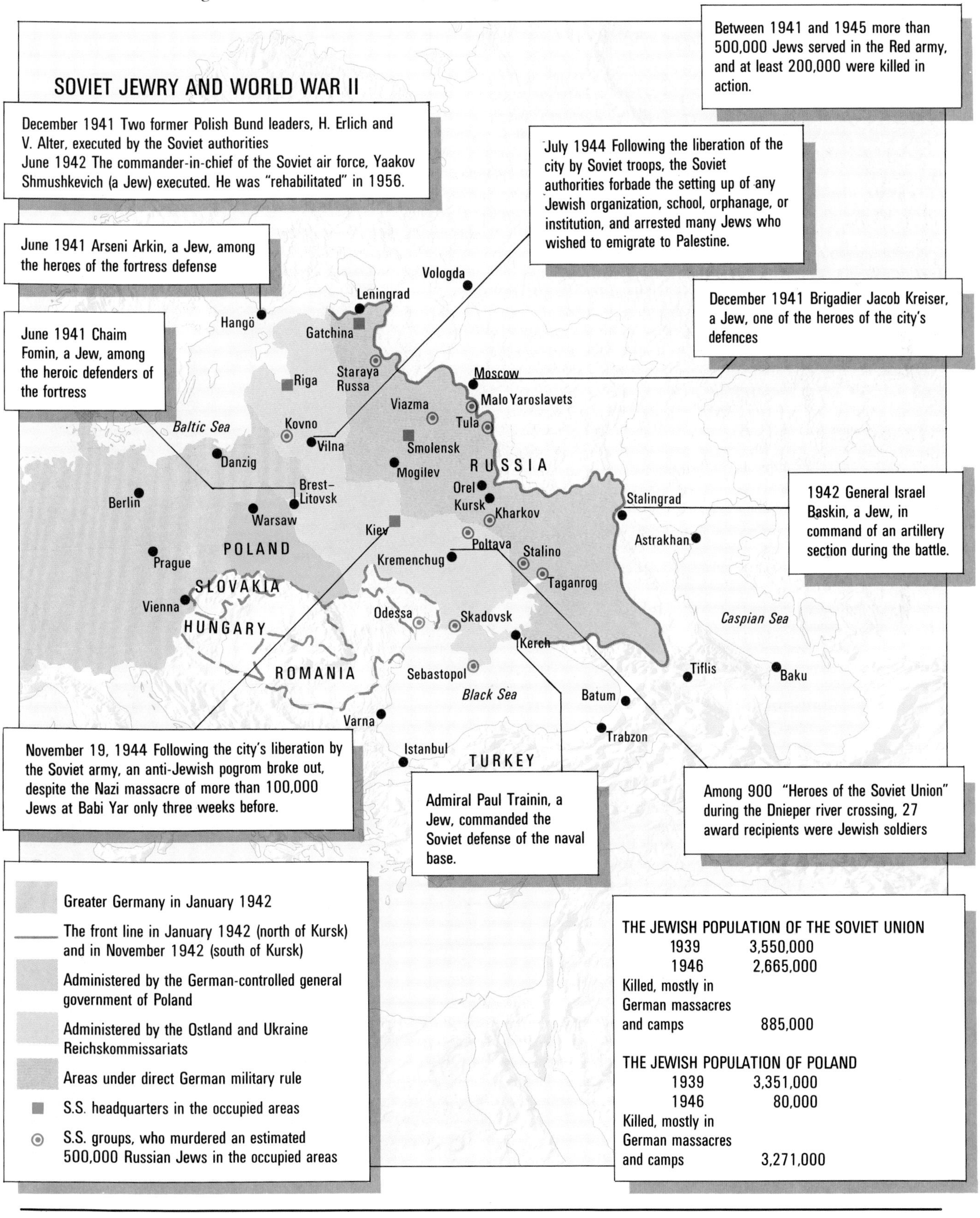
SOVIET JEWRY AND WORLD WAR II
Between 1941 and 1945 more than 500,000 Jews served in the Red army, and at least 200,000 were killed in action.
December 1941 Two former Polish Bund leaders, H. Erlich and V. Alter, executed by the Soviet authorities
June 1942 The commander-in-chief of the Soviet air force, Yaakov Shmushkevich (a Jew) executed. He was "rehabilitated" in 1956.
July 1944 Following the liberation of the city by Soviet troops, the Soviet authorities forbade the setting up of any Jewish organization, school, orphanage, or institution, and arrested many Jews who wished to emigrate to Palestine.
June 1941 Arseni Arkin, a Jew, among the heroes of the fortress defense
December 1941 Brigadier Jacob Kreiser, a Jew, one of the heroes of the city's defences
June 1941 Chaim Fomin, a Jew, among the heroic defenders of the fortress
1942 General Israel Baskin, a Jew, in command of an artillery section during the battle.
November 19, 1944 Following the city's liberation by the Soviet army, an anti-Jewish pogrom broke out, despite the Nazi massacre of more than 100,000 Jews at Babi Yar only three weeks before.
Admiral Paul Trainin, a Jew, commanded the Soviet defense of the naval base.
Among 900 "Heroes of the Soviet Union" during the Dnieper river crossing, 27 award recipients were Jewish soldiers
Vologda
Leningrad
Hangö
Gatchina
Riga
Staraya Russa
Moscow
Malo Yaroslavets
Viazma
Tula
Baltic Sea
Kovno
Vilna
Smolensk
Danzig
Mogilev
RUSSIA
Brest-Litovsk
Orel
Berlin
Kursk
Kharkov
Stalingrad
Warsaw
Kiev
Astrakhan
Poltava
Stalino
Prague
POLAND
Kremenchug
Taganrog
SLOVAKIA
Vienna
Odessa
Skadovsk
HUNGARY
Caspian Sea
Kerch
ROMANIA
Sebastopol
Tiflis
Baku
Black Sea
Batum
Varna
Trabzon
Istanbul
TURKEY
Greater Germany in January 1942
The front line in January 1942 (north of Kursk) and in November 1942 (south of Kursk)
Administered by the German-controlled general government of Poland
Administered by the Ostland and Ukraine Reichskommissariats
Areas under direct German military rule
S.S. headquarters in the occupied areas
S.S. groups, who murdered an estimated 500,000 Russian Jews in the occupied areas
THE JEWISH POPULATION OF THE SOVIET UNION
1939 3,550,000
1946 2,665,000
Killed, mostly in German massacres and camps 885,000
THE JEWISH POPULATION OF POLAND
1939 3,351,000
1946 80,000
Killed, mostly in German massacres and camps 3,271,000

Estonia, France (Natzweiler), Austria (Mauthausen) and Yugoslavia where Jews and non-Jews were starved, tortured, worked to death, and murdered.

BELOW: *The strategy for the "final solution of the Jewish problem" was worked out at a top-level meeting of Nazi bureaucrats under the chairmanship of Reinhard Heydrich in January 1942.*

The Germans required vast amounts of equipment to carry out their plan, and for the efficient running of the operation, it was important that the victims not realize their fate. Most of the Jews were shipped to their final destinations in cattle trucks, but in order

to keep up the pretense that they were simply being relocated, some Dutch Jews were sent to their deaths in comfortable passenger carriages.

When, in 1942, the truth about the mass murders reached the West, the governments of Britain, the United States, and the Soviet Union issued a public declaration setting out what was being done by the Germans and denouncing their "bestial crimes" against the

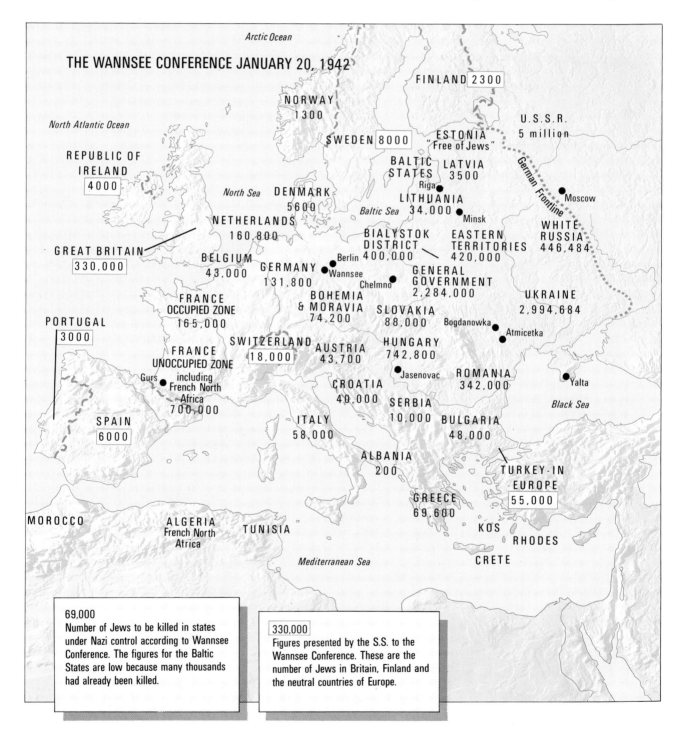

THE WANNSEE CONFERENCE JANUARY 20, 1942

FINLAND 2300

NORWAY 1300

U.S.S.R. 5 million

ESTONIA "Free of Jews"

SWEDEN 8000

REPUBLIC OF IRELAND 4000

BALTIC STATES   LATVIA 3500
Riga

DENMARK 5600
LITHUANIA 34,000
Minsk

NETHERLANDS 160,800

WHITE RUSSIA 446,484
Moscow

GREAT BRITAIN 330,000

BELGIUM 43,000

BIALYSTOK DISTRICT 400,000

EASTERN TERRITORIES 420,000

GERMANY 131,800   Berlin   Wannsee
Chelmno

GENERAL GOVERNMENT 2,284,000

FRANCE OCCUPIED ZONE 165,000

BOHEMIA & MORAVIA 74,200

SLOVAKIA 88,000

UKRAINE 2,994,684

PORTUGAL 3000

SWITZERLAND 18,000

AUSTRIA 43,700

HUNGARY 742,800

Bogdanowka   Atmicetka

FRANCE UNOCCUPIED ZONE including French North Africa 700,000
Gurs

Jasenovac

ROMANIA 342,000

Yalta

CROATIA 40,000

SERBIA 10,000

Black Sea

SPAIN 6000

ITALY 58,000

BULGARIA 48,000

ALBANIA 200

TURKEY-IN EUROPE 55,000

GREECE 69,600

MOROCCO

ALGERIA French North Africa

TUNISIA

KOS
RHODES
CRETE

Mediterranean Sea

Arctic Ocean

North Atlantic Ocean

North Sea

Baltic Sea

German Frontline

69,000
Number of Jews to be killed in states under Nazi control according to Wannsee Conference. The figures for the Baltic States are low because many thousands had already been killed.

330,000
Figures presented by the S.S. to the Wannsee Conference. These are the number of Jews in Britain, Finland and the neutral countries of Europe.

Jews. So horrified was the British House of Commons that its members stood in silence to honor the victims.

The Jews Fight Back

There were places where it was impossible for the Germans to keep their intentions a secret: the ghettos. Here, news eventually leaked back about where people were being taken after the mass round-ups. On July 22, 1942 the order came from the German Governor-General of Poland, Hans Frank, to liquidate the 500,000 Jews within the walls of the Warsaw Ghetto, giving the Nazi authorities there a daily quota of 4,500. Nine months later, the Jews who remained resolved to fight the Germans, despite the fact that this was tantamount to suicide.

On April 18, there was a massive resistance by everyone strong enough to hold

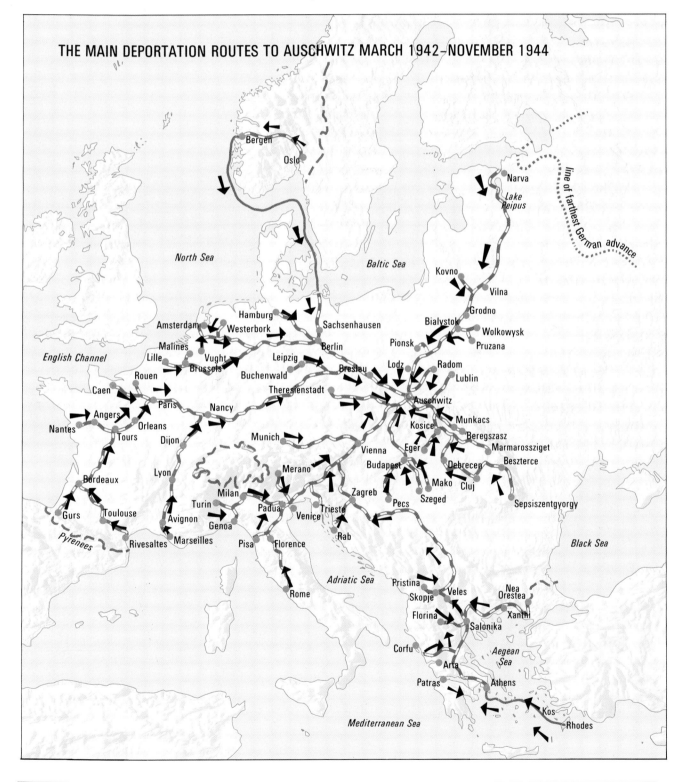

THE MAIN DEPORTATION ROUTES TO AUSCHWITZ MARCH 1942–NOVEMBER 1944

the few weapons that they had managed to smuggle inside. At first, to their utter astonishment, the Germans were repulsed. Then, in retaliation, the Nazis set fire to the ghetto and burned many of the inmates to death. Nevertheless, the resistance continued from the sewers and bunkers to which the survivors had retreated. In the end, although a significant number escaped, the Germans managed to round up another 20,000 people, who were all sent to their deaths.

The fate of Warsaw Jewry was chronicled by many of the inhabitants. Their records were preserved by a historian inside the ghetto, Emmanuel Ringelblum, who hid them in a sealed milk churn.

The Warsaw Ghetto uprising was by no means the only act of defiance by Jews.

Thousands joined the resistance fighters and partisans active all over Europe. There were even acts of resistance at the camps – such as at Sobibór in October 1943, when, in a mass escape, 150 were killed before they could get very far, but an equal number managed to elude Nazi capture; and at Auschwitz, where inmates managed to blow up two of the crematoria and cut their way out of the camp (all those who escaped through the wire were hunted down and killed). However, many incidents of bravery were never revealed because, after the war, there was no one left alive to recount them. Some camps – Treblinka, for instance – were razed by the Germans during their retreat and every inmate killed by the camp guards.

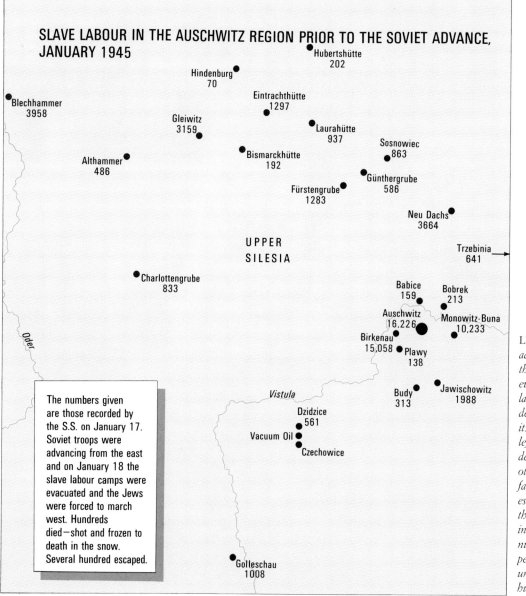

SLAVE LABOUR IN THE AUSCHWITZ REGION PRIOR TO THE SOVIET ADVANCE, JANUARY 1945

Hubertshütte 202

Hindenburg 70

Eintrachthütte 1297

Blechhammer 3958

Gleiwitz 3159

Laurahütte 937

Sosnowiec 863

Althammer 486

Bismarckhütte 192

Günthergrube 586

Fürstengrube 1283

Neu Dachs 3664

UPPER SILESIA

Trzebinia 641

Charlottengrube 833

Babice 159

Bobrek 213

Auschwitz 16,226

Monowitz-Buna 10,233

Birkenau 15,058

Plawy 138

Vistula

Budy 313

Jawischowitz 1988

Dzidzice 561

Vacuum Oil

Czechowice

Oder

Golleschau 1008

The numbers given are those recorded by the S.S. on January 17. Soviet troops were advancing from the east and on January 18 the slave labour camps were evacuated and the Jews were forced to march west. Hundreds died—shot and frozen to death in the snow. Several hundred escaped.

LEFT: *As Soviet forces advanced from the east, the SS ordered the evacuation of the slave labor camps and the destruction of Auschwitz itself. The first evacuees left on foot; many froze to death in the snow, while others, too weak to march farther, were shot by the escorting guards. More than 30,000 Jews were involved; the exact numbers of those who perished remains unknown, though a few hundred escaped.*

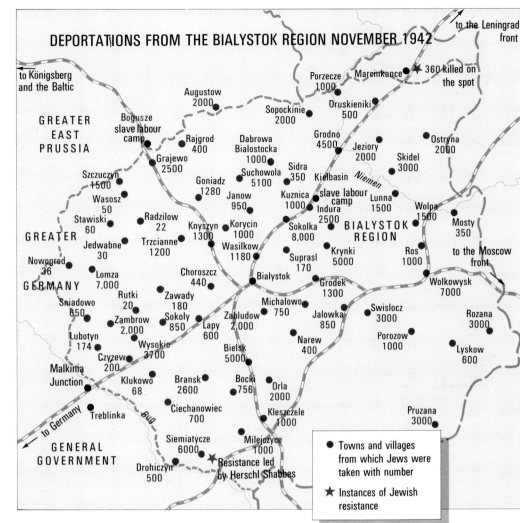

DEPORTATIONS FROM THE BIALYSTOK REGION NOVEMBER 1942

to the Leningrad front

to Königsberg and the Baltic

Porzecze 1000 — Marcinkance — 360 killed on the spot

GREATER EAST PRUSSIA

Augustow 2000

Sopockinie 2000

Druskieniki 500

Bogusze slave labour camp

Rajgrod 400

Dabrowa Bialostocka 1000

Grodno 4500

Jeziory 2000

Ostryna 2000

Grajewo 2500

Sidra 350

Skidel 3000

Szczuczyn 1500

Suchowola 5100

Kielbasin slave labour camp

Niemen

Goniadz 1280

Janow 950

Kuznica 1000

Indura 2500

Lunna 1500

Wolpa 1500

Wasosz 50

Stawiski 60

Radzilow 22

Knyszyn 1300

Korycin 1000

Sokolka 8,000

BIALYSTOK REGION

Mosty 350

GREATER

Jedwabne 30

Trzcianne 1200

Wasilkow 1180

Suprasl 170

Krynki 5000

Ros 1000

to the Moscow front

Nowogrod 36

Lomza 7,000

Choroszcz 440

Bialystok

Grodek 1300

Wolkowysk 7000

GERMANY

Rutki 20

Zawady 180

Michalowo 750

Jalowka 850

Swisłocz 3000

Rozana 3000

Sniadowo 650

Zambrow 2,000

Sokoly 850

Zabludow 2,000

Lubotyn 174

Wysokie 3700

Lapy 600

Bielsk 5000

Narew 400

Porozow 1000

Lyskow 600

Czyzew 200

Malkinia Junction

Klukowo 68

Bransk 2600

Bocki 756

Orla 2000

Pruzana 3000

to Germany — Treblinka

Bug

Ciechanowiec 700

Kleszczele 1000

GENERAL GOVERNMENT

Siemiatycze 6000

Milejczyce 1000

Resistance led by Herschl Shabbes

Drohiczyn 500

● Towns and villages from which Jews were taken with number

★ Instances of Jewish resistance

RIGHT: *German thoroughness is amply demonstrated in this map, showing the numbers of Jews deported from just one region in the east in 1942 (today on the western Russian border). Note the two slave labor camps and the siting of Treblinka, one of the most notorious of the concentration camps. All this effort had untoward military repercussions; railroad communications were often choked with trains carrying Jews, blocking vital military supplies.*

"The Righteous among the Nations"

Most of those in charge in the countries that capitulated to the Nazis – particularly in Hungary, Romania, and Croatia – helped them to deport and murder the Jews and other "undesirables": gypsies, socialists, Communists, homosexuals, Jehovah's Witnesses, the chronically ill, the handicapped, and the mentally ill. However, there were four notable exceptions: Finland, Denmark, Bulgaria, and Italy.

The Finns had joined the Germans in 1941 in the fight against the Soviet Union for possession of the province of Karelia, lost after Stalin's invasion of Finland in 1940. Yet the Finnish Commander-in-Chief, Field Marshal Carl Mannerheim, informed the Germans that if any of the 1,700 Jews in Finland were deported, the country would regard such an action against its citizens as an act of war and take the appropriate action. Consequently, all the Jews were saved.

In Denmark, King Christian X was one of many non-Jews who donned the yellow star of David. In addition, in October 1943, the Danish resistance organized a secret flotilla of small boats to spirit away more than 6,000 Jews by night to neutral Sweden.

Although the Bulgarian king, Boris III, signed away his Jewish citizens' rights and had most of their property confiscated, almost all 50,000 of them escaped deportation. Indeed, Bulgaria had a larger Jewish population at the end of the war than when it began. However, the 15,000 Jews of Thrace and Macedonia – respectively, Greek and Yugoslavian regions that the Nazis had given to Bulgaria as a bribe – were all sent to the Treblinka death camp in Poland.

In Italy, despite enormous German pressure to do so, Mussolini's Fascist regime refused to deport a single Jew. It was only after the fall of Mussolini and the subsequent surrender of the new Italian government to the Allies, when the Germans occupied the country, that the deportation of Jews began.

In addition, although France, Belgium, Holland, Norway, Yugoslavia, and Greece had their share of collaborators, they all also had sizable resistance movements, with the help of which a large number of Jews managed to escape.

The "Righteous Gentiles"

Some Jews survived the war by being hidden throughout the conflict by non-Jews. These people are known today as "Righteous Gentiles," a variation of the ancient Hebrew term meaning "the pious of the peoples of

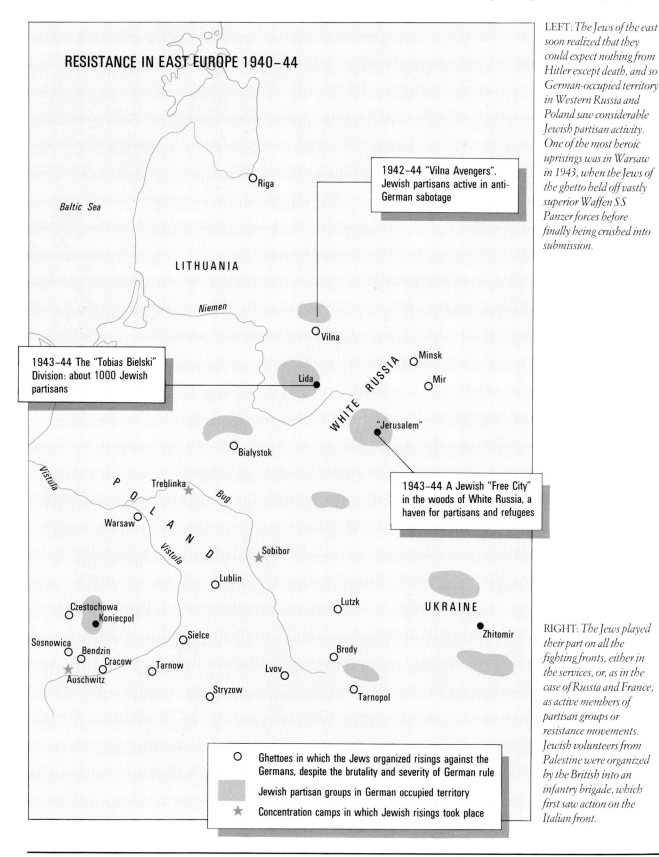

RESISTANCE IN EAST EUROPE 1940–44

1942–44 "Vilna Avengers". Jewish partisans active in anti-German sabotage

1943–44 The "Tobias Bielski" Division: about 1000 Jewish partisans

1943–44 A Jewish "Free City" in the woods of White Russia, a haven for partisans and refugees

Baltic Sea

Riga

LITHUANIA

Niemen

Vilna

Minsk

Mir

Lida

WHITE RUSSIA

"Jerusalem"

Bialystok

Vistula

P O L A N D

Treblinka

Bug

Warsaw

Vistula

Sobibor

Lublin

Lutzk

UKRAINE

Czestochowa
Koniecpol

Zhitomir

Sosnowica

Sielce

Bendzin

Brody

Cracow

Tarnow

Lvov

Auschwitz

Stryzow

Tarnopol

○ Ghettoes in which the Jews organized risings against the Germans, despite the brutality and severity of German rule

⬤ Jewish partisan groups in German occupied territory

★ Concentration camps in which Jewish risings took place

LEFT: *The Jews of the east soon realized that they could expect nothing from Hitler except death, and so German-occupied territory in Western Russia and Poland saw considerable Jewish partisan activity. One of the most heroic uprisings was in Warsaw in 1943, when the Jews of the ghetto held off vastly superior Waffen SS Panzer forces before finally being crushed into submission.*

RIGHT: *The Jews played their part on all the fighting fronts, either in the services, or, as in the case of Russia and France, as active members of partisan groups or resistance movements. Jewish volunteers from Palestine were organized by the British into an infantry brigade, which first saw action on the Italian front.*

the world." In medieval literature – and especially in the Zohar – it was claimed that all such good people have equal status with Jews; today, however, the term is taken to mean exclusively those Gentiles who helped the victims of the Holocaust.

The largest number of "divers" (as the hidden Jews were called) were to be found in Hitler's capital. Berlin, with its strong socialist tradition, had always held out against the *Führer*'s anti-Semitism and never applied the Nuremberg Laws as rigidly as did some other

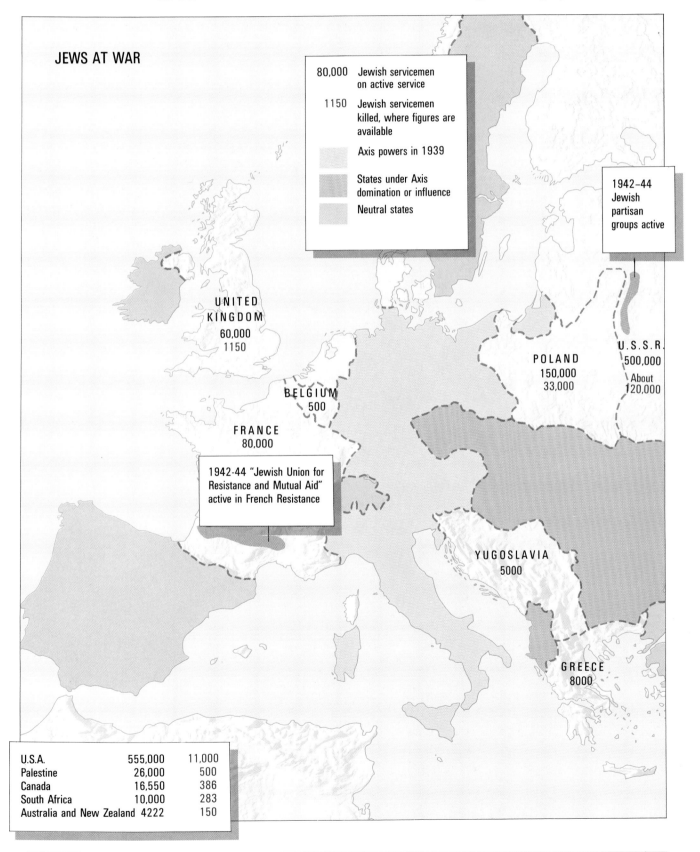

JEWS AT WAR

| 80,000 | Jewish servicemen on active service |
| 1150 | Jewish servicemen killed, where figures are available |

Axis powers in 1939

States under Axis domination or influence

Neutral states

1942–44 Jewish partisan groups active

UNITED KINGDOM
60,000
1150

BELGIUM
500

FRANCE
80,000

1942-44 "Jewish Union for Resistance and Mutual Aid" active in French Resistance

POLAND
150,000
33,000

U.S.S.R.
500,000
About 120,000

YUGOSLAVIA
5000

GREECE
8000

U.S.A.	555,000	11,000
Palestine	26,000	500
Canada	16,550	386
South Africa	10,000	283
Australia and New Zealand	4222	150

cities. Many Jews were also hidden with non-Jewish connivance in Amsterdam, although their hiding places were frequently discovered or betrayed, as in the case of Anne Frank and her family.

One of the most outstanding examples of the rescue of Jews by a non-Jew was the achievement of Raoul Wallenberg. A Swedish diplomat in Budapest, he worked with diplomats from Switzerland, Portugal, and other neutral countries to save the lives of thousands of Hungarian Jews by issuing them with *ad hoc* identity and travel documents. For a long time, it was assumed that Wallenberg's presence in Nazi-controlled Hungary was simply fortuitous, but it is now known that he had arranged to be posted there with the express purpose of saving as many Jews as possible. When Budapest fell to the Soviets in 1945, Wallenberg went to see the new occupying power and there he disappeared. Nothing more was heard of him until much later, when rumors began to filter through that he had been seen in various Soviet prison camps. The Soviet government finally admitted in the 1980s that Wallenberg had been imprisoned in 1945, but claimed that he had since died. The rumors about this particular "Righteous Gentile" still persist.

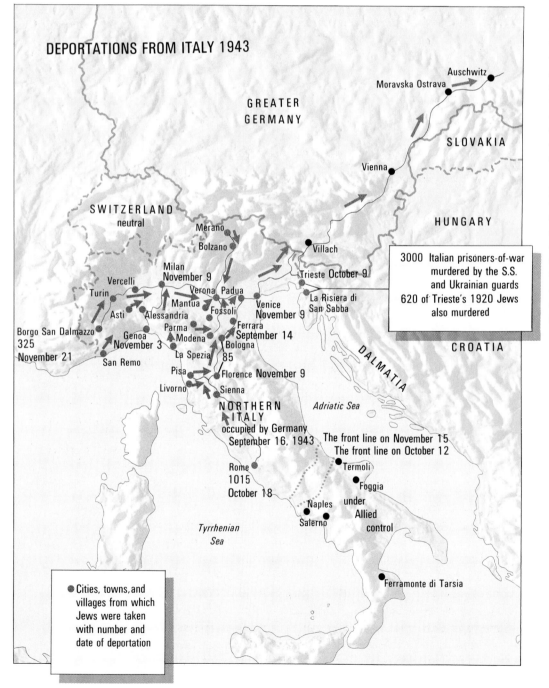

DEPORTATIONS FROM ITALY 1943

GREATER GERMANY

SLOVAKIA

Moravska Ostrava → Auschwitz

Vienna

SWITZERLAND
neutral

HUNGARY

Merano

Bolzano

Villach

Milan
November 9

Trieste October 9

Vercelli

Verona Padua

Turin

Venice
November 9

La Risiera di
San Sabba

Mantua

Asti

Alessandria

Fossoli

3000 Italian prisoners-of-war
murdered by the S.S.
and Ukrainian guards
620 of Trieste's 1920 Jews
also murdered

Parma

Ferrara
September 14

Borgo San Dalmazzo
325
November 21

Genoa
November 3

Modena

Bologna
85

DALMATIA

CROATIA

San Remo

La Spezia

Pisa

Florence November 9

Livorno

Sienna

Adriatic Sea

NORTHERN
ITALY
occupied by Germany
September 16, 1943

The front line on November 15
The front line on October 12

Termoli

Rome
1015
October 18

Foggia

Naples

under

Allied

Salerno

control

Tyrrhenian
Sea

Ferramonte di Tarsia

● Cities, towns, and
villages from which
Jews were taken
with number and
date of deportation

LEFT: *Until 1943,
Mussolini's Italy had
managed to resist German
pressure to take active
steps against the Jews. The
little legislation there was
remained largely
unenforced – indeed
Mussolini confided that he
had introduced it only for
"political reasons."
However, following
Il Duce's fall, the Allied
landings on the Italian
mainland, and Italy's
surrender, the Germans
acted quickly. Between
October 9 and November
21, a wave of deportations
took place throughout the
country.*

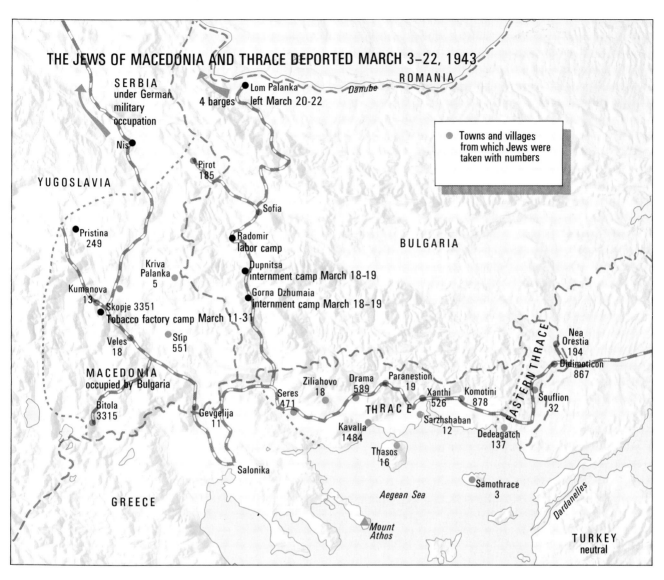

THE JEWS OF MACEDONIA AND THRACE DEPORTED MARCH 3–22, 1943

SERBIA
under German
military
occupation

ROMANIA

Lom Palanka
4 barges left March 20–22

Danube

● Towns and villages
from which Jews were
taken with numbers

Nis

Pirot
185

YUGOSLAVIA

Sofia

Pristina
249

Radomir
labor camp

BULGARIA

Kriva
Palanka
5

Dupnitsa
internment camp March 18–19

Kumanova
13

Gorna Dzhumaia
internment camp March 18–19

Skopje 3351
Tobacco factory camp March 11–31

Veles
18

Stip
551

MACEDONIA
occupied by Bulgaria

Ziliahovo
18

Drama
589

Paranestion
19

Nea
Orestia
194

Didimoticon
867

Bitola
3315

Gevgelija
11

Seres
471

THRACE

Xanthi
526

Komotini
878

Souflion
32

Kavalla
1484

Sarzhshaban
12

Dedeagatch
137

Thasos
16

Salonika

Samothrace
3

Aegean Sea

Dardanelles

GREECE

Mount
Athos

TURKEY
neutral

The End of the Holocaust

As the tide of the war turned and Soviet troops fought their way through *"Ostland"* (as the Nazis had renamed Estonia, Latvia, Lithuania, and Byelorussia), the Ukraine, and Poland, those prisoners in the German concentration camps who could walk were forced on death marches to camps farther inside the shrinking borders of the Reich.

By this time, nearly 6 million Jews had been murdered by the Nazis, who now were gripped by an insane desire to complete the job of totally destroying the Jewish people before Germany itself was overrun. The Commandant of Auschwitz, Rudolf Hoess, later testified, at his trial for crimes against humanity, that 400,000 Hungarian Jews were gassed in the three months of the summer of 1944. In addition, many of the Jews sent westward into Germany by train and those who survived the death marches died of starvation or disease in Dachau, Bergen-Belsen, and Buchenwald. In the autumn of 1944, as the Red Army approached Auschwitz, Himmler himself ordered that the extermination camps be closed down and the evidence of the appalling things that had been done there be destroyed. Fortunately, many of the camps were captured before the latter order could be carried out.

It was only when soldiers of the Allied armies liberated the camps and saw the piles of emaciated bodies that were barely recognizable as human that the full extent of the horror was finally revealed to the world. On April 11, 1945, when American troops overran Buchenwald in eastern Germany, they found 21,000 starving survivors, thousands of corpses, and the ashes of many more. In this and other camps, besides the physical evidence of the atrocities, such as warehouses full of shoes, jewelry, spectacles, and

ABOVE: *Between March 3 and 22, 1943, the Jews of Macedonia and Thrace were deported. As the tide of war turned against the German armies on the fighting fronts, Nazi fanatics stepped up their efforts to ensure that Europe became Jew-free.*

RIGHT: *Dutch Jews being rounded up by German occupation forces. In contrast to their practice in other parts of Europe, the Germans took a more subtle approach to the Jews of the Netherlands, with the result that Jews willingly cooperated in their own deportation, refusing to believe warnings that they would be worked to death.*

human hair, further investigation revealed undreamed-of horrors, including sterilizations and bizarre and disastrous medical experiments on live victims.

War Criminals and Collaborators

As the full horror of what the Nazis had done became apparent, the Allies rounded up as many of the perpetrators as possible. Some were tried for crimes against humanity by the International Military Tribunal at Nuremberg established by Britain, France, the U.S.S.R., and the U.S. (which gave rise to the "Nuremberg Trials"). These were carried out between November 1945 and October 1946. Twelve top Nazis were sentenced to death and executed, among them Alfred Rosenberg, Reich Minister for the eastern occupied territories and chief Nazi ideologist, whose racial theories contributed to the party's anti-Semitism; Ernst Kaltenbrunner, Austrian Nazi leader who, as head of the Security Police (SD), was responsible for the murder of millions of Jews; and Hans Frank, Governor-General of occupied Poland and responsible for the massacre following the Warsaw Ghetto uprising. Others – camp commandants, guards, and so on – were tried at other courts.

Many leading Nazis managed to escape execution. Sometimes this was through suicide: Goebbels emulated his beloved *Führer* by poisoning himself, his wife, and his

children in Hitler's Chancellory bunker; Himmler had taken poison soon after his capture by the Allies; Goering, although convicted at Nuremberg, committed suicide before his execution, using poison slipped to him by his German guards. Martin Bormann, who was thought to have escaped the fall of Berlin in May 1945, was tried and sentenced to death at Nuremberg *in absentia*, but after his skeleton was accidently discovered in Berlin in 1972, it was later decided that he, too, had committed suicide.

Others managed to escape justice with the help of Nazi sympathizers, notably the Auschwitz camp doctor Josef Mengele; Adolf Eichmann, the "Jewish expert" of the Reich Central Security Office and one of the masterminds of the "final solution"; and Klaus Barbie, the Gestapo chief of Lyon in France. However, they and their crimes were not forgotten. In 1960, Israeli agents captured Eichmann in Argentina and took him for trial to Israel, where he was executed in 1962. In 1983, as a result of pressure from the Nazi-hunting couple Serge and Beate Klarsfeld, the French extradited Barbie – the "Butcher of Lyon" – from Bolivia where he had been living since 1951. He was tried and convicted in 1987. (There have been reports of Mengele's death in South America; however, these have been treated with scepticism.)

Over the years, it has come to light that, in the wave of fierce anti-Communism that swept through the West immediately after the war, many Nazis were given sanctuary in the U.S., Britain, and other Allied countries because of the information on Communists and other left-wingers that they purportedly could trade. In addition, many Nazi collaborators from such places as Slovakia, the Baltic states, and the Ukraine were regarded as "refugees from Soviet Communism" and welcomed into the United States, Britain, Canada, Australia, and elsewhere with few questions being asked about their role in helping the Nazis. The cases of some of these are now under review.

Some people who became very prominent long after the war have, it has since been discovered, tainted pasts. The Nazi occupation of both Yugoslavia and Greece came under scrutiny with the election of Kurt Waldheim, former Secretary-General of

IN THE DEATH CAMPS

Teutonic efficiency showed itself to the full in the planning and the execution of the "final solution." Jews throughout Europe were forced to wear the Star of David for identification purposes; the child (below) is selling armbands with the star in the street, while the photograph (right) shows a selection of armbands from various countries. Once in the camps, the Jews were stripped of their clothes and personal possessions and issued with an official uniform (below right); the confiscated property was promptly recycled – furs, for example, finding their way to German troops fighting on the Russian front. The uniform itself was decorated with the appropriate badge or symbol; besides the yellow star for the Jews, there were badges for ordinary criminals, political offenders, Jehovah's Witnesses, and homosexuals. Further identification was branded on the arm.

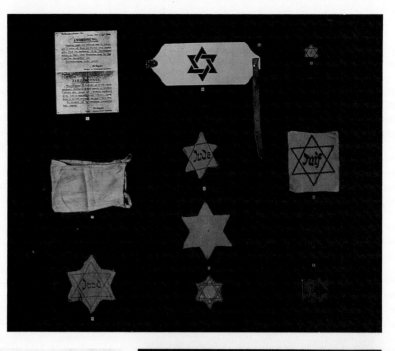

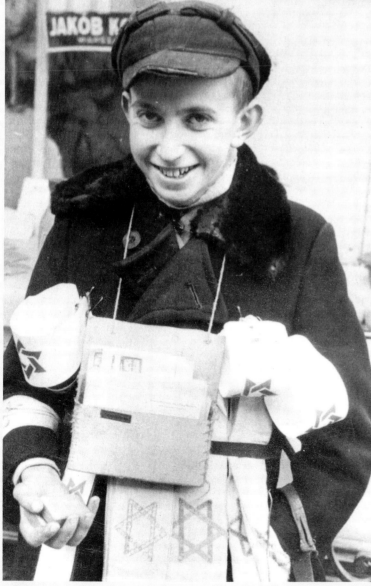

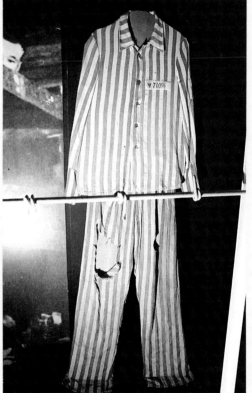

the United Nations, as Austrian president. Waldheim had stated in his autobiography that he had been registered as unfit for active service in April 1942 and spent the remainder of the war in Austria studying law. However, it was revealed that from that date he had, in fact, served in Croatia as a liaison between the German and Italian military staffs and then in intelligence in Greece, and had been decorated for his services to both the Croatian Fascists and the Reich during that period. There are claims – among many others, and all of which he has denied – that in 1943 he witnessed at first hand the deportations of Jews from Salonika, and at least knew of those from Rhodes, Crete, and Corfu in 1944.

As a result of these revelations, Israel withdrew its ambassador from Austria and refused to send a replacement as long as Waldheim remained president. The incident has also brought to the fore the role played by the Austrians after the 1938 *Anschluss* (annexation by Germany) and the fact that, many were active participants.

The same political turmoil persists in France. There, the examination of recently discovered wartime records has revealed that several so-called "patriots," in fact, collaborated with the Nazis.

The appalling destruction – both physical and psychological – caused by the Holocaust is incalculable, and the repercussions will be felt by Jew and non-Jew alike for many years

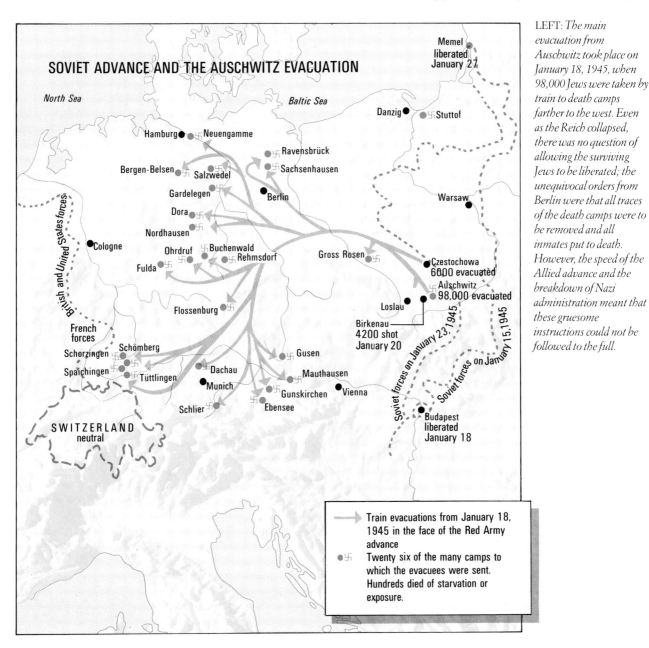

LEFT: *The main evacuation from Auschwitz took place on January 18, 1945, when 98,000 Jews were taken by train to death camps farther to the west. Even as the Reich collapsed, there was no question of allowing the surviving Jews to be liberated; the unequivocal orders from Berlin were that all traces of the death camps were to be removed and all inmates put to death. However, the speed of the Allied advance and the breakdown of Nazi administration meant that these gruesome instructions could not be followed to the full.*

SOVIET ADVANCE AND THE AUSCHWITZ EVACUATION

North Sea

Baltic Sea

Memel liberated January 27

Danzig ● Stuttof

Hamburg ● Neuengamme

Ravensbrück

Bergen-Belsen ● Salzwedel Sachsenhausen

Gardelegen Berlin

Dora Warsaw

Nordhausen

Cologne Ohrdruf Buchenwald Gross Rosen

Fulda Rehmsdorf Czestochowa 6000 evacuated

Auschwitz 98,000 evacuated

Loslau

Flossenburg Birkenau 4200 shot January 20

Soviet forces on January 23, 1945

Soviet forces on January 15, 1945

French forces

Schömberg Gusen

Schorzingen Dachau Mauthausen

Spaichingen Tüttlingen Munich Gunskirchen Vienna

Schlier Ebensee

Budapest liberated January 18

SWITZERLAND neutral

British and United States forces

→ Train evacuations from January 18, 1945 in the face of the Red Army advance

● ⌂ Twenty six of the many camps to which the evacuees were sent. Hundreds died of starvation or exposure.

to come. The exact Jewish death toll may never be known; many documents were destroyed, especially by the Nazis themselves. All that can be determined with any degree of accuracy is that, prior to World War II, Europe contained 9.2 million Jews, but by 1945, only 3.1 million were left.

In the words of the German historian Werner Keller:

The history of Germany will remain tainted for all time by the most atrocious crimes that human beings have ever inflicted upon helpless fellow human beings...No one will ever again be able to describe Germany as the land of Goethe and Bach, Kant and Lessing...It was also, and remains henceforth, the land of Hitler, Himmler and the death camps.

THE HOLOCAUST: JEWS KILLED AND SURVIVORS 1939–45

24,387	Estimate of Jews murdered 1939–45
1000	Survivors and those who returned.
----	Frontiers of 1937 (Northern Transylvania, in 1940)

NORWAY
728
1000

North Sea

SWEDEN

Baltic Sea

DENMARK
77
5500

NETHERLANDS
106,000
20,000

BELGIUM
24,387
40,000

LUXEMBOURG
700
1000

FRANCE
83,000
200,000

SPAIN

GERMANY
160,000
330,000

ITALY
8000
35,000

AUSTRIA
65,000
7000

FINLAND
11
2000

ESTONIA
1000

LATVIA
80,000

DANZIG
1000
8000

LITHUANIA
135,000

MEMEL
8000

BALTIC STATES
25,000

farthest German advance 1942

WESTERN SOVIET UNION
300,000

SOVIET UNION
1,000,000

POLAND
3,000,000
225,000

CZECHOSLOVAKIA
217,000
44,000

RUTHENIA
60,000

HUNGARY
200,000
300,000

YUGOSLAVIA
60,000
12,000

ROMANIA
40,000
430,000

BUKOVINA
124,632

BESSARABIA
200,000

NORTHERN TRANSYLVANIA
105,000

Black Sea

BULGARIA
50,000

ALBANIA
200
200

GREECE
65,000
12,000

THRACE
4221

MACEDONIA
7122

RHODES
1700
161

Mediterranean Sea

CRETE
260
7

LIBYA
562

In Germany 300,000 Jews survived the concentration camps.
On the rest of the European continent over a million and a half survived the war and Hitler's policies.

LEFT: *By the end of 1944, nearly 6 million Jews had been killed by the Nazis; many more died in the closing months of the war. In Germany itself, 300,000 Jews survived the concentration camps; in Europe as a whole, one and a half million Jews escaped the Holocaust. Many of these managed to escape before the outbreak of the war, while others survived because liberation came before the plans for their destruction could be completed. A significant minority were sheltered by non-Jews at the risk of their own lives.*

CHAPTER SEVEN

ISRAEL AND WORLD JEWRY FOLLOWING WORLD WAR II

The twentieth century has witnessed more upheavals in the Jewish population than ever before. Not a single Jewish community in any country has remained unaffected by persecution or emigration. That of the Pale of Settlement (which covered the Ukraine, Byelorussia, Lithuania, Latvia, and part of Poland) was, first, decimated by the pogroms, the German invasion during World War I, and consequent emigration; finally, it was completely eradicated by the Holocaust. The great Jewish communities of Egypt, Iran, and Iraq – the first centers of Jewish scholarship – have been reduced to a few hundred souls by emigration and, in some cases, executions.

Yet, from the mid-point of the century onward, the Jews of the world had cause for hope and pride. After almost 1,900 years, they once again had a homeland in Israel.

Post-Holocaust Anti-Semitism

The discovery by the civilized world that at least 6 million Jews had been exterminated in cold blood by Europeans – the Nazis and their partners – did not put an end to anti-Semitism.

At the end of the war, few Jews outside Britain remained in the same place where they had been when it had started. Most were sent to displaced persons' camps while the victorious Allies decided what to do with them. Few wanted to return to their homes because of the treatment they had received at the hands of their erstwhile friends and neighbors. Those who did return sometimes had an unpleasant shock. For instance, Jews

returning to Poland were met with open hostility, which in July 1946 led to a pogrom in the city of Kielce. A rumor had been started – and was confirmed by the parish priest – that Jews had murdered a Christian child for ritual purposes. Among the 42 Jews who were subsequently murdered by the mob were the occupants of a house used as a refuge by Jews returning to the city, including women and children. Film later smuggled out of Poland documented the incident, and local people who were interviewed expressed

ABOVE: *Inside the Caro synagogue in Safed. The synagogue is dedicated to the memory of Joseph Caro, a leading Safed scholar.*

RIGHT: *The collapse of Hitler's Reich did not benefit the survivors of the Holocaust in the east. Even as the Soviet armies advanced, pogroms followed in their wake.*

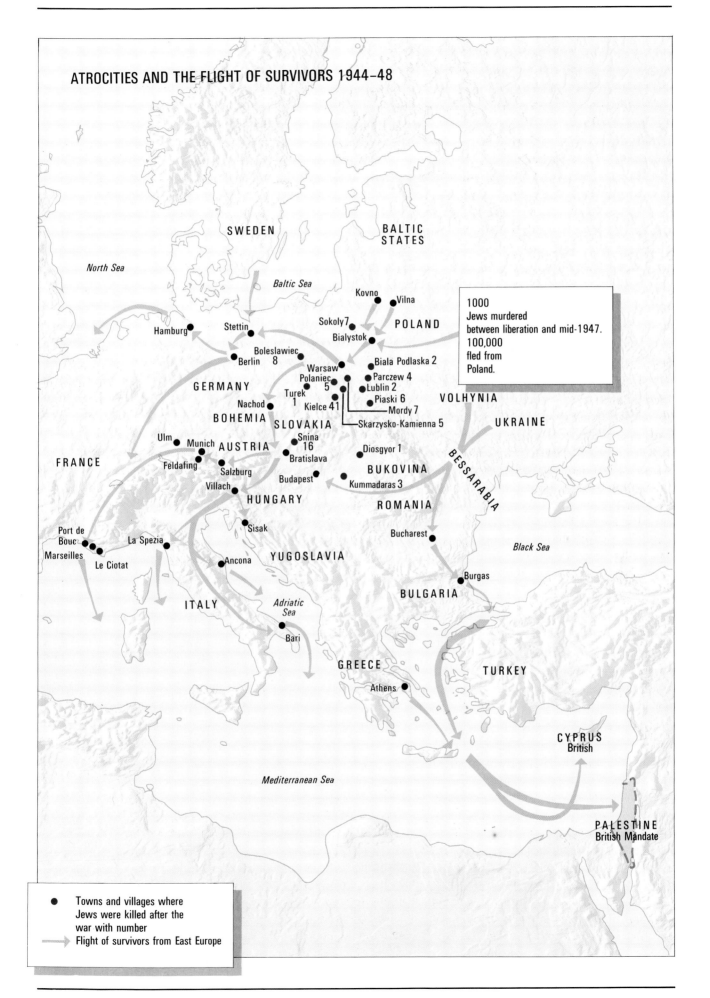

ATROCITIES AND THE FLIGHT OF SURVIVORS 1944–48

SWEDEN

BALTIC STATES

North Sea

Baltic Sea

Kovno
Vilna

Hamburg
Stettin

Sokoly 7
Bialystok
POLAND

Boleslawiec
Berlin   8

Biala Podlaska 2

Warsaw
Polaniec
Parczew 4
GERMANY   5   Lublin 2
Turek   Piaski 6
Nachod   1   Kielce 41
BOHEMIA   Mordy 7
SLOVAKIA   Skarzysko-Kamienna 5

1000
Jews murdered
between liberation and mid-1947.
100,000
fled from
Poland.

VOLHYNIA

UKRAINE

Ulm   Munich
Feldafing
AUSTRIA
Snina
16
Bratislava

Diosgyor 1

BESSARABIA

FRANCE

Salzburg
Villach
Budapest
HUNGARY

BUKOVINA

Kummadaras 3
ROMANIA

Sisak

Port de
Bouc
Marseilles
Le Ciotat

La Spezia

Ancona

Bucharest

Black Sea

Burgas

YUGOSLAVIA

Adriatic
Sea
Bari

ITALY

BULGARIA

GREECE

Athens

TURKEY

Mediterranean Sea

CYPRUS
British

PALESTINE
British Mandate

● Towns and villages where
Jews were killed after the
war with number
→ Flight of survivors from East Europe

satisfaction at what had happened; no one was ever punished. As a direct result of the Kielce pogrom, more than 5,000 Jews fled from Poland to make the difficult journey to Palestine.

Anti-Semitism is also considered by historians to be one of the motivating forces behind the "anti-Communist" witch-hunts that began in the United States shortly after the war and reached their peak in the early 1950s under the direction of Senator Joseph McCarthy. This is despite the fact that one of the prosecutors – and one of McCarthy's most enthusiastic supporters – was the young Jewish lawyer Roy Cohn. "Subversives" – Communists and anyone else with left-wing tendencies – were brought to testify before the House Un-American Activities Committee, and the careers of many of them – Hollywood film directors and writers and the physicist J. Robert Oppenheimer, among them – were ruined. Another consequence of the political atmosphere resulting from the McCarthy purge was the execution in 1953 of Ethel and Julius Rosenberg for passing nuclear secrets to the Soviet Union.

The ideas that motivated Hitler did not die with him. Those who have followed in his footsteps do not yet hold power, but they continue to desecrate Jewish cemeteries and the monuments to martyrs, and launch attacks on residents of Jewish neighborhoods. The resurgence of extreme right-wing politics in the last decade or so has been an unpleasant omen for the Jews. This trend includes the French National Front and its British counterpart (which, although officially disbanded in January 1990, lives on in a new guise: The Third Way), and the Republican Party in the German Federal Republic; much of the French press is also in the hands of anti-Semitic right-wingers.

Since the mid-1970s, a growing number of individuals – mainly in Britain, the United States, and France – have been producing apparently scholarly tomes to "prove" that the Holocaust either never actually happened, or that Hitler was not involved in its planning. In 1979, an organization calling itself the "Institute of Historical Review," based in San Diego, California, offered a prize of $50,000 to anyone who could prove that the Holocaust was fact. A survivor named Mel Mermelstein took up the chal-

lenge. His claim was substantiated by the American courts, but the Institute, not surprisingly, refused to hand over the money. Mermelstein sued and won his prize. The Institute has a branch in Britain, where it distributes anti-Semitic literature door-to-door and to schools, and it has even tried to carry its message to the Council of Europe.

The most disturbing manifestations of "intellectual anti-Semitism" and Holocaust denial today come from France, where the National Front has the greatest support of any right-wing party in Europe. For example, at Lyon University in 1986, the thesis of a candidate for a doctorate in history, which "proved" that the gas chambers had never existed, was marked "very good."

The Emergence of the State of Israel

The early settlers in Palestine strove to rebuild this forgotten wasteland against all odds, but they met with hostility from those who owned the land, many of whom were absentee landlords. The Ottoman Turks, who then ruled most of the Middle East and had entered World War I against Britain, France, and Russia, were also opposed to Jewish settlement; on December 17, 1914, Turkish troops entered Jaffa, arrested 500 Russian Jews – men, women, children, and babies – herded them onto ships under neutral flags and sent them to Egypt, then under British rule. Meanwhile the remaining Jews and Arabs suffered so greatly from famine and disease that when General Allenby and his British troops triumphantly marched into Jerusalem on December 9, 1917, the Jewish population of Palestine was by that time smaller than it had been at the beginning of the war.

The Zionist aim of a Jewish homeland came one step nearer its goal with the Balfour Declaration. This was a letter written on November 2, 1917, by Arthur Balfour, then the British Foreign Secretary, to Lord Rothschild, Chairman of the British Zionist Federation. In it, Balfour stated: "HM government view with favor the establishment in Palestine of a national home for the Jewish people." The problem with the Balfour Declaration is that this letter was sent to Lord Rothschild on an almost private basis, and its contents are vague and ambiguous – in particular, there have been

BELOW: The declining power of the Ottoman Empire coincided with the birth and growth of Zionism to make the future control of Palestine a matter of keen debate among the great powers. Matters came to a head in the First World War, when, to appease the Arabs, the Allies agreed to control the Holy Land themselves.

arguments ever since about what the British government meant by "a national home."

At the same time as giving hope to the Jews, the British government was also catering to the Arabs. The Emir Hussein ibn Ali, the Sherif of Mecca and held in high esteem by the Arab world, was strongly encouraged by the British to lead a revolt against Ottoman rule in the Middle East (a plan devised by Lloyd George); in exchange, he was promised that he would become monarch of a large independent Arab state after the war. Hussein complied, and in May 1916, he proclaimed the foundation of the

Hashemite dynasty, with himself at its head as king of the Arabs. With the help of T. E. Lawrence ("Lawrence of Arabia"), his son Feisal drove the Turks out of the holy places in the Hejaz (now part of Saudi Arabia). (Hussein was eventually thrust aside by Ibn Saud, who founded the kingdom of Saudi Arabia in 1926.)

Also in 1916, in the secret Sykes-Picot pact, Britain and France negotiated a division of the Middle East between themselves. Although the agreement was supposedly abandoned after the Armistice in 1918, some of its protocols were retained. One of these

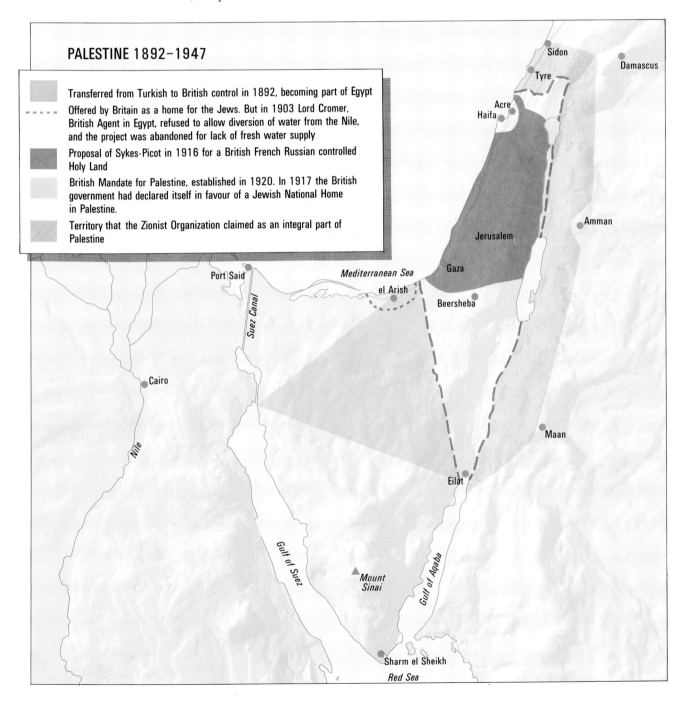

PALESTINE 1892–1947

Transferred from Turkish to British control in 1892, becoming part of Egypt

Offered by Britain as a home for the Jews. But in 1903 Lord Cromer, British Agent in Egypt, refused to allow diversion of water from the Nile, and the project was abandoned for lack of fresh water supply.

Proposal of Sykes-Picot in 1916 for a British French Russian controlled Holy Land

British Mandate for Palestine, established in 1920. In 1917 the British government had declared itself in favour of a Jewish National Home in Palestine.

Territory that the Zionist Organization claimed as an integral part of Palestine

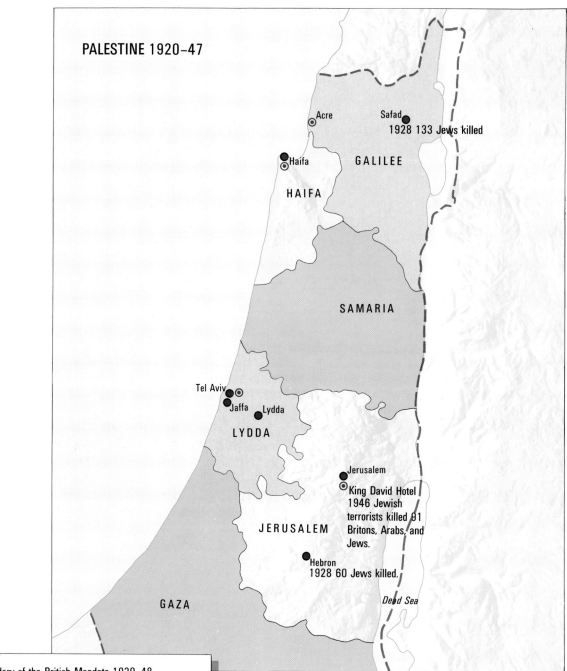

PALESTINE 1920–47

Acre

Safad
1928 133 Jews killed

Haifa

GALILEE

HAIFA

SAMARIA

Tel Aviv
Jaffa Lydda

LYDDA

Jerusalem
King David Hotel
1946 Jewish
terrorists killed 91
Britons, Arabs, and
Jews.

JERUSALEM

Hebron
1928 60 Jews killed.

GAZA

Dead Sea

- - - Boundary of the British Mandate 1920–48

District boundaries established by the British administration

● Principal Arab outrages against Jewish settlers

◉ Jewish terrorist activity, organized by Irgun and Stern groups, against British personnel and property. This violence was condemned by Zionist leaders. Over 300 British were killed 1944–48.

LEFT: *During the 28 years of British control, tensions between the Jewish and Arab communities continued to develop, especially with the increased Jewish immigration that resulted from the Nazi persecutions of the 1930s. The British tried to remain impartial, proposing a partition plan in 1936, but this was rejected by the Arabs.*

Eventually, the quotas imposed on Jewish immigrants led to guerrilla activity and the demand for British withdrawal.

RIGHT: *The Temple Mount as seen from the South. With the conquest of the old city from the Jordanians in the Six Day War, Jerusalem finally came under Jewish control for the first time since the days of the Romans.*

ABOVE: *The tomb of Abraham, Hebron. Abraham has a dual role in the Jewish story, being both the father of the people and the founder of Judaism.*

Court: "[Dr. Weizmann] has been a great helper of our cause, and I hope the Arabs may soon be in a position to make the Jews some return for their kindness." However, in July, Feisal was deposed by the French and forced to leave Syria. In compensation, the British gave him the throne of Iraq.

The British had control of both sides of the Jordan through their League of Nations mandate over Transjordan, which began in 1920. A large part of this area – known as eastern Palestine – was within the homeland claimed by the Jews (for instance, the territories of two of the Twelve Tribes, Gad and Manasseh, had been on the east bank of the river), but Winston Churchill, the British colonial secretary, handed over the mandated territory to Abdullah, another of Hussein's sons, as its emir.

Faced with immediate Arab opposition to Jewish immigration – Arab riots first broke out in 1920 – the British temporarily restricted the entry of Jews into Palestine that year to 16,500. In May 1921, the then High Commissioner for Palestine, Sir Herbert Samuel – himself a Jew – ordered the complete cessation of Jewish immigration. This decision was soon revoked, but it led to the production of the first of the infamous White Papers.

Published in June 1922, under the aus-

placed Lebanon and Syria within the French sphere of influence, thus making these two areas unavailable to the British to hand over to their allies.

Nevertheless, the British ensured that Hussein's son, Feisal, was proclaimed King of Syria in March 1920. Chaim Weizmann, later the first president of the state of Israel, had negotiated with Feisal over Palestine, and Feisal supported the Zionist claim. On March 1, 1919, the latter wrote to Felix Frankfurter, the prominent American Zionist leader and later Justice of the U.S. Supreme

pices of Winston Churchill as colonial secretary, this was an attempt at clarifying (in the light of the ambiguity of the Balfour Declaration) British policy regarding a Jewish national homeland. Jews were to remain in Palestine "as of right and not on suffrance"; however, the autonomous Jewish administration of the country was not to receive official recognition, and immigration was to be restricted to "the normal absorption capacity." This new ambiguity was to cause even more problems than had the Balfour Declaration in the first place.

Hostility between Arabs and Jews grew, reaching a peak in 1929, when more than 60 Jewish inhabitants were massacred in the holy city of Hebron, where both Jews and Arabs still worship at the tombs of the Patriarchs. As a result of the commission of inquiry set up in the wake of the massacre, the British produced the most famous of the White Papers (dated 1929 although published in 1930), in which major restrictions on Jewish immigration were again proposed. The 1929 White Paper caused turmoil even in Parliament, where Lloyd George accused the Prime Minister, Ramsay MacDonald, of breaking Britain's promises to the Jews, and eventually the immigration clause was dropped. By 1935 the number of Jews legally allowed into Palestine was more than 61,000 per year and by 1936, the Jewish population there had reached 400,000 – one third of the total. However, in November 1937, the British government, in the face of increasing Arab unrest, announced that immigration was to be restricted, between August 1937 and March 1938, to only 8,000.

The last of the White Papers, known to the Jews as the "Black Paper," was published on May 17, 1939, when Nazi oppression was at its height. It envisaged immigration of 15,000 Jews per year for the following five years and then a total halt. By now, the trickle of legal Jewish immigrants to Palestine, mainly children, was being supplemented by as many illegal boatloads as the Jewish community could organize. In 1939 alone, more than 30 ships carrying a total of nearly 17,000 refugees had made their way from Black Sea ports in Romania and Bulgaria to the Mediterranean and the seaports of Greece and thence to Palestine. This operation – known as *Aliyah Bet*, literally "Immigration B," as

opposed to "Immigration A," legal immigration – was managed by the forerunner of the Mossad, the Israeli intelligence service of the present day.

Many boats were intercepted by the British before or just as they reached the Palestinian shore, and the refugees were sent to detention camps in Cyprus or Mauritius for the duration of World War II. Others suffered even worse fates. In 1940, the *Patria* – a French liner to which "illegals" had been transferred for transportation to Mauritius – was blown up by the underground Jewish defense force – the Haganah *(see below)* – in Haifa harbor; the explosives, intended only to immobilize the ship, proved too strong and the ship sank, drowning 252 immigrants. In 1942, the *Struma*, on its way from Romania, was torpedoed and sunk – probably by a German submarine – off the coast of Turkey with the loss of most of the 769 refugees abroad.

ABOVE: *Haj Amin El Husseini, the Grand Mufti of Jerusalem, photographed in 1946. He was one of the first spiritual leaders of the Arab world to call for a holy war to drive the Jews out of Palestine; his anti-Semitic views led him to seek Nazi support before and during the Second World War.*

Jewish Social Organization within Palestine

Unlike the earlier settlers to Palestine, those who arrived in the first decade of the twentieth century did not come for religious reasons, nor was their immigration organized by a philanthropist such as Baron de Hirsch or Baron Edmond de Rothschild. These new settlers were committed socialists who realized that the inhospitable land of Palestine – consisting of swamp, desert, and rock-strewn, barren hills – could only be farmed collectively if it could be farmed at all. They began by organizing themselves into agricultural and laboring cooperatives.

In 1909, two momentous events occurred. One was the foundation of the first all-Jewish city, Tel-Aviv, which started as a group of tents on the sand dunes near Jaffa. The other was the formation of the first *kibbutz*, Um Djuni (later called Degania), on malarial swampland by the Sea of Galilee, which by 1914 had more than 50 members.

A kibbutz is a cooperative in which the members' work is centrally allocated and everything, except clothing and a few personal possessions, is shared. There is no money within the community – members take whatever items they need from the kibbutz store – nor are wages paid. From the beginning, members' children lived from birth in a special children's house, visiting their parents at least once a day, and this is still the case on many kibbutzim; however, in recent years, some kibbutzniks have decided to have their children living with them at home. There are now some 270 kibbutzim in Israel with a total population of 116,000.

The rigors of kibbutz life proved too difficult to accept for some, and for them an alternative way of life was devised. A *moshav* is a planned community – a cluster of houses surrounded by fields. The houses are rented to their occupants, who farm the land allocated to them and make use of the collectively owned machinery and processing plants. However, members of a moshav have many more personal possessions than those on a kibbutz, which they buy at the village cooperative store or elsewhere, and they operate a market economy. But like kibbutzniks, some moshavniks work in the towns and contribute part of their salaries to the upkeep of the farm. The first moshav, Nahalal, was founded in 1922 on a tract of land in the Jezreel valley bought from its absentee owners.

The early colonists, encouraged by the British, began to organize as soon as they arrived, using their official link with the British authorities – the Jewish Agency – to found hospitals. In 1912, the Hungarian–American Henrietta (in Hebrew "Hadassah") Szold arrived in Israel to set up a healthcare network for the whole country, beginning with a medical training center in Jerusalem. When the Hebrew University was opened on Mount Scopus in Jerusalem in 1918, the Hadassah Medical School became part of it.

Besides ensuring the health of the immigrants, there was also a great need to ensure the defense of their farms against attacks by neighboring Arabs. The Watchmen (*Ha-Shomer*), founded in 1909, was the forerunner of the Haganah, the Jewish Agency's defense force, established in 1920 and later to be the foundation of the Israeli army.

Also in 1920, a parliament of the Jewish settlers was set up, called the *Asefat Nivharim* ("Assembly of Representatives"). The systematic purchase of land for farming purposes was initiated in the 1920s through the World Zionist Organization, again with British encouragement, and in 1924, the various land-purchasing bodies previously

BELOW: *An aerial view of Nahalal, the first cooperative village, or* moshav, *to be founded in Israel. The circular building pattern was deliberately devised to allow for better defense. Today, there are around 450* moshavim *in Israel, each occupied by an average of 60 families. Each is allocated a house, essential furniture (unless they already possess it), and a tract of land to cultivate. Decisions on what to grow are made in common, while associated costs are shared between the entire community.*

ABOVE: *The tomb of Theodor Herzl, founder of modern Zionism, in Jerusalem. Appalled by the vicious anti-Semitism he witnessed in France during the Dreyfus affair in the 1890s, Herzl decided that Jewish assimilation in Europe was impractical and that the only solution was the foundation of a Jewish national state. He organized the first Zionist World Congress in 1897 and served as president of the World Zionist Organization until his death in 1904. His remains were moved from Vienna to Israel in 1949.*

established by philanthropists, such as Rothschild's Palestine Colonization Association, were amalgamated into the Joint Palestine Appeal, known in Hebrew as the *Keren Ha-Yesod* (the "Founding Fund"). The Jewish Agency, which had taken over the functions of a civil service and organized immigration and land settlement, was enlarged in 1929.

By the 1930s, the Jewish community in Palestine was thriving – self-sufficient and completely autonomous. The country had gradually begun to flourish, and exports, particularly of oranges, began to flow from the port of Jaffa. As a result, Arabs from neighboring countries were attracted to settle in Palestine and share in the new economic activity.

Jewish Fighting Forces

The first specifically Jewish fighting force since Roman times was formed within the British army in 1915 during World War I. This was the Zion Mule Corps, a section of the 38th Battalion of the Royal Fusiliers. It was led by a former Russian officer, Captain Joseph Trumpeldor, who was a firm believer in the ability of the British to open the way to Jewish settlement in Palestine through conquest. Comprising over 500 volunteers and commanded by five British and eight Jewish officers, the Corps distinguished itself during the 1915 Gallipoli campaign.

This alliance with the British was in stark contrast to the *modus operandi* of David Ben-

Gurion and other early Zionist leaders, who put their faith in the Turkish rulers and asked to form a Jewish legion within the Ottoman army. They were imprisoned for their pains.

During World War II, the Palestinian Jews wanted their own fighting force to participate – as Jews from the Jewish homeland. Reluctantly, in 1939, the British permitted the formation of a Palestine Regiment as part of the East Kent Regiment ("The Buffs"). In 1941 and 1942, 5,000 Jewish soldiers, dressed in British army uniforms with shoulder flashes bearing the word "Palestine," fought in Cyrenaica (now northeastern Libya) against the Germans and Italians, distinguishing themselves at the battle of Bir Hakim as they fought alongside the Free French forces of General Koenig; they also took part in the Allied landings in Italy, which were launched in September 1943.

It was not until September 1944 that Churchill announced in the House of Commons the creation of a completely separate Palestinian Jewish fighting force: the Jewish Brigade. This was posted to Italy in May 1945 and helped in the mopping-up operations in the north, where Brigade soldiers first encountered Holocaust survivors. After marching triumphantly through the Arch of Titus in Rome, built to celebrate the Roman emperor's victory over the Jews almost 1,900 years earlier, the Brigade turned its efforts to helping survivors of the concentration camps. It was disbanded in 1946.

After the war, there were about 150,000 survivors of the Holocaust who wished to emigrate to Palestine. However, despite this relatively small number and the fact that the world now knew of the horrors that they had suffered, the British refused to increase Jewish immigration into Palestine, the new Labour government under Clement Attlee holding to the restrictions of the White Paper of 1939, even though they had opposed this policy at the time. Speaking in the House of Lords in July 1946, Victor, Lord Rothschild told the assembled peers how the maintenance of the 1939 White Paper restrictions was regarded by Jews as "a betrayal of previous promises." He went on: "And when the scales seemed once more to be weighted against them, the last tenuous threads snapped and they said: 'There is no hope; therefore let us die fighting.'"

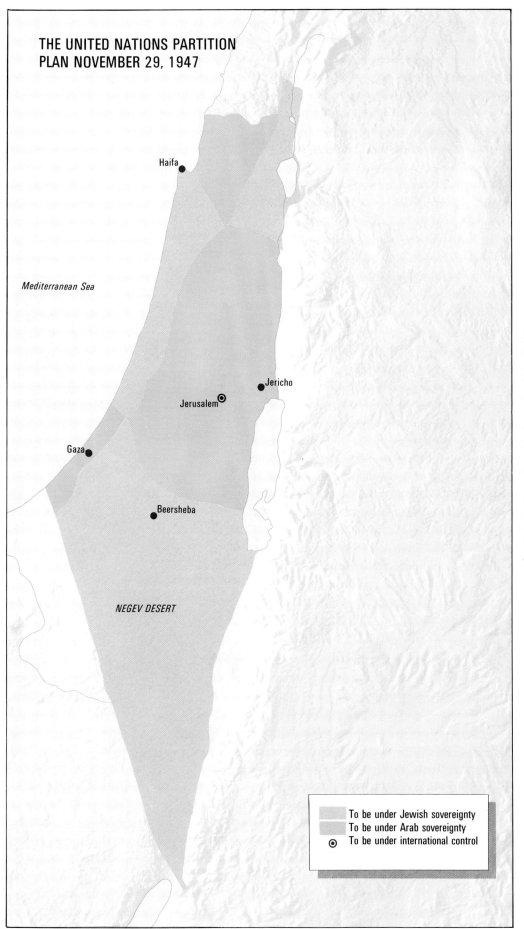

THE UNITED NATIONS PARTITION PLAN NOVEMBER 29, 1947

Mediterranean Sea

Haifa

Jericho

Jerusalem

Gaza

Beersheba

NEGEV DESERT

To be under Jewish sovereignty
To be under Arab sovereignty
To be under international control

LEFT: *Palestine after the war was a troubled land, as British attempts to put down unrest failed. In November 1947, the United Nations approved a partition plan; 33 nations supported the plan but Britain abstained. Though the plan allocated much of the best land in Palestine to the Arabs, it was rejected by them as totally unacceptable. The result was open war after the final British withdrawal in May 1948.*

Among those who decided to "die fighting" were the members of the Irgun and the Haganah. Formed in 1937, the *Irgun Zvai Leumi* ("National Military Organization") had, in January 1944, called upon the Jews of Palestine to revolt against the British. In August, they raided several police stations in search of arms. However, considering that the Allied victory against Hitler was of paramount importance, the Irgun leader, Menachem Begin (later prime minister of Israel), decided against attacking military installations as long as the war with the Nazis was still in progress. This semi-truce lasted until May 1945. The following September, the Haganah, until then a relatively moderate group, allied itself with the Irgun, and with the activities of the even more extreme Stern Gang (officially, the "Fighters for the Freedom of Israel," founded in 1940 by Abraham Stern), a wave of terrorism against the British – and reprisals by the British against the Jews – began, which was not to end until the British troops departed in 1948.

● On July 13, 1945, the Irgun attacked a British Army truck carrying gelignite fuses and killed the constable on duty; on the 25th, they blew up a railway bridge.

● The British shot an unarmed high school student in the hip while he was pasting up anti-British posters. Refused medical treatment in Acre Jail, he died of blood poisoning.

● On 16 June 1946, the Haganah blew up nine bridges and damaged the Haifa railway works. In retaliation, the British sealed up the Jewish Agency buildings, seizing their archives, and arrested 3,000 Jews throughout Palestine, including most of the senior Zionist leaders.

● On July 22, 1946, the Irgun blew up the King David Hotel in Jerusalem, killing 91 people: British administrators, Arabs, and Jews.

● Jews caught by the British in possession of arms were arrested, imprisoned, and sometimes flogged. On December 29, 1946, after one such flogging, the Irgun seized a British major and three sergeants and flogged them. On January 1, 1947, they attacked a police post, killing one policeman.

● On May 4, 1947, the Irgun and Stern Gang attacked Acre Jail, releasing 41 prisoners; three of those involved were captured by the British, who hanged them. Two days later,

on July 31, the Irgun murdered two British sergeants and booby-trapped the ground underneath their bodies.

The Birth of the State of Israel

In 1947, realizing that, after the Holocaust, world opinion would be overwhelmingly in favor of Jewish resettlement in their homeland, and mindful of the terrorism and resulting repression that was occurring in Palestine, the British government decided to hand the problem over for the United Nations to resolve. On November 29, 1947, the General Assembly voted on whether Palestine was to be partitioned and the Jews granted a national homeland, with Jerusalem under international trusteeship. However, the U.N. plan was unworkable: the Arabs were to be given such huge sectors of land that one quarter of the Jews of Palestine, some of them in well-established Jewish settlements, would be outside the area of Jewish statehood. Nevertheless, both the United States and the Soviet Union voted in favor of the motion; Britain was one of 11 abstentions. The final vote was 33 to 13 in favor. Those who voted "No" were the six Arab states who were then members of the U.N., as well as four non-Arab Muslim states – Afghanistan, Pakistan, Turkey, and Iran – plus India, Greece, and Cuba.

Attacks on Jewish settlements by Arabs, who also opposed the U.N. settlement, increased between the time of the U.N. resolution and the declaration of Israeli independence five and a half months later. Although the defense of these settlements – many of them islands within territory with an Arab majority – was vital, Britain continued to ban the Haganah, which thus had to arm and train itself in secret.

On May 14, 1948, the British mandate in Palestine came to an end, and the last British high commissioner departed. On that day, Israel was declared independent by its first Prime Minister, David Ben-Gurion, at the Museum of Modern Art in Tel-Aviv.

Confident of victory, the armies of Transjordan, Iraq, Syria, Lebanon, and Egypt immediately invaded, and Jerusalem came under siege. Transjordan's Arab Legion under the command of Sir John Glubb ("Glubb Pasha") was able to seize a large portion of the land west of the Jordan, the

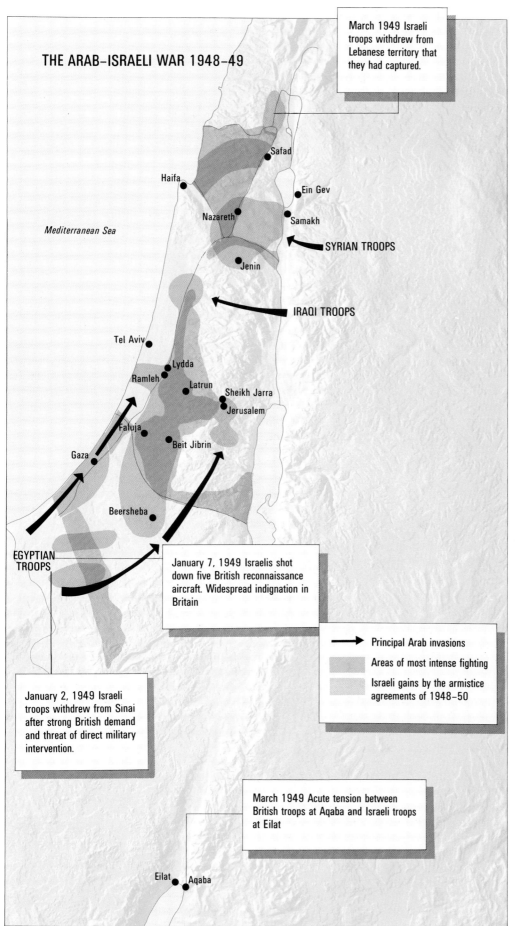

THE ARAB–ISRAELI WAR 1948–49

March 1949 Israeli troops withdrew from Lebanese territory that they had captured.

Safad

Haifa

Ein Gev

Nazareth

Samakh

SYRIAN TROOPS

Jenin

Mediterranean Sea

IRAQI TROOPS

Tel Aviv

Lydda

Ramleh

Latrun

Sheikh Jarra

Jerusalem

Faluja

Beit Jibrin

Gaza

Beersheba

EGYPTIAN TROOPS

January 7, 1949 Israelis shot down five British reconnaissance aircraft. Widespread indignation in Britain

January 2, 1949 Israeli troops withdrew from Sinai after strong British demand and threat of direct military intervention.

→ Principal Arab invasions

Areas of most intense fighting

Israeli gains by the armistice agreements of 1948–50

March 1949 Acute tension between British troops at Aqaba and Israeli troops at Eilat

Eilat Aqaba

LEFT: *Few outsiders expected the Israelis to hold their own against the well-equipped Arab armies that attacked them, following British withdrawal. Nevertheless, despite minor Arab gains, the Israelis managed to retain all the territory allocated to them by the U.N. and even gain slightly more, notably the western half of Jerusalem.*

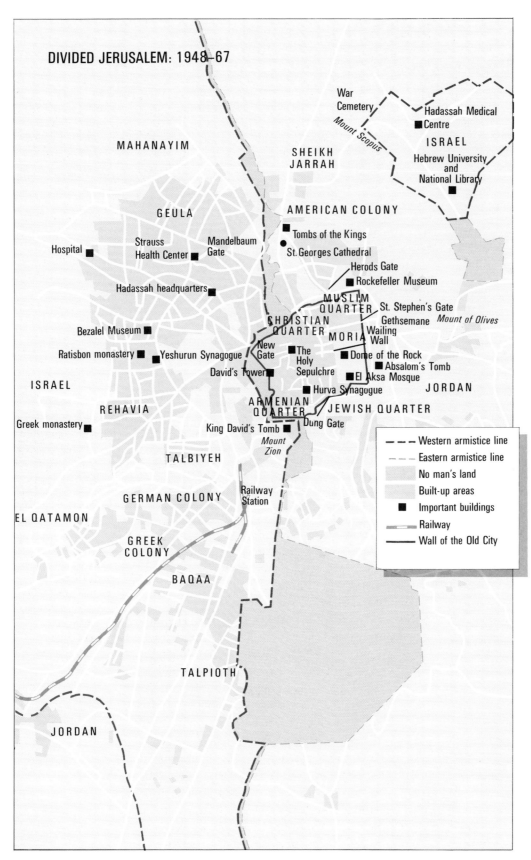

DIVIDED JERUSALEM: 1948–67

MAHANAYIM

SHEIKH JARRAH

War Cemetery

Mount Scopus

Hadassah Medical Centre

ISRAEL

Hebrew University and National Library

GEULA

AMERICAN COLONY

Tombs of the Kings

Hospital

Strauss Health Center

Mandelbaum Gate

St. Georges Cathedral

Herods Gate

Rockefeller Museum

Hadassah headquarters

MUSLIM QUARTER

St. Stephen's Gate

Gethsemane

Mount of Olives

Bezalel Museum

CHRISTIAN QUARTER

MORIA

Wailing Wall

Ratisbon monastery

Yeshurun Synagogue

New Gate

The Holy Sepulchre

Dome of the Rock

Absalom's Tomb

ISRAEL

David's Tower

El Aksa Mosque

JORDAN

REHAVIA

Hurva Synagogue

Greek monastery

ARMENIAN QUARTER

JEWISH QUARTER

Dung Gate

King David's Tomb

TALBIYEH

Mount Zion

GERMAN COLONY

Railway Station

EL QATAMON

GREEK COLONY

BAQAA

TALPIOTH

JORDAN

- - - Western armistice line
- - - Eastern armistice line
- No man's land
- Built-up areas
- ■ Important buildings
- Railway
- Wall of the Old City

LEFT: *After the first Arab-Israeli war, control of Jerusalem was divided, Israel holding the west of the city and Jordan the east. This included the Jewish quarter of the old city, which Israelis were forbidden to visit until 1967, when they occupied it in the Six Day War. In between, the Jordanians had desecrated Jewish graves and destroyed synagogues in the former Jewish quarter.*

"West Bank," which had been designated by the U.N. as a future Arab state; this was annexed and Transjordan was renamed the "Hashemite Kingdom of Jordan."

The Jews were fighting to retain control of the whole of Palestine, at least west of the Jordan. By 1949, they had managed to retain all the territory allocated to them under the U.N. resolution and even gained slightly more. Casualties were heavy: between November 1947 and May 1948, more than 4,000 Jewish soldiers and 2,000 Jewish civilians were killed – a total of more than 6,000 dead out of a Jewish population of 650,000. When a ceasefire was agreed in 1949, the Gaza Strip (also intended for the Arab state) had been taken by Egypt, and Jerusalem, proposed as an international city, had been split in half, with Jordan holding the eastern part and the Old City, and Israel the western half. More than half a million Arab Palestinians lost their homes; most were sent to U.N. refugee camps, with only Jordan granting some of them citizenship.

Despite implacable Arab hostility, the new state of Israel struggled and survived. The most effective long-term damage that the Arab nations have been able to do has been unquestionably in the economic sphere, with the imposition of a trade boycott. This not only covers their own trade; the Arabs have also put heavy pressure on other countries and with their vast purchasing power, they have had enormous success.

The Years since Independence

The Jews who had managed to survive the Holocaust and World War II, whether inside the camps or outside in hiding or on the run, had now to experience another challenge: starting new lives thousands of miles from their birthplaces and bereft of any possessions. The traumas suffered by survivors, both concentration camp deportees and others, have been extensively documented by psychologists and sociologists, as has their ability or inability to cope with normal life after liberation.

ABOVE: *Burned-out armored trucks on the road to Jerusalem, from the time of the 1947 struggle for independence. This area of Palestine saw some of the fiercest fighting of the war, involving Israeli forces and the crack units of the British-trained Jordanian Arab legion.*

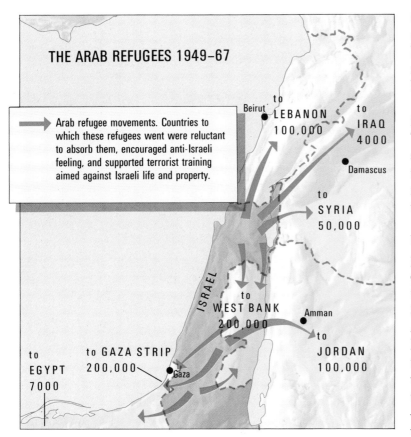

THE ARAB REFUGEES 1949-67

Arab refugee movements. Countries to which these refugees went were reluctant to absorb them, encouraged anti-Israeli feeling, and supported terrorist training aimed against Israeli life and property.

Beirut
to
LEBANON
100,000

to
IRAQ
4000

Damascus

to
SYRIA
50,000

ISRAEL

to
WEST BANK
200,000

Amman

to
JORDAN
100,000

to
EGYPT
7000

to GAZA STRIP
200,000
Gaza

Gaza Strip which they had occupied, the attacks ceased and the *fedayeen* moved their bases to Syria and Lebanon. U.N. forces moved into the Gaza Strip to form a buffer between the two countries.

Between 1956 and June 1967, attacks increased on Israel's northern settlements. Throughout the 1960s, the kibbutzim were subject to systematic shelling from Syria in the northeast, and there were also terrorist raids from Lebanon on Israel's northernmost towns and even on targets well inside Israel.

In 1967, Nasser decided to defy the United Nations by ordering out the U.N. peace-keeping force posted, under the terms of the Suez settlement, in the Strait of Tiran, the strategic area on the southern tip of the Sinai peninsula at the entrance to the Gulf of Aqaba. This effectively blocked access by Israeli shipping to the port of Eilat, and was therefore construed by Israel, as an act of war. Nasser then adopted an even more threatening stance, inviting other Arab states – Syria, Iraq, and Jordan – to help him wage war on Israel.

With Israel's independence, restrictions on immigration were abolished. Approximately 702,000 people arrived between 1948 and 1951, putting a great strain on resources. The newcomers included not only the remnants of European Jewry, but also people from the ancient communities of Iraq (Babylonia), Syria, Lebanon, and north Africa, whence they had been ejected by anti-Jewish regimes, as well as from less hostile countries such as Turkey. Jewish communities established well before the Christian era were now abandoned for ever. In Egypt, for example, many Jews decided to leave after General Mohammed Neguib overthrew King Farouk in 1952.

Neguib's successor, Gamal Abdel Nasser, nationalized the Suez Canal Company in July 1956, and a combined Anglo-French operation was organized to reopen the canal. Israel took advantage of the situation to launch its own attack in an attempt to stop raids by *fedayeen* (Arab guerrillas), which had made the whole of the southern part of Israel – from Beersheba to Eilat – virtually uninhabitable. Although, the following year, the Israelis were forced, through pressure from the U.S. and the U.N., to withdraw from the

FAR LEFT: *Between the War of Independence and the Six Day War 580,000 Palestinian Arabs fled from Israel to seek refuge in Gaza, on the West Bank, Jordan, Syria, and Lebanon. In contrast to the Jews displaced from Arab lands, the Palestinian refugees remained isolated, neglected, and unabsorbed, often as a deliberate act of policy by their host countries. The result was a ready-made guerrilla army, willing to be used to attack Israeli life and property. The problem was aggravated by the subsequent territorial expansion of Israel as a result of the Six Day War and intervention in Lebanon.*

LEFT: *Israeli tanks rumble past the old city wall of Jerusalem, leading a military parade to mark the 20th anniversary of the country's independence in 1968. Even today, despite moves toward peace in the Middle East, Israel is still constantly on the military alert; its defense forces, though highly successful in action, place a considerable strain on the nation's budget.*

RIGHT: *More than 650,000 Arabs quit Israel after independence, many of them settling in refugee camps, which speedily became a focus for anti-Israeli feeling. It was from such camps that the principal Palestinian liberation movements drew their strength.*

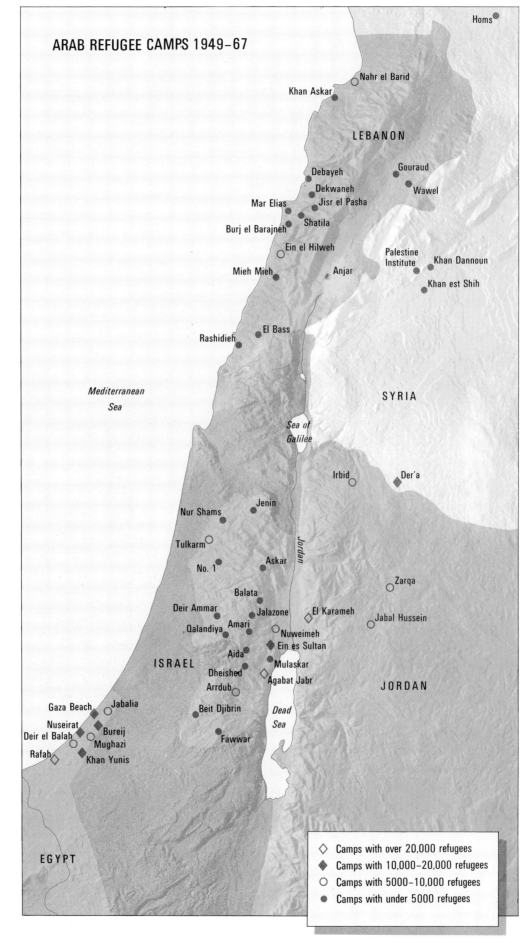

ARAB REFUGEE CAMPS 1949–67

Homs

Nahr el Barid
Khan Askar

LEBANON

Debayeh
Dekwaneh
Mar Elias
Jisr el Pasha
Shatila
Burj el Barajneh
Ein el Hilweh
Mieh Mieh
Anjar

Gouraud
Wawel

Palestine Institute
Khan Dannoun
Khan est Shih

Rashidieh
El Bass

Mediterranean Sea

SYRIA

Sea of Galilee

Irbid
Der'a

Jenin
Nur Shams
Tulkarm
No. 1
Askar
Balata
Deir Ammar
Jalazone
El Karameh
Qalandiya
Amari
Nuweimeh
Aida
Ein es Sultan
ISRAEL
Mulaskar
Dheished
Agabat Jabr
Arrdub

Jordan

Zarqa

Jabal Hussein

JORDAN

Gaza Beach
Jabalia
Nuseirat
Deir el Balah
Bureij
Mughazi
Rafah
Khan Yunis

Beit Djibrin

Dead Sea

Fawwar

EGYPT

◇ Camps with over 20,000 refugees
◆ Camps with 10,000–20,000 refugees
○ Camps with 5000–10,000 refugees
● Camps with under 5000 refugees

Again, the Israeli forces were well prepared. On June 5, 1967 a pre-emptive strike destroyed Nasser's air force on the ground, and in a pincer movement, the massed Egyptian army was surrounded in the Sinai and cut off from its supplies. The Syrians were repulsed and the Israeli army advanced to within 40 miles of Damascus; the Jordanians were also beaten back. At the end of just six days – hence the name "Six Day War" – Israel occupied the West Bank, the Sinai peninsula, the Gaza Strip, the Old City of Jerusalem, and the Golan Heights, the high plateau in Syria that overlooked the Israeli settlements on the northern border.

The Yom Kippur War of 1973, so called because the attack took place on the Day of Atonement (October 5), was the Egyptians' and Syrians' counter-offensive. At first, it was successful and caused heavy Israeli losses, but the Israelis recovered and regained some of the land they had lost. After the war ended

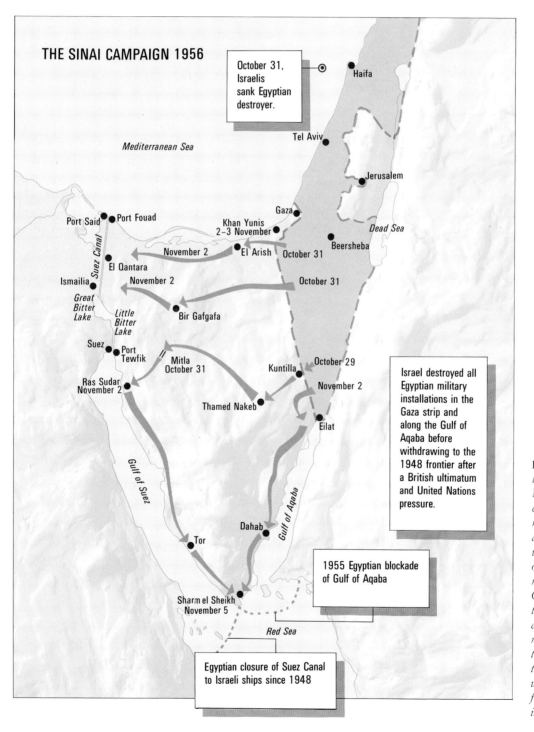

THE SINAI CAMPAIGN 1956

October 31, Israelis sank Egyptian destroyer.

Haifa

Mediterranean Sea

Tel Aviv

Jerusalem

Gaza

Port Said · Port Fouad
Khan Yunis
2–3 November

Dead Sea

November 2 · El Arish
October 31 · Beersheba

El Qantara

November 2

Ismailia
October 31

Great Bitter Lake
Little Bitter Lake

Bir Gafgafa

Suez · Port Tewfik
Mitla
October 31

Kuntilla · October 29

November 2

Ras Sudar
November 2

Thamed Nakeb

Eilat

Israel destroyed all Egyptian military installations in the Gaza strip and along the Gulf of Aqaba before withdrawing to the 1948 frontier after a British ultimatum and United Nations pressure.

Gulf of Suez

Gulf of Aqaba

Dahab

1955 Egyptian blockade of Gulf of Aqaba

Tor

Sharm el Sheikh
November 5

Red Sea

Egyptian closure of Suez Canal to Israeli ships since 1948

LEFT: *Increasing Arab terrorism and threats from Nasser's Egypt led to clandestine Israeli negotiations with Britain and France, both of whom were determined to overturn Nasser's nationalization of the Suez Canal. The Israelis were the first to strike, destroying all Egyptian military installations in the Gaza Strip and along the Gulf of Aqaba before withdrawing to their 1948 frontiers under international pressure.*

RIGHT: *An Israeli gunner on the Golan Heights looks out over Syria. Today, the threat to Israeli security is internal as well as external. Success in war has brought its own problems, the Arabs of the occupied territories having launched what they term an* intifada *("shaking off") of Israeli rule. This has led to major riots and civil disturbance.*

on October 24, tension remained high in the region. The United States finally stepped in, with President Jimmy Carter pledging to try to bring peace to the Middle East. He managed to make considerable progress, thanks largely to the Egyptian president, Anwar Sadat, who, in 1977, took the unprecedented step of journeying to Jerusalem to make peace with Israel. In March 1979 Sadat signed a peace treaty with Israel's prime minister, Menachem Begin, at Camp David, the presidential retreat in the U.S., under the auspices of President Carter.

Sadat was assassinated by Arab extremists in 1981, but his successor, Hosni Mubarak, has continued to pursue Sadat's moderate policies. In April 1982, Israel signed an agreement giving back to Egypt all but a tiny fragment of the Sinai peninsula. This fragment – the small town of Taba, which had been developed as a seaside resort by the Israelis – was handed over to the Egyptians in 1989.

While peaceful diplomacy was being carried out between Israel and Egypt, Israel's relations with its other Arab neighbors were worsening. In 1981 it staged a bombing raid on Iraq to destroy the nuclear reactor that that country was building with French help. Israel claimed that the nuclear capability would be aimed at itself.

Then, in 1982, following increasing terrorist attacks across their northern border, the Israeli government decided to occupy part of Lebanon. The army advanced as far as Beirut, occupying the south of the country, including the major cities of Sidon and Tyre, which were important bases for the Palestine Liberation Organization. The invasion of Lebanon was the first military action fought by Israel that did not have the universal support of its citizens, some of whom considered it to be an act of aggression and not of defense, and there were several instances of Israelis refusing to fight. The invasion of Lebanon, in which the Israelis suffered the loss of 580 lives, was by no means a victory, as previous military engagements had proven to have been. In 1984, the invasion and its cost in casualties for Israel provoked a government crisis and Prime Minister Begin resigned. The Israeli army was eventually withdrawn to the south.

In late 1988, the Arab populations of the West Bank and the Gaza Strip started a series of demonstrations and riots that have come to be known as the *intifada* (Arabic for "shaking off"). The discontent was perhaps the inevitable result of the way in which the Arabs had been forced to live in the territories conquered during the Six Day War: under Israeli military rule for 20 years with no sign of a peace settlement that might give them some right to self-determination.

Israel's Contribution to the World

Just over a quarter of the world's Jews now live in Israel – in fact, about the same proportion as during the Second Temple period. However, despite its relatively small population (4.1 million in 1985), small size (the area of Wales or Massachusetts) and the fact that it has fought five wars/conflicts since independence in 1948, Israel has made a significant contribution to world economic development and culture.

Both the kibbutz and the moshav have served as examples for voluntary collective settlements in different parts of the world. In France, for instance, there has been an experiment called Kibbutz Pardeilhan, in which non-Jews live a kibbutz-style existence. In addition, Israeli experts have brought the moshav idea to developing countries – for example, Sierra Leone, the Central African Republic, Cameroon, Ghana, Nigeria, and Sri Lanka – where it has proved effective in helping farmers make the best use of their land and resources.

Israel has also been in the forefront of the development of new techniques in agriculture and livestock raising, especially in advanced water-saving methods such as hydroponics and drip-feed irrigation. The results of this work include new strains of citrus fruit, as well as a joint program with the Egyptians to farm the African fish called the tillapia, which thrives in the brackish waters of the Great Bitter Lake, part of the Suez Canal.

The arts are greatly encouraged in Israel. There are academies of music and dance,

BELOW: *The tomb of the Patriarchs at Hebron, where Abraham, his wife, Sarah, and Isaac were buried. Today, this cave at Machpelah is not only a hallowed Judaic site; it is also honored by Muslims and Christians.*

RIGHT: *Faced by vastly superior Arab forces and the threat of imminent attack, Israel's response was a surprise strike, directed primarily against Egypt, whose airforce was caught and destroyed on the ground. The result was complete victory in six days of warfare.*

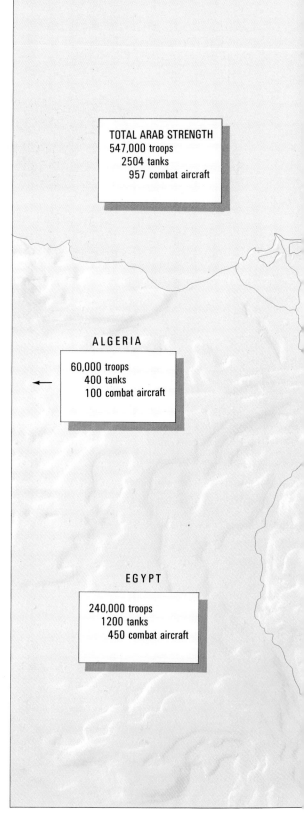

THE MIDDLE EAST CRISIS 1967

TOTAL ARAB STRENGTH
547,000 troops
2504 tanks
957 combat aircraft

ALGERIA
60,000 troops
400 tanks
100 combat aircraft

EGYPT
240,000 troops
1200 tanks
450 combat aircraft

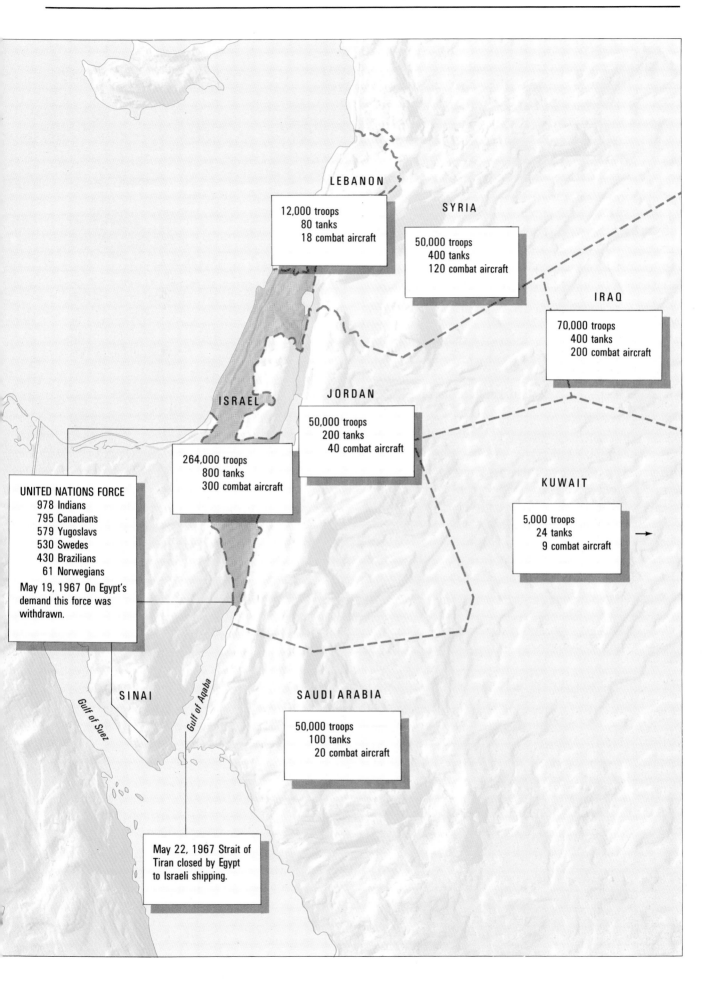

LEBANON

12,000 troops
80 tanks
18 combat aircraft

SYRIA

50,000 troops
400 tanks
120 combat aircraft

IRAQ

70,000 troops
400 tanks
200 combat aircraft

ISRAEL

JORDAN

50,000 troops
200 tanks
40 combat aircraft

264,000 troops
800 tanks
300 combat aircraft

KUWAIT

5,000 troops
24 tanks
9 combat aircraft

UNITED NATIONS FORCE
978 Indians
795 Canadians
579 Yugoslavs
530 Swedes
430 Brazilians
61 Norwegians

May 19, 1967 On Egypt's
demand this force was
withdrawn.

SINAI

Gulf of Suez

Gulf of Aqaba

SAUDI ARABIA

50,000 troops
100 tanks
20 combat aircraft

May 22, 1967 Strait of
Tiran closed by Egypt
to Israeli shipping.

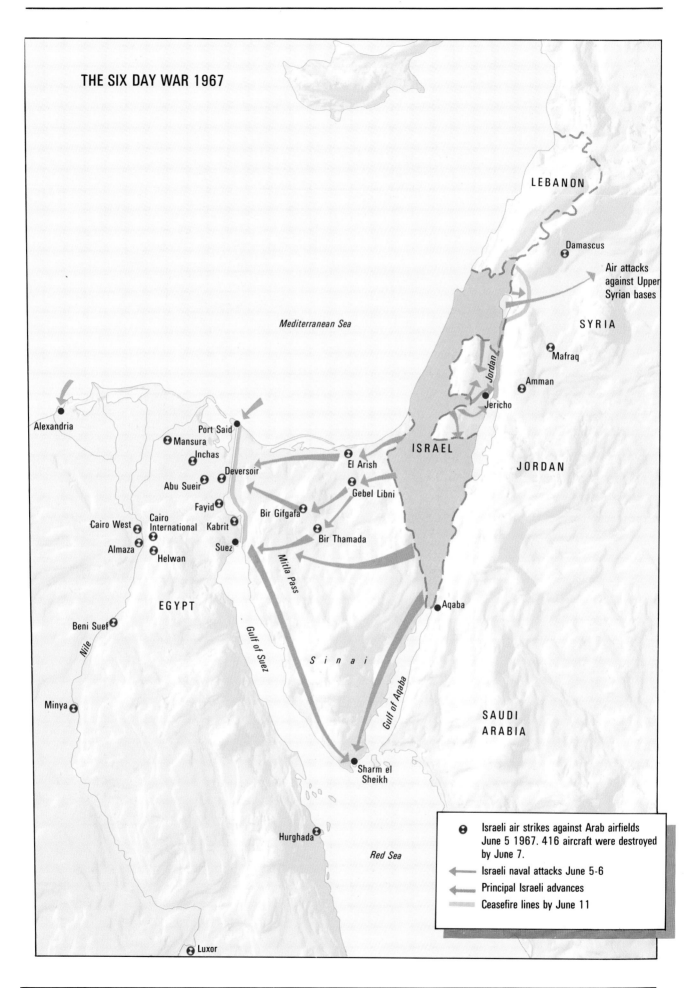

THE SIX DAY WAR 1967

LEBANON

Damascus

Air attacks
against Upper
Syrian bases

SYRIA

Mediterranean Sea

Mafraq

Jordan

Amman

Jericho

ISRAEL

JORDAN

Alexandria

Port Said

Mansura

Inchas

Deversoir

El Arish

Abu Sueir

Gebel Libni

Fayid

Bir Gifgafa

Cairo West

Cairo
International

Kabrit

Almaza

Suez

Bir Thamada

Helwan

Mitla Pass

Aqaba

EGYPT

S i n a i

Beni Suef

Nile

Gulf of Suez

Gulf of Aqaba

SAUDI
ARABIA

Minya

Sharm el
Sheikh

Hurghada

Red Sea

	Israeli air strikes against Arab airfields June 5 1967. 416 aircraft were destroyed by June 7.
←	Israeli naval attacks June 5-6
←	Principal Israeli advances
	Ceasefire lines by June 11

Luxor

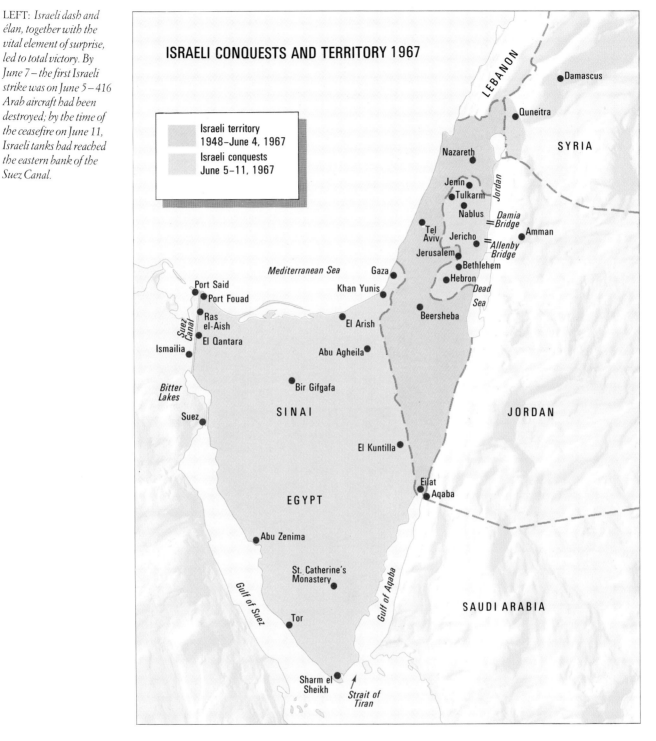

ISRAELI CONQUESTS AND TERRITORY 1967

Israeli territory
1948–June 4, 1967

Israeli conquests
June 5–11, 1967

DAMASCUS · Damascus
LEBANON
Quneitra
SYRIA
Nazareth
Jenin
Tulkarm
Nablus
Damia Bridge
Amman
Tel Aviv
Jericho
Allenby Bridge
Jerusalem
Bethlehem
Gaza
Hebron
Khan Yunis
Dead Sea
Mediterranean Sea
Beersheba
Port Said
Port Fouad
Ras el-Aish
El Qantara
El Arish
Ismailia
Suez Canal
Abu Agheila
Bitter Lakes
Bir Gifgafa
JORDAN
SINAI
Suez
El Kuntilla
EGYPT
Eilat
Aqaba
Abu Zenima
Gulf of Suez
St. Catherine's Monastery
Gulf of Aqaba
SAUDI ARABIA
Tor
Sharm el Sheikh
Strait of Tiran

ABOVE: *A glance at this map shows the extent of Israeli success in 1967. Not only had the Egyptians been driven back to the west bank of the Suez Canal, but the Jordanian enclave had been eliminated, while the Golan Heights had been captured from Syria. However, this success brought its own problems in its wake, with many more resentful Arabs coming under Israeli rule.*

a multitude of art galleries, and three art schools, the oldest of which – the Bezalel School in Jerusalem – was founded in the nineteenth century.

Israel has produced a number of distinguished musicians, among them Yitzak Perlman, Daniel Barenboim, Pinchas Zuckerman, and one of the few women conductors, Dalia Atlas. The Israel Philharmonic Orchestra, now one of the leading orchestras in the world, was founded as the

Palestine Orchestra (or Palestine Symphony Orchestra) by the violinist, Bronislaw Huberman, in 1936, and Jewish musicians from Europe flocked to join it. Arturo Toscanini was its first conductor of international repute, and it has also performed under the batons of Leonard Bernstein and Zubin Mehta.

In painting, Mordecai Ardon's works hang in the Tate Gallery in London, and those of Yaakov Agam have been installed in the Elysée Palace, the French president's residence. Israeli literature (written in Hebrew) by such fine writers as Amos Oz, Aharon Appelfeld, and David Grossman has also reached the outside world, being widely translated into foreign languages.

The Decline of the Jewish Languages

The cultural heart of Yiddish – in Poland, the Ukraine, and, to some extent, Romania – was almost entirely eradicated in the Holocaust. In the Soviet Union under Stalin, Jewish secular culture was vigorously repressed, even though official ideology permitted the cultural expression of other ethnic minorities. Even in the outlying republics of the U.S.S.R., the Jewish dialects of Georgia, Daghestan (on the Caspian Sea) and Bukhara (in central Asia) were banned and the teaching of them – and of Hebrew – prohibited by the Soviet authorities.

If World War II signalled the death knell of Yiddish culture in Europe, assimilation and acculturation have caused the rapid decline of Yiddish in the rest of the world. Today, there is only one major Yiddish institution: YIVO, the Yiddish Scientific Institute, in New York. The *Jewish Daily Forward*, which had been the only daily Yiddish newspaper in the United States, became a weekly in 1985; in 1920, it had 200,000 readers, but today this figure has shrunk to only 30,000. Two daily Yiddish newspapers and one weekly are still published in Paris, all of them distributed elsewhere in the world. In Israel itself, where Hebrew and Arabic are the official languages, Yiddish is frowned upon as divisive since it is only spoken by one segment of the Jewish community, and in some cases, it is even banned – for instance, Yiddish words in Hebrew advertising on radio and television.

The only place where Yiddish is a living language and there is a thriving market for Yiddish books is South America, in both the Spanish-speaking countries (chiefly Argentina) and Brazil. Yet even here, the younger generation are abandoning Yiddish in favor of the vernacular.

Despite this decline in the use of Yiddish as an everyday language, Yiddish theatre has managed to survive, and in 1987, a new company was formed in Poland. However, there is little to perform except such classics of Yiddish drama as *The Dybbuk* by An-Ski and *Mirele Efros* by Jacob Gordin: no new literature of any significance is being written. Actors who made their names in the American-Yiddish theatre, such as Theodore Bikel and Mike Burshtein, have been working in English for years. The one exception to the dearth of new Yiddish works in the performing arts was the 1974 film *Hester Street*, which told the story of Jewish immigrants coming to live in New York in the 1890s. The almost entirely Yiddish screenplay, written by the film's director Joan Macklin Silver, received an Academy Award nomination.

Perversely, now that Yiddish is dying, it is enjoying a modish revival among Jews in the English-speaking world, where its decline has been the most rapid. Some American and British universities are establishing departments in Yiddish studies, and in Israel, where there has been a sudden realization that a very important part of the Jewish cultural heritage is in danger of extinction, all the universities now have chairs in Yiddish. These attempts at reviving the language are, however, probably too little too late, for this activity is unlikely to reverse the accelerating decline of spoken and written Yiddish.

The story is the same with the other Jewish languages. Yahud was the language of the Jews of Baghdad, and Judezmo and Ladino were two variants of the Spanish-based language of the Sephardi Jews; the Jews of Iran also had their own dialect and continued to use an archaic Hebrew script. Today, almost all the native speakers of these languages have either moved to Israel, where they are encouraged to speak Hebrew, or to other countries where they have adopted the vernacular. In the Balkans and Turkey, Ladino is spoken by the older generation, but not by the young, who are also abandoning their Ladino first names – e.g. Gracia,

ABOVE: *A street sign in three languages – Hebrew, Arabic, and English – in Jerusalem. Use of Hebrew is on the increase, though many speak English. Yiddish is also seeing a revival in many countries.*

cially enriched by their presence.

Although many Jews in the Western world have moved politically farther to the right of their socialist ancestors, the Jewish tradition of championing the underdog and fighting for civil liberties continues. In South Africa, Helen Suzman, the veteran Progressive Party leader (now retired), and the writer Hilda Bernstein, are outstanding examples, and many of the conscripts who have gone to jail rather than fight to support the apartheid regime have been Jewish. In the United States, Jews (including rabbis) were in the forefront of the civil rights movement of the 1960s. And in Argentina, the journalist and newspaper publisher Jacobo Timmerman was imprisoned for his outspoken critiques on the right-wing military junta that ruled in the 1970s and 1980s.

Jews have become particularly prominent on the English-language literary scene. In the United States, these include such luminaries as Saul Bellow (winner of the Nobel Prize for literature in 1975), Herman Wouk, Leon Uris, David Mamet, Bernard Malamud, and Philip Roth; in Canada, Mordecai Richler; and in Britain, Frederic Raphael, Harold Pinter, Arnold Wesker, Bernice Rubens, Danny Abse, Brian Glanville, Clive Sinclair, Gerda Charles, Michelene Wandor, and Anita Brookner. French literature has also been given an added Jewish dimension by such writers as André Schwartz-Bart and Albert Mémi, and the works of the anthropologist Claude Lévi-Strauss have had a worldwide influence. In addition, twentieth-century thought has been undoubtedly enriched by the journalism and books of the Italian survivor of Auschwitz Primo Levi.

Fortuna, Vidal – in favor of local names for "patriotic" reasons.

Attempts are being made to study these languages while speakers of them are still alive, and to revive their use. At Haifa University, the Institute for the Study of Jewish Languages publishes a weighty annual compilation of questions, answers, and observations. (Significantly, this is written in English, and the words of Jewish languages are not written in Hebrew characters but are transliterated into Roman letters.) In Madrid, the Instituto Arias Montano was established to study the Spanish-Jewish heritage and publishes a journal called *Sepharad*, the Hebrew and Ladino name for Spain.

The Jewish World Today

Since 1945, Jewish life in the free world (with the exception of West Germany) has returned more or less to its pre-war state. The refugees who fled from the pogroms and the Nazis made a remarkable contribution to the countries that took them in. In science, for example, there was the work of such theorists and researchers as Albert Einstein, Lise Meitner (who, with Otto Hahn, discovered the fission of uranium), and Ernst Chain (the co-developer, with Howard Florey, of penicillin as a widely available antibiotic). Britain and the United States, in particular, have been artistically, scientifically, and commer-

The Decline of the Ancient Communities

The most ancient Jewish communities outside Israel, in Egypt and Iraq, have been reduced to fragments since the establishment of the Jewish state and subsequent hostilities. Today, there are only 300 Jews in Egypt and 400 in Iraq. Many were airlifted to safety from the latter by the Israelis in "Operation Ezra and Nehemiah" in 1950, but a number of those who stayed behind were publicly hanged as "Israeli spies" after the present repressive Ba'ath regime took power in 1968. As many as 4,500 Jews remain in Syria, but as in Iraq, they are prisoners of the regime,

JEWISH POLITICAL LEADERS

In the twentieth century, Jews have played an active part in the political life of many nations, starting in Russia, where many of the original Bolshevik leadership were Jewish or of Jewish descent. Leon Trotsky (below right) was a prime example. He organized the Bolshevik armies in their struggles against the White Russians and later, after Lenin's death, was Stalin's chief rival for supreme power. Forced into exile, he was eventually assassinated in Mexico in 1940. Léon Blum (right) led the Popular Front, a coalition of left-wing political parties, to power in France in the 1930s. However, his social reforms – and his

Judaism – aroused the hostility of the French middle classes, and a favorite right-wing catch phrase of the time was "Better Hitler than Blum." Israel has produced its own leaders of world stature; David Ben Gurion (above) led the new nation in its formative years, while Golda Meir (far right, top) saw Israeli arms triumph in the Six Day War. In the U.S., Henry Kissinger (bottom right) served as head of the National Security Council and then as Secretary of State. He was instrumental in negotiating U.S. withdrawal from Vietnam and in opening diplomatic relations with mainland China. Israel has enjoyed substantial U.S. backing and support; the Jewish lobby is a potent force in U.S. politics.

living in fear of their lives and unable to leave or communicate with anyone in the outside world.

The same applies to the Jews of Iran who settled in ancient Persia even before it became part of the Babylonian Empire. The Jewish kingdom of Adiabene existed for 100 years from the first century b.c.e. in parts of what are now northern Iran and northern Iraq. Iranian and Iraqi Jews have much in common, as the oldest diaspora. The Jews of Kurdistan lived in territory that was later split between both countries.

In 1950, there were 100,000 Jews in Iran, of whom ten per cent were wealthy or middle class, while the rest lived in poverty, especially the Kurdish Jews in their remote mountain villages. The Alliance Israélite Universelle ran schools in Tehran, Isfahan and Shiraz. Mashhad had a community of secret Jews, all of whom have now left for Israel or the English-speaking world. When the Shah was deposed in 1979, half the Jewish population fled overnight. Some emigrated to the United States, others were helped to escape by Israeli emissaries. Once the Islamic State had been declared, Jews were refused permission to leave, trapped as they had been in Iraq and Syria. By the mid-1980s, only about 1000 Jews were left. In 1999, 13 Jews from Shiraz and Isfahan were arrested for "spying for Israel". Ten were found guilty and sentenced to long terms of imprisonment.

In 1960, the Jewish community of Afghanistan, living mainly in Kabul, Herat, Kandahar, and Balkh, numbered 32,000. They had survived the fanatical Muslim regimes that followed the assassination of the king in 1933. Jews were expelled from small towns and villages and deprived of their citizenship. When emigration was briefly permitted in the 1960s, the majority left, mostly for Israel. By the time the Taliban took over in 1996, there was only one synagogue remaining, in Kabul. The rabbi, who claims to be the last remaining Jew, lit Chanukah candles in December 2002 after the Taliban were overthrown.

Ethiopia has a unique Jewish community, numbering about 100,000 in 1990. These dark-skinned Jews – called Falasha, meaning "stranger" in the national language, Amharic – have many religious practices that differ from those of other Jews, implying that they must have long been isolated from the rest of the Jewish world. Some walked to Israel in the nineteenth century, but Israel only officially recognized them as Jews (and thus allowed them to return) in 1975. When the Emperor Haile Selassie was overthrown and the famine struck in 1985, the remaining Falashas found themselves at the mercy of both the Eritrean rebels and the Marxist regime of Colonel Haile Mengistu Mariam. In 1991, the Israeli authorities organized "Operation Moses" to airlift the Falashas to Israel. Unfortunately, details of the operation were leaked, and it had to be halted prematurely due to the embarrassment it caused the Sudanese government that had allowed Israel to use its air space. Although as many as 20,000 Jews were airlifted out of Ethiopia in a single day, another 20,000 remained. The Israeli authorities are in the process of bringing the remaining Falashas to Israel, reuniting the many families and friends that were separated as a result of the 1991 airlift.

The Ethiopian rescue was based on two previous airlifts. The first of the missions to save Jews from persecution by flying them to Israel was "Operation Magic Carpet," which brought the Yemenite Jews to Israel in 1949. Jews had lived in the Yemen, in southern Arabia, since before Islam and there was a Jewish kingdom in Yemen in the early Middle Ages. Yemenite Jews were completely cut off from the rest of the Jewish world, and suffered from discrimination, though the fortunate few who found themselves under British rule in the former colony of Aden were able to become British citizens. Once the British granted Aden independence, in 1967, and it united with Yemen, all these Jews emigrated, mostly to Israel.

The second airlift, "Operation Ezra and Nehemiah" (named after the Babylonian Jewish scribe and prophet who led the Jews back to their homeland), from 1950-51, enabled the Jews to escape from Iraq. Although Jews had lived in Iraq for 2,700 years, ever since the Babylonian Exile, their lives had never been easy for them, especially after the Abbasid conquest in 750, when Baghdad became the capital of the Islamic world. In 1258, the Mongols invaded and massacred the citizens of Baghdad with impunity. Under Ottoman rule, Jews were relegated to the status of dhimmi, non-Muslims who had far fewer rights than that of the Muslim majority. They were also forced to live in Jewish quarters, and their houses could not be higher than those of the Muslims.

A small number of Jews, mainly Baghdadi merchants, grew extremely wealthy. Iraqi and Iranian Jews were often merchants travelling the Silk Road from China, a trade route that was used from Roman times until the late Middle Ages. In the late eighteenth and early nineteenth centuries, with the founding of the British Empire, Jewish merchants expanded their trading operations into British India and even China. Famous dynasties were founded wherever they went, Sassoon in Bombay, and Kadourie in Hong Kong. In 1918, with the break-up of the Ottoman Empire, Iraq became a British mandated territory. The British restored the monarchy and ended discrimination against Jews, who rose to positions of power in the government. But anti-British riots broke out in 1941, in which the Jews were made scapegoats. Order was restored, and there was a brief respite that ended when the British withdrew in 1948. With the establishment of the State of Israel, "Zionism" became a capital crime. Pogroms were orchestrated by competing factions of the ruling Ba'ath party, culminating in the public hanging of eleven Jews in Baghdad in January, 1969. Scores more died in prison and under torture. By 2002, only 100 Jews were left in Iraq, living mostly in Baghdad, a city whose population had at one time been one-fifth Jewish.

The Indian Sub-continent

About 25,000 Jews lived in the Indian subcontinent before Partition in 1947. They were divided into three very distinct communities, the Bene Israel, the Jews of Cochin, and the Iraqi Jews, many of whom were traveling merchants.

The Bene Israel community is believed to be descended from a group of Yemeni Jews who were shipwrecked off the Konkan coast, West Maharashtra, in Bombay state, the area in which they live to this day. Although they themselves claim to be descended from Jews from the Holy Land who arrived during the First Temple period, other authorities date their arrival from much later. The fact that

they are unaware of the festival of Hanukkah and the Fast of the Ninth of Av, however, makes it seem likely that they reached India thousands rather than hundreds of years ago. The Bene Israel community has even been allocated a caste. Their traditional occupation is that of oil-presser but many have become leather-dressers. When the Bene Israel began emigrating to Israel in the 1950s, there was some controversy over their status as it was claimed that many had converted to Christianity. About 5,000 Bene Israel remain in India, living mainly in Thana, a suburb of Mumbai (Bombay).

The Jews of Cochin, in Kerala state on the southern tip of India, are divided into two communities, the "black Jews" and the Paradesi or "white Jews". The former are the older community, probably arriving along the trade routes from the Arabian peninsula in the eighth century c.e. As early as 970, they were granted privileges by the ruler of Malabar, and prospered greatly under Dutch rule (1663-1795), when they were joined by the "white" Jews, mostly exiles from Spain who came via circuitous routes. The two communities maintain separate synagogues and do not intermarry.

The community that left its mark most heavily on the Indian sub-continent, from Bombay to Rangoon, are the so-called Baghdadi Jews who came not only from Iraq, but also from Syria and Iran. They settled mainly in Bombay and Calcutta and a few, such as the Sassoon family, became immensely wealthy. The founder of the Sasson dynasty, David Sassoon, arrived in 1832. He and his descendants left many fine public buildings that still stand in Bombay, such as the Sassoon Library, the clock tower in the Victoria Gardens (now known as Jijamata Udyan), the Sassoon Docks (founded by David's son), and the David Sassoon Industrial Institution and Reformatory, a home for orphaned and destitute boys. Another son, Abdullah, changed his name to Albert and married a Rothschild. Albert's son, Alfred, was the father of the English poet, Siegfried Sassoon.

Although the Jews of the Indian sub-continent were never subject to discrimination, the majority emigrated to Israel upon Indian independence, while others left for the United Kingdom, the United States, and

Australia. Today, there are no more than 5000 Jews in the whole sub-continent – India, Pakistan, Burma, and Bangladesh.

North Africa

The ancient Jewish communities of North Africa were greatly reduced in size after the founding of the state of Israel and by France's subsequent withdrawal from her colonies in the Maghreb. The Jewish community in this region is either descended from Spanish Jews who fled the Inquisition, or from Berber tribes who converted to Judaism just when Christianity was gaining ground in the rest of the Mediterranean – a phenomenon of which the second-century Christian writer, Tertullian, and St. Augustine complained bitterly. These Jews preserved their religion despite the spread of Islam. They live in isolated communities in the Atlas Mountains, and retain their traditional dress and customs.

The majority of the 203,000 Jews of Morocco left the country when the State of Israel was established and a wave of anti-Jewish hostility swept through the Arab world. However, when King Hassan II ascended the throne in 1961, the political climate improved. Morocco has some allegiance to the Arab cause, but the country's remaining Jews, most of whom live in Casablanca, enjoy equality and prosperity. As the situation on Morocco's frontiers deteriorated at the turn of the millennium, many Jews left for France, Israel, and Canada, and it is estimated that the population has reduced to 5,700.

The Crémieux decree of 1870 accorded Algerian Jews French citizenship, unlike their Muslim compatriots. As a result, the Jewish population, numbering about 230,000, closely identified with France, and when Algeria became independent in 1962, 115,000 of them left, mostly for France and the French-speaking world, or Israel. The rioting and mass killings that followed the cancellation of the Algerian elections in 1999 and the rise of the Islamic extremists caused the remaining Jews to emigrate.

Of the 105,000 Jews who lived in Tunisia prior to independence from France in 1956, about 7000 are left after emigration to France, Canada, and Israel. Most live in the ancient community on the island of Djerba,

with its magnificent synagogue, the Ghriba, and there are also small communities totaling around 1500 in Tunis, Sfax and Sousse. Although Jews have not suffered from overt persecution, the uncertainty of the country's political future after the death of President Habib Bourguiba makes their situation precarious.

The other ancient Jewish communities of north Africa are those of Libya and Egypt. Under Colonel Ghaddafi, though himself rumored to have had a Jewish mother, the Jews could expect no mercy and there are believed to be no Jews left in Libya. The community had been a thriving one whose roots went back far beyond Roman times and it thrived under the Italian occupation of 1911. Libya was in the front line in World War II and Jews were subject to terrible oppression by the occupying Germans, especially when they occupied Benghazi in 1943. Even under British occupation, the pogroms continued. After the establishment of the State of Israel, the British, who effectively ruled Libya, made emigration illegal. However, after it was legalized again in 1949, at least 30,000 Jews fled the country.

The 1956 Sinai Campaign was the pretext for expelling almost 25,000 Jews from Egypt and confiscating their property. Under the rule of Gamal Abdel Nasser (1918-1970), former Nazis were welcomed into the country and given high office, assisting Egypt in developing rocketry and even nuclear weapons. Leopold Gleim, a Nazi war criminal sentenced to death in absentia, controlled the Egyptian secret police.

In 1979, the Egyptian Jewish community became the first in the world to be allowed to establish official ties with Israel, at the same time as the Peace Treaty with Israel was signed. Israel established an embassy in Cairo and a consulate in Alexandria. Relations have been shaky from the start, however, and repeated anti-Semitic outbursts, once confined to the unofficial press, have spread even to official newspapers such as Al-Ahram. A few hundred Jews still remain in Egypt.

Southern Africa

The largest Jewish community in Africa is now that of South Africa. It is very different from the north African Jewish community.

Dutch and English Jews were among the early settlers in South Africa and many came with other European settlers after the two World Wars, but the majority of South African Jews originated in Lithuania and arrived after the Boer War. Before the founding of the state of Israel, South African Jewry had the largest percentage of Zionists of any Jewish community. Their contributions to the State of Israel ranked second only to that of the United States and was proportionately three times larger. Another great South African Zionist was Jan Smuts (1870-1950), who was a personal friend of the first President of the State of Israel, Chaim Weizmann. Smuts played a significant role in persuading the British foreign secretary to issue the Balfour Declaration of 1917. The South African government made great efforts to smuggle food, medical supplies, money, arms, uniforms, and aircraft to the Haganah, the secret Jewish army, before Israel's War of Independence. When the Nationalist Party came to power in 1948, the Jewish community was worried as many Nationalists had been Nazi supporters and anti-Semitism was rife among party members. However, South Africa became the first country to formally recognize the State of Israel and even allowed the Jewish community to officially send money there. After 1948, the Jewish population of South Africa remained more or less static at 118,000, though there was a steady trickle of emigrants to Israel, a flow which quadrupled in 1961 following the Sharpeville massacre. By the turn of the millennium, more than 15,000 South African Jews had left, mainly for Israel and the English-speaking countries. Jews constituted the majority of the liberal-leaning, anti-racist elements in South Africa. Joe Slovo and Dennis Goldstein were among the many Jews imprisoned for their fight against Apartheid. The Jewish population of South Africa was estimated to be about 79,000 in 2001, of whom at least 10,000 are black, Indian, or "mixed race".

The Jews of Zimbabwe, the former Rhodesia, are mostly of British or South African origin. Sir Roy Welensky (1907-1991) was a Jew, originally from New Zealand, who was prime minister of the Federation of Rhodesia and Nyasaland but resigned when the Federation was dissolved and Britain attempted to hand over rule to the black majority. The country, now Zimbabwe also contains the largest number of Lemba, a black tribe who claim to practice Judaism, though the majority Zimbabwean Jewish population does not entirely accept them. There are Lemba in other parts of Africa, notably South Africa. Many Jews have left Zimbabwe for Israel and the English-speaking world due to the famine and political unrest.

At one time more Israelis lived in Africa than locally born Jews. In the 1960s, when Israeli aid to Africa was at its height, as many as 25,000 Israelis were resident in sub-Saharan Africa, working mainly in the military and agricultural fields. In the 1990s, increasing influence from hostile Arab countries, and the rise of Islam in West Africa, reduced the Israeli presence. A notable example is Liberia. With the success of the 1989 rebellion lead by Charles Taylor and funded by Ghaddafi's Libya, the close relationship between Israel and Liberia came to an abrupt end. Though the numbers have diminished, there is still a sizeable Israeli presence in Africa, even in countries that do not dare to maintain diplomatic relations with Israel.

South America

Immigration to Argentina consisted mainly of Jews of Russian and Polish origin who fled from the pogroms in the late nineteenth and early twentieth centuries. They were joined later by north African Jews and other Sephardim whose integration into Argentinian society was facilitated by the fact that they spoke Ladino, a Spanish-Jewish dialect. Baron de Hirsch purchased land in Argentina and started a Jewish colonization plan in 1892, enabling poor Jews to become farmers in the Pampas. Although these farms were successful for a number of years, they later faced the same economic problems that beset the rest of Argentinian agriculture, and consequently, two-thirds of the Jewish population – numbering 450,000 – now lives in Buenos Aires. Argentina, Brazil, and Paraguay are among the South American countries with a significant population of former Germans who have continued to sympathize with the Nazis and offer sanctuary to war criminals fleeing justice.

The right-wing demagoguery of the Peronist government of Argentina, used the Jews as scapegoats for their own failings and corruption. One of the regime's most famous victims, newspaper editor Jacobo Timmerman, has written extensively about the persecution. The explosion that rocked the Jewish community center in Buenos Aires in 1994, preceded by the bomb at the Israeli embassy in 1992, both incidents for which no one has ever been brought to justice, renewed the anxiety of the remaining Jewish population. In 2001-02, the appalling economic crisis in Argentina caused large numbers of Jews from all over Argentina to emigrate to Israel. It is estimated that however bad the political and economic situation in Israel becomes, 20,000 Jews will make the journey from Argentina by 2010.

Most Brazilian Jews are Ashkenazim. There are 40,000 in Rio de Janeiro and the same number in Saõ Paolo. Smaller communities exist in Bahia, Belem, Manaus, Porto Alegre, Recife, and elsewhere. Argentina and Brazil are the last bastions of Yiddish culture outside New York, and this has created a bond between the Jewish communities of Argentina and Brazil. The Brazilian government has always enjoyed friendly relations with Israel.

The United States and Canada

The Jewish population of the United States is estimated at 5-5.5 million but no reliable statistics are available because – unlike any other Jewish community – there is no overall Jewish body representing all strands of religious observance and cultural affiliation. Jews live in every state of the Union, including Alaska and Hawaii, but the majority congregate in the biggest cities, New York (where the population of Manhattan is estimated to be twenty per cent Jewish), Chicago, and Los Angeles. Jews have been and continue to be prominent in every sphere of American public life, and have been advisors and senior officials to every president, Republican and Democrat since World War II, and also to Jefferson Davies, President of the Confederate States. Despite this, institutionalized and unofficial anti-Semitism were both rife in the United States before World War II. Jews were excluded from "Ivy League" universities, country clubs, and the best hotels. Some of the world's biggest companies denied Jews employment. The best residential areas were "zoned" to keep out undesirables (which often included Jews, Catholics, and non-whites. To the administration's considerable embarrassment, the first Israeli ambassador's residence in Washington D.C. in 1949 was found to be zoned to exclude Jews!). Overt discrimination ended with the anti-segregation laws of the 1960s.

Unquestionably, the home of Jewish scholarship has shifted from eastern Europe to the United States, and all the major Jewish theological institutions now have their headquarters there. In New York, the Yeshiva University represents the modern orthodox tradition, and the Jewish Theological Seminary trains rabbis for the conservative movement, The Hebrew Union College, headquartered in Cincinnati, Ohio, trains reform rabbis. Chicago also has the largest Jewish museum, the Spertus Museum. Parts of Brooklyn – Williamsburg and Boro Park – have become the preserve of ultra-orthodox Jews, who wear the traditional eastern European dress of black kaftan, broad-brimmed hat and sidelocks (peyos). The revival of Yiddish in the 1990s was largely an American initiative, and secular institutions such as the Arbeiter Ring in New York have done much to assist the promotion of Yiddish culture.

A large number of immigrants from the former Soviet Union and a few from Eastern Europe have swelled the American-Jewish population. When Jews first began leaving Russia in significant numbers in the 1980s, many settled in the Coney Island area of Brooklyn, which has become known as "Little Russia". Fairfax Avenue, in Los Angeles, also has a large number of Russian-Jewish shops; the Persian Jews tend to favor Beverly Hills.

Canada has about 300,000 Jews, most living in Toronto and Montreal. They are largely of eastern European origin and identify with the English-speaking community, but French-speaking north African immigrants tend to live in Quebec province.

France

The 660,000 Jews of France now constitute the second largest community in Europe,

after the former Soviet Union, thanks to the influx of some 300,000, the majority of the Jewish population of North Africa, who have come since the 1950s. Half of all French Jews live in Paris and there is a large community in Marseilles. Kosher butchers and Jewish bakers and bookshops abound as never before. The Jewish Quarter of Paris, the Marais, favored by the aristocracy prior to the Revolution that turned progressively into a slum, began its revival in the 1970s and is one of the most fashionable districts in the city enlivened by Jewish restaurants, cafés, and cultural institutions. Jo Goldenberg's restaurant has faithfully preserved bullet holes from a terrorist attack.

The Front National and Muslim extremists have recently made concerted efforts to attack the Jewish community. Incidents include the desecration of the ancient graveyard at Carpentras, in Provence, in 1990 when 35 graves were damaged and a corpse was dug up (four men were caught and imprisoned). French Jews seem disinclined to leave, however, and the greatest danger to the community is assimilation.

The Former Communist Bloc

The second-largest Jewish community in the world experienced an upheaval in the 1990s, when the Soviet attitude towards the West, Jews and Israel changed abruptly. Mikhail Gorbachev, the last ruler of the Soviet Union, liberated the satellites from the yolk of Communism, resulting in the fall of the Berlin Wall, the eventual overthrow of Communism in Russia, and the velvet "revolutions" or bloody revolutions throughout the former Soviet bloc.

Communism became a viable movement at almost the same time as Zionism, and both competed for support among the impoverished Jewish masses of eastern Europe. Many Jews had supported the Decembrists in 1905, and even more participated in the Russian Revolution of 1917. They could now leave the Pale of Settlement and they rushed to settle in the cities of Russia and the Ukraine from which they had formerly been banned. Their freedom was short-lived, as during the civil war that followed they suffered terribly at the hands of the "white" Tsarist and counter-revolutionary forces, more than 200,000 being massacred in the Ukraine alone. Then followed the starvation years of the 1920s, when Jews died in their thousands, along with the rest of the population.

From the outset, the Communist party line in the Soviet Union was that Jews had the right to a cultural but not a religious identity. For Marxists and many others on the extreme left, Zionism was, and continues to be, an utterly unacceptable "bourgeois nationalist" solution to the "Jewish question". Stalin was clearly anti-Semitic even from the beginning of his rule. In fact, his essay *Marxism and the National Question* (1913), which deals with Jewish nationalism, first attracted Lenin's attention to him, and once he gained supreme power in 1927, he put his theories into practice. These included the establishment of an autonomous Jewish region, the first Jewish homeland of the modern era, established in a remote swamp in far-eastern Russia called Birobidzhan. The region was rumored to be rich in natural resources, however, and settlement was needed to counter the threat from neighboring China and Japan. The Communists and Labor Zionists had always shared the belief that one reason for latterday anti-Semitism was the fact that Jews were not farmers (in most countries Jews had not been allowed to own or farm land). Since local hostility in the former Pale of Settlement would prevent Jewish agricultural settlements being established there, it was argued, Jews could be given large tracts of land to work collectively in their own, autonomous region. A huge campaign was organized to attract Jews to the region, money was collected, lotteries were held to raise funds, and Jews from as far away as Argentina flocked to the new settlements. The plan failed, however, due to very poor planning. Gradually, the non-Jewish populations who had also emigrated to this virtually empty region, outnumbered the Jews. Today, there remains a single synagogue in the capital, also called Birobidzhan, and the Jewish population can be numbered in the hundreds.

Elsewhere in the Soviet Union, the Jews were subjected to a series of repressive measures designed to make the Jewish religion disappear. All private Jewish religious observance — circumcision, the teaching of Hebrew, religious education, bar mitzvahs (the coming-of-age ceremony for 13-year-old boys), the training of rabbis, and the public celebration of festivals were banned. Although, in theory, synagogue services were permitted, every Jewish organization had to be registered with the authorities. Approximately 1000 synagogues were in existence in 1917, of which barely 60 survived into the 1980s – in Riga, Latvia, in 1989, there was only one synagogue for a population of 28,000 Jews – and most of them had no rabbis.

In what might seem at first to be a change of heart, Stalin decided to grant Jews a separate nationality when he introduced internal passports in 1933. However, this was merely a ruse to stigmatize the bearer of Jewish passports that were stamped with a large "J". Unlike other "nationalities" – Georgians, Uzbeks, Tadjiks, Ukranians, and inhabitants of the Baltic States – Jews were denied any cultural or national privileges. Instead, even secular Jewish culture was ruthlessly suppressed. Books in Hebrew, Yiddish, and other Jewish dialects were banned and there were no facilities for kashrut (the observance of the dietary laws).

From the earliest days of Communism, more Jews were active party members than those from any other ethnic group, so they suffered proportionately more in Stalin's purges of loyal party members, even though these were not aimed specifically at Jews. However, the Stalinist purges of the higher party echelons in the late 1930s and the post-war period were certainly anti-Jewish in their intent. They rid Stalin of all the leading Jewish intellectuals, including Lenin's closest associates, Kamenev and Zinoviev, as well as intellectuals such as the writers Osip Mandelstam and Isaac Babel. Leon Trotsky, a Jew and Stalin's main rival for power after Lenin's death, was assassinated on Stalin's orders in Mexico in 1940.

The worst anti-Semitic excess occurred after Stalin supposedly foiled the so-called "Doctors' Plot" of 1952, and these were mirrored in the Slansky trials in Czechoslovakia. A number of doctors accredited to the Kremlin, almost all of them Jewish, were arrested on the spurious charge that they had attempted to poison members of the Supreme Soviet, including Stalin himself, on "international Zionist" instructions. Fortunately, Stalin died three months after the doctors' arrests; the purge was stopped and those who were still alive were released. Yet official anti-Jewish measures continued under all of Stalin's successors until 1985.

Throughout this period, many Jews tried to leave the Soviet Union but emigration by anyone was regarded as a form of treason. The number of Jewish "refuseniks" eventually totalled about 9000. Labeled "prisoners of conscience" in the West, many were jailed

BELOW: Natan Sharansky, Israel's Minister of Housing and former Soviet refusenik. He founded Israel BeAliyah, a political party primarily of Russian immigrants that has enabled them to play a full role in Israel's political life at local and national level.

and all were dismissed from employment, leaving them destitute. The most famous of such prisoners is Anatoly Sharansky, founder of an emigration campaign which resulted in his release on February 11, 1986. Freed on the border of the still-divided Germany, Sharansky was met by the Israeli ambassador who immediately presented him with an Israeli passport under his Hebrew name of Natan Sharansky. Sharansky went on to found a new political party of Russian immigrants, Yisrael be'Aliyah, and has been a minister in several Israeli governments.

The reversal of the 70-year-old Stalinist policy towards the Jews, under the leadership of Mikhail Gorbachev, was spectacular. From the moment Gorbachev became general-secretary of the Party in 1985, Soviet Jewry was allowed to flourish. Although organizations still had to be registered, it was estimated that, by the end of 1990, there were about 135 Jewish congregations in Russia, and cultural institutions have similarly burgeoned. For instance, on February 12, 1989, the Solomon Mikhoels Cultural Center opened in Moscow, much of the funding for which came from the Australian Jewish community. (Mikhoels, the leading Yiddish actor of his day, toured the United States and Britain in the early 1940s to win support for the Soviet fight against the Germans, only to be murdered by the Soviet regime after the war.) In addition, Jewish groups were allowed to visit Israel; a Lithuanian contingent attended the 1989 Maccabiah, the Jewish sports festival.

Russian Jewry officially numbers 1.5 million. A further 1 million have chosen to register their nationality as non-Jewish, although they are of mixed parentage. Despite their new-found freedom, there is a dark side. With the coming of glasnost and the subsequent fall of Communism, official, anti-Semitic nationalistic groups such as Pamyat ("Memorial") have come out in the open. One Pamyat member told the playwright Alexander Galin in the summer of 1989: "You're a Jew, aren't you? I'm telling you now: you've got two years to live."

In the rest of eastern Europe, the break-up of the Eastern Bloc has produced an improved attitude towards the Jews and Israel. Most Communist countries broke off diplomatic relations with Israel after the Six Day War in 1967 but the new governments have restored them.

In East Germany and Hungary, the tiny post-war Jewish communities were allowed to exist in relative freedom, despite some official hostility towards Israel. In 1989, Hungary resumed diplomatic relations with Israel. Romania was the only Communist country to maintain trade and other relations with Israel uninterruptedly and to permit Jewish emigration. Approximately 30,000 Jews still live in Romania; there were 800,000 prior to World War II and 350,000 in 1945.

In Poland, home to 3 million Jews in 1939, only 50,000 survived the Holocaust, the majority of whom left after pogroms occurred even after the war, notably in Kielce and Lagow. There were even disturbing hints of anti-Semitism from the pro-democracy Solidarity trade union before it was banned and martial law imposed in 1981. However, after the defeat of Communism and the victory of Solidarity in 1989, successive Polish governments have been more favorably disposed towards the Jews, and Poland has re-established diplomatic ties with Israel. It is ironic that "Jewish" restaurants and souvenir shops, run by non-Jews, have opened in what were once the Jewish quarters of Cracow and Warsaw, to cater for those Jewish tourists seeking their roots and any remnant of their lost families or visiting the concentration camp memorials. A major effort is being made to restore Jewish cemeteries and other Jewish remains but many priceless treasures, such as the heavily painted and decorated wooden synagogues were consigned to the flames.

Klement Gottwald, president of Czechoslovakia between 1948 and 1953, was a devotee of Stalin. After a visit to the U.S.S.R. in June 1950, he had most of the leading Jewish members of the Czechoslovak Communist party hierarchy arrested, including his second-in-command Rudolf Slansky, who was tried and executed in December 1952. The others who were sentenced to long terms of imprisonment were eventually rehabilitated, as was Slansky (posthumously). Several prominent figures of the Prague Spring of 1968 were Jewish – a fact that was stressed by opponents to discredit the attempted reforms. President Vaclav Havel, the first president of the Czech Republic after the end of Communism has conferred high office on many Czech Jews. The historic Jewish Quarter of Prague, which the Communists at one time carefully omitted from the tourist map, is now packed with visitors. Its attractions include the Altneu Shul, the Old Jewish Cemetery, the oldest active synagogue in the world, and the Pinkasova synagogue. The latter has a wall on which the names of all the Czech Jews who died in the Holocaust are listed; this synagogue was long "closed for repairs" by the Communists.

Nowhere have the numbers of post-war European Jewry increased so dramatically as in Germany. They live mostly in Frankfurt and Berlin. Few are of German origin, they are mainly from the former Soviet Union, Iran, and Iraq. The cantor of the Berlin synagogue, the Greek-born Estrongo Nachama (1918-2000), an Auschwitz survivor, and community leader Ignatz Bubis (1927-1999) did much to strengthen the community. To quote the BBC, "Few people could ever have imagined that 55 years after the end of World War II, Germany would have the fastest growing Jewish population in the world" (outside Israel). An estimated 98,000 Jews lived in Germany in 2001.

The Aftermath of the Holocaust

Clearly, Jews have experienced more upheavals in the second half of the twentieth century than at any time in their history. Even the destruction of the First and Second Temples was not as traumatic as the events that affected the Jewish people between 1933 and 2000.

Jewish demography had been largely stable since the Expulsion from Spain in 1492, but this changed radically from the second half of the nineteenth century, when all over the world, from Iraq to the Pale of Settlement and beyond, the Jewish minority was again used as a scapegoat by despotic rulers. All the libels resurfaced, there were show trials (the Damascus Blood Libel in 1840 and the trial of Mendel Bayliss in Kiev in 1912) and a series of pogroms initiated in Russia by unpopular rulers, the worst of which was the 1909 Kishinev Pogrom. The result was the mass emigration of Jews from East to West. Such mass movements of populations had been impossible in the past, but improved communications, notably the Hapag (Hamburg-America) shipping line under its Jewish general manager Albert Ballin, made this possible. His ships accounted for almost all the emigration, Jewish and non-Jewish, from central and eastern Europe between 1880 and 1918.

During the interwar years, anti-Semitism became "fashionable" even in western Europe and the United States where right-wing demagogues demonized the Jew. The Nazis could never have succeeded in their mission to destroy European Jewry had they not had plenty of willing collaborators in the countries of German occupation and fellow-travelers elsewhere. They managed to exterminate six million Jews but left another six million so physically and mentally damaged that their lives were destroyed for ever. Many, like the author, Primo Levy, committed suicide after surviving the death camps.

This terrible tragedy marked a turning point for the Jewish people, just as the destruction of the Second Temple and Roman persecution had done nearly two thousand years previously. Once again, the survivors were reinvigorated, they found new directions and new beginnings, most notably the establishment of the State of Israel. The United States now has the largest Jewish population of any country, even than that of Israel. In western Europe, the Jews are deeply involved in rediscovering their cultural identity; there is a revival in Jewish education, history, and folklore even among the secular sections of the Jewish community. More Jews are sending their children to Jewish schools and there are many cultural and teaching institutions in the communities. In the former Soviet Union and Eastern Europe, there is new hope for the surviving remnant of Jewry. Jews are once again allowed to practice their religion openly and their ties with Israel extend to sending students to study at Israeli universities and rabbinical seminaries.

At no time in the past 2000 years has anti-Semitism been completely absent from all parts of the world, although there have been lulls between the worst excesses. The question remains as to whether anti-Semitism is experiencing its first major revival since World War II. Terrorist attacks against Jews outside Israel – first by Palestinians but increasingly by Muslim fundamentalists of other nationalities – have become common-place. In the former Eastern Bloc countries, such as Romania where Prime Minister Petre Roman is often abused for his Jewish back-ground (he is only half-Jewish), anti-Semitism may have merely gone to ground, as it has in the Baltic states. In Slovakia, which was under Nazi control during the war years, there is a resurgence of anti-Jewish feeling. Although the atrocities committed in former Yugoslavia did not directly affect the Jewish population, it caused many Jews to emigrate. Serious damage was caused to Jewish property, such as the picturesque syn-agogues of Sarajevo and Dubrovnik (Ragusa) and some Jews have vowed to remain to keep these ancient communities alive. In Russia, anti-Jewish propaganda persists, as do threats from the nationalistic groups, such as Zhirinovsky's Social Democrats.

Nowadays, unlike the poet Heinrich Heine (1797-1856) or the composer Gustav Mahler (1860-1911), Jews do not consider conversion to Christianity as the solution to the problem of European anti-Semitism. The Nazi hunter, Simon Wiesenthal, has often remarked on how most Viennese Jews, like their German counterparts, considered Hitler to be nothing more than a bad joke in the early days. Never again will Jews be caught off guard in the same way.

BELOW: Nearly 60 years on there is a determina-tion that the Holocaust should never be forgot-ten. A potent example of this is the site of the pro-posed Holocaust Memorial in Berlin, near the Brandenburg Gate on what was once nomansland between East and West Berlin.

Israeli Demographics at the Turn of the Millennium

If the turn of the millennium has been eventful for the Diaspora, it has been even more so for Israel. The massive influx of Russian Jews has increased the population of Israel, so that it has leaped from 650,000 in 1948 to 4,389,600 in 1987, of whom about 82 percent were Jews, and on the eve of the 52nd anniversary of independence, in the year 2000, it stood at 6.3 million. There are currently 4.9 million Jewish citizens and 1.1 million Arab citizens. Of the 63 per cent of the Jewish population born in Israel, 43 per cent are second-generation Israelis. According to data published by Israel's Central Bureau of Statistics in 2000, approx-imately three million citizens have immigrat-ed to Israel since the establishment of the State, one million of whom arrived from the former Soviet Union in the 1990s. Of the 1.1 million Israeli Arabs, 81 per cent are Muslim, 10 per cent Christian, and nine per cent Druze.

The absorption of such a huge number of immigrants from the former Soviet Union has proved almost as problematic as the mass immigration of the early 1950s, when Jews flocked to Israel from the Displaced Persons camps of Europe and from the Arab world. This time, there is an additional dimension. Due to the ban on religious observance dur-ing the Communist era, it was ruled that immigrants with one Jewish grandparent could claim the right to settle in Israel under the Law of Return. As a result, many obser-vant Christians are classed as olim (Jewish immigrants). This situation has even led to greater toleration by orthodox Jewry who wield enormous political power, and there are moves towards recognition of Conservative and Reform Judaism, includ-ing a jointly-run "school for converts".

The population of Israel has been further swelled by so-called "illegal immigrants," foreign workers originally invited into the country in 1995 during the first Intifada to do work previously done by Arabs. Most have remained in Israel beyond their visa expiry date. They are believed to number around 30,000, originating mainly from the Philippines, west Africa, and eastern Europe.

Israeli Politics

Politics in Israel is complex in the extreme. Israel has a multitude of single-issue and broad-issue parties covering the whole political spectrum, each jostling for power under the unwieldy direct proportional representation system. For a political party to govern alone it must have a two-thirds majority, almost an impossibility, and one that has never been achieved. The result is always a shaky coalition and political parties that emerge, merge, and dissolve with alarming frequency. There are also anomalies such as the election of Samuel Flatto-Sharon, who stood for the Knesset in 1978, just to gain immunity from prosecution, and actually won enough votes for a second seat!

Nevertheless, the centrist socialists, under various names, managed to retain power between 1948 and 1977 when, Menachem Begin's right-wing Herut party (later part of the Likud Haleumi) finally won the majority of votes and formed a government. This marked a sea-change in Israel's political life. The Jewish settlement in Palestine and the State had been built on socialist and collectivist principles. Many of the largest enterprises, including Klal the construction firm and the Egged bus company, were cooperatives. Capitalism gradually began to take over and by the 1980s, many of the cooperatives, including the *kibbutzim* (collective farms), were struggling for survival. Their future is anyone's guess, but their value to Israeli society, past and present, should never be underestimated.

In the 1990s, following the assassination of Yitzhak Rabin, Shimon Peres became prime minister for a brief period. However, the Labour Party lost the election that followed, this time to the Likud party under Binyamin "Bibi" Netanyahu, who was educated in the United States. Despite Netanyahu's promises that the atrocities of the Intifada — the bombs planted in buses, cafés, and crowded markets that were the hallmark of Palestinian terrorism — would cease if he were elected, they grew even worse. In the 1999 election, the population voted overwhelmingly for the Labour Party under Ehud Barak, hoping for renewed momentum in the Peace Process. But peace has been long in coming and at times seems to be an unresolvable issue.

"Peace, Peace and there is no peace"

Once the Soviet Union and its allies no longer helped the Arab states to maintain hostilities with Israel so as to divert their populations from their justifiable grievances, peace looked like a viable option. In 1989, the Palestine National Council formally declared acceptance of UN Resolutions 242 and 338, a tacit recognition of the existence of the State of Israel. This was preceded, in 1988, by the Hamas Charter. Ironically, the Israelis had originally supported Hamas because it opposed the Palestine Liberation Organization. Yet the Hamas Charter stated that Palestine belonged solely to the Muslims and could only be liberated by *jihad* (holy war).

Negotiations between the Palestinians, Jordan, and Israel began secretly in the early 1990s. On September 13, 1993, the Precursor of the Declaration of Principles, known popularly as the Oslo Agreements, was signed between Israel and Palestine, with the support of the United States and the CIS. The series of agreements is named

ABOVE: *Germany has a burgeoning Jewish population. The restored synagogue in the Oranienburgerstrasse in what was once East Berlin has a golden dome that is a prominent city centre landmark. The banner reads "We love our Jewish fellow citizens! No anti-Semitism".*

RIGHT: *The United Kingdom was the first country outside Israel to officially declare a National Holocaust Remembrance Day, in 2000. Scottish Secretary of State Helen Liddell inaugurated a ceremony in Glasgow at the Royal Concert Hall in 2002.*

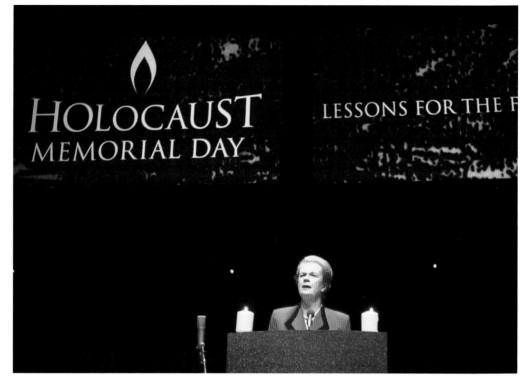

after the capital city of Norway, the country which brokered the accords and hosted many of the secret meetings.

In 1994, Jordan and Israel signed a peace treaty. At the time, it was revealed that the two countries had been in negotiations for many years and there had been secret meetings between King Hussein and a succession of Israeli prime ministers, but the time had not been right for an open settlement. King Hussein and then prime minister Rabin had actually been personal friends. In that same year, arrangements were made in Cairo for Gaza and Jericho to enjoy autonomy, and at the end of a five-year transition period, 90 per cent of the West Bank and Gaza Strip would be under autonomous Palestinian control.

The assassination in 1995 of Prime Minister Yitzhak Rabin, hero of the Six Day War and architect of the Peace Process, rocked Israeli society to its foundations. Rabin was shot as he was giving a speech at an historic peace rally in the center of Tel-Aviv. The horror and shame of the event left an indelible mark on the Israeli nation who realised how deeply the citizenry were divided on the issue of peace with the Palestinians. The majority of the population remained committed to peace but there were notable hardliners who would not tolerate ceding an inch of land to the Palestinians. They were either secular right-wingers or members of the reli-

gious parties, the National Religious Party or the more extreme Agudat Israel.

Despite this opposition, "Oslo II", the Interim Agreement was signed by Israel in 1995 and details of the redeployment of Israeli forces in the West Bank and Gaza were arranged. Leadership elections were held in the West Bank and Gaza the following January and Yasser Arafat was elected chairman of the Palestine Authority. There was much rejoicing on all sides, but the rejoicing was short-lived. The election of a right-wing government in Israel in 1996 led to a delay in the implementation of the Hebron redeployment, and each side hardened their attitudes. Arafat freely admitted that if the Peace Process were to run its course, he was liable to be killed by members of such hardline Palestinian groups as Hamas, Islamic Jihad, and the Popular Front for the Liberation of Palestine, who refused to recognize Israel and wanted to "drive the Jews into the sea".

In 1996, the Israelis mounted the "Grapes of Wrath" operation in Lebanon, in retaliation for the Hisbollah attacks on northern Israel. When Ehud Barak later undertook the promised withdrawal from Lebanon on May 24, 2000, this was unfortunately interpreted as a sign of Israeli weakness.

Throughout the late 1990s the Palestinians continued to plant bombs and perpetrate terrorist attacks in the heart of Israel. The

Israeli public became ever more disillusioned as PLO intransigence mounted. The Palestinians now demanded the right of "return" for three million Palestinians (the Arab population of Palestine had numbered only 650,000 in 1948). The Wye River Memorandum negotiated in 1998 seemed to offer hope of a "second redeployment" (the first had never been implemented) but 1999 came and went without the Final Accord being signed. In the year 2000, Arafat and Barak met President Clinton at Camp David one final time. Knowing that his term of office was nearly over, the U.S. president tried his utmost to persuade the two leaders to reach a settlement but to no avail. A final attempt was made by Barak to reach an agreement over the refugee problem in a meeting at Taba, the Sinai resort in Egypt, but it was clear that the gulf between the sides was unbridgeable.

On December 10, 2000, Barak offered his resignation. In the snap election that followed, his right-wing arch-rival Ariel Sharon, won the premiership. This enraged the Palestinians who linked him with the massacres in the Sabra and Shetila refugee camps that had been conducted by Israel's Falangist allies in Lebanon, when Sharon had been Minister of Defence in the Begin government.

Palestinian reaction to the new right-wing regime in Israel was not long in coming. Using the pretext of a visit by Ariel Sharon to the Al-Aqsa Mosque on September 28, 2000, the Arabs began a second Intifada, which they called the Al-Aqsa Intifada. There were gunfights and rocket attacks by the Israeli army and the Palestinians, resulting in many Palestinian casualties, including young boys and even children who had been encouraged to take part in the fighting. Israeli settlements on the West Bank were routinely attacked and Hebron became a battleground. Israeli incursions into West Bank towns where suspected terrorists were hiding were among the reprisals meted out by the Sharon government. Yasser Arafat was prevented by the Israelis from attending midnight mass at the Church of the Nativity in Bethlehem at Christmas 2001, and kept a prisoner in his compound in Ramallah.

The bitterness between the Israelis and the Palestinian Arabs has become so deep at the time of writing that it is hard to see

where forgiveness lies, although peace is the only possible solution. The Palestinians have widespread support from around the world for their territorial "struggle". However, the Israelis believe that they have already conceded the disputed land, and see the Palestinians real goal as the destruction of the Jewish state. As long as this remains the case, it is hard to predict a peaceful resolution.

The Jewish future

It took a long time for the majority of Jews to support the idea of a national homeland. Many were still sceptical long after the establishment of Israel in 1948 and remain so today; others claimed that once the state was established, there would be no need for Zionism. Yet even the non-Zionist Jewish organizations have to admit that the very existence of Israel as a haven for oppressed Jews is a guarantee of the safety for the whole Diaspora. Never again will doors be shut in the faces of desperate people fleeing persecution as they were during World War II, when unoccupied Europe and the rest of the world abandoned most Jews to their fate.

The survival of the Jewish people, unprecedented among the nations, is due to its extraordinary ability to confront adversity with positivism, and its infinite ability to adapt and start afresh. The great communities of Spain, eastern Europe, Babylon (Iraq), and Persia have gone forever. The English-speaking world, France, and Israel are the future home for world Jewry.

TOP: *Israel's foreign minister, Shimon Peres (left) with his close friend the late prime minister Yitzhak Rabin, who was assassinated in 1995. His assassin, Yigal Amir, a law student and right-wing political activist, was aided and abetted by several accomplices including his brother.*

ABOVE: *In contrast to the situation today, hopes for peace were high at a press conference in Camp David in 2000. U.S. President Clinton is flanked by Israeli Prime Minister Ehud Barak and Yasser Arafat, who stands next to Egyptian President Hosni Mubarak.*

INDEX

Page numbers in italics indicate captions.

CREDITS

Quarto would like to thank the following for their help with this publication and for permission to reproduce copyright material. While every effort has been made to trace and acknowledge all copyright holders, we would like to apologize should any omissions have been made.
J. Catling Allen 20 bottom, 33 right, 52, 60, 64, 65

Sammy Avnisan, Jerusalem 170 (all © Yad Vashem), 181 top & middle right, middle left (© Yad Vashem)
BIPAC 54
Werner Braun, Jerusalem 14, 44, 46, 48, 49, 113 top right, 186, 191, 192, 197, 204, 207, 208 top right & middle left
Bridgeman Art Library 8, 12 top & bottom, 24 top & bottom, 25 bottom left, 26, 33 bottom

left, 37, 72 top & bottom, 81, 100 top & bottom, 101, 117 bottom, 122 top & bottom, 130, 133, 134 bottom right
Brotherton Library, Leeds 89
J. Allan Cash 66 bottom left, 69 top, 83 bottom, 208 bottom, 210 Mary Evans Picture Library 82, 104 bottom left & right, 109 right, 113 bottom left & middle left, 120 bottom, 124, 125, 134

top left, 137, 156, 180
Archiv Gerstenberg 66 top right, lower right, 69 bottom, 76 top, 78 top & bottom, 83 top, 86, 88, 90, 92, 97, 98, 103, 104 top, 113 middle left, 117 top left, 128, 129, 131, 132, 136, 139 top & bottom, 140, 143 top, 149 top left & right
Mander & Mitchenson Theatre Collection 109 bottom

Mansell Collection 25 top right & bottom right, 38
Photoresources/C.M. Dixon 9, 11, 20 top, 28
Popperfoto 106, 107, 120 top, 143 middle, 163, 166, 190, 198, 200, 208 top left & middle right, 219
Zev Radovan, Jerusalem 32, 41, 75 top right, 189 top & bottom
Wiener Library Archives, London 160, 164, 165, 167